MW01633241

Museums and Centers of Contemporary Art in Central Europe After 1989

Museums and Centers of Contemporary Art in Central Europe After 1989 is a comprehensive study of the ecosystem of art museums and centers in the Czech Republic, Hungary, Poland, and Slovakia. Focusing on institutions founded after 1989, the book analyses a thirty-year boom in art exhibition space in these regions, as well as a range of socio-political influences and curatorial debates that had a significant impact upon their development.

Tracing the inspiration for the increase in art institutions and the models upon which these new spaces were based, Katarzyna Jagodzińska offers a unique insight into the history of museums in Central Europe. Providing analysis of a range of issues, including private and public patronage, architecture, and changing visions of national museums of art, the book situates these newly founded institutions within their historical, political, and museological contexts. Considering whether – and in what ways – they can be said to have a shared regional identity that is distinct from institutions elsewhere, this valuable contribution paints a picture of the region in its entirety from the perspective of new institutions of art.

Offering the first comprehensive study on the topic, *Museums and Centers of Contemporary Art in Central Europe After 1989* should be of great interest to academics, researchers, and postgraduate students engaged in the study of museums, art, history, and architecture.

Katarzyna Jagodzińska is an Assistant Professor at the Institute of European Studies at Jagiellonian University, Krakow, Poland. She also works in the International Cultural Centre, Krakow. She is an expert in museum studies of Central Europe.

Museums and Centers of Contemporary Art in Central Europe After 1989

Katarzyna Jagodzińska
Translated by Carolyn C. Guile

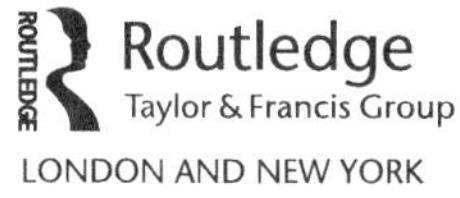

LONDON AND NEW YORK

First published 2020
by Routledge
2 Park Square, Milton Park, Abingdon, Oxon OX14 4RN

and by Routledge
52 Vanderbilt Avenue, New York, NY 10017

Routledge is an imprint of the Taylor & Francis Group, an informa business

© 2020 Katarzyna Jagodzińska

Translated by Carolyn C. Guile

British Library Cataloguing-in-Publication Data
A catalogue record for this book is available from the British Library

Library of Congress Cataloging-in-Publication Data
A catalog record for this book has been requested

ISBN: 978-1-138-55431-3 (hbk)
ISBN: 978-1-315-14890-8 (ebk)

Typeset in Sabon
by Apex CoVantage, LLC

This translation was made possible with support from the Ministry of Science and Higher Education's National Programme for the Development of Humanities – Universalia 2.1, in 2017–2018, project number 21H 16 0033 84.

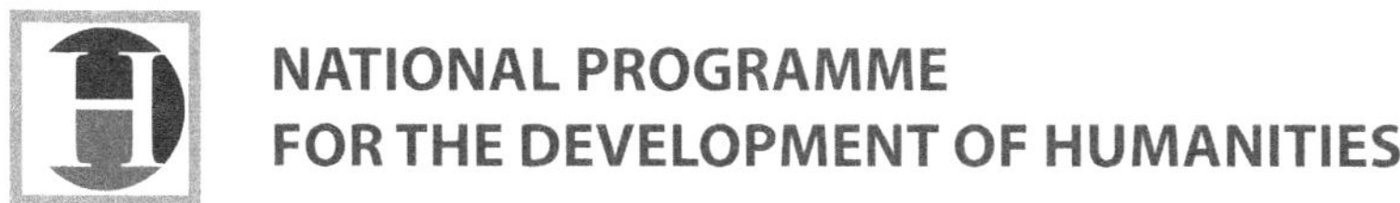

Contents

Acknowledgments

I became interested in Central Europe as a perspective for research in 2005 when I started working at the International Cultural Centre in Krakow. The ICC, which according to its mission statement resides at the center of international dialogue and interdisciplinary research on culture and heritage in Europe and in the world, uses Central Europe as one of its key concepts. The cultural heritage of Central Europe – variously defined, yet not fully definable – constitutes for the ICC not only a topic in itself, but also a starting point for looking at the processes taking place in other geographic regions and disciplines alike. The optics of Central Europe often allow for a more insightful and holistic view of global processes originating in mainstream regions.

I owe credit to Professor Jacek Purchla, founder and long-time director of the ICC, for this Central European perspective, and the pursuit of a wide (i.e. extending beyond the realm of the local) perspective and synthesis. Professor Purchla was not only my employer at the ICC, where under his guidance I carried out various projects set in the region; he was also the supervisor of my doctoral thesis at the Jagiellonian University, whose theme – just as in the present book – was museums and centers of art in Central Europe. In 2014, the ICC published the book that resulted from those studies entitled *Czas muzeów w Europie Środkowej. Muzea i centra sztuki współczesnej (1989–2014)* (The Museum Age in Central Europe. Museums and centers of contemporary art [1989–2014]). I thank the Professor very much for the kindness, faith in success, and friendship that he has given me.

The Museum Age in Central Europe was the point of departure for the writing of the present book – which, however, has been fully rewritten. With respect to new institutions for art, the dynamics of change in the region are so great that the huge body of new material I have accumulated in the four years that have passed since the publication of the Polish edition demanded a new approach and new conclusions, the identification of other points of emphasis, and the documentation of subsequent openings and closures, successes and failures of the institutions.

The development of this powerful material would not have been possible without the kindness of many people who shared knowledge, insights, and remarks with me. In 2007, I set out on my first and longest tour of Central

Europe to collect materials and visit the institutions being researched. Subsequent tours and visits took place each year until 2018, when I finished writing the book. Some of the conversations took place via Skype, telephone, and e-mail, as in many cases it was the only possible way to obtain information and statements. I would like to thank all those who have made it easier for me to collect materials and thus become a part of this book. In particular, I would like to thank Dr. László Baán, Dr. Jiří Fajt, Prof. Dorota Folga-Januszewska, and Dr. Alexandra Kusá, who agreed to an interview for this book, and Gábor Ébli, who discussed with me meanders of Hungarian museum scene and offered comments to fragments of this book, as well as Richard Adam, Marek Adamov, Vladimír Beskid, Zuzana Bodnárová, Jadwiga Charzyńska, Sebastian Cichocki, Nóra Deák, Richard Drury, Peter Fertőszögi, Eszter Göttinger, Richard Gregor, Lucia Gunišová Pavuková, Dr. Péter Inkei, Balázs Jelinek, Werner Jerke, Hana Jirmusová-Lazarowitz, Grzegorz Klaman, Alicja Knast, Prof. Milan Knížák, Šárka Komedová, Ábel Kónya, Katarína Kosová, Prof. Vojtěch Lahoda, Petra Lekešová, István Márta, József Mélyi, Dr. Jacek Michalak, Helena Musilová, Joanna Mytkowska, Petr Nedoma, Magda Němcová, Vincent Polakovič, Veronika Polakovičová, Jiří Pospíšil, Dr. Maria Anna Potocka, Sandra Průša, Petr Pudil, Stanisław Ruksza, Katarína Rusnáková, Michaela Šilpochová, Marcela Straková, Jarosław Suchan, Dr. Miklós Székely, Krisztina Szipőcs, Aneta Szyłak, Leoš Válka, and Tomáš Vlček.

This book could not have been created without funds for translation, which were granted as part of the National Program for the Development of Humanities – Universalia 2.1 (Narodowy Program Rozwoju Humanistyki – Uniwersalia 2.1). Its publication in English by a prestigious international publishing house would not have been possible without the interest of Routledge's editors in my subject.

I would like to thank Dr. Carolyn C. Guile, who took up the difficult task of translating the book from Polish to English. Many hours of work on translating the nuances of the Polish language have produced a great effect.

I express special words of gratitude to my parents, with whom I visited the world's largest museums as a child. The memories of these visits proved to be the greatest inspiration. Thank you for your continued motivation and unwavering patience. Thank you also – last but not least – to my husband, who tirelessly accompanied me on numerous trips through Central Europe, and showed great support and understanding in the difficult time when this book was being created.

If not for you, there would be no book!

Introduction

Central Europe is filling up with museums. The boom in museum construction, which began at the dawn of the nineteenth century, was without precedent in this part of Europe. There can be no doubt that museums became an important part of the urban panorama, associated with decisions about a building's form, and how the museum is received by its audience. And this meaning changes, just as museums themselves change. Museums as temples, museums as cemeteries, museums as mausoleums, museums as places of entertainment, museums as meeting places, museums as forums. Such comparisons have been made since the nineteenth century and are well illustrated by the changing attitude toward museums. The perception of the museum as a temple went hand in hand with nineteenth-century museum architecture typologies. In a 1988 press release issued on the occasion of the presentation of the Museum of Broadcasting in New York, Philip Johnson stated that "museums have taken the place of churches in our culture" (Davis 1990: 196). J. Pedro Lorente in his book dedicated to museums of contemporary art, *The Cathedrals of Urban Modernity*, claims that not only the impressive architecture of museum buildings encouraged associations with cathedrals, but also, museums – like cathedrals – became strictly urban phenomena. According to him, museums devoted to contemporary art in particular fully deserve this name (Lorente 1998: 1, 15). Stanisław Lorentz (1999: 10), director of the National Museum in Warsaw for nearly fifty years referred to the phrase, "museum as sister of the church", stating that museums (as had other scientific and educational institutions) increasingly were assuming the role of the cultural center, which churches and monasteries had fulfilled in the past.

Irrespective of whether the assessments of museums are merely expressions of exaggerated optimism or brutal criticism, the fact remains of their prestigious place and important role they play in the built environment, as well as in the cultural, social, and sometimes political and economic spheres.

Theme

In the pages of this book, I look at museums – specifically, museums of modern and contemporary art, as well as centers of contemporary art and

Kunsthallen – as a modern phenomenon, until recently an absent or under-represented element of the contemporary city. What is important to me are the motives and mechanisms that drive the creation of a new institution or the construction of a new building; the relationships that the museum builds with its surroundings; the challenges, dilemmas, and social barriers that accompany its creation; and social demand. I chose to focus on Central Europe (as a region, not the sum of its individual states), which remains largely absent from the literature of museum studies.

Central European museums and exhibition institutions follow directly from global museums, and on many levels are derived from foreign – particularly Western – models. My point of departure was based on the hierarchies of the so-called vertical narrative in art history. Piotr Piotrowski characterized it in this way:

> The city or cities where the paradigms of specific artistic tendencies are created constitute its [hierarchical approach] heart. Those are generally the great cities of the West: Berlin, Paris, New York. It is assumed that from there, models of artistic practice spread throughout the world, eventually reaching the peripheries. Therefore, art of the centre sets up the paradigm; art of the peripheries adopts models developed in the artistic metropolitan centres. The art canons, hierarchies of value and stylistic norms are all created in the centre; on the peripheries those canons, norms and values are at best received and assimilated. It can happen, of course, that significant artists appear within the margins of the artistic geography, but their recognition and art historic consecration must happen within the centre, though Western exhibitions and publications.
>
> (Piotrowski 2012: 26)

Of course, the concepts used in art history and museology cannot be used interchangeably. In my view, however, the development of museums may be looked at through the vertical and horizontal narratives of the history of art – particularly as regards the type of museum of contemporary art I have chosen, which in Central Europe (standing in this narrative periphery) materialized suddenly and numerously.

The main hypothesis with which I entered into the study is the conviction that almost all museums dealing with modern and contemporary art created since the 1990s in Central Europe are an imitation of formulae emerging in the center. The tradition of erecting modern museum buildings, as well as the creation of institutions dealing with the collection and presentation of the newest artistic creations, halted during the communist period, supports this conclusion. Due to the temporal shift and geographic distance from mainstream culture, the Central European peripheries emulate the models belatedly. Collective historical experiences render the circumstances of formation, structure, and function of the museums and centers of contemporary art similar, although the local interpretation of the Western models rarely produces new solutions. An interdisciplinary approach to the subject that places the projects within their historical context permits the tracing of both the process of their creation in relation to actual regional political-economic conditions, and the degree to which Western models were adopted. My goal was the creation of a picture of the region in its entirety from the perspective of new institutions of new art. I located the boundary of time in the year 1989. The year 2018, when I completed this book, offers nearly a thirty-year perspective of the development of museums after the time of political transformation.

Central European museums in existing literature

The art of Central Europe, Central and Eastern Europe, Eastern Europe, irrespective of nomenclature, is researched often by art historians from within the region (e.g. Fabiański 2000) and beyond (see Kaufmann 2004). However, it is poorly represented in international museum discourse. Until recently, Western publications rarely took into account European post-communist institutions; if this region was mentioned, it was only cursorily. An early example of its inclusion in sociological research on the museum public is in Pierre Bourdieu and Alain Darbel's *L'Amour de l'art. Les musées d'art européens and leur public* (1969). The research was carried out in five countries: France, Greece, Holland, Poland, and Spain. The exhibition, *Museums in the 21st Century: Concepts, Projects, Buildings*, attempted an overview of new museums at the beginning of the twenty-first century, and opened in several countries between 2006 and 2011. It was accompanied by a catalog published in several editions. It is striking that it did not include a single example from Eastern Europe. It was not, of course, a comprehensive exhibition or publication, as Scandinavian museums are similarly absent. But the curatorial decision is symptomatic, and shows how insignificant to Western publishers the region has been with respect to these new museum investments.

J. Pedro Lorente is the author of two important publications directly related to the subject of this book, that take Eastern European museums into consideration. *The Cathedrals of Urban Modernity. The First Museums of Contemporary Art, 1800–1930* (1998) and *The Museums of Contemporary Art. Notion and Development* (2011) offer a substantial introduction to contemporary art museums and present key moments in their history. But the author maintains a predominantly Western focus, making only passing reference to Central and Eastern European developments. From 2010–2013 under the direction of Peter Aronsson from Linköping University in Sweden, the substantial international project, Eunamus (European national museums: identity politics, the uses of the past and the European citizen), was undertaken and financed by the European Commission. Researchers from eight universities "explored the creation and power of European national museums. The focus was on understanding the conditions for using the past in negotiations that recreate citizenship, and on the understanding of layers of territorial belonging" (Eunamus Research n.d.). The project encompassed the range of museums from the whole European terrain, such that Central and Eastern Europe were represented on equal terms with Western Europe in the research (empirical and literary). A number of publications resulted from this project, the crowning achievements of which were the book project, *National Museums and Nation-building in Europe, 1750–2010* (Aronsson and Elgenius 2015), as well as nine extensive reports available in open access on the project website. Similarly, this part of Europe has become an integral part of Simon Knell's research devoted to national galleries in various parts of the world, as represented in *National Galleries. The Art of Making Nations* (2016). Among those studies mentioned here, only Lorente's are directly related to the present book.

The tendency toward regional ignorance dominated for years also among authors working in Central and Eastern Europe. It was only in the second decade of the twenty-first century that studies of museums in the region started to appear more frequently, in both national and English languages. The volume, *From Museum Critique to the Critical Museum* (2015), edited by Katarzyna Murawska-Muthesius and Piotr Piotrowski, addresses the issue of the criticality of museums, with special attention devoted to museums in Central and Eastern Europe. My publication, *Czas muzeów w Europie Środkowej. Muzea i centra sztuki współczesnej (1989–2014)* (The Museum Age in Central Europe. Museums and Centers of Contemporary Art [1989–2014]) (in Polish), was the first monograph to treat Central European museums comprehensively; the present publication is based on it. In 2016, Gábor Ébli published the volume, *Múzeumánia. Egy kulturális élménygyár európai modelljei* (Museumania. European Models for Generating Cultural Experience) (in Hungarian). A section comprising twelve chapters treats the East-Central European countries; the other two sections address the Western European countries as well as other "peripheral" ones such as Portugal, Greece, and Scandinavian countries. One of his conclusions is that there are fairly strong parallels among museum developments in the European periphery. Ébli also published several articles devoted to this theme, including substantial texts in the Romanian journal, *Revista ARTA*: "Collecting Contemporary Art in Eastern Europe, I: Museums in Regional Rivalry?" (2016a) and "Collecting Contemporary Art in Eastern Europe, II: Do Institutionalised Private Collections Measure up with Museums?" (2016b). His perspective is the widest, as he looks at Eastern Europe as a whole. However, this naturally means that he limited himself to the most important institutions and phenomena. Margaret Tali's book, *Absence and Difficult Knowledge in Contemporary Art Museums* (2018), is also geographically located in East-Central Europe. The author takes up collection practices of contemporary art museums through the example of four institutions: the Ludwig Museum in Budapest, the Hamburger Bahnhof in Berlin, Kiasma in Helsinki, and Kumu in Tallinn, which problematize the issue of absence. Beyond this are individual articles dedicated to a comparative approach within the region. Tali and Laura Pierantoni (2011: 167–82) engage the subject of contemporary art museum architecture in Estonia, Hungary, and Croatia in their article; the museums chosen for analysis are regarded as monuments that relate to the construction of new narratives of identity and statehood. In contrast, Miklós Székely (2014) focuses on the strategic building of contemporary art collections in East-Central Europe, and looks at select museums in Hungary, Poland, Czech Republic, Slovenia, Serbia, Croatia, and Romania.

There is also a growing number of publications on specific museums and museum buildings, as well as literature devoted to specific subjects such as museum education. But these are usually limited to the perspective of one country, and are written in the national language; when they go beyond this, the points of reference are usually Western, not Central European. An exceptional, because it is cross-cultural, example that includes both Western and Eastern Europe, as well as other regions of the world, is Zdzisław Żygulski, Jr.'s canonical book, *Muzea na świecie* (Museums in the World) (1982). Despite the fact that nearly three decades have passed since its publication, it remains the most complete synthesis of museology published in Polish.

Key concepts: Central Europe

> Central Europe means trauma and ambivalence. But it is also a repository of values which the West has long forgotten. It is the lesson of communism, the criticism of the idea of progress, the ubiquity of history, the complicated geography and politics, the cultural diversity and strong nationalism, the inferiority complex of the periphery; but is it also the creativity of the frontier. Central Europe is a difficult dialog with neighbors.

So wrote Jacek Purchla (2009a: 7) in the introduction to the Polish publication of a collection of essays by Csaba G. Kiss on the idea of Central Europe. This definition contains the essential features of this part of the continent that are important to the theme of the present book. Thomas DaCosta Kaufmann (2004: 186) refers to Central Europe as an artistic region, pointing out that its definition "does not need to be taken as fixed" and is dependent upon context, period, and subject. In writing about Central Europe, I have four countries in mind: the Czech Republic, Hungary, Poland, and Slovakia. It is a region with its own legitimate history, politics, and culture; however, extant literature most often defaults to an East-West opposition. Central Europe is most often analyzed as a part of the East (which was formally behind the Iron Curtain). There is no shortage of voices such as that of Emil Brix, who maintains that, "the identity aspects of the East are not moving from the West" (Brix 2001: 17). There is an extensive literature on the political concept of Central Europe, some of which stems from Friedrich Naumann's notion of Mitteleuropa (1915) (e.g. Delanty 1995; Elvert 2003). The same is true of cultural concepts, among which Milan Kundera's essay *The Tragedy of Central Europe* (1984) is central.

I invoke here only one construct, the political, which served as a frame for determining the geography that is the subject of this book. The Visegrad Group (V4), as it is named, was established in 1991 by Czechoslovakia (since 1993, the Czech Republic and Slovakia), Hungary and Poland. It refers to the reunion of the kings of the Czech Republic, Hungary, and Poland whose rulers met at the Visegrad Castle in Hungary in 1335 and decided to cooperate closely in the areas of politics and trade. The aim of the cooperation undertaken after the fall of communism was the entry of these countries into NATO and the European Union (EU), as well as building European security and preserving the cultural community. After 1 May 2004, when all members were admitted to the EU, the Group's legitimacy was called into question. The prime ministers of the four countries met on 12 May to confirm that the collaboration would continue, and that it would focus on regional activity and initiatives aimed at strengthening Central European identity. First among the areas of cooperation undertaken by the V4 was culture (Declaration of Prime Ministers 2004).

The usefulness of the concept of Central Europe, as well as those of Eastern and Western Europe, to describe cultural phenomena after the fall of communism often has been doubted and even questioned. Timothy Garton Ash (1999: 10), for example, states that "as Poland, Hungary, and the Czech Republic transform into typical Western European capitalist democracies, join NATO and finally the EU, the dividing line between Central and Western Europe is gradually blurred". A number of terms apply to the description of this part of Europe. Piotr Piotrowski in his canonical book, *In the Shadow of Yalta: Art and the Avant-garde in Eastern Europe, 1945–1989* (2011a, Polish ed. 2005) wrote about East-Central Europe, discussing the work of artists in the territories of Czechoslovakia, Yugoslavia, East Germany, Poland, Romania, and Hungary as well as parts of Bulgaria. In the subsequent *Art and Democracy in Post-Communist Europe* (2012: 10–11, Polish ed. 2010), regarding art after 1989 he wrote about "the eclipse of 'Eastern' and especially 'Central'", replacing these terms with "post-communist" Europe. Instead of a geographical approach, Piotrowski proposed taking a topographical approach to artistic phenomena, following from the de-regionalization of this part of Europe. Slovene art historian Igor Zabel devoted a great deal of attention to the subject of the "former East" on the basis of art and artistic criticism. He wrote,

> Eastern Europe is politically correctly described as the "former East." Why "former"? The geographical position, and also cultural traditions of the "former Eastern" countries remain the same. What can be called "former" is the socialist system that has been abolished. This system, in

spite of being abolished and absent, obviously still determines the identity of these countries and their cultural production. Eastern Europe now belongs to the same political, economic and cultural frameworks as the western countries, yet inside that framework it remains essentially different from them. The parallelism with the idea of the post-communist tradition is, I think, obvious. The end of the communist system, [the] introduction of a market economy, a democratic political system etc. do not put the post-communist countries on the same level with democratic western society. Communism has obviously not been replaced by a fully functional system of democracy and free market, but by a post-communist system that is and is not equal to the system on the West.

(Zabel 2004: 81–82)

This lengthy citation supports my assumption about the distinctiveness of the Central European region from Western countries. The similar geopolitical situation, historical relationships, the segregation from Western culture for forty years by the curtain of communism, and the common aspiration to shake off civilizational backwardness in order to make up for lost time – as well as the compulsion toward Western culture – have rendered the Central European countries similar to one another, justifying their comparison as regards the phenomenon of museums in the region. Resolving or exhausting the concept of "Central Europe" is not of key importance to me here.

Key concepts: the contemporary turn in museums

Like Central Europe, "contemporary art" is a vague notion. Due to its constantly changing nature and the need to define it anew, it is difficult to pinpoint its turn. Conversely, the character of a museum is such that it is not in a position to react quickly to changes (in contrast to art centers); as regards a collection, it is simply impossible, hence it quickly takes on an historical character.

The beginnings of the contemporary art museum reach back to the first half of the nineteenth century, and even then, it was accompanied by a dilemma concerning the temporal scope of the collected works. The very problem of establishing the boundaries of contemporary art launched the history of the Museum of Modern Art in New York. Its first director, Alfred Barr, wished for the museum to have a purely contemporary character, hence he planned that the collection would evolve; the older works would be removed after a determined period of time (ten, twenty, thirty, fifty years), in order to make space for new works. However, this did not happen and the museum began to create a historical collection. Later, in opposition to the MoMA, the MoCA (Museum of Contemporary Art) type emerged.

Although the title of the book includes the term "contemporary art", I am not limiting myself to the institutions of the newest art, and I am also including museums of twentieth-century art. In Central Europe, disputes arose over the distinction between museums of modern and contemporary art, particularly regarding the creation of the Museum of Modern Art in Warsaw (see Atlas 3.18) and the temporal boundaries of its future collection. The arguments borne out are symptomatic of decisions regarding the turning point of new museums. The choice of name was important, because it would determine the character of the collections and the exhibition program. Krzysztof Pomian (2005: 26) stated that the name, "museum of contemporary art" suggests the display of Polish visual culture regarded as being of our time, whereas the "museum of modern art" amounts to the avant-garde art museum. Reflecting on the contemporary turn, he suggested four possible starting points of artistic significance: 1918, the break with Young Poland symbolism and the entrance of the artistic avant-garde onto the scene; the first half of the 1960s, the breakthrough in global art and the striving for new materials and techniques; as well as dates of specifically political meaning, namely the years 1945 and 1989. He opted for 1918 for the museum's collections. The Preliminary Concept of the Warsaw Museum of Modern Art of 2005 comprising the programmatic objectives adopted the working name, "Warsaw Museum of Modern Art". The document stipulates that the museum would present the accomplishments and transformation of twentieth- and twenty-first-century Polish art in an international context, uniting the European achievement with those considered most valuable in Polish art of the time. (Wstępna koncepcja warszawskiego Muzeum Sztuki Nowoczesnej 2005: 5, 9). Ultimately the Museum of Modern Art was chosen, but typologically speaking, it is a museum of contemporary art.

The year 1989 marked a turning point for many of these new museums, but it is more of a point of reference rather than a conventional boundary beyond which these institutions did not reach.

Museums in the context of post-1989 cultural policy

For all countries in the region, 1989 ushered in the first processes of transformation, bringing new cultural possibilities, not least for museums. The marketization of some sectors of culture has only just ended (it took over twenty years!); in some areas, the term does not apply at all. That said, all sectors and related institutions are subject to constant change, starting from the creation of heretofore non-existent institutions, to providing them with a suitable base for their modernization and changing orientation. Their needs and expectations are central.

Institutions change – in their appearance, and in their ways of managing, creating, and implementing programs. The audience, for which all types of institutions and cultural industries compete, also changes. Likewise, the markets for particular cultural production are evolving all the time. Private institutions (especially theaters, as well as art centers) arise in the sectors hitherto dominated by public institutions; projects for institutions operating under public-private partnerships emerge, while many institutions were run by foundations and associations.

Robert Chrabąszcz, Jerzy Hausner and Stanisław Mazur (2003: 13) noticed that economic reforms, privatization, and measures for economic stabilization undertaken in the spirit of neoliberal ideology turned out to be a shock to society. Economic programs were established mainly on the basis of so-called Washington consensus, whereby the recommendations included the abolition of state subsidies and a preference for budgetary spending on education and healthcare. Culture was also harnessed to the process of adapting to free market economic principles. Jacek Purchla (2009b: 8) emphasized that, "in most countries of our region undergoing the difficult processes of transformation, culture was perceived above all as ballast, as a traditional burden on the budget, and not as a catalyst for change". Other priorities, and the perception that culture was a matter of excess, meant that in large part, the 1990s were lost years for institutions of art. The awareness of culture as an essential element of economic development is bred in political circles with the advent of a new age; nevertheless, the application of economic thinking to the management of cultural institutions, especially those "inherited" from the preceding era, is a long-term process. Jarosław Suchan rightly pointed out that in the context of Polish cultural policy,

> in the nineties, public authority generally did not have a mind for culture, and as a consequence supported it only to such an extent that it neither was allowed to fall nor was able to grow. More and more often today, politicians and government are beginning to see the value of culture and to support it more willingly than they had done thus far. But at the same time, they are instrumentalizing it as a tool for political marketing, and as a means to economic ends, including among others the development of tourism.
>
> (Mazur 2011)

Such a role may be ascribed to the opening of museums, which frequently arise from a political initiative. Much more often, historical museums and the vision of history they present are subject to heated political discussions. However, as the examples in this book demonstrate, the instrumentalization of art museums in the period of systemic transformation is a phenomenon occurring in every Central European country. In the nearly thirty years that have passed since the breakthrough of 1989, fundamental changes have taken place in Central European museums; the investment in infrastructure (new premises, modernization) has facilitated the adaptation of global exhibition standards from which new types of institutions have emerged, such as museums of contemporary art and – especially in Poland – historical museums (commemorating wars, martyrdom, and national liberation). More and more often, new technologies are used in exhibitions and displays; there is also more attention paid to their educational function and to issues of public comfort (leisure spaces and services).

Despite the various solutions integrated within the cultural policy of individual Central European countries, as well as the different priorities and dynamics these changes introduced, one can point to the common denominator that connects Czechoslovakia (from 1993, the Czech Republic and Slovakia), Poland, and Hungary after 1989. Above all, the point of departure is similar: the single-party system, limited freedom, a command economy, and centralization, from which there has been a transition to parliamentary democracy, civic freedoms, and market economies.

Where Poland is concerned, Kazimierz Krzysztofek (1999: 272) writes that an excessively optimistic belief in market mechanisms and too hasty a retreat from public patronage accompanied culture management at the state level. This was carried out without adequate synchronization of the scope and pace of withdrawal from the process of creating new structures of patronage. Dorota Ilczuk (2015: 6) in a compendium treating Polish cultural policy after 1989, formulated six key axes, around which she concentrated attention on specific ministers of culture and documents that formulated these policies at specific moments. These points, to which the whole of Central Europe may be compared, bearing in mind that their realization occurred at different times and in varying scope, are:

- the decentralization of the powers of public administration concerning culture;
- the transference of the majority of cultural institutions from the central government to local governments;
- the privatization of the majority of government-owned cultural industries (publishing, film, galleries, etc.);
- the abolition of censorship (including waiving the requirement for formal authorization to undertake artistic and cultural work);
- the cessation of detailed coordination and control of all levels of public spending on culture (especially by the Ministry of Culture and Voivode (representatives of Polish government in each region of Poland)); and
- general changes in the administration and regulations of the government that have had a major impact on culture.

The organizational framework for institutions operating in the field of culture in Poland is set out in the Act of 25 October 1991 (amended on 31 August 2011). It includes theaters, operas, operettas, philharmonics, orchestras, film institutions, cinemas, museums, libraries, cultural centers, artistic centers, art galleries, and research and documentation centers. In addition, a portion of these institutions – museums and libraries, as well as the film industry – operates on the basis of laws pertinent to them in specific ways (the Act of 21 November 1996 concerns museums, amended in 2007). Recommendations brought by The White Book, created in 1996, which was based on a study focused on relations between the state and culture in European countries, served as a source of inspiration in preparing strategic documents on culture in the Czech Republic. In Hungary, there is no act that addresses cultural activity as a whole; the Law on Culture is referred to as Act CXL of 1997 on the Protection of Cultural Property, Museum Institutions, Public Library Services and Community Culture. The state's cultural policy strategy, announced in 2002, defined Slovakian cultural policy as a hybrid model.

Decentralization in the field of cultural institutes went hand in hand with administrative reform. In Poland, territorial reform was divided into two stages: in 1993, the municipalities were charged with the responsibility of running cultural institutions entered into the voivods' register, and then in 1999 subsequent layers of self-government were added: the district authorities and the self-governing voivod adopted the operation of the majority of institutions, which hitherto had public status. Among the centers of art, which remained under the purview of the Minister of Culture, were the Zachęta State (presently National) Gallery of Art and the Ujazdowski Castle Center for Contemporary Art in Warsaw, as well as the National Museums in Krakow, Poznań, and Warsaw. In 2000, in accordance with the Constitution, the territory of the Czech Republic was divided into fourteen regions. Within the administrative decentralization, the management of a major part of museums, art galleries and libraries was transferred from the state to regional governments. This important shift was echoed in the new Museum Act of 2000 (the Act No. 122/2000 Coll., on protection of collections of a museum nature and on amendment to certain laws) and the *"Concept of More Effective Care of Movable Cultural Heritage in the Czech Republic 2003–2008"*. Many regional museums of art (galleries) were established in the late 1950s and the early 1960s, so that twentieth-century art represents a cardinal part of their collections. Museums transferred from the government's hand onto the regional administration included the Czech Museum of Fine Arts in Prague, the Gallery of Modern Art in Roudnice nad Labem, and the Gallery of Modern Art in Hradec Králové. The Ministry of Culture has retained the management only of key institutions of national importance. The thirty-one cultural institutions which remained within the authority of the Ministry of Culture after the decentralization, encompassed fifteen museums, two of them being art museums (the National Gallery in Prague and the Moravian Gallery in Brno) (Petrová 2011: 2).

In Slovakia in 1989, in order to ensure the continuity of local and regional cultural institutions, and until the completion of the transformation of public administration and reform of the tax system, all of them fell under the direct control of the ministry: they increased in number from 152 to 230 in 1992. Changes in the cultural sector were the effect of the strategy for the reform of public administration adopted in 1999. In 2002, the decentralization of cultural organizations managed thus far by the Ministry was completed.

In Hungary, most cultural functions, especially the maintenance of museums and libraries, were given to the cities in 2011. However, this is considered by some as a move in opposite direction. Péter Inkei indicates that instead of decentralization it was a step in the recentralization process. Most of the competences of the nineteen counties were removed at that time and this way some of their functions went to the cities, others were taken back to the central level (Personal communication with Péter Inkei 2018).

The belief in the necessity of state intervention in culture is evident in the first document on cultural policy adopted by the Polish government in 1993, the "Principles of State Cultural Policy", which stated that "an introduction into the culture of full commercialization would be shameful. We consider it necessary to assert that the state cannot resign from its function as a patron. But moderate commercialization does not have to be a threat to culture" (Krzysztofek 1999: 272–273). In the "Narodowa Strategia Rozwoju Kultury na lata 2004–2013", the following strategic areas were considered: the promotion of reading and the support of the book and publishing sectors; the protection of cultural heritage; the development of artistic education; the increased efficacy of artistic institutions in the creation of the cultural sphere, including the promotion of Polish creativity; and the establishment of a system supporting contemporary artistic creation. The latter included the creation of institutions for documentation, collection, and sharing (Narodowa Strategia Rozwoju Kultury na lata 2004–2013: 115). This is the only moment in the period following the transformation during which contemporary art and its institutions were granted such an elevated position in national cultural policy. On these grounds the program, "Znaki Czasu" (Signs of the Times) was created for the promotion and development of regional contemporary art collections, which leavened a later series of museums and centers of art. The Museum of Modern Art in Warsaw was launched. But the Ministry quickly retreated from this, shifting its focus to museums having an historical emphasis. Nevertheless, the spirit of that translated into the dynamic development of museums and art centers.

The first document devoted to cultural policy in the Czech Republic, was the 1999 "Strategy of Effective Cultural Support". In 2001, an updated and amended version of the aforementioned documented was adopted under the title "Cultural Policy in the Czech Republic (for the Years 2001–2005)". In 2008, the government adopted the "National Cultural Policy 2009–2014". The 2001 National Cultural Policy laid emphasis on acquisition of contemporary cultural objects; the two benefits resulting in preservation of testimony of the present for the next generations on the one hand and supporting living artists on the other hand (Cultural Policy 2001: 26). Prepared in 2006, the "Concept of More Effective Support of the Arts, 2007–2013", presented the SWOT analysis (a popular method used in management presenting strengths and weaknesses of a project) of the Czech cultural sector. It contained several weaknesses: insufficient social dialogue on the subject of contemporary art; the absence of reflection on how to increase interest in art; insufficient of subsidies for the presentation of contemporary art in museums, galleries, and exhibition spaces; inadequate facilities for presentation and storing contemporary art including new media; and the absence of institutions capable of engaging in international cooperation at the highest level within the European cultural infrastructure. On the other hand, as opportunities, two points were considered: a deliberate emphasis on the presentation of art in public or unconventional spaces, which are intended to facilitate public dialogue not only regarding art, but also to foster the presentation of art, music, and theatrical production in public and urban spaces; and second, the improved use of historical and industrial buildings (*Concept for More Efficient Support of the Arts in 2007–2013*, 2006: 47–50).

From the 1990s onwards, the state's support of the museums, galleries, and historic buildings it funded resulted in a spectrum of projects. These ranged from re-installation of long-term exhibitions through reconstruction of the institutions' premises in accordance with advanced museum standards to the acquisition of new buildings and their adaptation for the museum's use (e.g. new branches of the National Gallery in Prague: Trade Fair Palace and Kinsky Palace). The National Gallery gradually acquired new buildings – the Schwarzenberg Palace and the Salm Palace, which were reconstructed and brought up to advanced museum standards. A new entrance connecting these two neighboring edifices was built, such that the two previously mentioned palaces and the opposite Sternberg Palace comprise the Museum Triangle next to the Prague Castle. The Moravian Gallery in Brno also benefited from state funding as evidenced, for example, by the acquisition of the Governor's Palace and its adaptation for museum premises, and the reconstruction of the Pražák Palace, the current Gallery's headquarters (Personal communication with Magda Němcová, 2018). Other regional institutions were transformed (including GASK in Kutná Hora and the Gallery in Hradec Králové). The "Concept for the Development of Museums in the Czech Republic for 2015–2020" was adopted in 2015 and represents a landmark strategic document that consciously embraces all aspects of museums' functions. way.

Culture enjoyed a particularly high status in Hungarian politics during the period of center-right government in the years 1998–2002. At that time, the National Theater building was erected, and the Palace of Arts was also begun; Millennium Park, serving educational and cultural functions, was also created. In 2003, the ministry undertook the implementation of a strategic medium-term plan, "The Imperative of Rebuilding-Modernizing Museums", the emphasis of which was the protection of collections as well as the implementation of the notion of the user-friendly museum. In turn, in 2004, the "Alpha: Program for Modern Museums" was implemented, under which, among other things, the Holocaust Emlékközpont (Holocaust Remembrance Center) was opened (Museum Policy in Hungary 2003).

In 2006, Hungary faced an enormous financial deficit. It was argued to be the reason for the consolidation of cultural administration at the ministerial level: independent from 1998–2006, the Ministry of National Cultural Heritage merged with the Ministry of Education, and in 2010 was converted into a state secretariat within a larger Ministry of National Resources (similar secretariats covered health, education, social affairs, family and youth, as well as sports). In 2011, the state's priority was the creation of a museum district on the grounds of the City Park, interpreted by many observers of cultural life in Hungary as a government arrangement to take over the central wing of the former Buda Castle and empty it for administrative and protocol functions (Interview with József Mélyi 2018; Personal communication with Péter Inkei 2018); on the other hand, it was presented as a cultural, economic, and branding asset of Hungary (see interview with László Baán, Chapter 2). The new constitution of Hungary adopted in 2011 emphasized the key role of the Hungarian Academy of Arts (established in 1992 as a non-governmental association) in the current cultural policy. The Act on the Hungarian Academy of Arts (Act CIX), passed in 2011, upgraded it to the rank of a public foundation which gained the leading position in all major decision-making procedures in culture (Inkei and Vaspál 2014: 6–7). This conservative institution controls several cultural institutions (e.g. Hungarian Museum of Architecture and Műcsarnok) and occupies jury seats in many important bodies, such as the National Cultural Fund (Interview with József Mélyi 2018).

The political and economic situation of Slovakia after the transitions of 1989 and 1993 was the most unstable. Government policy, formed after the 1994 elections, resulted in the weakening of the pace of economic transformation, a constant conflict between the president and the prime minister, and the tightening of policy towards national minorities. In 1996, the US Congress excluded Slovakia from the group of countries eligible for financial assistance connected to joining NATO; ultimately it was not even considered among the group of states eligible for the second round of the enlargement of the Alliance. The commencement of talks about joining the EU was also in question. It was not until December 1999, after the change in government in the previous year, that Slovakia started negotiations (Gruszczak 2004: 801–803).

The divorce with the Czechs gave the Slovaks long-desired independence and subjectivity on the international stage, but it dealt a blow to cultural activity whose public was suddenly reduced from more than fifteen million to just over five million citizens. The reduction in consumers struck the publishing industry most especially, and met its reflection in the plastic arts as well. Bratislava, a much smaller, younger, and weaker cultural center, remains in the shadow of Prague. The Ministry of Culture in Slovakia had established the so-called national methodological centers for specific areas of culture (theater, music, galleries, monuments, museums, audiovisual centers, public education, media), while regional centers of culture were created at the local level. Cultural policy likewise became subject to the "Strategy for State Cultural Policy and the Action Plan for its Implementation", discussed in

2004; its central tenets were laid out in the "Program Declaration of the Government of the Slovak Republic in 2006–2010" (Smatlák 2011: 4–7). Finally, in 2006, the government adopted the "Strategy on the Development of Museums and Galleries in the Slovak Republic", in place until 2011. And in 2013 the new "Strategy for the Development of Culture of the Slovak Republic for the Years 2014–2020" was adopted, followed by the "Action Plan for its Implementation 2015–2017".

The turning point for the Central European countries was 2004, when they gained membership within the European Union. This made them eligible to apply for funds earmarked for the implementation of investment projections, including museum infrastructure. Their intended use was for the construction of key museum investments: the Museum of Modern Art building in Warsaw, as well as museum buildings for the City Park in Budapest. But this did not happen, and the financing was taken over by the city of Warsaw and the Hungarian government, respectively.

Centers founded by George Soros played an essential role in Central European countries, serving as a bridge between communism and its limitations, and capitalism, whose rules had to become known. Soros – raised in Hungary, educated in England, and from 1956 residing and working in the United States – directed his philanthropic activity toward the ends of promoting a global open society. In 1979, he founded the New York Open Society Foundations. The first one in Eastern Europe was founded in 1984 in Hungary and followed three years later in the Soviet Union, with others in the region soon after. In 1993, the financier opened the Open Society Institute, which supports a network of sixty foundations operating in Europe, Asia, Africa, South America, and the United States. Art was an important field of Soros's Eastern European activity. In 1985, the Soros Foundation operating in Műcsarnok opened the Center for the Documentation of Fine Arts in Budapest. Its task was to support avant-garde art through scholarships, purchases, exhibitions, and catalog publications. In 1991, the organization was transformed into the Soros Center for Contemporary Arts (SCCA), which in addition to collecting documentation about artists, dealt with the organization of exhibitions, project implementation and the distribution of grants to support contemporary Hungarian artists. Between 1991 and 1999, several analogous centers were opened in Central and Eastern Europe.[1] One of the important activities of the center in Hungary was the organization of the juried annual exhibition. The Hungarian center was transformed in 1996 into C[3]: the Center for Culture and Communication, which until 1999 belonged to the SCCA network.

SCCA-Prague was founded in 1992. Its purpose was to provide support for contemporary art as an essential component of civil society's harmonious development. Its activities encouraged unrestricted artistic creativity and the restoration of its social role. (Introduction 2000: 9). The most visible activities of the foundation were the annual exhibitions (based on open competition), which emphasized new media (the center provided artists with access to state-of-the-art computers). The organization has created a spacious documentation center with an art library, materials on contemporary Czech artists, and a grant program for artists. In 1999, SCCA-Prague was transformed into two separate organizations: the Center for Contemporary Arts Prague, and the Foundation for Contemporary Arts Prague.

SCCA-Bratislava was established in 1993. The scope of its activity was similar to that of the other organizations. In 1999, the center changed its name to The Foundation – Centre for Contemporary Arts. Since 2002, the foundation has been organizing an annual auction of contemporary art, a percentage of the proceeds of which is allocated to the grant program.

Soros's activity in Poland was of a different nature. In 1988, a foundation was established under a name different than the others, the Stefan Batory Foundation, conceived primarily as a granting body. The Center for Contemporary Art operated as part of this foundation in 1992–1994. It subsidized exhibitions, catalog printing and the development of contemporary art monographs, and maintained an archive and library. Its work was handed over to the Ujazdowski Castle Center for Contemporary Art in Warsaw (Fundacja im. Stefana Batorego 15 lat n.d.).

In 1998, Soros announced the decision slowly to withdraw from the Central European countries, indicating that the revolutionary moment was already behind them (Smolar n.d.: 8). From that moment, regular financial support for foundations was successively reduced – and in 2003, it ceased.

Methodology

I have been collecting materials for this book systematically since 2006. Since then, I have completed several research trips to almost all the museums and art centers included here. In many of these institutions, I conducted interviews and discussions with directors, curators, or those responsible for educational activities. My sources were catalogs of collections and exhibitions issued by these institutions, annual reports, informants, and unpublished internal materials. I also drew on the daily and specialist press. In 2012, the material I developed took the form of a doctoral dissertation (for which the outer historical endpoint was 2009), published in Polish in 2014. As the landscape of art institutions in Central Europe is constantly changing, I am continuously observing and documenting it.

In 2017 and 2018, I conducted a series of conversations with directors and curators of museums and art centers, as well as researchers and observers of cultural life, so as to look at institutions operating in different countries through their eyes. On one hand, I wanted to capture the changes that are occurring in the context of art institutions in the region; on the other, to learn about the problems, challenges, achievements, and expectations that museums and centers of contemporary art are facing today. Despite the huge jump that took place over the previous decades with respect to infrastructure, management models and program concepts, e.g. in the realms of education and work with audiences, the picture of these conversations that emerges is not unequivocally positive. The statements of my interlocutors assist me in delineating a common landscape of museums and centers of modern art in Central Europe.

Arrangement of the book

The book consists of nine chapters. Each is devoted to a different issue of importance, in my estimation, for the development of museums in Central Europe. Not a complete list of issues that should be conjoined with museums in this region, I have chosen each in such a way so as to show the fullest possible spectrum of museums and centers of modern and contemporary art.

Chapter 1 introduces the context for the discussions appearing in the subsequent chapters. It outlines the panorama of institutions dealing with contemporary art in the region before 1989, and the necessary changes they faced in order to meet the challenges of the twentieth and twenty-first centuries, are an important reference point for all recently established institutions. Further in the chapter, I mention new investments in individual countries, showing their number and place on the map of Central Europe. Finally, I present the condition of contemporary museums and art centers in the region. I discuss the changes taking place, the challenges they face, and the durability of the museum boom in this area.

In Chapter 2, I give voice to people who are direct observers and initiators of change within museums: Dorota Folga-Januszewska, Jiří Fajt, Alexandra Kusá and László Baán. From the four interviews I conducted with representative interlocutors from the Visegrad countries, a dynamic and complex picture of the region's museums emerges. The similarities and differences between museums in individual countries, the challenges, problems, and needs, but also the achievements and possibilities, are indicated here.

In Chapter 3, I discuss the issue of the museum as icon. The phenomenon of massive interest in the creation of new institutions, especially in Poland, in relation to which the term "museum boom" may be safely applied, is associated primarily with the expectation for iconic museum buildings. The architecture of museums has provided an opportunity to present the circumstances of their creation, as well as the motivations and expectations of various interest groups.

The architecture of museums is also presented in Chapter 4, whose subject is the adaptation of existing buildings, especially those of post-industrial and residential character, for the needs of museums and art centers. In many cases, despite the ambition to erect new buildings, taking over existing buildings proved to be the only option for undertaking or continuing operations.

I devote Chapter 5 to the cultural complexes and museum districts under which museums dedicated to contemporary art operate. In particular, many such places are found in Hungary, where the process of their creation provides an opportunity to present the relationship between cultural institutions and politics.

Chapter 6 discusses places for art created by private individuals and non-governmental organizations. Institutions of this kind are significantly fewer in Central Europe than institutions of art financed with public funds; statistically, Slovakia and the Czech Republic have the highest numbers.

Whereas the earlier chapters pertain to specialized institutions dealing exclusively with the art of the twentieth and twenty-first century, four large museums of national art in Warsaw, Prague, Bratislava, and Budapest are the subject of Chapter 7. Presented here at the time of change, each case took on a different character and was undertaken in different circumstances, but concerned contemporary art.

Chapter 8 is a case study of a Polish program supporting contemporary art in the regions of "Znaki Czasu". Announced by the Ministry of Culture, it resulted in the creation of collections and new art institutions to house them.

In Chapter 9, I summarize Western inspirations for the creation of the museums referred to in the previous chapters and point out the specific features of the institutions, in particular the interest in the art of the region as demonstrated through program activities and collectors' strategies.

An atlas of museums and contemporary art centers created after 1989 closes the book.

Note

1 In Belgrade, Bratislava, Bucharest, Kiev, Chişinău, Ljubljana, Moscow, Odessa, St. Petersburg, Prague, Riga, Sarajevo, Skopje, Sofia, Tallinn, Warsaw, Vilniuas, and Zagreb, as well as in Almaty in Kazakhstan.

1 The ecology of art museums before and after the 1989 political transition

An overview

The Central European museum boom that started toward the end of the 1990s belongs to the global phenomenon that had been underway since the 1970s and 1980s. The difference, however, is that in this part of Europe, museums abruptly became an essential part of the cultural landscape and urban panorama. After 1989, a new type of museum arose: the museum of contemporary art. Quite frequently, centers for contemporary art emerged independently from museums, both the Kunsthalle type and autonomous collections. Cities rode the wave of new plans and investments, but disputes also erupted among political dissidents, investors, architects, and cultured communities. A portion of those proposals awaits completion.

The aim of the following chapter is to delineate the institutional background of museums and centers for art created after the political transformation of 1989. A number of these institutions demonstrate the rich museum tradition of the region; but at the same time, they show the dearth of institutions dedicated to the newest art, which in the 1990s was particularly visible. The chapter also serves to document and contextualize the proceeding chapters of the book. I begin with the twentieth-century traditions; here the institutions are presented across place and in chronological order, commencing with Poland where they appeared with the greatest frequency (as a consequence of the country's considerable size and population), and followed by examples in Hungary, the Czech Republic, and Slovakia. I then treat the development of institutions that arose (or that acquired new buildings, thanks to which their activity gained momentum) after the transformations of 1989. This enumeration shows the extraordinary number of investments that had been undertaken in the Central European territories in a relatively short period of time – just under twenty-five years beginning from the opening of the first contemporary art museums in the Czech Republic (1995) and Hungary (1996), through the establishment of a museum of contemporary art in Gdańsk (2017). In the final section, I discuss the context of art institutions after 1989 as well as mention the most important functional challenges and problems.

Twentieth-century tradition

New museums and centers of art emerging since the 1990s did not arise from within a vacuum. From a statistical point of view, the assessment of those institutions engaged with modern and contemporary art in the individual Central European countries before 1989 is not the worst, although these are almost exclusively institutions established for the collection and presentation of art in general; twentieth-century art represents only one area of interest. There were just a few specialized institutions: the Muzeum Sztuki in Łódź (which in addition to twentieth-century art also houses works from earlier periods), Zachęta Gallery in Warsaw, and Műcsarnok in Budapest. Also worthy of mention is a network of galleries that emerged across Poland during the 1950s and 1960s, whose goal was to collect and exhibit contemporary art. In addition, regional art museums in Czechoslovakia focused predominantly on the twentieth century. Not only specialist institutions dedicated to the newest works of art, but all museums covering twentieth-century art of different periods provide the context for the emergence of institutions of modern and contemporary art.

The longest-standing tradition among the institutions engaged with contemporary art in the partitioned Polish lands is the Society of the Friends of Fine Arts, established in 1854 in Krakow; analogous in form was the Society for the Encouragement of Fine Arts in Warsaw, which from 1860 became one of the most important institutions of art in Poland. This latter institution played a key role in mounting exhibitions during both the nineteenth and twentieth centuries, as well as after 1989. In its first period of activity, Zachęta occupied a rented space, but since 1900 has been located in a Neo-Renaissance building on Małachowski Square in Warsaw according to a project by Stefan Szyller. The Society's activity ceased in 1939, when it was converted to the "House of German Culture" (its holdings were spared by their transport to the National Museum, a portion of which entered into its permanent collections).

After the war, the Society was not reinstated. Initially, the headquarters of the General Directorate of Museums and Monuments Protection was located in the building, and from 1951 it contained the Central Bureau of Art Exhibitions (Centralne Biuro Wystaw Artystycznych – CBWA) established two years earlier. Its goal was the popularization of art and the organization of artistic life throughout the country. An administrative network was created to serve this purpose. In 1949, offices were established in Katowice, Krakow, Poznań, and Bydgoszcz; Łódź, the delegation of the Krakow branch in Zakopane, Gdańsk, Szczecin, and Wrocław in 1951; in 1958, Olsztyn and Opole. The CBWA was involved in planning and organizing exhibitions both in Warsaw and for the individual branch offices. It also controlled the entire exhibition activity in the country. Over the space of forty years, the CBWA organized many significant, individual exhibitions of the most important Polish and foreign artists (Mansfeld 2003). It also created a collection with "politically correct" works purchased from exhibitions and competitions, but from the 1970s, art was acquired for educational purposes, giving rise to a professional collection (Stepnowska 2003: 205). In 1962, eleven branches of the CBWA were transformed into the Bureaus of Art Exhibitions (Biura Wystaw Artystycznych – BWA) and subordinated to the provincial authorities. From 1975, when the new administrative division of the country took effect, there were forty-one; together the delegations and branches they numbered forty-nine, to correspond with the number of provinces. The CBWA did not formally supervise the offices, which functioned independently, but on the principle of unwritten law, close cooperation continued as the CBWA still coordinated the major exhibitions according to a "tradition of established authority" (Meschnik 2001: 16). The quality of exhibitions organized by the BWA was uneven; the galleries staged valuable exhibitions, but many extra-artistic considerations decisively impacted the organization, whose offices functioned as a support structure for the local art scene regardless of artistic merit. Officially, the CBWA functioned until 1994. At that time, the statute of the institution was changed, establishing the Zachęta State Gallery of Art (from 2003, the Zachęta National Gallery of Art). The liquidation of the CBWA, however, did not entail the liquidation of individual BWAs, many of which decided to continue operations under the existing name.

The creation of the Muzeum Sztuki (Museum of Art, see Atlas 3.10) in Łódź marked an unprecedented event in Central Europe (see Turowski 1998; Ojrzyński 1991, 2004; Jurkiewicz-Eckert 2006). This is the oldest museum in the region focused on modern and contemporary art, having been the only independent museum of its kind in the region until the creation in 1996 of the Ludwig Museum in Budapest. Its initiator was the internationally respected avant-garde artist Władysław Strzemiński, who on 15 February 1931 officially handed over a collection of international modern art comprised of Polish and foreign artists' gifts to the Department of Education and Culture of the City of Łódź. Two rooms opened a year earlier in the Łódź City Hall as the Museum of Urban History and Art, named after Julian and Kazimierz Bartoszewicz, became the place for the presentation of the collections.

While still living in Soviet Russia, Strzemiński observed the development of museums of artistic culture (operating from 1919–1922) that combined the features of art research institutes and museums with extensive didactic ambitions. After arriving in Poland, the idea of creating a museum that would present not only the works of Polish artists, but also those of artists from broader Europe, matured in his mind. He never left for Western Europe, but his work and theoretical writings were well known thanks to exhibitions and the art press. In Paris, Henryk Stażewski and the poet Jan Brzękowski, as well as the painter and art critic Michel Seuphor, co-created the collection through their acquaintances and friendships in the art world. In sum, forty-four artists – including thirty-three from the Parisian milieu – initiated

International Modern Art Collection, but there were no works by artists from Russia and Central Europe, except Poland. During the Second World War, the collection was designated as Degenerate Art by the Nazis. 24 pieces out of 111 were stolen and destroyed. After the war, Strzemiński, together with his wife Katarzyna Kobro, donated most of their surviving work to the museum. In 1946, the museum received a new seat from the city in the former palace of Maurycy Poznański at Więckowskiego Street in Łódź. The opening of the permanent exhibition in the new building took place in 1948, and presented art from the Middle Ages through international modern art. There, the famous Strzemiński Neoplastic Room was established. In 1950, the museum was taken over by the state and renamed the Muzeum Sztuki in Łódź. Also that year, the display was closed for its incompatibility with the principles of socialist realism, and the Neoplastic Room was destroyed. Modern art slowly returned to the museum rooms in 1956, but the new permanent display was not opened until 1960.

The creation of the Muzeum Sztuki in Łódź did not eliminate the plans for the establishment of a museum in Poland devoted exclusively to contemporary work. In 1966, Jerzy Ludwiński, the initiator of the most radical concept for such a museum, announced the program of the Museum of Recent Art in Wrocław. The museum he proposed would act as a "constantly changing open system" that would "react to artistic facts at the time of their creation;" it would "provoke artistic facts" in which "a new art would be born". Ludwiński also described the formal issues of such an institution: not too large, and no excessive financial outlays, where "the existence of a collection should not be the most important thing" (Ludwiński 2008: 21). Following this concept, the "museum" staged two exhibitions in 1967 (Ludwiński 2008: 4).

The encyclopedic museums – national, regional, and municipal – are important to collecting and disseminating twentieth-century art, although Marcin Szeląg noted (2005: 34) that these museums "treated [it] incidentally, and accumulated it more through the implementation of specific state policy towards living artists and socialist propaganda, rather than by the real conviction that there was space for it in museums". In 1985, the Ujazdowski Castle Center for Contemporary Art in Warsaw (see Atlas 3.17) was formally established, although its proper activity developed only after 1990. Since the first exhibition opening in 1992, it began to play the role of substitute for the contemporary museum missing in the capital.

The thirty-year effort after 1989 to establish new institutions dealing with modern and contemporary art and to construct new buildings also marks a period of struggle between institutions established in the nineteenth and twentieth centuries to improve the infrastructure around the premises and funds for collecting activities. The National Museum in Warsaw is struggling with the problem of the limitations of the exhibition space; in 1995–1996, a comprehensive concept for a building extension was created. Although approved by the Ministry of Culture, it was not carried out. The collections of contemporary art occupied only a few rooms, and thus in 2007, only the so-called collection highlights were displayed; in 2012, after the renovation, the Gallery of Twentieth- and Twenty-First Century Art was opened there. Similarly, the National Museum in Krakow is seeking to enlarge its exhibition space through the addition of a new wing to the main building. In 2005, the five-year renovation project of the Gallery of Twentieth-Century Polish Art was completed, but this did not solve the problem. In November 2017, the opening of the major Stanisław Wyspiański exhibition, which temporarily occupied almost the entire space, meant that the gallery ceased to exist for more than a year (only a small exhibition of highlights from the collection was organized). In 2001, a new wing of the National Museum in Poznań was opened, which included a permanent display of Polish contemporary art after 1945. In the years 1989–1992, the building of the Museum of Contemporary Sculpture was erected at the Centre of Polish Sculpture in Orońsko. In 2011, a permanent exhibition of Polish modern and contemporary art was opened to the public in the converted attic of the National Museum in Wrocław.

After Poland, Hungary had the greatest number of museums. An analogous institution to the Warsaw Zachęta is Műcsarnok (a Hungarian translation of the German word *Kunsthalle*), which was founded a bit later than Zachęta by the Hungarian Society of Fine Arts in Budapest (1877). The society itself was founded in 1861 with the goal of "promot[ing] every branch of our native arts to the highest possible perfection, to improve artistic taste, and to extend the love of art" (Regős 2000: 27). In the beginning, the society lacked proper headquarters and the name "Műcsarnok" appeared only in the title of its published bulletin. In 1865, it received five rooms in the building of the Hungarian Academy of Sciences, then in 1877 it moved to a specially built palace on the prominent Andrássy Boulevard. In the following year, international exhibitions took place in spring and winter on a regular basis.

It soon turned out that the society's headquarters was insufficient, thus initiating a new building project. Favorable circumstances accompanied the demand for the new building as the state prepared to celebrate the millennium of the Hungarian state, sparking a number of investments including museums (Museum of Applied Arts, and Museum of Fine Arts). In 1894, the National Assembly of the Royal and Metropolitan City decided that in the place where the Andrássy Boulevard meets the city park, an area of 4,000 square meters would be developed as a fine arts exhibition space (Gábor 2000: 5). A national exhibition, open for half a year, occupied the center of the millennium celebrations. Part of the exhibition presented cultural production and art documenting the state's current status and economic progress, while the other offered a historical retrospective. Fine arts were included in both (Gábor 2000: 6).

Műcsarnok was designed by architect Albert Schickedanz, in keeping with the Neo-Renaissance style. He also provided designs for many other contemporaneous investments. After the commencement of construction on Műcsarnok, he was entrusted with designing the Millennium Monument at the Andrássy Boulevard terminus. In 1899, he was commissioned to design the Museum of Fine Arts across from the monument and opposite Műcsarnok. The resulting square created between these two cultural sites, located at the intersection of a park and a boulevard, was later called Heroes' Square. However, it was impossible to achieve a uniform concept for the square owing to uneven investment activities by multiple entities. According to the plan, the building was to resemble a cathedral, with a nave and two aisles, terminating in a semi-circular apse, with a columned portico at the entrance. The opening took place in 1896, the millennium year.

During the First World War, the building housed a military hospital, but the program of regular exhibitions was continued in the entrance hall. As the restoration work came to an end, the Second World War began, bringing with it serious damage to the building. Post-war reconstruction was carried out in 1962–1965. Losing its monopoly on the implementation of regular exhibitions for the National Association of Hungarian Fine Arts after the war, the Society began to organize large thematic exhibitions. In 1952, the name Műcsarnok was changed to the Institute for Organizing Exhibitions, and then to the less awkwardly worded Exhibition Institutions. The exhibition system in Hungary had been completely centralized. The Exhibition Institutions organized all exhibitions that took place in the provinces, including cyclical and traveling exhibitions in train wagons, which during the holiday season would stop for a time at the Lake Balaton resorts. They also organized exhibitions abroad, as well as receptions for foreign exhibitions (Frank 2000: 36–47).

The Ernst Múzeum founded by the Budapest collector Lajos Ernst at the end of the nineteenth century was the first private collection in Hungary that was transformed into a private museum (1912). It was assigned to the Exhibition Institutions in the middle of the twentieth century. Its creator collected both works of art and historical artifacts (hungarica). The functional idea had been to combine the museum with a tenement house, which was to provide financial resources for its activities as well as to aggrandize the collection. The museum was located on the first floor of a tenement house (Gyula Fodor, architect) located in the city center; a cinema and shops were opened on the ground floor, while other floors were designated for flats. The collection was presented in fourteen rooms, ten of which were devoted to ten centuries of Hungarian history as a gesture toward the unrealized plans of the Millennium Exhibition. Since its opening, the museum was one of the premier cultural centers of Budapest (Róka 2002: 24). As the rental income from the apartments turned out to be insufficient to finance the museum's needs, it undertook to organize an art auction. In the late 1920s, the museum owner's serious financial problems resulted in the sale of the building, followed by the collection in 1932. The institution was still active, not as a museum but as exhibition space. For forty years beginning in 1953, the Ernst Museum served as an additional exhibition space for contemporary art from the former Műcsarnok.

A revolutionary change in the functioning of Műcsarnok took place in 2007 as a result of governmental budget reform, when it ceased to be a publicly financed institution. As a non-profit institution, it continued to implement all of its previous goals, tasks, and obligations. Two hitherto independent institutions – the Ernst Museum and Dorottya Gallery – became an integral part of Műcsarnok. The Ernst Museum ceased to exist in 2013, its space in the building taken by the new Robert Capa Contemporary Photography Centre.

Beyond these specialized institutions of modern and contemporary art, universal museums also engaged twentieth-century art. The largest of them, the Hungarian National Gallery (Magyar Nemzeti Galéria) was founded in 1957 for the collection and presentation of Hungarian art. In 2011, it was merged with the Museum of Fine Arts and awaits relocation to a new building, where the Hungarian and international collections from the nineteenth century to the present will be combined. Next to this state museum, the Municipal Gallery of Budapest (today located in the Kiscelli Múzeum; initially housed in the Karolyi Palace) also specializes in twentieth-century and contemporary art. Apart from Budapest, the most important collections of twentieth-century art are found in the regional museums in Pécs and Győr. The Modern Hungarian Gallery (Modern Magyar Képtár), operating as part of the Janus Pannonius Museum in Pécs, holds the second largest collection of Hungarian modern art in the country. It, too, opened in 1957, but in contrast with Hungarian National Gallery, which documents the entire cross-section of art from this period, the gallery in Pécs is focused on selected and progressive artistic trends. With funding running out since the regime change, the museum in Pécs has lost significant ground. Gábor Ébli points out that "[i]ts symbolic distance from Budapest has multiplied by now. Pécs was very close to Budapest in the 1980s, the intelligentsia would regularly commute to Pécs to see new artists. Now, Pécs is almost off the map" (Interview with Gábor Ébli 2018).

Similar to Zachęta and Műcsarnok is the somewhat younger institution in the Czech Republic, the gallery of Rudolfinum, whose history is inseparable from the beginnings of the Czech National Gallery. In 1796, the Association of Patriotic Friends of Arts founded two institutions: the Academy of Fine Arts and the public Picture Gallery of the Association of Patriotic Friends of the Arts. As the latter was not able to meet expectations for the representation of contemporary art, in 1902 the Modern Gallery of the Kingdom of Bohemia (see Vlnas 1995) was established. It was founded by Emperor Franz Joseph I as his private foundation with a view to creating a collection of twentieth-century art. Truly modern, avant-garde art found its way there in the first years of operation; later purchases were concentrated primarily on nineteenth-century art. In 1918, the collection of the Picture Gallery attained status as the main art collection of the new Czechoslovak state. In his role as director from 1919, Vincenc Kramář limited the project to works created before 1800, while later works ended up in the Modern Gallery. In 1923 a significant purchase of modern French art took place. During the

Second World War, the gallery assumed the name of the National Gallery. In 1942, funds from the liquidated Modern Gallery were directed to the Gallery of the Czech-Moravian Lands (the official name of the National Gallery). In 1929, the Picture Gallery had to vacate the Rudolfinum, finding a temporary home in the attic of the Municipal Library a few years later. In the 1950s, the collection expanded to include a donation of Chinese works and paintings by Picasso and Braque.

The second largest collection of nineteenth- and twentieth-century art in Prague after the National Gallery was the Prague City Gallery. Formally, it was established in 1963, but efforts to create it began as early as the second half of the nineteenth century. After 1989, the City Gallery acquired a number of exhibition spaces for the presentation of twentieth- and twenty-first-century art.

The then Central Bohemian Gallery was founded in 1963 (after 1989, it changed its name twice) as a museum of modern and contemporary art based in Prague and at Nelahozeves Castle north of Prague. A long-time curator of the museum, Richard Drury, remembers that in the 1960s "our gallery had a modern permanent art collection, while in Prague at that time there wasn't one. People took the train and went up to Nelahozeves. Until it was terminated for ideological reasons in 1971, our permanent collection was a kind of cultural Mecca" (Interview with Richard Drury 2017). From 1973, the museum has had its own building (offices and exhibitions for temporary shows) in Prague; since 2010, it has operated in Kutná Hora.

The largest Czech art museum outside of Prague is the Moravian Gallery in Brno (see Lehmannová and Březinová 2011; Tomášek 2011; Zapletal 2011). The history of the collection of contemporary art here and the Picture Gallery functioning within it dates back to the Moravian Museum, established in 1817. In 1961, the latter separated from the museum; then, as the Moravian Gallery it was combined with the Museum of Applied Arts. Also in Brno, the House of Art must be mentioned, an exhibition space for contemporary art whose origins date back to the time of the Moravian Art Association (Mährischer Kunstverein, established in 1871). Opened in 1911, the Art Nouveau building received the name of the Kaiser Franz-Josefs-Jubiläums Künstlerhaus; after the Second World War, it was renamed the House of Art.

The third important center of art in the Czech Republic after Prague and Brno is Olomouc, whose Fine Art Gallery was established as part of the Regional Museum in 1952. In 1990, it gained independence and began to create its own permanent display. Two years later, its name was changed to the Museum of Art. In 2006, with the opening of the Archdiocesan Museum, the existing headquarters became the specialized Museum of Modern Art, focusing on art of the twentieth and twenty-first centuries, and housing both permanent and temporary exhibitions.

In terms of its organization, the aforementioned network of regional art museums dealing mainly with contemporary art of a given region resembles a network of Bureaus of Art Exhibitions established in Poland during a similar period. In the Czech Republic, the museums were establishing collections, while in Poland, temporary exhibition spaces were created. In 1953, the Gallery of Modern Art in Hradec Králové was opened, with a collection including representative Czech works from the turn of the nineteenth and twentieth centuries to the present. The Gallery of Modern Art in Roudnice nad Labem (1910) similarly specializes in modern art.

Slovakia was the last in the region to develop its state art collections. The first institution that adopted the name, "National Gallery of Slovakia" was founded in 1933 as part of the Slovak National Museum in Martin.[1] The next "Slovak Gallery" functioned from 1943 as a branch of the Bratislava Slovak Museum. It was not until 1948 that the Slovak National Gallery (SNG) appeared, which, despite many attempts, never merged with the National Museum and remained independent. The SNG has created a cross-sectional collection of mainly Slovak art, although from the very beginning, its attention was directed broadly toward twentieth-century art. The gallery's headquarters are the so-called Water Barracks on the banks of the Danube dating to the mid-eighteenth century, adapted for exhibition purposes in the years 1950–1955. But space turned out to be insufficient for the SNG's needs; hence, in 1963, an architectural competition was organized for the construction of a new museum wing. Vladimír Dedeček produced the winning entry; he proposed a wing suspended over the ground that would close off the courtyard from the side of the river at the height of the first, second, and third floors. The modernist wing was opened in 1977 (the project was not implemented in its entirety), and the permanent display was presented there until 2001, when owing to design defects, it was necessary to close for security reasons. Two architectural competitions have been carried out to modernize the closed wing and adapt the courtyard to a fully open public space. Construction work began in 2015.

The second most important institution of art in the capital, the Gallery of the City of Bratislava opened in 1961 in two locations, the Mirbach Palace and the Pálffy Palace. Its collection spans from the Middle Ages to the present. The other important art museums include the Jan Koniarek Gallery in Trnava, presenting twentieth-century Slovak art and the work of Ján Koniarek. Until 1991, it operated in rented spaces; after three years of adjustments, it was opened to the public in 1993, in the Neoclassical Kopplová villa. A new wing opened in 2002 on the occasion of the fiftieth anniversary of Koniarek's death. In 2004, the gallery obtained for exhibition purposes a late nineteenth-century synagogue, in which it opened a branch of the Synagogue – Center of Contemporary Art.

The museum boom since the 1990s

In the 1990s, few new art institutions emerged. The museum boom in this respect was marked only by the arrival of a new age and favorable circumstances related to the financing of new cultural investments. The gift of German collectors to Hungary in 1989 initiated the creation of the first independent museum of contemporary art in Central Europe, the Ludwig Museum, which opened in Budapest in 1996. In Prague, the role of the modern art museum is played by the powerful branch (1995) of the local National Gallery dedicated to art from the end of the nineteenth to the beginning of the twenty-first century and located in Veletržní palác. In Warsaw, the Museum of Modern Art was formally established in 2008, but it is still waiting for a proper building. In Bratislava, the Kunsthalle was established in 2014; the remodeling of the Slovak National Gallery, which brings together the objectives of a number of types of artistic and cultural institutions, began earlier. These four museums serve merely as an introduction to a long list of new institutions, new buildings, and important public discussions that have taken place and have continued since the 1990s.

The new institutions were the most popular in Poland. According to Joanna Mytkowska, director of the Modern Art Museum in Warsaw, "access to contemporary culture seems to be essential in order to be able to function in a complicated modern world. Compared with the development of this type of institution in our western neighbors, four museums for such a large country is not that many" (Interview with Joanna Mytkowska 2017). Similarly, Maria Anna Potocka, director of MOCAK Museum of Contemporary Art in Krakow, points to the positive aspect of the existence of many museums: "It is good even when there is more than one museum in the same city. Paris has several contemporary museums and they mutually drive the audience and justify their own existence" (Interview with Maria Anna Potocka 2017). Aneta Szyłak, proxy for the NOMUS New Museum of Art in Gdańsk, says that the creation of other institutions of modern art may be more and more difficult due to the termination of European funds and cultural policy that is focused on the past. But also, in her opinion, "you have to try, because it seems to me that contemporary art is an amazing tool that supports understanding the world. Artists are able to find a visual language for things for which we do not yet have words" (Interview with Aneta Szyłak 2017). In terms of institutions of modern and contemporary art, Poland is the most decentralized country in the region. Szyłak emphasizes that "there are more and more competent people in the field. It seems to me a very interesting tendency that we are no longer afraid of working outside the centres".

Chronologically, the first museum of contemporary art in Poland to adopt the name was established in Radom in 1990, as a branch of the Jacek Malczewski Museum (see Atlas 3.13). In addition to Warsaw, all major and many smaller cities have begun to create museums and art centers, or to expand existing museums to serve art of the twentieth and twenty-first centuries. In Krakow, the MOCAK Contemporary Art Museum was created in 2010, the only institution in the period under discussion to receive a dedicated building. In Wrocław, the Contemporary Museum was opened in interim headquarters (2012), followed by the Four Domes Pavilion Museum of Contemporary

Art, a new branch of the National Museum (2016). The Muzeum Sztuki in Łódź acquired a new building named ms² (2008), making it possible to present the collection properly. The Leon Wyczółkowski District Museum of Art in Bydgoszcz was also built, and within it a Gallery of Modern Art (2009). The new headquarters of the Cricoteka Center for the Documentation of the Art of Tadeusz Kantor was established in Krakow (2014), featuring not only exhibitions of Kantor's art, but also contemporary art referring to it. A new building of the Muzeum Śląskie (Silesian Museum), an artistic and historical museum, was opened in Katowice (2014); modern and contemporary art figures prominently. The NOMUS New Museum of Art in Gdańsk has started activity in its temporary location (2018). The only private museum of modern art in Poland, Villa la Fleur was founded in Konstancin-Jeziorna near Warsaw (2010).

The art center also became a popular type of institution. Five such centers were created in Poland: the LAZNIA Centre for Contemporary Art in Gdańsk (1998), the Wyspa Institute of Art in Gdańsk (2004), the Znaki Czasu Centre of Contemporary Art in Toruń (2008), the TRAFO Trafostacja Sztuki in Szczecin (2013), and the Elektrownia Mazovian Center for Contemporary Art in Radom (2005, 2014). The previously mentioned Ujazdowski Castle Center for Contemporary Art in Warsaw was also created. Galleries, whose activities are largely reminiscent of art centers, arose: Atlas Sztuki in Łódź (2003–2017), Art Stations Gallery in Poznań (2004–2016), and Szyb Wilson Gallery in Katowice (1998). After 1989, a few galleries that were part of the network of BWA built strong regional brands, such as the Arsenal Gallery in Białystok and BWA Tarnów.

In Hungary, apart from the Ludwig Museum, no museums dedicated to twentieth- or twenty-first-century art were created. In Dunaújváros, the Institute of Contemporary Art was established through the initiative of art historians and artists (1997); in Debrecen, the MODEM Modern and Contemporary Arts Center was created (2006) and from the beginning exhibited the private collection; in the town of Paks, a municipal gallery of contemporary art took shape (1991, since 2007 in a new building). The Municipal Museum of Art in Győr has been enriched with new collections of twentieth-century art by Béla Radnai and János Vasilescu, presented in dedicated buildings (opened in 1997 and 2006, respectively). In Budapest, the private MEO Contemporary Art Collection Art existed for almost six years (2001–2007); the private gallery KOGART focused on modern art (it was opened in 2004 and has been operating since 2013 also in Tihanyi). In Veszprém, two galleries were created for private collections: the Gallery of Modern Art for the László Vass Collection (2003), and in the Dubniczay Palace, the Károly László collection (2006).

In Prague, apart from the constantly expanding National Gallery, two museums of twentieth- and twenty-first-century art arose: first, the Museum Kampa, established by the Jan and Meda Mládek Foundation (2001), and later the Artbanka Museum of Young Art, in operation for less than two years

(2011–2013), which presented the newest art. Coming out of the Prague-based Czech Museum of Fine Arts, GASK was established (the Gallery of the Central Bohemian Region) in historic Kutná Hora. Within Prague, three art centers specializing in contemporary art were created: DOX (2008) and FUTURA (2003), as well as MeetFactory (2001, 2007), a center of contemporary art and culture. Prague is one of the cities in Central Europe most saturated with twentieth- and twenty-first-century art institutions, with new institutions constantly emerging. It also anticipates the opening of the new, private Kunsthalle Praha as well as other new museums initiated by private collectors. The National Gallery in Prague is planning to relocate part of its contemporary art collection to smaller centers by involving regional museums in cities such as Ústí nad Labem, České Budějovice, Hradec Králové, Pilsen, and others operating in Prague's shadow. The idea is based on the Artists Rooms program implemented by the Tate Gallery. The Egon Schiele Art Center (1993) in Český Krumlov presents Schiele's works and organizes exhibitions of modern and contemporary art. In Brno, a gallery space was created on the site of Friedrich Wannieck's former machine factory, first operated by the collector Richard Adam (2006–2015), and then location of the Fait Gallery (since 2016).

Three private museums of twentieth-century art were created in Slovakia: the Danubiana Meulensteen Art Museum, located in the small town of Čunovo (2000); then shortly after this, the Milan Dobeš Museum in Bratislava (2001–2016); and finally the ZOYA Museum in the village of Modra (2009). In addition, three Kunsthallen were created: Kunsthalle/Hala umenia in Košice (2013), Kunsthalle Bratislava (2014) and Nová synagóga/Kunsthalle Žilina (2015). In addition, the project space in Banská Štiavnica – Banská St a nica was also formed (2011). In Bratislava, the Nedbalka Gallery was created for the private collection of modern art (2012). The Tatra Gallery (1993, 2009) was opened in Poprad. In addition, the monographic Andy Warhol Museum of Modern Art opened in Medzilaborce (1991).

In sum, a very large number of new institutions have dramatically changed the cultural landscape of Central Europe. Each of the museums and art centers has a different profile, different dynamics, and a different scope; they differ in size; in whether they work with or without a collection, and in the intensity and ambition of their program. All have significantly influenced the shifting of cultural life towards twentieth- and twenty-first-century plastic arts. In the following chapters, these institutions appear in the context of the trends, phenomena, and discussions occurring in Central Europe after 1989.

The condition of Central European art institutions since the turn of the century

The dynamics of emerging new institutions, and the transformation of existing ones are a direct result of the political situation in and cultural policy of individual countries, which in the space of almost thirty years began to move in various directions. With respect to the functioning of cultural institutions, we can point to periods of prosperity, stagnation, and recession in each of the four countries after 1989. A milestone for the entire region was its entry into the European Union, influencing the influx of financial resources in all spheres of life, including culture.

Museums in all countries faced the problem of autonomy; private institutions, some of which began to build collections, emerged alongside public museums and galleries; private collections also began to supply public museums, and collectors cooperated with public institutions; finally, the challenge of establishing relationships with an audience occupies an increasingly central position in museum strategy.

In the 1990s, the Ludwig collection in Hungary became the *spiritus movens* for establishing a new museum specializing in contemporary art. It was also then that private galleries were developing intensely, many of which would close with the advent of the new century. A breakdown occurred in 2010, when the conservative Fidesz party won the parliamentary elections, and the Hungarian Academy of Arts started to occupy a key position in the cultural field. The Academy took over the management of Műcsarnok, the main exhibition space for contemporary art in Hungary. These changes have influenced the programs of exhibitions and projects. "All state institutions, including the Ludwig Museum, Műcsarnok and the Hungarian National Gallery, are somehow frozen", said museologist Miklós Székely (Interview with Miklós Székely 2018). "Contemporary art is to provoke, ask questions, generate debates, and that is not happening now". Due to the limited autonomy of public art institutions (there has been a high turnover in directorial positions), the politicization of granting bodies that prefer conservative projects, and the influence of people with links to the government, the modern art industry in Hungary has shifted to the private sector (Interview with József Mélyi 2018). The most important artistic project coloring the contemporary art scene is OFF-Biennale in Budapest, the first edition of which took place in 2015. This is a grassroots project, financed independently, whose overarching objective is to "help [re-establish] the foundations of an independent Hungarian art scene" (OFF-Biennale Budapest). Its stage is private apartments, vacant shops, industrial buildings, alternative theaters, and various public places. In addition, private galleries began to play the role of public institutions of contemporary art (József Mélyi lists acb Gallery, Vintage Gallery and Kister).

Art institutions' lack of independence from political influence is a problem in Slovakia, as well. This is particularly visible in regional museums, where the rotation of directors and main curators has prevented program continuity. Changes in positions are made for political reasons and managers, as Alexandra Kusá, general director of the Slovak National Gallery, points out (see the interview in Chapter 2), lack formal education and experience in the field of art. According to Katarína Rusnáková, a museum researcher and former director of the Collection of Modern and Contemporary Art at the National Gallery in Prague, the director of a well-functioning museum or art center should be:

> a visionary person, a skilled and experienced art historian, a curator and manager, who is a respected authority in the local environment as well as abroad. But permanent problems, however, are frequent conflicts of opinions between these personalities and the cultural and political elite.
>
> (Interview with Katarína Rusnáková 2018)

This disturbing practice has meant that the art museums in the provinces "have remained in a strange, frozen state", according to Vladimír Beskid, independent curator and artistic director of the European Capital of Culture Košice 2013. "These galleries are co-creating a stagnant, sour environment" (Interview with Vladimír Beskid 2018).

In the Czech Republic, an example of interference by regional authorities in the museum's structure is GASK – Gallery of the Central Bohemian Region (see Atlas 1.4), which since 2000 has been a contributory organization of the Central Bohemian Region. In 1998, the museum acquired the large historical building of the Jesuit College in Kutná Hora, enabling the presentation of the collection which previously had not been possible in Prague due to space constraints. A disagreement over the timeframe of opening the Jesuit College as a museum of art brought about a conflict between the institution and its financiers, leading to the subsequent replacement of the director and almost the entire staff; this resulted in a radical change in the gallery concept for the building's use. The original aim had been to create the Kutná Hora Arts Center for the display of the museum collection, also presenting a collection of Baroque Jesuit paintings, an exhibition devoted to the history of the Jesuit college and a presentation of Czech animated film by Krátký film Praha (Neumann 2001 [13]). A separate plan was devised in 2009 by the then Central Bohemian Governor, who also wished to house a new university in the Jesuit College. Insisting on opening the institution quickly, the Governor of the Central Bohemian Region dismissed the director in 2009. This in turn resulted in the replacement of the whole team of employees.

Political connections are visible not only at the regional level. In 1999, Milan Knížák, the director of the National Gallery in Prague, enjoyed the strong support of President Václav Havel. Art historians and art critics assessed his directorate very negatively (more on this in Chapter 7).

Exceptionally favorable conditions in Poland in 2004 led to the development of contemporary art institutions: a nationwide program to support the development of the collections "Znaki Czasu" was established (discussed in Chapter 8), which gave rise to two contemporary art museums, one art center, and collections that powered existing museums; the process of the creation of the Museum of Modern Art in Warsaw also began. These events generated lively debates about museum architecture, the need to develop existing museum collections, and the backwardness of infrastructure, as well as management, education, working with the audiences, and the museum's social role. Art institutions focused on the present were priority for the government only briefly, as the cultural policy of the ensuing decade was focused on museums of history and martyrdom. Nonetheless, this moment initiated a process of intense change that led to the participation of the municipal authorities.

Private museums in Central European countries separated from the West by an Iron Curtain did not arise; hence, their appearance is associated with the need to create places for the public presentation of private collections. However, private art institutions in Central Europe are few in number. In the Czech Republic and Slovakia, private capital produced several dynamically operating private museums, art centers and large non-commercial galleries, and private art collections gave rise to new public institutions or branches of existing museums.

Although the topic of museum audience is an enormous one not only in Central Europe, there the museums have been confronted with the urgent need to attract visitors. As Gábor Ébli states,

> [T]he public of museums began shrinking as mandatory school class visits were no longer organized, and people went for other pastimes. Museums in the 1990s in Hungary slowly came to understand that they will have to fight for visitors, as it is no longer automatic that pensioners' groups will come, or the government would be funding research activities, etc.
>
> (Interview with Gábor Ébli 2018)

The competition for audience turned out to be difficult, due on the one hand to the low level of visual literacy in contemporary art across the region, which museums and art centers had to address; and on the other, to the reluctance of many museums to change their attitudes to a visitor and to working with their audience, so as to give the matter a weight comparable to the care of collections. In Ébli's opinion, the need to transform the Hungarian National Gallery – the largest museum of Hungarian art – was one of the main reasons for its loss of autonomy and its merging with the well-managed (in terms of public relations and attendance numbers) Museum of Fine Arts. He states,

> [The] strong move from the ivory tower-like old museum model towards a visitor friendly institution, part of the culture industry, performed by the Museum of Fine Arts has been the number one issue in the country's museum arena, with much media coverage, for more than a decade now.

Vladimír Beskid says that in Slovakia in general, culture is not a social priority, and art – especially contemporary art – occupies a much lower position than theater, literature, or the protection of monuments (Interview with

Vladimír Beskid 2018). Mytkowska points to the growth of the audience interested in contemporary art, but also says that in the face of changes in the Polish education system resulting in the removal of subject matter pertaining to the participation in culture from the school curriculum, "We reach the limit of viewers who have some preparation" (Interview with Joanna Mytkowska 2017), which she asserts may translate into an undesirable elitism of these institutions.

Note

1 From the second half of the nineteenth century, Martin (at that time Turčiansky Svätý Martin) was the spiritual capital of Slovakia. In 1863, Matica Slovenská (whose activity suspended in 1875–1919) was established here, constituting the nucleus of the national library, museum, scientific society and publishing house, which for a long period was the only Slovak intellectual center, an institution that nurtured national traditions. See Niedziela (1995: 55–56).

2 The transformation of museums in Central Europe

Conversations about changes and challenges

In this chapter, I would like to give voice to those who contribute to the region's museum landscape. At the end of 2017, I conducted four interviews with museum researchers and professionals devoted to the development of museums in Central Europe after 1989. I invited four people from various Visegrad countries to share their perspective on the development of art institutions in their countries. Each of these conversations offers a look at another aspect of the museums' operation in Central Europe; they refer above all to the museum infrastructure, the public, and management issues.

I talked with Dorota Folga-Januszewska about the specificity of museums in the Central European region. My interlocutor worked for thirty years at the National Museum in Warsaw performing functions from superintendent to director; currently she is the deputy director of the Museum of King Jan III's Palace in Wilanów. She is one of the leading experts and authorities in the field of museology in Poland and the Central European region. For over ten years, she has been the chairperson of the ICOM Poland and is also active in the international arena (including the Central European ICOM Group). Her professional experience and scholarly interests revolving around Central European and world museums in both their historical and present forms allowed her to look at Polish museums in the context of issues relevant to museums in different countries. In our conversation, she drew attention to topics that have not yet been exhausted by museums in the region – the identity of museums, their reactions to mainstream practices, their survival rate, as well as communication and collecting strategies.

Jiří Fajt discusses changes taking place in the National Gallery in Prague, where he has been general director since 2014. He mostly refers to the planned rebuilding of the Trade Fair Palace (Veletržní palác), which is a branch devoted to modern and contemporary art, and its change of focus to be more oriented towards Central Europe. He also sketches the scene of art institutions in Prague and the Czech Republic in a broader sense. Before coming to the NG as director, my interlocutor worked at the University of Leipzig and as a curator.

Alexandra Kusá looks at Slovak museums through the prism of the Slovak National Gallery in Bratislava, which she manages. She talks about the changes taking place in Slovak museums, many of which follow Western models, as well as related cultural policy. She devotes great attention to the social role of museums and to working with the public. Kusá has extensive experience in museum work (she started at the SNG as an assistant working with a collection of modern and contemporary art); she has also worked at the auction house and at the Moravian Gallery in Brno.

The last of my interlocutors, László Baán, is primarily a cultural manager with experience working in high positions, first in the office of the mayor of Budapest, and then in the Ministry of Culture, where he was responsible for finances. Since 2004, he has been the director of the Museum of Fine Arts in Budapest. He has been serving since 2011 as the Government and Ministerial Commissioner for the new Museum Quarter in Budapest, as well as president of the Városliget Ltd. Company that is implementing this investment. The conversation is primarily about this great undertaking, whose momentum and complexity are unmatched in Central Europe. He comments on this investment largely from an economic point of view, and presents museums as an asset that have an impact on public revenue and tourism.

Interview with Dorota Folga-Januszewska

> Prof. Dr. Dorota Folga-Januszewska was a long-standing President ICOM Poland, and is a member of SAREC – Strategic Allocation Review Committee ICOM. She is also Professor at the Academy of Fine Arts in Warsaw, where she is the Chair of the Theory Department in the Faculty of Graphic Arts. She is the deputy director at the King Jan III Palace Museum in Wilanów, Warsaw. An art historian, art critic, and museologist, she served from 2010–2012 as director of the Institute of Museology at the Wyszyński University in Warsaw, where she was also the Founder of the program in museum studies. She also lectured at Warsaw University. From 1979–2008, she worked in the National Museum in Warsaw (in 2007–2008, she was general director). She is the author of 340 books and catalogues, and curator of fifty-four exhibitions.

After the turn of 1989, and especially over the last dozen years or so, fundamental changes have taken place in museums. Which changes from your perspective seem the most fundamental, with regard to museums in our part of Europe in particular?

I think that first of all, you need to be aware of the changes that have taken place in our environment – I am thinking here of the Polish situation, of Central Europe, but also of changes all over the world. The most important ones include: connecting people with extensive networks, as did the Internet in the 1990s, as well as supra-cultural phenomena arising from this new way of communicating. Social networks also emerged. These gave birth to a new type of organization, and "horizontal" structures connected people interested in certain phenomena. Here we can jump to museums – the great new phenomenon of the end of the twentieth and the beginning of the twenty-first centuries has been global "museumization". After a two-thousand-year period of museum development, a boom in these institutions took place. Museums from Africa to Australia, from both Americas to Asia, and course including those lying within Europe, had become "symptoms" of civilization in past decades. Natural, anthropological, historical, artistic, technical, scientific, cosmic museums, science fiction, literary museums, artists and sports museums – all of them are *signum temporis* – spaces for a new form of active education. It did not happen immediately, one can even say; it took a long time, at least from the *mouseion* age, that is, the Beotian festivals, the Mouseion, the places of ancient education, through dozens of historical, intangible, and material forms, to active social centers based on the exchange of ideas, as are many museums around the world today.

From today's point of view, what seems to me to combine these ancient beginnings and recent changes is the re-recognition of the importance of intangible heritage in museums, as well as the professional protection of material exhibits. All of this is done within the active "environment" of museums; that is, the social, cultural, and natural environment in which museums operate on a daily basis. This two-way street – that is to say, the impact of audience expectations on museum programs and the impact of museums on the environment, realized consciously – is in my opinion the essence of the ongoing changes. Perhaps the word "audience" is no longer appropriate. We are talking rather about communities in which and for which museums exist.

The virtualization of the world and digital communication led, in a very short time, to the fact that on one hand, museums dominated by multimedia forms of presentation were "tiring"; but on the other, the same processes strengthened the widespread expectation of free access to information. So we have a new model of the museum, which should be an interestingly designed space, and in it, there are encounters with artifacts of the whole animate and inanimate world, interestingly presented information ingested by the recipient's mood, education, or free time. I think that this type of change applies to us in Central Europe, as well as to museology in many other parts of the world.

Do you feel that museums in Central Europe, especially those that are newly emerging and lack the tradition and "ballast" of the nineteenth or twentieth century, are different from the Western European or American museums?

I wonder if today (in the second decade of the twenty-first century) the point of reference is still museums in the United States and Western Europe. Is it not that new trends in museum institutions are currently being created and developed in Asia – Japan, China, South Korea, India – as well as in Australia or Canada? I don't know! I have the impression that the economic, mental, and political changes that have taken place in Central Europe (from the Vistula to the Rhine, from the Baltic to the Carpathians?) are only in the "beginning of conscious reflection" phase. Central Europe in the twentieth century experienced dramatic events and, as shown in recent years, the wounds are not yet healed. On the contrary, the demons of "guilt and punishment" are constantly awakening, directly impacting the creation of many new museums and memorial sites. It also brings Central Europe closer to other "post-transition" nations that are often geographically distant (China, Central and Northern African countries), but which experience similar problems.

Many museums in our region are museums of anxieties that are not understood and are difficult for outsiders to "read". When I was working on the guide for *1,000 Museums in Poland* (2008–2010, 2011 ed.), I traveled to many places where new institutions were created, and I talked (often incognito) with their employees. Then it occurred to me that a frequent motive for founding new museums is the need to document harm: lost collections, nationalized estates, places of execution, destroyed factories, devastated natural areas. Although more than seventy years have passed since the Second World War, and since the transformations of 1989 – also over quarter century – our memory cannot dispose of the "unresolved" topics. This applies to historical, ethnographic, and anthropological museums, as well as to artistic and even technical ones. In recent years, this phenomenon is worsening thanks to the "policy of remembrance" promoted by the authorities. The memory of trauma, however, is revealed not only in historical museums; it is also present in regional museums, it influences the way these places are organized, and the language that these institutions use to communicate with their surroundings. Because we live in an era of open communication on many levels, these emotions – rarely positive – are spreading faster and more effectively. They affect not only the sense and content of the message, but also influence the form architecture takes, the means of spatial planning, and the visual design of exhibitions.

Of course, this does not apply to all museums, but all you need to do is enter several museums of modern and contemporary art – in Warsaw, Prague, Budapest, Berlin, Vilnius, Vienna – to encounter at least three generations of artists who – although working or having worked in other conditions – are not able either to omit or suppress some measure of anxiety.

Once I thought that this anxiety is a Polish specialty, but the more I travel around Slovakia, Hungary, Austria, or the Czech Republic, I see that even in these areas, museologists are constantly struggling with the problem of how to exhibit this type of emotion. Central Europe has many museums that need to "survive", to be reconceived, and understood.

And in this I see the biggest difference. The museums of Italy and France; those in many German lands (especially western and southern Germany); the British, Dutch, and Spanish museums, of course to some extent also, are devoted to various wars, dramas, and religious conflicts. But the biggest difference I can feel in the design, arrangement, selection, and presentation of exhibits in these countries consists in the goal of people organizing these museums to offer the communities for whom they work something that can be termed, the "pleasure of knowledge", regardless of the dominant subject.

This sensory approach to the design of form and meaning gives the museum audience a certain type of comfort. And because people like when something is a bit "pleasant", these museums are visited frequently and constitute an inherently participatory element of community life. Of course, there are big differences – for example, as between museums in different regions of Italy, Spain or France – but their common feature is this neuro-aesthetic line of positive experiences, possibly resulting from a certain stage of cultural history.

These two types of "programming of emotions" can also be felt in the arrangement of museum architectures large and small. We know that the form of space has a huge impact on our experiences and their interpretations. Maybe in this respect it is worth analyzing museums erected in our part of Europe?

The very investigation into the architectural form – namely, architectural competitions and discussions over the selections – was a source of great emotions and broad social interest. But do you have the impression that they want to deal with the region and engage in cooperation with its institutions, or is this path subordinated to foreign, especially mainstream culture?

It is very difficult to answer this question unambiguously. We must remember that museums, like all spaces of creativity, can be very strongly personalized. The personalities of their creators – architects, directors, curators – are largely reflected in the program and language of the environment. This difference and uniqueness overlaps with the specificity of the region (both in the sense of community and foreignness towards the environment); with understanding the role of the museum as a creator of values and mediator; but also with regional policy, social, national, religious, and political problems. There are no two similar examples. There are places like the famous Muzeum Sztuki in Łódź, which is on one hand the fruit of the most magnificent traditions of pre-war Łódź and the heir to the avant-garde. But on the other hand, being embedded in the particularities of the formerly working-class city, it had to grapple for many years after the Second World War with the local society's lack of interest. The legendary "a.r." collection of modern art was well known outside of Poland, appreciated and invited to exhibitions in Paris (Centre Pompidou), but the museum complained about low local turnout. It worked for the region, but it took many years of effort to build a new headquarters so that the museum's relations with youth, schools, and local governments eventually resulted in something that could be called a relationship of mutual sympathy.

There are also completely different examples. During the Solidarity uprising in 1980–1981, social protests called for the restoration of the Muzeum Śląskie in Katowice and its magnificent holdings of Polish painting collected by Tadeusz Dobrowolski as proof of the Polishness of Upper Silesia – a so-called social objective. In 1984, the museum the Germans destroyed in 1940 was revived, and regional funding made it possible to set up this museum, interestingly, on the site of the "Katowice" mine, underground. It was opened in 2014. All the work shown in the exhibitions, especially the exhibition presenting the history and culture of Silesia, was accompanied by heated, sometimes shocking discussions and debates – the best proof of how important this museum was becoming to the community.

I have other examples in mind. When I went to see the Andy Warhol Museum of Modern Art in Medzilaborce, Slovakia (see Atlas 4.8) for the first time, I became aware of the phenomenon mentioned in your last question – but it has many facets. Warhol – born in Pittsburgh, treated as a star of American art, son of Julia Zavacká and Ondrej Warhola, and very close to his mother who never learned English (Andy talked to her always in Ruthenian, they took part in the ritual year in the Orthodox church in Pittsburgh) – becomes in the 1990s the epitome of the Central European emigrant success story. At the great exhibition of Warhol's works, which I put on at the National Museum in Warsaw in 1998, the then-director and creator of this museum in Medzilaborce, Michal Bycko showed up. Soon an association was formed – Spoločnosť Andyho Warhola – bringing to life numerous programs for children and youth in the region of the Carpathian Mountains in eastern Slovakia. Has the museum influenced the community? Probably, although apparently among the more than ten thousand visitors this museum hosts annually, the majority are Poles (the border is close). The museum building itself in Medzilaborce is a typical box structure of the social realist houses of 1970s and 80s. Adjacent to the church, it looks like it dropped in from another planet.

Museums that would accentuate the art of Central Europe in their collections and exhibitions are scarce. Do you think that this Central European-ness is too seldom compared to other areas of interest?

I am not sure if I can now recognize this "Central European-ness" as a phenomenon. At the beginning, I mentioned the anxiety that was constantly circulating in Central Europe after the Second World War. Today, in the second half of 2017, we see that the situation of museums around the world has changed a lot, new problems have arisen, and tensions have moved to the Middle East, Korea, Ukraine, Spain, and Catalonia, Great Britain and Scotland. At the same time, museums around the world have created horizontal relations within the industry. There are separate associations of museums of technology and science, museums of natural history and living nature, university museums and a separate committee of museums of modern art ICOM (CIMAM). This influenced the dissemination of experiences and the blurring of strong program differences, especially in the area of modern and contemporary art. Perhaps the most striking example is when the Museum of Modern Art in Warsaw (MSN) organized "an action" *To be Found* in 2014. Located in the Sculpture Park in Bródno, it was one of the elements of the conceptual program of the Chinese artist Ai Weiwei (his total program was implemented in dozens of places around the world). Lately, and more and more often, I have the impression that museums of contemporary art in particular work just like modern media – high-profile material is sold simultaneously through hundreds of channels. It has become such a race for overnight success. When the employees of these museums look for a different, more individual path, they do not find support from their organizers who finance museums and expect their popularity. It is a vicious circle.

On the other hand, as if in response to the increasing criticism of the "art world", there are waves of small social initiatives, bottom-up, often flowing from artists themselves. They are local, regional, and private, and participation in them is sometimes the privilege of integrated social networks and specific knowledgeable individuals. In this way, the world of individual cells, of which rarely something is known and of which little is spoken, is growing. There is on the one hand globalization and surveillance, and on the other a specialization and a desire to be enclosed within a small circle.

We are dealing not only with the boom for museums and exhibition institutions, but also with their turnover. One institution is closed down, another emerges. Not only in Poland. Is there anything else missing from this landscape of art institutions? Or is it enough to build and create new institutions?

This disappearance and creation of new institutions is perhaps a more frequent feature in this part of Europe than elsewhere. But of course it happens all over the world. I do not know if someone has ever collected data indicating how many new museums or galleries appear and disappear every decade. I can think of many interesting places that do not exist anymore. Even when I was writing the *1,000 Museums in Poland*, I had to remove three or four museums at the turn of 2010 and 2011 because they ceased to function. Rather, the "persistence" of cultural institutions is something extraordinary, a phenomenon that proves either the good patronage of the state, local governments, foundations, associations or the determination of individual people and the community. Some collectors, after accumulating works, declare their willingness to convey them to the "gaze" of the audience, but it also happens frequently enough that in not finding a partnership in one place, they disappear with their collections and open a museum somewhere else. After the failure of talks in Warsaw, Grażyna Kulczyk chose Susch in Engadine, Switzerland, where an institution is being created that serves as both the museum and studio space for artists, to be opened in the winter of 2018–2019. Located near the road leading to St. Moritz, in the very center of the beautiful ski and tourist areas, the museum certainly will find its audience, although it must be remembered that in Switzerland, there is no shortage of private collections and museums. How long will it last? This is also difficult to assess at present.

On the question of whether it is enough to build and create new museums and galleries in Poland or in Central Europe, I will answer emphatically – no, that is not enough! The more that are created, the better the testimony to the level of social education and needs. Of course, only a small number of those will remain – those that find an audience, develop the right language for dialogue with the environment, these will be the necessary ones . . .

The maintenance and development of large and valuable collections and museums, the scale of which necessitates public support, requires more care. That is why I am concerned that some large state and local museums have slowed down the pace of collecting contemporary art, both Polish and European, as well as from other parts of the world. The National Museums in Warsaw or Wrocław, Krakow, and Poznań organize exhibitions, but not much is heard about their collections policies, or new acquisitions of contemporary art. The new institutions such as MSN in Warsaw do not play this role to the right degree. You can, of course, explain the reasons for the trouble – the lack of space and financial resources – but in fact it is rather a lack of vision and determination that leads to "holes" in collections that will be difficult to fill in the future. What is missing for me? I guess the vision of development, program, a strength in decision-making, determination, and wider cooperation with creators – not only with one well-known milieu, but also with different environments. I am missing something like consistently implemented "program risk", whose fruits are often great collections, the value of which is revealed fully only after many years.

12 October 2017

Interview with Jiří Fajt

> Jiří Fajt is a Czech-German art historian, curator, university teacher, and, since 2014, General Director of the National Gallery in Prague. He specializes in Medieval and early Renaissance culture in Europe north of the Alps, with a special focus on the fine arts and architecture. He has headed science, research, exhibition, and publishing projects at the Leibniz Institute for the History and Culture of Eastern Europe at the University of Leipzig, and has authored numerous treatises, catalogues and books devoted to the art patronage of the Luxembourg and Jagiellonian ruling dynasties in Central Europe, as well as prepared a number of international exhibitions for various institutions including the Metropolitan Museum of Art in New York, the Städel Museum in Frankfurt, the Art History Museum in Vienna and the National Gallery in Prague.

Prague does not have a museum of contemporary art. There is Museum Kampa, but that has been built around a private collection reflecting the interests of the collector and is thus not fully representative. Can we say that the Trade Fair Palace substitutes for a museum of modern and contemporary art in the Czech Republic?

I would not say it is a substitute, but that it is indeed a museum of modern and contemporary art which is part of the National Gallery. The programming of this museum corresponds with that of any other autonomous museum of modern and contemporary art, so it does not matter whether from the organizational point of view it is part of a bigger institution.

The Trade Fair Palace has a long history. How has the National Gallery (most importantly the branch at the Trade Fair Palace) been changing since 2011 after the directorship of Milan Knížák, in particular?

There have been general changes which affected the whole inner structure of the gallery. I do not think there were any definitive changes when Knížák left. I took over in 2014, and since that time, I have been organizing the whole institution. We have created a new inner structure so it can fulfill the expectations of a twenty-first-century art museum. We have established a membership program and a very attractive sponsorship program which are already yielding good results; we have pointed out the importance of the scientific activity of the museum and created a separate section that deals with scholarly activities.

There is no change that could be defined as specific to the Trade Fair Palace and the collection that is housed there. However, there has been a great change in terms of the programming of the Trade Fair Palace, which is reflected in the increased number of visitors. The number of visitors to the whole National Gallery grew from 250,000 in 2014 to 720,000 in 2015, so it has almost tripled in recent years. That corresponds to the income of the National Gallery, which has also more than tripled. This is a very distinct change which I would say came about from the reinvigoration of the Trade Fair Palace, so that is specific to the Trade Fair Palace.

When I came to the National Gallery, I indeed gave my full attention to the Trade Fair Palace. I decided to focus on this building and invite the young generation here. The building was almost empty when I took over, and now you see many young people there who visit the collections and stay in the coffee shop. It is probably thanks to our new general partner, Komerční banka, which has supported us in such a way that it has allowed us to make the gallery free of charge for anyone up to the age of 26. That has had a great impact on the viewership numbers.

What are your priorities and specific focus regarding the collection areas of modern and contemporary art?

The national character of the collection is actually quite interesting, because in addition to a very strong focus on Czech and Slovak art, there is also a very strong focus on the international scene in terms of modern and contemporary art. This is based on the governmental acquisition scheme of the late 1920s. At that time, the government decided to acquire a substantial number of French artworks directly from artists' studios, so thanks to this we have one of the most important collections of paintings by Picasso (twenty-five paintings and more than sixty works on paper). I would like to keep up this acquisition tradition, not only for Czech art, which is of course the backbone of our acquisition policy, but we would like to focus on the whole region of

Central and Eastern Europe, i.e., the former Soviet bloc countries. We would like to expand this profile by acquiring individual pieces by classic masters of modern and contemporary art.

Is the focus on the former Soviet bloc countries also reflected in the programming?

Yes. Twice a year, we organize an exhibition focused on the youngest generation of artists coming from the whole region. It is called *Introducing* and takes place in the Trade Fair Palace. The young artists are coming from different parts of the world, but mainly from Central and Eastern Europe. We collaborate closely with Berlin, Vienna, and Dresden. We have a very close partnership with the Staatlichen Kunstsammlungen Dresden – we are exchanging our people, inviting appropriate programming from them, and jointly developing concepts for exhibitions. We are very well-linked to the whole region. I have close contacts with Poland, Hungary, and Slovakia based on my former activities in Germany, where I am still living.

Has this regional focus always been important for the Trade Fair Palace, or has it appeared recently?

I do not think it was previously as important for the National Gallery. This is a new strategy that came with the new leadership – I implemented this strategy when I took over.

What challenges do you have to face in running the National Gallery and specifically the Trade Fair Palace?

Some of those challenges are of a general nature. We are fighting some legal limitations. Along with the Czech Philharmonic and the National Theater, we are trying to change the legal status of this institution. We hope our new legal status will be very much like what we know from, for example, the German-speaking countries. I think what is quite crucial is to have a certain freedom in offering salaries to the people who are to be employed by the National Gallery. We need to be on a comparable level with the international market, which is not the case at the moment. I would say that the most complicated situation is with the salaries – how to hire people from abroad. That is an important condition for the good programming of a national gallery. We work with the international public and we invite many curators from different countries. I hired Marius Winzeler [director of the Municipal Museums Zittau in 2009–2015] as the Director of the Old Masters Collection, and then I hired two people coming from the United States, namely Milena Kalinovská [director of public programs and education at the Hirshhorn Museum and Sculpture Garden in Washington, DC in 2004–2015], who became the Director of the Collection of Modern and Contemporary Art, and Adam Budak, who was born in Krakow, spent 12 years in Graz [Curator for Contemporary Art at the Kunsthaus Graz in 2003–2011] and two years in Washington, DC [Curator for Contemporary Art at the Hirshhorn

Museum and Sculpture Garden in 2011–2012], and who has become the Curator for special projects of the National Gallery.

Do you find it hard to attract the Czech public with contemporary art, especially local, Praguers?

It is quite challenging. People are not used to contemporary or modern art. It is quite new to the local public. However, I think it is possible to achieve certain results, and I do believe people will become more interested in what we are doing. We simply need time to open their minds and their eyes, to invite them to the National Gallery and to persuade them that it is worth visiting the institution and paying attention not only to modern art, but also to contemporary art. From time to time, contemporary art is not comprehensible enough, and many people do not feel it speaks to them. That is why educational activities are necessary in institutions such as the National Gallery, so we are working on a variety of academic, educational programs with a special focus on contemporary art. We have started a close collaboration with the Austrian foundation Thyssen-Bornemisza Art Contemporary (TBA21), established by Francesca von Habsburg. We signed an agreement for five years with them and the result of this partnership will be an exhibition of their outstanding collection of internationally acclaimed artists. The whole collection will move to Prague and we are now reshaping one of our venues, the Salm Palace, which is located directly in front of Prague Castle, i.e., a very prestigious location, in order to host this fantastic collection of 800 pieces. This represents another focus on contemporary art.

If you were to compare the National Gallery in Prague to the National Gallery in Bratislava, the Hungarian National Gallery in Budapest and the National Museum in Warsaw, what are the particular features of the National Gallery in Prague and in what ways is it similar to those institutions?

I think that all these institutions are facing similar problems – the insufficient exhibiting of some works of art, of international modern and contemporary art. I also think that every museum in this region can complain of a lack of finances. I do not think there is such a lack of finances in the Czech Republic, and in the case of the National Gallery there is a great potential for fundraising. One needs to come up with an attractive program. As I mentioned in the beginning, we have put in place a well-functioning sponsorship program which makes enough money to cover the expenses of the international exhibitions. The great challenge is to create conditions which would be attractive for people coming from abroad, from the Western part of the world. Among the similarities there is, possibly, the legal situation of the institutions. Many of my colleagues are facing the same problems with the legal status of their institutions and there have been some attempts to change it – for example, the National Museum in Warsaw having a board of trustees – but I do not think this really works now.

Regarding the differences, there are of course different collections which form the basis of these institutions, and the institutions themselves have to create specific programming. Certain differences can stem from different political situations. I know the impact of politics in Hungary is quite strong, and unfortunately, the changes there are very much politically influenced. Slovakia and the Czech Republic are quite similar. Personally, I have not experienced any political interventions since I took over, and as far as I know, the situation in Slovakia is very much so.

Is there room, in your view, for another institution dealing with contemporary art in Prague and in the Czech Republic? I do not mean a gallery, but rather a bigger institution such as a museum, or center of contemporary art, or a Kunsthalle.

I think so. The whole artistic scene in Prague is developing quickly. There are several projects coming into being, like a private Kunsthalle which is going to be opened within two or three years near Prague Castle. There are also other private museums that are going to be created in the years to come. It is a very good sign for the whole artistic scene. I do not think there is a great deal of opportunity or room for the state to come up with a new public institution – I mean a museum with collections. The structure of the state institutions is sufficient. There were some questions about whether the state should run institutions such as the Rudolfinum, but in my opinion, it was a very good decision made at that time to found a state Kunsthalle. The programming of the Rudolfinum is very good. When the National Gallery was not functioning well, the Rudolfinum was the only institution that was relevant on an international scale. There is certainly space for private initiatives.

Since all these new initiatives are coming into being in Prague, which is already well-developed in terms of modern and contemporary art, does it not mean that the provincial cities are becoming more and more underrepresented?

You are right, there are very few initiatives taking place outside of Prague. I agree that regarding the programming focusing on contemporary art, regional cities are underrepresented. That is why my colleagues and I are thinking about how to get away from Prague and bring contemporary art to the regions, to smaller cities. I know quite well what happened in the UK with the Tate, when they came up with the program of artist rooms ten years ago. I have already invited one of the curators who was in charge of the artist rooms to come to Prague and share her experience with us. We are now developing a program on how to bring contemporary art from Prague to these small places. You are absolutely right that there is a lot going on in Prague, but it is not an ideal situation for the future understanding of contemporary art in the whole country.

The number of those new initiatives means that there is still a museum boom, and we have only discussed contemporary art. Does it mean there are new museums to be created within other types of museums, such as

historical museums, natural history museums, etc., or is this just a phenomenon regarding art and particularly contemporary art?

I think this only concerns the visual arts, contemporary art. I do not know if we can speak about a museum boom because it is focused only on this specific type of institution.

I already asked about the challenges for the National Gallery. Now I would like to ask about the challenges for Czech museums in general.

The most important challenge for every museum, not just Czech ones, is to find a proper way to approach the visitor. The former discourse on this topic in museology was very much focused on the works of art themselves because they are the natural basis of every museum and we are obliged to take care of our collections. However, the main concern of every institution nowadays is to pay attention to the visitor. The visitor is located at the center of all of our activities. We have to adapt our programming to the needs of our visitors, which doesn't mean lowering the quality of what we do. There is still much left to be done in Czech museums. I think that there are many people who have not yet realized this change in the main discourse about museums. This is one point. And the second point is that the institutions will have to come up with really interesting programming. That does not necessarily mean populist programs. A museum should be based on scholarly approach, i.e., every exhibition should be prepared on comprehensible but deeply academically based research. That is not the case in many museums, not just in the Czech Republic, but worldwide. The intellectual quality of the project is what we need to support – intellectually well-prepared exhibitions which would present new topics and new messages to society, often even against the mainstream. That is one of the main challenges and potentials for cultural institutions in a globalized world at the moment.

5 January 2018

Interview with Alexandra Kusá

Note: Jiří Fajt was removed from the position of the director general in April 2019.

> Dr. Alexandra Kusá received her Masters degree in Art History at the Faculty of Arts of the Comenius University in Bratislava, and later her doctorate on the subject of Socialist Realism. She gained her professional experience as curator of the SOGA Gallery and the Collection of Modern Art (an auction house in Bratislava), and then moved to the Slovak National Gallery where she started as assistant curator of the Modern and Contemporary Art collection. There, she later became curator, chief curator of the Collection of Architecture, chief curator of the Modern and Contemporary Art collection, and finally the General Director (since 2010). She is still active as a curator. Since 2006, she has been lecturing in the Art History Department at Comenius University.

Comparing the Slovak National Gallery to other Central European national galleries – the National Gallery in Prague, the Hungarian National Gallery in Budapest, the National Museum in Warsaw – how would you characterize it, briefly?

We are definitely the smallest museum in terms of collection, tradition, and building. Because of this, we are less prominent on the international scene. We were created in 1948, which is very late for a national gallery, owing to Czechoslovakian politics. A positive aspect of this fact is that we are not weighed down by tradition, and so we can be more creative and freer in terms of how we work with the collections. Also, our museum is not in the politicians' sites; therefore, the director position and the exhibition plan are not under pressure from political parties.

The SNG is now in the process of major redevelopment. You will not only recover space that you lost when a whole wing was closed in 2001 due to its poor technical state, but you also will gain the new courtyard space. How do you imagine the institution at this moment?

We are thinking very hard right now about how we are going to work, because the role of museums in the contemporary world is changing. Right now, much of our space is closed. It is difficult for us to mount exhibitions because we do not have a transit depository, a photo studio, all of the invisible infrastructure needed to make professional work. We decided that we are going to call this period a "creative provision". We are using it to become more advanced, to try new things. We do not need to be conservative, because we are not fully formed. Now, we can be more creative – we can try many more programs, and test how we can work in the future. For example, five years ago, we decided to make a summer pavilion. We turned the courtyard of the former gallery into a space that was to serve the public from spring until late autumn. And it worked perfectly! That is why we included this experience in the reconstruction plan; we simply changed it so that this space can serve the public in a better way.

How did the temporary pavilion work?

We decided to erect an architectural structure with built-in opportunities for various activities. We actually received an architectural prize for it. We prepared special gallery programs there, and made the space available to other institutions. Normally in galleries many things are prohibited, so we decided to work with these rules in a positive way, turning them into slogans proclaiming that everything was allowed: "sitting on the ground is allowed!", "doing nothing is allowed!", "touching things is allowed!". It served as a public space for two years, and was connected neither to the collection nor to the building.

This way, through opening up practices, you embrace changes that are visible in museums all over the world.

Everything in galleries around the world is changing now. Institutions are opening up. We have experience with this, and it really can be very progressive. We know from Vienna and elsewhere, as we steal and share ideas from all over Europe, how we do and do not want our gallery to work. I hope we are clever enough to do it. Now when I travel, I usually do not look at art first; I usually look at how an institution is working, how it deals with audience, how the object labels are made, how the shop is working, what the programs are.

Vienna is very close to Bratislava. Does this mean that Viennese museums in a general sense are a pattern for you?

In referring to Vienna, I specifically mean the MuseumsQuartier because it is very familiar to the Slovak public, who of course will make the comparison. The MQ is a whole area with different functions. It is a very popular place, but popular as a public space. One has a similar feeling at the Tate Modern, in the Turbine Hall – a feeling of community space not necessarily connected to the collections. This is something we want to recreate in the Slovak National Gallery, only on a smaller scale. I think it is realistic. When we made the "creative provision", we had only one space, the "Berlinka". We decided that we did not have enough money to create our own programming. Throughout the city, there are plenty of fine institutions and programs, but without space. Now, we are a platform for all kinds of cultural activities; we secured good partnerships and do not need to do everything by ourselves. That is what we learned from this bad situation – that sharing is the perfect solution for us. We have even transferred this idea into the digital realm when we created WebUmenia, a website that contains most of our collections. For this the Rijksmuseum was our model, as well as the "sharing is caring" movement. The number of digital visitors is currently half of the number of actual ones, and is increasing.

And what is that that you do not want to recreate from the MQ?

The connection of public space with the galleries there is very weak, as it was completely steamrolled by free activities. This is probably due to the fact that there are several institutions there and that MQ is not only a gallery, but also an umbrella for various activities. As a consequence, it is hard to promote a single theme.

Do you think that the proximity of Vienna influences the programming of art institutions in Slovakia?

Yes, for big projects it is too close. Vienna is always the first choice as a partner for traveling exhibitions.

One of the priorities now for museums worldwide is audience engagement and inclusion. Do you observe this trend in Slovakia?

It is hard for me to say, but as far as I can see, we are far and away the only ones dealing with this type of question. Most Slovak museums and galleries are focused simply on surviving.

Let us speak for a moment about the more general situation surrounding museums in Slovakia. How have museums been changing here since the early 1990s? What are the milestones?

The biggest changes were in the areas of finances and audience. For a few years after the transformations of 1989, the main focus was on economics and the role of culture diminished. This was happening, I suppose, across Eastern Europe. I had the same experience when I worked in the Czech Republic. In the museums in the West, there were crowds of visitors, art was part of their life; while in Eastern Europe, the situation was very different. Things have started to change. Three or four years ago, the number of visitors to our gallery finally started to grow. Another major change is in the area of political connections. Cultural politics was a big issue in socialist countries. During the Vladimír Mečiar period (1990s), the situation in Slovakia was really bad, and the museum scene was saved by non-state activities and money from entities like the Soros Foundation or the Pro Helvetia Foundation. We inherited a huge lacuna in exhibition programs and collections. Until 1989, galleries dealt mostly with social realist art and not with neo-avant-garde art from the 1960s, 1970s, and 1980s. So it took a lot of work to figure out how to fill these gaps.

And what does the interest in Central European art look like? Is it an important direction, or it is largely overshadowed either by national art or by Western directions?

It very much depends on the people working in the institutions, and not on any Central European focus. It is always about how people who are preparing the project are educated and what they can manage. The Soros foundation's network did some very good work back in the 1990s. I know the names of curators and artists from that time very well. When we researched what people would like to see, they clearly said, Slovak art. But maybe this is because they were not so educated and simply lack awareness of other types of art. This is our big task – to teach them, to show them, to explain to them why this should be interesting for them. We usually realize this through curatorial projects.

What are the current challenges museums are facing? Or what are the current issues pertaining to museums?

First, we need to deal with very basic problems, since there have been few changes or investments in museum buildings. Today, people do not want to go to a museum just for an exhibition. It is more complex than that; they want to come to a gallery to have a coffee, to post an interesting picture on social media, to buy a postcard, maybe take part in a program, or simply to be in inspiring surroundings. When you go to the Tate Modern, you can spend something like four hours seeing the collection, grabbing new books, having a coffee, sitting in the Turbine Hall and just watching people. I like this cultural experience. Sometimes I do not even go to the exhibitions; I simply sit and watch people, how they behave, how they simply feel good being in a cultural institution. People travel, and they know what museums look like elsewhere. They usually travel to big cities, where there are big museums with diverse offerings. They want to have a similar experience at home.

It may sound funny, but the first change I made when I started as director was to change the bookshop, not the exhibition program. It was the year 2010, and we had a counter bookshop. Soon after we prepared the new front desk, a creative atelier for kids, a place to have coffee, the summer pavilion, and finally two years ago we decided to do the last basic thing – to renovate the toilets. The old ones were serving us well, but they looked like something from 1973, so we actually should have labeled them. These simple things show people that the gallery is really part of their contemporary life. In a gallery, you should have the experience you are used to, plus the art. Now we are thinking about what to do with the old ladies who are monitoring in the gallery. They are not always nice, and it is quite complicated to explain to them that visitors are guests, and that we need to treat guests with a different attitude. But because we are small, it is easier for us to make these changes. Now we know what is working and what is not, what is necessary and what is not.

And how are other museums in Slovakia dealing with these kinds of changes?

The biggest progress is being made in private institutions and initiatives not funded by the government, like cultural institutions located in the railway stations in Banská Štiavnica and Žilina. The regions own most galleries, and the regions are very different. There is a new, scary tendency to replace directors with new ones who are not art historians. This is due to regional politics.

When you look at the ecosystem of Slovakian museums, what do you miss most?

I miss a perfect traditional museum. As I am getting older, I like the traditional museums more and more. I love the Kunsthistorisches Museum in Vienna, all of those cases from the nineteenth century with animals. The mixture of the old and new world. There are a lot of contemporary activities in Bratislava, but I miss the conservative program. I would like to see something old-fashioned, for instance an exhibition about Bratislava, to see historic collections connected with Slovakia. If I want to see a perfect exhibition of contemporary art, I fly to London. For Leonardo, I can go to Poland, for good drawings to Vienna to the Albertina. It is a forty-minute drive. So I miss a good installation of our history and at least one complex institution. I would like to go somewhere where I could spend four hours looking through collections and temporary exhibitions, have a coffee and read a paper. I was hoping that the castle in Bratislava would turn into something like that, but there is no such institution. On the other hand, we are a small city and I am not sure if two or three big institutions would attract enough of an audience.

22 November 2017

Interview with László Baán

Dr. László Baán holds a Masters in Economics, a Masters in Philosophy, and a doctorate in Economic Sciences. He began his professional career as research assistant at the Institution of Social Sciences in Budapest, but quickly transferred from an academic career to become a civil servant. In 1995–1997, he served as the Cultural Commissioner at the Mayor's Office in Budapest; in 1998–2000, he was Deputy State Secretary for Finance in the Ministry of Cultural Heritage; in 2000–2002, he served as Permanent State Secretary; and in 2002–2004 as Deputy State Secretary for Finance. Since December 2004, he has been General Director of the Museum of Fine Arts in Budapest. Right from the start, his aim has been to completely redefine the organization and the activity of the institution in order to meet visitors' new, twenty-first century expectations. Since October 2011, Baán simultaneously has served as Government and Ministerial Commissioner for the new Museum Quarter in Budapest.

You are the driving force of the Museum of Fine Arts' international success. What was the museum like when you started your directorship? What did you do to transform the museum into a destination?

Despite having one of the most important collections in East-Central Europe, up to the mid-2000s, the Museum of Fine Arts had been seriously underperforming. It failed to exploit its potential with regard to the exhibitions organized for the Hungarian public, and also with regard to its efforts in the international arena. Just as a comparison: up until the mid-2000s, the museum had an average of 200,000–250,000 visitors annually, but after its restructuring it attracted 500,000–600,000. The most successful year in the institution's history was 2007, when with its more than 750,000 visitors the museum was among the top fifty most frequented museums in the world, i.e. on the same level as the Guggenheim in New York, or the Rodin Museum in Paris, for example. In the last ten years, the Museum of Fine Arts' solo exhibitions have toured Europe's most prominent museums, including the Musée d'Orsay in Paris, the Musée du Luxembourg, the Thyssen-Bornemisza Museum in Madrid, the Royal Academy of Arts in London, the Kunstforum in Vienna, the National Gallery of Modern Art in Rome, and the Palazzo Reale in Milan, taking its collection to hundreds of thousands.

Let us put the Museum of Fine Arts in the broader context of Hungarian museums. How have the Hungarian museums changed since the political transformations of 1989?

For reasons that are well known, during the communist era, the Hungarian museum scene did not – since it could not – follow the Western trends of the time. This lack of synchronicity continued into the period after the change in the political and economic system, and by the end of the 1990s, there had been an increasing hiatus between the attitudes of the Hungarian museum world and the main Western trends, and also a discrepancy with the changed expectations of the Hungarian public. While the international museum sphere was experiencing one boom after the other from the 1980s onwards, in the 1990s the average numbers of visitors to Hungarian museums plummeted to half of what they had been in the decade before. Unlike other social arenas after the changes of 1989 in Hungary, the museum sphere did not open up towards the best practices of the international museum scene, and made little effort to meet visitor needs; on the contrary, with the exception of a few commendable although isolated examples, it fell into a deep [Sleeping Beauty] -like sleep. Virtually no changes were introduced in the decades-old and obsolete domestic museum practices in an environment where almost the entire Hungarian society, and many of its cultural segments, had undergone a thorough transformation.

The major art museum established in the 1990s is the Ludwig Museum, operating initially within the Hungarian National Gallery, then independently next door within the complex of the Buda Castle, and after the turn of the century in a new cultural complex. The other publicly funded art museums have awaited transformation.

These deficient museum practices were radically changed by the Museum of Fine Arts, Hungary's only comprehensive collection of European art, which adopted the institution's overall reorganization as its openly declared strategy in 2005. Its top priority was to bridge the gap created by lagging behind for two decades, thus serving as an example for other museums and challenging the whole institutional system. We wanted to prove that the Hungarian public had not lost interest in museum-going in the preceding one and a half decades, but it was a considerable percentage of Hungarian museums that were lagging behind the visitors' needs since they were unable to learn a new language of communication with the much-changed environment around them. We firmly believed that if we, the museum, truly changed, our reception by the public, the media, and the business sector would also radically change. The reorganization was modeled on the practices of the biggest Western museums. Among other things, the Museum of Fine Arts' operation with a new function required changes in its financing system. Of all the museums in Hungary, the Museum of Fine Arts was the first to establish a separate profit center managed by professional staff with its scope extending to handling almost all the income (sponsorship, museum shop, and leasing halls) apart from revenues from ticket sales. This reorganization also contributed to the museum soon becoming the best-sponsored cultural institution in Hungary, when previously it had received a negligible amount of financing from the business sector. Although the amount of government support received by the Museum of Fine Arts did not increase, its budget rose almost twofold, with the institution's own income exceeding the government funds allocated to it. The budgetary restructuring went hand in hand with organizational changes:

new departments linked to the new functions were set up or expanded – e.g. exhibition organization, legal, public relations, museum education – and many young people were recruited as managers. From 2005 onwards, the museum significantly enlarged its already existing network of international relations and exploited it far more efficiently than before; the most spectacular development took place in the area of loaning.

The Liget Project will bring huge changes to the ecosystem of museums in Budapest. Its scope cannot be compared to any other enterprise in Hungary or in the whole region. Many people were saying that it is unrealistic, considering the cost and the country's financial difficulties. How did you manage to convince the state authorities to realize your vision?

Cultural development projects are investments with a long-term return. The truth of this is not only borne out by a famous line written by Count István Széchenyi, referred to as the greatest Hungarian – "The number of educated minds is the real power of a nation". Hungary will actually enjoy tangible, material benefits thanks to the developments. According to the impact study made in the planning phase of the project by KPMG, an international consultancy firm, this investment will produce a 100 percent return in the medium term, i.e. fifteen years, thanks to the surplus income it will generate in the tourism sector. It is estimated that the renewed Városliget (City Park) will attract 300,000 overnight visitors from abroad every year, and thus Budapest's position on the market of cultural experience tourism, and within that the market in family city breaks, will be strengthened. The Liget Budapest will be a unique and market-leader attraction in family tourism. Indeed, there is no other big city in Europe that can attract domestic and international visitors with a network of institutions in a single, distinct urban space set in 100 hectares that is as diverse and as high quality as the renewed Városliget. Thanks to the Liget Budapest project, this has been the capital's public park that has been a venue for culture and recreation for more than one hundred years.

Considering the number of tourists spending at least one visitor night at a commercial tourist facility, cities in the same category as Budapest – e.g. Vienna, Prague, Milan, Amsterdam, and Barcelona – produce far better indicators: this figure in Budapest is still only 3.5 million, while in the cities mentioned it is more than six million. The arguments used in the preparatory material made for the decision-making convinced the government that the Liget Budapest will be a unique, family-friendly attraction of outstanding quality – and as such will equally cater to the needs of the local residents and at the same time represent a tourist attraction with a market-leading potential in its own segment. Hence, supporting it from the country's national resources is definitely worthwhile.

The new museum quarter will greatly enrich the Hungarian ecosystem of museums, offering them new infrastructure, new exhibition space, new depository

space. Is there in your opinion a need to create any other museum buildings or establish new museums in Hungary?

It is well known that museums almost everywhere have become institutions displaying and preserving one of the most important aspects of the identity of local and national communities. This is precisely why the expansion of museums or establishing new ones is an extraordinarily intensive ongoing process all over the world right now, and one that will almost certainly continue into the future. This is taking place at different levels of intensity in different places depending on numerous factors, including economic, political, or cultural historical and others. The Liget Budapest Project is currently one of the biggest museum development projects in Europe, so any other projects that will be realized in the future will obviously be on a smaller scale, but by no means small projects in themselves. Let me just point out, for example, the Museum of Applied Arts, which was the third institution of its kind in the world after those in London and Vienna, is now in the early stages of comprehensive renovation and expansion. Another one I could mention is the Museum of Transport in the Városliget, which will move into a brand new complex with a far greater floor space that will be constructed in the coming years. I can also mention the planned interactive museum institution called the Hungarian House of Innovation that will be established in the renovated building of the Museum of Transport in the Városliget and will be similar to La Vilette in Paris. And I could continue this list with institutions of contemporary art and of private collections as well as new institutes of rural or local history that will definitely be augmented in the near future.

What challenges can you see ahead for Hungarian museums, in a broader sense?

A top-ranking challenge and task before the museums – and indeed the entire European institutional system – in the future will be to master the new language already spoken by generations Y and Z, i.e. adopting the logic and means of digital communication in the information society. If we cannot meet this challenge, an unimaginably high percentage of the canon of the European cultural treasure accumulated since the Age of Enlightenment, will be reduced to a dead, "out-of-date", uninspiring mass of objects and letters within a matter of decades.

15 November 2017

3 The iconic museum for Central Europe

Although the core of a museum is its collection and its building, a museum is more than this. Its architecture changes with the institution's character. Looking at the historical development of museums, it may be said that its corresponding architecture inherently reflects an institution's philosophy and nature in a given era, moving from the metaphor of the temple, palace, and fortress to forum; from sacred to profane, from elite to common.

As a rule, regardless of the moment in time, the museum seeks a prestigious place in its local context or in nature, its status emphasized through architectural form. In the twentieth century, buildings having unique forms that fulfilled particular roles on their sites were deemed icons. Often, museums have iconic pretenses. The global desire to build architectural icons unsurprisingly has touched Central Europe, as well, where at the turn of the century investors and architects embraced this fashion and entered the race for iconic contracts and projects.

The last decade of the twentieth century and first decade of the twenty-first century can be termed not only "the time of museums", but also the "time of the quest for museum icons" – a quest, because only some museums aspiring to iconic status actually achieved it. Ground-breaking investments in big cities such as New York, Berlin, Paris, and London provided the point of entry and in many places the architecture of contemporary museums aims to play the role of a landmark. It also happens that a building starts to function as a landmark or icon in its setting when there is no such expectation.

In this chapter, I raise the issue of the museum as icon through the example of those being created in Poland, Hungary, and Slovakia. In Poland particularly, the appearance of museums has become the topic of public debate, at the center of which resides the history of the construction of the Museum of Modern Art in Warsaw. The architecture of museums is of particular importance for shaping the image of cities in countries where, along with political transformation, a construction boom started in the context of residential and service buildings, as well as public architecture. A museum, together with such public institutions as a town hall, theater, philharmonic, library, hospital, bank, railway station, university, a representative palace complex, and cathedral, make up the resources of a modern city.

The theme of the chapter is the appearance of the museum in relation to its function. I present the creation of selected museums that underlined the public expectation for iconic architecture, as with the Guggenheim Museum in Bilbao. I reference social debates in which various positions and visions clash. I also seek to answer the question: is a Central European Bilbao possible?

Temple, fortress, sculpture, box: the changing shape of the museum

As a peculiar hallmark in the landscape, museum architecture of an iconic and symbolic character is not created primarily to serve a collection, but to provide recognition for cities, regions, and even nations. It has a much more important role to play in cultural policy and cultural tourism than in the world of art. As Suzanne MacLeod (2013: 1) argues, "Governments all over the world are recognizing the power of culture, and particularly cultural buildings, to spark international interest speak of economic investment and growth". The iconic museum is a signpost on the map of global tourism. "Museums have become one of the most desirable commissions for architects to win, now that cities have discovered museums as a marketing factor", writes Thierry Greub (2008: 9) in the catalog accompanying the traveling exhibition *Museums in the 21st Century. Concepts, Projects, Buildings*. The museum boom, which can be observed in various parts of the world especially in the decades immediately before and after the turn of the millennium, is based largely on the pursuit of exceptional architecture.

Michaela Giebelhausen (2011: 225–231) introduced the notion "The Museum as Monument" for the description of the first buildings erected to serve museums' needs. The prestige of the museum depended on an architecture that embodied permanence (Giebelhausen 2011: 231), as well as on the prominence of site. The nineteenth-century museums usually took the form of a Greek or Roman temple (Żygulski 2004: 111). With this, the notion of the temple of art was necessarily conjoined with the museum of art. The arrangement of the museum was codified by Jean-Nicolas-Louis Durand, who in his *Précis des leçons* drafted a plan for an ideal museum: "four wings arranged in a square into which a Greek cross and central rotunda were inscribed. Each of the wings had a separate entrance accentuated by a long portico with forty-six columns" (Giebelhausen 2011: 225). Leo von Klenze in designing the Glyptothek in Munich (1815–1830), and Karl Friedrich Schinkel in the Altes Museum project in Berlin (1823–1830), attempted this model. The classical style was manifest in somewhat later museums in London – the National Gallery, the British Museum, the Tate Gallery; it also spread throughout Europe, as well as other continents where European influence was strong. The classical style persisted until the middle of the twentieth century, evident in the designs of Metropolitan Museum of Art in New York (1874), the Art Gallery of New South Wales in Sydney (1909), and the National Gallery in Washington (1937). In the nineteenth century, buildings erected in Neo-Renaissance, Neo-Gothic, Neo-Romanesque and Neo-Byzantine styles were also popular. The Bayerisches Nationalmuseum in Munich, the Nordiska Museet in Stockholm, and the imperial museums in Vienna also embraced the classical style.

The twentieth century brought with it unprecedented dynamics with respect to a new perspective on museum architecture. At least a few museum buildings can be described as revolutionary for the ways in which they introduced a new style of museum architecture or constituted its culmination. These museums have achieved icon status.

First, they gradually began to depart from the temple and palace type in favor of geometric forms largely derived from the achievements of the Bauhaus. The museums created in this spirit were simple, functional, and devoid of ornament, with painted white exhibition halls that would not interfere with the reception of the art. Żygulski (1982: 153) lists two main, opposing tendencies prevailing in museum architecture from the mid-twentieth century and still prevailing in the twenty-first century: completely closed, bunker-like blocks isolated from the outside world, and constructions employing glazed walls evocative of enormous windows. An important marker of the new museum architecture of the fortress type was Le Corbusier's unrealized project for the world museum in Geneva, Mundaneum, commissioned by the League of Nations in 1929. The building was to take the shape of a ziggurat straight from Babylon. Frank Lloyd Wright referred to this project in the design of the Guggenheim Museum in New York (which opened in 1959). The building's majestic, completely white silhouette in the shape of an inverted ziggurat, with a ramp along which works of art are suspended along the inner atrium, is as much an architectural stunt as an indelible signature. While the architecture was greatly valued for its appearance, it was criticized for its lesser utilitarian potential. In this same category of museums may be included the cylindrical Hirshhorn Museum in Washington (Gordon Bunshaft 1974), the new wing of the National Gallery in Washington (Ieoh Ming Pei 1979), and the Museum of Modern Art in Frankfurt am Main (Hans Hollein 1991). In turn, the master of "transparent architecture" is Mies van der Rohe, designer of the New National Gallery in Berlin (1968). For the first time, the exhibition gallery was completely glazed on four sides, and the interior was free of all supports.

The beginning of a rapid global shift towards new museums can be dated to the 1970s. Numerous, often contradictory trends are beginning to appear in museology, which include discourse about both the architecture of the buildings, and their location and character. Josep Maria Montaner and Jordi Oliveras (1986: 9–10), analyzing museums created in the years 1975–1985, pointed to the changing nature of the museum institution. They observed that museums have ceased to be sacred places, that they are opening up to the public more and more. This has meant that they are becoming less and less places for the direct contemplation of art, and more and more sites that provide space for work, education, and study. The increasing number of visitors to these institutions forced changes in their spatial arrangement. First, it became necessary to design extensive entrance halls capable of fulfilling new functions and services such as a gift shop, a café, and a restaurant.

In the second half of the twentieth century, museums were increasingly compared to shopping malls and amusement parks. Victoria Newhouse (2006) introduced the notion of "the museum as entertainment" in order to discuss museums whose architectural solutions are conducive to leisure and pleasure. It included the Centre Pompidou, an exhibition space at the disused Fiat Lingotto factory in Turin (Renzo Piano, from the 1980s–2002), the Groninger Museum in Groningen (Alessandro Mendini, Michele de Lucchi, Philippe Starck, Coop Himmelblau 1994) and The J. Paul Getty Museum in Los Angeles (Richard Meier 1997). The Centre Pompidou (Renzo Piano and Richard Rogers 1977) was a milestone in the field of museum architecture. As Nathan Silver (1994: x) writes in his monograph of the building popularly referred to as Beaubourg: "Upon opening, it at once became, as foreseen, a principal focus of art and knowledge in France, and, as not entirely foreseen, one of the most popular tourist attractions in Europe".

Newhouse (2006: 260), writing about museums created since the end of the 1980s, points to the growing importance of architecture for the identity of museums:

> Whereas museums have always identified with their collections – the Louvre is the *Mona Lisa*, MoMA is *Les Demoiselles d'Avignon* – the new museum is identified with its architecture: the dominant image is the container rather than the contents.

According to Lampugnani (2011: 259), museum buildings erected since the 1990s "are indisputably works of art that absorb other works of art". Many researchers have come to similar conclusions, the Guggenheim Museum in Bilbao being the most frequently cited example.

Discussions around architectural icons

In Britain, the debate about iconic buildings gathered momentum in 2004 when a group of architectural critics and architects began attacking building complexes emerging on the banks of the Thames, known as the Costa del Icon (Jencks 2006/2007: 48). The key figures in this discussion are Charles Jencks, architect, theoretician, and architectural critic; and Deyan Sudjic, an architecture critic previously for *The Observer* and director of the Museum of Design in London.

Jencks combines the fashion for iconic buildings with the weakening role in society of religion and various ideologies (Jencks 2008). In his *The Iconic Building* (2008), he discussed specific buildings and evoked conversations with "starchitects", listing the requisite features of a building-icon. He is neither a proponent nor an opponent of the type. From among a large number of construction projects around the world, he chose those that are icons or aspire to that name, showing what this iconicity consists of, which buildings are well-designed icons, and which are mere caricatures. In his view, this is a long-lasting global trend which for commercial and spiritual reasons is strengthened by the twilight of traditional religions and historical iconography. He writes: "The iconic building is not going to go away, and may indeed increase in volume, as long as these widespread forces continue" (Jencks 2008: 195).

According to Jencks, the iconic building "is meant to upset the context, overturn convention, challenge the hierarchy" (Jencks 2008: 16), to evoke emotion-laden experience (for example, the Jewish Museum of Daniel Libeskind, which became one of the main icons of the nineties) (Jencks 2008: 55), and "mixes different codes, that is languages and meanings from different walks of life – not just architectural or technical references" (Jencks 2008: 165). "The successful building is, in effect, a giant iconostas asking to be decoded, which is why people come back again and again to try to fathom the meaning" (Jencks 2008: 182). "Like the sacred icon in front of the Russian altar, the iconic building often occupies a prominent place in the city or carries out a function regarded as important although [. . .] today that can mean almost anything" (Jencks 2008: 22). "The successful landmark has to be both enigmatic and expressive, it must suggest much more than it names, and leave the final interpretation, if it ever comes, up to the critics, the public, and the detectives of mystery" (Jencks 2008: 203); "the successful iconic building grows from the inside to the outside, and takes up new metaphors from this growth", for example as with the Disney concert hall in Los Angeles by Frank Gehry (Jencks 2008: 203). He describes the nature of icons through the examples of specific buildings, starting with Sydney Opera House (which he finds reminiscent of sails, shells, fish, and waves) and the TWA terminal at Kennedy Airport in New York (which evokes a beak, wings, and air flow). Graham Morrison (2004) – the source of the notion, the "Costa del Icon" – noted in his article in *The Guardian*, "The true architectural icon is a building that is unmistakable, often provocative, and carries cultural signals far beyond its purpose". He considers the unequivocal icons to be the Sydney Opera House, the Centre Pompidou, and the Scottish Parliament, each of which initially disappeared: "They convey the spirit of their age; they are both useful and memorable" (Morrison 2004).

For Jencks, the symbol of architecture that breaks down conventions and restrictions is the Guggenheim Museum in Bilbao. "Thomas Krens and the Basques said they needed a 'hit' there, like the Sydney Opera House. They needed the building to do for Bilbao what the Sydney Opera House did for Australia", noted Frank Gehry (Jencks 2008: 12). In the post-Bilbao era, everyone wants such a thing. According to Jencks, the iconic building is not necessarily required to take an unusual shape, as exemplified by the Swiss Re office in London designed by Norman Foster (2000–2004), a bullet-like form that is also a rational and functional building (Jencks 2008: 185). The Swiss Re building has at the same time all the hallmarks of an iconic building: a striking, reduced profile, the perfect location, and a wealth of visual connotations (Jencks 2008: 185).

Jencks (2008: 145) also introduced a distinction between the icon and the landmark (although he does not stick to it rigorously, and uses the concepts interchangeably): the landmark influences the audience, but it is also familiar, while the icon is always foreign, disturbing, and new, its reception difficult. He also introduced the category, "the Iconic Icon" – a doubly iconic building that on the one hand is an essentialized image, like a logo, and on the other reveals relationships between visual images (Jencks 2008: 28). The first example of an iconic icon was, according to Jencks, the Guggenheim Museum building in New York. In turn, in referring to the works of Peter Eisenman, the author uses the term, "anti-icon icon" (Jencks 2008: 162). According to Jencks, Eisenman's buildings look like something struck by an earthquake. The investment that best fits this new category is the "non-buildings" complex of the City of Culture of Galicia in Santiago de Compostela. "Santiago wanted to produce a secular tourist attraction, other than the religious one they have, and they saw how successful Bilbao was for the economy of the Pays Basque. They wanted an alternative to the figural object of Gehry, so we gave them a landscape – a project totally 'other than Bilbao'" stated Eisenman himself (Jencks 2008: 164). Ultimately, the complex consisted of six pairs of structures joined in the landscape, buried in three "mounds".

As an ardent critic of the fashion for icons, Deyan Sudjic presents a much more extreme position than Jencks. He writes with sarcasm about competitions in which icons and landmarks are required of architects:

> Competitions [. . .] have become ubiquitous, leading all but inevitably to the kind of architecture that looks best reduced to a logo on a letterhead or to the confined spaces of one of those Eiffel-Tower-in-a snow-storm paperweights. It claims to be about inspiration but ends only in the obvious. The search for the architectural icon has become the ubiquitous theme of contemporary design.
>
> (Sudjic 2003)

In an architecture based on such principles, "every sensational new building must attempt to eclipse the last one. It leads to a kind of hyperinflation" (Sudjic 2003). In his article for *The Observer*, Sudjic quoted Paul Finch, Chairman of Board of Commissioners, Commission for Architecture and the Built Environment, who noted that "it is history that decides what is going to be an icon. The buildings that have become iconic are not designed to be icons, they are designed to be good buildings" (Sudjic 2003). It is difficult to disagree with this, although there are certainly exceptions – Gehry's museum in Bilbao, for one.

An important aspect of discussion on iconic architecture is the phenomenon of so-called starchitects – celebrities of the architectural world who, through their well-known, delightful or shocking iconic structures, have tremendous market appeal. According to Lenartowicz (2006: 398), architecture clients are also looking for a recognizable brand, a big name. The figures of Renzo Piano and Richard Rogers, whose careers flourished after the opening of the Centre Pompidou (McClellan 2008: 87), were perhaps the first in this phenomenon. An important milestone on the path to stardom is winning the Pritzker Prize, granted annually to living architects since 1979 and commonly referred to as the architectural Nobel. This award not only recognizes current activity, but also fuels further career development. The majority of the laureates have created international museum icons: Ieoh Ming Pei, Richard Meier, Hans Hollein, Oscar Niemeyer, Frank Gehry, Tadao Andō, Norman Foster, Rem Koolhaas, Jacques Herzog and Pierre de Meuron, Zaha Hadid, Richard Rogers, Jean Nouvel, Peter Zumthor, Kazuyo Sejima and Ryue Nishizawa from the SANAA studio, Shigeru Ban.

In the case of a museum building, virtually every interested party – architects, artists, curators, investors – is driven by different goals and expectations. Karsten Schubert (2002: 94) writes that the museum is an architect's statement, his announcement that "this is his building, reflecting his own architectural thinking and philosophy, his signature". Artists, on the other hand, would prefer an architecture that is subordinate to the work of art and allows it to be the center of attention. Curators expect buildings to be flexible, in order to respond to changing artistic requirements and curatorial strategies. Last, politicians and investors, like architects, desire something stately. For them, museums clearly illustrate national or environmental aspirations and financial strength, making them the most desirable status symbols. Politicians, however, writes Schubert (2002: 98), "often lose interest in their new cultural toys the moment the ribbons have been cut and the television crews have moved on".

An icon for the center of Warsaw: the Museum of Modern Art

In trying to find its place on the map after 1989, Central Europe has needed modern buildings whose unique architectural expression will bring together the names of cities with unique forms. The term "icon" has become the key word for the discourse about museums in Poland. In almost all cities that have undertaken museum design, competition proposals, investors, politicians, and the media have made reference to symbolic architecture. But this has been done without deeper reflection on the appeal of Bilbao's success and the possibility of its transplantation – on a smaller scale – both in Warsaw and in the Polish provinces. The need for architecture that will attract the eye and influence the identity of the city has been stated; hence the fashion for icons traveled to Central Europe from Western countries.

The Guggenheim Museum in Bilbao is not the only source of inspiration, although probably no museum has generated nor will generate so much printed and media attention. This icon is considered by some to be the symbol of the twilight of the twentieth century, and by others the symbol of the beginning of the twenty-first century. The term, "Bilbao effect" arose from its success – a unique architecture that is an economic and public relations triumph, and that plays a decisive role in the revitalization of post-industrial areas or in the ennoblement of so-called under-developed districts.

The Museum of Modern Art (MSN; see Atlas 3.18) in Warsaw stood at the center of the Polish museum debate. It was to be the largest museum project in Poland since 1989, eclipsing everything that had been built in Poland to that point. A document entitled, "Preliminary Concept of the Warsaw Museum of Modern Art" adopted by the Museum Program Council in 2005 begins with these words:

> Warsaw is the only European capital that does not have a museum of modern art. Since the building of the Warsaw National Museum (1938), no single museum building dedicated to art has been created in Poland, despite the requirements of creative communities in such important centres as Silesia and Łódź as well, that have called repeatedly for the creation of art museums since 1945.
>
> (Wstępna koncepcja warszawskiego Muzeum Sztuki Nowoczesnej 2005: 3)

The propagandistic nature of the introductory part of the document accounts for its generalizations,[1] but it clearly expressed a great need to establish such a museum. The importance of the investment, the controversies swirling around it, the formal problems and foment in the circles of architects, museum workers, and those employed in the culture industry made this debate a point of reference for all subsequent Polish museum and exhibition projects. The expectation that the museum building would play the role of a modern icon in Warsaw resided at the center of this debate. When in 1990 Frank Gehry stayed in Warsaw in connection with his exhibition at the Ujazdowski Castle, he agreed to design a museum for Warsaw at the time: "Bilbao could stand in Warsaw, because he had matured at that point into this architectural concept" (Już trudno 2013: 170). The hunger for the Western fashion for architectural icons among art historians, critics, and architects triggered, on the occasion of the capital museum, a need for discussion in the Polish public sphere that went beyond this one project – a discussion about no less than the place of Polish architecture within global architecture. The question has been asked, indirectly, as to whether Polish architecture (and more specifically, Polish museum architecture, whose tradition had been interrupted for several decades in the twentieth century) may be considered avant-garde. The question is whether the resumption of this tradition will mean reaching for the patterns employed by Western countries for a dozen or so decades, or whether Polish architecture may be included among the new and fresh Western trends.

Placeholders for the museum of contemporary art in Warsaw were the Ujazdowski Castle Centre for Contemporary Art (opened in 1985, housing a collection of contemporary art and conducting exhibitions), Zachęta, and the National Museum. The advent of the twenty-first century brought an actual opportunity to create an institution that would consistently build a representative collection of contemporary art for Poland and also showcase a museum building. In March 2005, it was determined that the museum would be established as the product of the cooperation between the City of Warsaw and the Ministry of Culture and National Heritage. This decision was made shortly after the announcement of the ministerial program, "Znaki Czasu" (see Chapter 8), during a particularly favorable period for Polish contemporary art. An international architectural competition was set up and an institution established (the statute was announced, and a director, program council and museum board were appointed). Presumably, if not for the controversy related to the architectural competition, the issue of building a museum would not have received so much attention, and would not have been the subject of such critical fanfare in the press. As a result of the adoption of overly strict formal requirements, most foreign architectural teams were excluded from participation in the competition. In an atmosphere of scandal, the competition was canceled.

The winner of the first prize in the second iteration of the competition was Christian Kerez, an architect from Switzerland who proposed a clear, minimalist project reminiscent of two juxtaposed cubes, with fully glazed lower stories whose only ornament was a sculptural roof treatment (invisible from the street level). After the previous, ineffective appeals to the city authorities and the minister, the museum director resigned, followed by the entire program council as a form of protest against the jury's selection. The first prize was awarded for, among other things, "an avant-garde approach to the architecture of the object, for the creation of a new, expressive spatial form" ([Muzeum Sztuki Nowoczesnej w Warszawie] Pierwsza nagroda 2007: 75). The project was accepted for implementation and a new director was appointed. However, in 2008, the city authorities halted the design work for almost six months to consider an idea to situate another institution within the building, the Rozmaitości Theater. Finally, in 2009, the architect returned to the design with the additional task of placing a theater room in the building. The next three years were consumed by problems with land ownership on Defilad Square and delays in the delivery of the construction project by the architect. In 2012, as a result of a long-lasting conflict, the city of Warsaw broke the contract with the architect and brought the case to court.

The two main threads of the social debate that flared up in connection with the project are the issue of its name and the related issue of the nature and temporal limit of art presented there, and the role that the institution and building should play. It is this second problem that is crucial for this chapter, as it invites analysis of other Polish institutions of contemporary art.

The terms of the architectural competition stipulated that,

> Architecturally, the building of the Museum should be a formal and meaningful counterpoint for the Palace of Culture, and its shape, a globally recognizable symbol of Warsaw. The museum together with the adjacent square and park will become the most important public place in the revitalized center of Warsaw.
>
> (Regulamin konkursu na opracowanie koncepcji architektonicznej budynku Muzeum Sztuki Nowoczesnej w Warszawie2005: 7)

The "Preliminary Concept" also mentions this symbolic aspect:

> The changes planned in the surroundings of the Palace of Culture and Science are aimed at giving the center of the capital a more elevated standing both with the new urban shape and the new significance of this place. The hieratic Defilad Square – once a symbol of single-party power, and after 1989 transformed spontaneously into a public market – will become in the near future an expression of political transformation, a place integrating Warsaw's society around cultural events of the highest order, held in a new, attractive and friendly urban space. The symbol of these changes, and the new symbol of Warsaw as well, should also be the Museum of Modern Art building, which – by being located in the vicinity of the Palace of Culture – will engage in an aesthetic and ethical discourse with its past.
>
> (Wstępna koncepcja warszawskiego Muzeum Sztuki Nowoczesnej 2005: 3)

The museum director, Tadeusz Zielniewicz, said before the announcement of the results, "The team working on the organization of the museum dreams that the building in a sense would be the first exhibit. That it would be a value in itself" (Statement for *Dziennik*, after Piątek 2007: 66). The expectation of a new symbol was so great that the lights of the Palace were to be symbolically extinguished at the time of signing the letter of intent between the city and the ministry, signifying that it was to give way to the museum in the future (Zielniewicz, Borkowski and Mazur 2006).

The selection of Kerez's project unleashed a weeks-long media storm. Extremely negative comments dominated the online forum on the architectural competition website. In a survey conducted by the Public Opinion Research Centre among the residents of the capital, on the order of the museum, over 60 percent of respondents favored the project that received a honorable mention, and just over 20 percent the Kerez project (CBOS 2007). Two camps representing extreme positions were identified – a critical, "pro-icon" stance, promoted by the museum director and almost the entire program council, urging them to abandon the selected project; and the "minimalist" position, which approved of the jury's selection. A member of the museum's program council and then-president of the Polish AICA section, Dorota Monkiewicz, repeatedly voiced her criticism of the project. On behalf of the council, she stated: "This project is in our opinion not feasible. The building is arrogant, it repels spectators, it does not answer our slogan, 'Museum of Modern Art attracts'" (Jarecka 2007b: 14). Adam Budak, then curator of Kunsthaus Graz, admitted that Kerez managed to contend with the Palace, but "what he proposed is too camouflaged, too close to the architecture of department stores" (Piątek 2007: 70).

Kerez's building was associated most with socialist architecture's gray blocks that filled the cities and provinces of the Eastern Bloc countries. In a section in a book devoted to Kerez's work, Marcel Andino Velez (2008: 87) noted that in modern Poland the only type of buildings with a simplified, rectangular shape are hypermarkets: "corrugated steel structures, dotted with the logos of global brands, are widely associated with cheap, instant-profit-driven development". It is hardly surprising that one of the online commenters associated Kerez's project with the architecture of the temple of consumption; after the results were announced, the press reprinted the visualization of the museum building with the Carrefour logo. This association was probably evoked not only by the architecture of the edifice, but also by its close proximity to the shopping centers on Marszałkowska Street, with their glazed ground floors and obscured higher stories, as well as the fact that according to the original vision (expressed in the conditions of the competition), the museum's ground floor would be the commercial space. Andy Warhol's words are apt here: "All department stores will become museums, and all museums become department stores" (Jencks 2008: 44).

Attacked by a wave of criticism after the announcement of the competition results, Christian Kerez defended himself in the project's copyright description posted on the competition website:

> The new museum is not big enough to compete with such a gigantic building [the Palace of Culture and Science]. Therefore, this new building can also be seen as an extension of the Palace of Culture in Warsaw. [. . .] However, the proposed new building does not submit to the neo-classical structures of its immediate surroundings – the new Museum of Art is rather the antithesis of the 1950s architecture [. . .]. Contrasting with the vertical skyscrapers from that time, the Museum of Modern Art consists of horizontal surfaces arranged one on top of the other.
>
> (Kerez n.d.)

The Swiss architect emphasized that the Palace of Culture is a sculpture, hence it would be a rather bad joke and a big failure if a solid, expressive sculptural gesture stood near the Palace of Culture. [. . .] The modesty of

this building is justified. I say this not because I like such modest buildings, but I share something with minimalism. It results from reading the
situation of this square and the neighbourhood of the Palace of Culture.

(Jarecka 2007a: 14)

The mass, in turn, is a product of the local development plan and the
restrictions regarding its dimensions recorded in the competition conditions.
Some critics and journalists, sharing the architect's arguments, defended
the project. In 2007 in the pages of *Obieg*, Katarzyna Hołda, not without
a note of sarcasm, wrote that another flashy building in this place would
deepen chaos and anxiety:

> whether we like it or not, the PKiN [Palace of Culture and Science] is an
> icon of Warsaw also because of what is associated with it. You may treat
> it as a symbol of a dark past, or you may see it as a happy ending symbol.
> Either way, building something equally dominant next to the Palace will
> introduce a cacophony, but it will not drown it out, because – let's face
> it – it cannot be drowned out.
>
> (Hołda 2007)

Zofia Herman (2008: 14), seeking the cause of the social indignation, said
that it may be due to the fact that the project did not fulfill the "dream of
destroying the Palace of Culture". Dorota Jarecka (2007d: 16) wrote sarcas-
tically in *Gazeta Wyborcza*:

> Kerez has designed a building that does not emphasize anyone's unique-
> ness: the place, the country, the nation or the group of people that make
> up the museum. He does not stress the messianic idea of introducing a
> great change in the lives of Poles through art. He says the opposite –
> there is nothing special about the fact that a modern state in a modern
> city there is a modern art museum. Could it have been more offensive
> to us?

Adam Szymczyk, who was a member of the competition jury and also a
member of the program council, said that "this form has a chance to become
a new icon of Warsaw. The simplified form may have a stronger effect than a
complicated, mangled one" (Jarecka 2007c: 17). He added at the same time
that the architecture of the building itself, without work on the museum's
program, would not attract a million viewers a year.

The museum itself defended Kerez, noting in the texts accompanying the
exhibition, *Christian Kerez: New Projects of the Museum of Modern Art in
Warsaw* (July–September 2008) that the museum building "concentrated on
delivering a unique interior" (Christian Kerez New Projects 2008). It was
this aspect of the museum that Bogna Świątkowska had closely attended
to much earlier, saying, "Kerez's building may seem ineffective from the

outside, but it enchants with its idea for the interior. Do we have an icon? The question is whether the icon must be externality, the façade" (Piątek 2007: 71). Kerez himself complained: "This is the problem with the so-called icons – they are too spectacular from the outside to engage interest in the contents" (Nie używam flesza 2007: 73). The sculptural interior of the gallery space, the uniqueness of which is the roof structure, was supposed to provide not only functionality, but also individuality of expression. On the basis of the photographs of the exhibition halls, the space of the Warsaw museum could be easily identified.

Just after the competition was settled, Ewa Porębska, editor-in-chief of *Architektura-Murator* monthly, wrote that the architecture of the building "may turn out to be too avant-garde and clean, I do not know whether it will be understood in Poland" (Miała być nowa ikona Warszawy 2007: 14). This is an accurate diagnosis of what happened. Kerez's project was for many people the end of a dream about a museum icon in the center of the capital, the sobering up after the party, megalomania and madness of global museum architecture. It came at a time when architecture began to turn away from obscure forms that overwhelmed content. The design of the Warsaw museum is a good example of the fact that while Central European architecture does not have to take over well-worn patterns from the West, it can fit into those developing trends. "The cool architecture [of the Kerez building] is worthy of the most spoiled and bored European societies, sophisticated 'cultural excess'", wrote Grzegorz Piątek (2007: 66). The history of this competition meant, however, that Warsaw would miss the spectacular architecture of a museum in general.

One may wonder whether the reason for the confusion around the MSN project had not been, above all, the imprecise wording in the competition requirements: "recognizable in the world, a new symbol of Warsaw". Likewise implicit in the statements of the majority of jurors and the public, nothing that the winning design does not represent has been added – an exuberant shape, a sculptural, organic, and gaudy form, a colorful or shiny coating. The international jury chose the project that is best for the given location (it should be noted that the fact that the Kerez project meets the first of the conditions is not questioned: the building "should be a formal and meaningful counterpoint to the Palace of Culture") and for the specific moment in time. The judges invited to sit on the jury, (apart from Poland) representing Switzerland, Great Britain,[2] Germany, and Luxembourg, acknowledged that the countries of the West and the world in general were already saturated with museum spectacles. Now, in line with the current trend in Switzerland and Austria, not to mention Japan, each representing a different cultural milieu, the world of art needed quiet, calm, and balanced buildings. These features, combined with an appropriate solution for the Warsaw museum's interior, could determine its iconicity for the twenty-first century rather than for the end of the previous one. The odds of this are good if one looks at the Kerez project through the prism of the characteristics of the iconic building listed by Charles Jencks. Even if the building was not in the position to meet them all, it: 1) refuted the context, overturned the conventions, questioned the hierarchies, 2) took the prominent place in the city space and carried an important function, and 3) evolved from the inside out.

The seven years that have passed since the first competition for the museum was announced to the termination of the contract with the architect whose project won, despite the loss of time and money, translated into a much-needed reflection on the spatial situation of the capital's center, the expectations concerning a museum building there, and the nature of the institution being created. It seems that this time was necessary to arouse public interest in architectural matters and to start working on the foundations that MSN had laid, for example through the implementation of the *Warsaw Under Construction* festival, which largely filled the gap regarding public education about aesthetics and design. The fact cannot be escaped that despite the imbroglio associated with the construction of the building, the museum was able to implement its exhibition program in temporary offices and build a collection. Since 2008, its headquarters are the back of the furniture pavilion "Emilia" (initially only a warehouse, in the years 2012–2016 the entire pavilion), located near the intended site; and from 2017, a temporary exhibition pavilion on the Vistula River (loaned by the Austrian foundation Thyssen-Bornemisza Art Contemporary). The four-year exhibition activity in the furniture pavilion "Emilia" helped establish momentum, and the location in the immediate vicinity of the Palace of Culture made it possible to learn about the neighborhood – its challenges, problems, and public. The pavilion's fully glazed elevations provided the opportunity to observe the Palace in a way that will be similar from the newly erected building.

In the second half of 2013, a new (third) architectural competition was announced for the design of the building housing the museum and theater. This time, the competition framework clearly stated that the goal of the project is not to search for an iconic building, but to build social bonds,

> The Museum building is not meant to be an icon or a monument – the aim is to create a place of contact between residents and modern art in Warsaw, as well as meeting places for Varsovians and visitors to the capital. This social situation alone will be the best monument for the city.
>
> (Wytyczne programowe 2014: 8)

As well as become "an important place for education, entertainment, leisure and meetings, helping the public from various environments participate in culture and experience architecture and public space" (Wytyczne programowe 2014: 8).

At the same time, it was announced:

> This place can define a new centre of gravity for the whole city. The new building should oppose dichotomies such as lack of transparency – transparency,

> inhuman scale – human scale, glamor – simplicity, anti-social – pro-social;
> instead of history, it should be directed towards the future.
>
> (Wytyczne programowe 2014: 7)

Another procedure was also employed whereby the architect implementing the project and not an anonymous architectural concept was selected. US-based Thomas Phifer and Partners studio won the competition in 2014 for showing, according to the competition commission, "the highest understanding of the functional program" for both designed institutions. The announcement posted on the museum's website states:

> The understanding of ideas such as openness, transparency and the convincing simplicity of proposed solutions presented in the architect's concept give hope that when such long-awaited buildings are created [. . .], they will become, through the values they communicate and the attitudes they strengthen, and in contrast to the monumentalism and architectural pride of the Palace of Culture, a symbol of modern Warsaw.
>
> (Pracownia Thomas Phifer and Partners zaprojektuje 2014)

Therefore, the hope for a symbol at this point was not completely abandoned. This project, like the criticized vision of Kerez, seems visually anti-iconic. This time, however, there was no popular mobilization against the outcome, and it is also difficult to identify voices of withering criticism. It seems that in spite of the attenuated battle over the museum, and the possibility at one point that the project would not be implemented, social consensus formed around the belief that any building would be better than none.

The museum project was born over the next several months, entailing close cooperation with the museum team and the designer's understanding of the character and logic of architecture, urban planning and the social space of Warsaw. As a result, a minimalist design of two boxes emerged – a white museum and a black theater. They are devoid of architectural ornament, they affect their own simplicity, elegance, and texture of materials. Their form is to be cut off from the architecture of the Palace, but also from the modernist and modern commercial buildings of Warsaw. The Centre Pompidou is the point of reference for the MSN project in terms of the openness of the building and the relationship it builds with the adjacent square. One of its important features was accessibility from all sides. There had also been no main entrance (several years after opening the entrance from the north and south were blocked. [Silver 1994: 179]). The square in front of the building in Paris, also designed by the building's architects, has become an important meeting place and stage for artistic events. The landscape became an integral part of the concept, and the view onto it from the observation deck, escalators and elevators was directly incorporated in the building's program. In Warsaw, this aspect will be generated by the so-called city rooms – places of rest opening onto views of the city. In the main space on the ground floor, there will be a large auditorium, which will be open visually up to the level of the exhibition rooms. This is an element taken from museum's temporary location in the pavilion "Emilia", in the center of which there was an atrium and in it an auditorium. From the exhibition spaces there, one could look down at the auditorium and participate in organized events. "This element of the project indicates that these meetings, this audience presence, are to constitute the institution", noted Mytkowska (Interview with Joanna Mytkowska 2017).

There are more links to be found with the Centre Pompidou. Enthusiastic reception from the jurors did not translate into the public and media moods related to the new edifice. The Piano and Rogers project, chosen from 681 applications (desiring to raise the profile of the winning project, second and third prizes were not awarded) was attacked and criticized both after the announcement of the results of the competition, as well as after the opening in 1977 (the negative reception began to change only a year later). One of the critics was Jean Baudrillard (1994), who wrote about Beaubourg as a hypermarket of culture. Despite that, in the first year of operation, the Centre was visited by six million people (the museum itself is visited by two million visitors a year).

Although the new vision of MSN included other priorities, and its design stems from the museum's real needs and possibilities, the area and city, and the symbolic and iconic role that the edifice might play there have not disappeared into oblivion. Mytkowska, in relation to the new project, herself admitted that,

> The museum has the potential to be a contemporary icon, only if we understand the meaning of this concept otherwise. The building with white, translucent material, deprived of ornament, can redefine Defilad Square as a contemporary, attractive place where urban life will finally come back, while at the same time the city will be able to experience art and community.
>
> (Joanna Mytkowska o nowym budynku muzeum 2015)

The anticipation of an icon in the Polish provinces

According to the original assumptions, MSN was to be the first new, postwar edifice erected for the needs of contemporary art in Poland. It turned out, however, that other cities that did not attract media attention leapt over Warsaw in this respect. In 2008, the Znaki Czasu Centre of Contemporary Art (CSW) in Toruń and the new building of the Muzeum Sztuki in Łódź, ms², were opened; two years later, the MOCAK Museum of Contemporary Art in Krakow. Other construction projects in other cities were at various stages of development: the Elektrownia Mazovian Centre for Contemporary

Art in Radom, the Muzeum Śląskie in Katowice, the Wrocław Contemporary Museum, and the (ultimately unrealized) Special Art Zone in Łódź. All of them are connected by the hope that a given building will be an urban hallmark, that it will become a source of a new city identity, that the structure will act as a tourist magnet and will locate the city (as similarly as it did in Bilbao) on the Polish cultural map, at least, if not in Europe and the wider world as well. Comparisons with Bilbao have been repeated on various occasions.

The Znaki Czasu CSW building in Toruń (see Atlas 3.16) symbolically opened the way to new premises for Polish museum institutions. The building (architect Edward Lach) blends in with the historic buildings of the city through its scale and brick treatment of the façade. Architecturally, however, it is not a building-icon, although these were the expectations. Even before the architectural competition was announced, the director of CSW, Michał Korolko, explained:

> The new infrastructure will give us the opportunity to create a cultural institution with a European dimension. We will not feel like poor relatives at foreign museums. I suspect that the side effect in Toruń will be the same as after the creation of the famous Guggenheim Museum in Bilbao. The rank and attractiveness of this institution draw crowds of art lovers to this Spanish city every year.
>
> (gg 2006)

In studies conducted by the Institute of Sociology of the Nicolaus Copernicus University in Toruń on the reception of modern art and the demand for high culture in Toruń and the region just before the public opening of the center, respondents praised the incorporation of the building into an urban layout, but did not hide their disappointment that the building was "too avant-garde for the purposes for which it was built" and that it was "not so impressive that it would inspire the residents of the city, and above all tourists" (Szlendak 2008: 4). The local community expected a unique architecture that would generate discussions and serve as a magnet to attract local audiences, tourists, and the media. CSW did not set up an architectural spectacle but rather an exceptional exhibition and educational program, which was carried out in the first years of operation. Innovative actions on the ground in Poland, and emphasis on inter-disciplinarity and virtual presence, did not translate into audience engagement – the media reported on the attendance fiasco in the first and second year.

An icon was also awaited in Radom. The competition jury in 2007 awarded first prize to Andrzej Kikowski's project for the transformation of the municipal power plant into the Elektrownia Mazovian Centre for Contemporary Art (see Atlas 3.12). The justification for the decision was that, "The object, being a work of art in itself, offers a very interesting spatial foundation, giving hope that it will become an icon of Radom"

(Internetowy Serwis Architektoniczny Ronet.pl 2007). Agata Morgan, acting director of the institution, stated in 2007, "I hope that the Elektrownia Mazovian Centre for Contemporary Art will become a cultural icon of Radom" (gas, cig 2007).

The architectural solution for the new building of the Muzeum Śląskie in Katowice and its highly symbolic location takes up the old architecture and mining tradition, creating an icon for the whole of Silesia. Already at the design stage it played a symbolic role, changing the image of the city from the capital of the region, whose economy for decades was based on heavy industry, to a city dedicated to services, knowledge, and culture. The museum, buried in the ground, refers to the region's mining traditions and places the exhibits where coal, representing its wealth, had been mined to the surface. However, it does not cut itself off from the outside world, and it uses a natural light source. In the jury's opinion: "going down to the harvesting level, visitors have the feeling of discovering what the earth conceals, without losing contact with the daylight that flows from above" (Jasiński 2008: 76), by way of towers positioned on the surface. Visitors to the museum will be able to extract sensations from exhibits installed in the exhibition halls, just as coal earlier stood nearby the surface of the "Warszawa II" shaft.

The discussion related to the creation of the Museum of Contemporary Art in Krakow was also related to the concepts of icon and symbol. Ultimately, the chosen location – the Oskar Schindler's Factory – has a symbolic dimension, thanks to the success of Steven Spielberg's film *Schindler's List* (based on the book by Thomas Keneally, *Schindler's Ark*). Subdued, minimalist architecture is inscribed in an irregular factory plot, hidden behind the administrative building of Schindler's Factory which houses a historical museum and behind a high wall-curtain separating museum buildings from the street. It is a kind of "sign" in the landscape of the district that undergoes transformation. The contentious issues surrounding the Krakow museum were not about architecture, however, as it remained in the shadow of the ongoing battle for location. The aim was to choose the most worthy place for the presentation of contemporary art, ennobling art in a city aspiring to be the cultural capital of Poland. On the one hand, the Krakow debate exposed the deep division and crisis of the artistic, museum and cultural environment, and on the other, chaos and institutional confusion on the part of municipal officials. The Museum in Krakow was not imagined as an architectural icon; its symbolic meaning is mainly ideological, although the architectural expression and connection with the place of special interest to Polish history suited those things to that role.

The third museum after Warsaw and Krakow devoted to contemporary art is the Wrocław Contemporary Museum. The aspirations to create such a museum in this city were actualized in 2004 with the establishment of the "Znaki Czasu" Dolnośląskie Society for the Encouragement of Fine Arts. The Society started the construction of the collection as well as the efforts to create a museum for its presentation. A competition in 2008 resulted in the selection of a project by the Warsaw architects Mirosław Nizio and Damian Cyryl Kotwicki. The site for the black cube twisted around its own axis is the plot next to the Museum of Architecture, which had taken over the buildings of the former church and Bernardine monastery in the immediate vicinity of the Panorama Racławicka building, near the National Museum and the Academy of Fine Arts. Another museum in this place will strengthen its potential as a museum district.

As in Warsaw, Wrocław (see Atlas 3.19) also anticipated an exceptional building; however, unlike Warsaw, the establishment of a museum institution and the construction of a museum remained a local issue, not involving national public opinion. The choice of location, architectural competition or discussions around the program concept were not accompanied by such lively emotions as were similar issues in Warsaw and Krakow. Shortly after the announcement of the competition, the director of the Cultural Division of the Municipal Authority, Jarosław Broda, said, "We dream that this building in itself would be a work of art and would have a positive impact on the image and development of the city. Just like the Guggenheim Museum in Bilbao" (B.a. 2008). The mayor of Wrocław, Rafał Dutkiewicz, also shared his expectations: "An attractive, modern building can be a tourist attraction, which will also encourage you to visit us and our collections of art" (Saraczyńska 2008). The publication put out by the Municipal Authority of Wrocław, *MWW Muzeum Współczesne Wrocław. Koncepcja programowa* [MWW Contemporary Museum Wrocław. Program Concept], opens with a statement that the museum "is designed as an image-building undertaking for the city" (Krajewski and Monkiewicz 2007: 6).

The 2007 conception refers to museum activity, meaning, and function, and not architectural structure, which suggests that regardless of the architectural design selected in the competition, the creators of the museum wanted to give it status worthy of an "ambassador" of the modern city. The same document also sets out the expectations related to the museum building: "attractive and unique architecture of the MWW building with a recognizable body, shaped coherently, but without monotony, with a friendly but at the same time representative character" (Krajewski and Monkiewicz 2007: 19). In the justification of the selection, the jury stated that the first prize was awarded, among other reasons, for the "synthetic form of the iconic building, which constitutes the proper identification of the object" and for "shaping the facade in a manner corresponding to the rank of the object" (The I Prize 2008: 42). In anticipation of the new museum building, as in Warsaw, it began its operations in temporary headquarters.

In the context of Polish museum buildings of iconic value, one should also mention the new branch of the Muzeum Sztuki in Łódź – ms² (see Atlas 3.10), located in a post-industrial building in the Manufaktura center. The museum occupies a special position in Polish museology for its collection of international modern art. Just as MoMA is a signpost in the world of modern art, so too is the Łódź Muzeum Sztuki in Poland. It is a point of reference for other Polish collections and currently emerging art.

The creators of this museum, like those of many others created during this period in Poland, referred to the Bilbao effect. Director Jarosław Suchan stated:

> Bilbao was a small city in the north of Spain, unknown in wider Europe. This art museum made this city famous in Europe and in the world. The benefits for the city and its inhabitants are tangible. The new building of the Łódź Museum is obviously not a project of this scale, but it certainly has a chance to become one of the pillars of Łódź's promotion, just as with Manufaktura or lofts.
>
> (ms² 2007)

Awaiting the "Bilbao miracle" seems to be the most justified in Łódź's case, although this may refer rather to the failed construction of the Special Art Zone (SSS, abbreviation from Specjalna Strefa Sztuki) in the underground area of Łódź Fabryczna railway station and next to the revitalized EC1 power plant. The complexity and diversity of the investment covering 90 hectares – a combination of objects serving various aspects of culture (art, film, music, cultural education), residential buildings and transport infrastructure justifies the comparison with Bilbao while at the same time creating a new market square. In the architectural competition at the SSS in 2007, an exceptional architecture was expected. "The competition was to solicit an object that would become an icon of Łódź", it was recorded in the annulling document signed by the City of Łódź Office. According to the jurors' decision, none of the works met all of the competition objectives. The next round took place in 2008. Its statement reads:

> The Special Art Zone should be a living place, where contemporary art is permeated with the life of the city. Architecturally, the building of the Special Art Zone should be a significant, distinctive accent of the New City Centre.
>
> (Regulamin Konkursu na Opracowanie Koncepcji Architektonicznej Specjalnej Strefy Sztuki 2008: 6)

It is impossible to resist the impression that the expectations and rhetoric of commissioners are the mirror image of the slogans from the competition regulations for the MSN. In the second version, the design of the German studio Möller Architekten + Ingenieure BDA was chosen, which proposed the construction of a rectangular cuboid wrapped in a glass tube. This concept would allow the envelope to be used for exhibition purposes, and the transparency would make the art displayed there visible from the outside at the street level. In an interview for *Gazeta*

Wyborcza, Maria Poprzęcka compared the Łódź project to the investment carried out in Bilbao, where

> The Guggenheim Museum is just the heart of a larger whole that pushes energy into the bloodstream of the entire city. It's exactly the same with SSS. The big glass tube, which won the competition for the SSS project, has a chance to be not a competitor with the Gehry building, but an extremely impressive new logo for Łódź. [. . .] In Bilbao, this great reconstruction after the collapse of the shipbuilding industry caused the city to change to culture and tourism, becoming a flywheel for the new economy of the city. [. . .] In Łódź, the Special Zone of Art is to be the heart of the whole project and its flywheel.
>
> (Bomanowska 2008)

One icon is not enough: the momentum in Budapest

The slogan "icon" in the context of museums appeared in Hungary only with the building of a new museum district in Budapest (discussed in Chapters 2, 5, and 7), which has been under development since 2007. The original project entailed the construction of an underground museum, precisely, an extension of the already-existing underground level of the Museum of Fine Arts. But this met with criticism voiced by a group of prestigious art historians. One of the arguments against it was a conviction that an investment financed with public funds should be visible in the city space, not hidden underground. The second project, introduced when the initial underground expansion was halted, was based on iconic buildings destined to fill the City Park. The creator of this concept, director of the Museum of Fine Arts and state commissioner for the construction of a new museum district, László Baán, commented on it in 2012, even before the architectural competition was launched: "The complex of buildings to be erected must be of such iconic value whereby, together with the collections held and exhibited, it could become a new emblem of Budapest and, indeed, Hungary" (Interview with László Baán 2017).

A wide-ranging vision, acknowledged by many as not very realistic, was widely criticized by cultured persons. Nevertheless, in 2013, a competition was opened for the idea and spatial parameters of the museum district within and on the outskirts of the City Park. The existing buildings of the Museum of Fine Arts and Műcsarnok (Kunsthalle) are located at its entrance, and the Hungarian Museum of Transport in the park itself. Then, in 2014, four architectural competitions were announced for the construction of five new museum buildings: the building for the New National Gallery and the Ludwig Museum, the Ethnographic Museum building, a complex of two separate buildings for the Hungarian Museum of Architecture and Photomuseum (finally, it was decided that the latter two would not be located within the park) and the building of the House of Hungarian Music. The competition parameters (Liget Budapest Competition Programme 2014: 9) included the following guidelines for applications regarding the new architecture:

> [to] provide a lasting aesthetical experience for visitors at the highest level of contemporary architecture and contribute to the enrichment of the architectural heritage of Budapest [. . .] are composed of buildings conveying specific and strong architectural ideas, [to] create a clearly recognizable and identifiable building complex that is able to improve the international fame of Budapest and Hungarian culture.

The project, operating under the name Liget Budapest Project, also includes the revitalization of the entire park and other facilities already on its premises. In the first iteration of the competition, the winning design of the edifice intended to accommodate the New National Gallery and the Ludwig Museum could not be selected. At the end of 2014, a new competition was undertaken, but this time it was not an open call; instead, only large international architectural studios were invited to participate. In 2015, two projects were selected *ex aequo*: the Norwegian studio Snøhetta and the Japanese SANAA. Both projects were conceived as icons. Snøhetta proposed a building consisting of two connected ramps that are an extension of the public space of the park. The roof of both parts is an operational staircase. This element particularly appealed to jurors who stated that the building "returns the land occupied [by] the park by creating a new public space" (Városliget Zrt. 2015: 12). In this sense, it resembles the Oslo Opera building also designed by this studio. The SANAA project consists of sloping planes and concave roofs, the whole being reminiscent of white boxes and paper cards arranged one on top of the other in a light jumble. In this case, the jurors emphasized the "strong contact [of the building] to its environment" (Városliget Zrt. 2015: 12). The jury's opinions seemed to favor the Snøhetta project. The statement of justification for the first prize notes: "This emblematic building matches [the] dominant role to be played [by] the Liget Project, and it can also become an international symbol" (Városliget Zrt. 2015: 12). Finally, the SANAA studio was invited to design the museum building. Upon the selection of the architectural studio, as a result of the discussion, it was decided not to connect the New National Gallery and the Ludwig Museum, which in effect will not move it to the park.

The competition for the Ethnographic Museum, which the French workshop of Vallet de Martinis DIID Architectes originally won, was rerun. The reason for this was the change in the museum's location. In the second competition, a design by the Hungarian studio Napur Architect was selected unanimously. The jury's statement praised "an extremely simple, emblematic building that can also become a symbol at the international level" (Liget Budapest Néprajzi Múzeum 2016: 10). Its shape resembles a huge ramp for skateboards. The roof of the museum was conceived in its entirety as a public space constituting an extension of the park with greenery, benches, and walking paths. The building blends into its surroundings, while its larger part is underground.

The icing on the cake of iconic edifices is the Hungarian House of Music project by the Japanese architect Sou Fujimoto. Glazed walls were covered with a spread roof resembling a mushroom cap. Numerous holes in the roof picturesquely bring light into the interior, and under the cap there is also green park – the crowns of the trees appear through oval roof openings.

The schedule of the construction is gradually shifting. As of 2018, the investment project involving the erection of new buildings, modernization of existing buildings and revitalization of the park is planned for 2021.

The landmark on the Danube: the Dutch galley near Bratislava

The only discussion around the museum icon in Slovakia concerns "the bridge" wing of the Slovak National Gallery designed during the socialism period by Vladimír Dedeček. The architecture of the Danubiana Meulensteen Art Museum in Čunovo (see Atlas 4.5) is a clear contemporary sign in a space that can be read in terms of an icon, albeit unintentionally.

The investment site was the artificial peninsula on the Danube in the immediate vicinity of the dam, located in Čunovo 15 kilometers from the center of Bratislava. The founder of the museum, Vincent Polakovič, often recalls the symbolism of this border area which connects three Central European countries: Slovakia, Austria, and Hungary. The site was determined by the exhibition program, geared towards Central Europe on the one hand through the proximity of its neighbors, and on the other towards international art due to the washing of the Danube Peninsula shores by a body of water that flows through ten countries and four European capitals. Not only is the location symbolic, but also the architecture of the museum has been blended into the river context. Polakovič and painter Peter Pollág drew up a vision of a museum resembling the shape of a Roman galley, and the well-known Slovak architect Peter Žalman was chosen for its implementation. As Pollág (2001: 8) writes, "Today, Europe's largest natural artery still serves as a bond between the old continent's nations. And, with its ambition to unite nations and cultures, it is precisely this ancient bond that the new riverside museum wants to nurture". The museum is located near the ancient *limes Romanum*, also not far from the place where archaeologists have discovered the remains of a ship.

The architect developed a vision, depicted by the painter, of a boat-shaped lens with oars leaning against the hull, a compact, two-story construction in five colors – red, blue, white, gray, and yellow – whose shape corresponds to the elongated form of the peninsula. The main part of the ground floor is occupied by a high, open two-story exhibition space. Polakovič himself (Žalman 1999: 20) mentioned similarities to and inspirations from other, Western art museums, above all in Louisiana in Denmark, which also inspired him to name the museum Danubiana. The sculpture park surrounding the building is an extension of the exhibition space. When asked about the iconicity of the building, Polakovič deliberately omits the word "icon", claiming that "the functionality of the space has always been of primary importance for us" (Interview with Vincent Polakovič 2017). However, it is hard to resist the impression that the appearance of the building was at least as important as the functionality, with curved walls which certainly do not serve the presentation of paintings.

The museum was created at an extremely fast pace; by the end of 1998, the patron of the entire undertaking, Gerard Meulensteen, approved the location, and in 2000, the finished building was opened. It soon turned out to be too small; hence, in 2013–2014, a wing was added. At that time, the whole was repainted in white.

Summary

The pursuit of architectural icons is a noticeable, global trend. A public museum lends prestige to an iconic investment. The function ennobles the architectural form. Central Europe, especially Poland, became a victim of the fashion for the fanciful museum shapes – a victim in the full sense of the word, because the wait for a museum building that would function for Poland as a visual revelation attracting millions of tourists turned out to be a fantasy. The visions of politicians, officials, and specialists in tourist marketing have diverged with those of jurors of architectural competitions and architects themselves.

The vast majority of new museum buildings are not works of art of Baroque proportions, but rather subdued and austere boxes, giving priority to the art presented in their interiors. The critics of sculptural icons claim that in Western countries, there is a weariness with this tendency; therefore, Poland should draw rather on functional, subdued architecture, remaining in the avant-garde instead of being a belated follower. On the other hand, might it be asked whether sculptural architecture must be reserved for shopping centers, football stadiums, and residential and office buildings, so often accused of lacking proportion, moderation, and taste? Perhaps it would be good if one of the museums, particularly for the contemporary art that seems predestined for it, could be a vibrant sculpture? And this is not necessarily for international tourists, but for the local audience for whom art has to be taken down from its temple pedestal to become part of everyday (not merely festive) knowledge. Might this kind of building overcome the barrier of inaccessibility to become a real calling card for contemporary art in societies wherein it fights with notions of hermeticism and elitism?

These questions relate primarily to Warsaw, where a new (not adapted) building was erected and its central location was ensured. Within individual environments, there was no agreement about the nature of the architectural expression of the building. A significant limitation in this regard was also introduced by location. Nevertheless, after the experience of other cities – for example, the building in Toruń incorporated into the urban fabric, the adapted buildings in Łódź and Krakow (although in the latter case with a large share of contemporary architecture), new but subdued buildings of the museum in Katowice and a minimalist building in Wrocław awaiting completion – it is perhaps time for a building in the capital that would fill the gap between the West and the East, and that with its aesthetics would refer to the lush 1990s and early years of the twenty-first century, in the spirit of Gehry, Calatrava, and Libeskind?

On the other hand, could such a building, regardless of its form, be original, unique, and well-designed at the same time? This is equally dangerous, as it will likely fall into architectural kitsch which, laced gigantomania, will render the museum a caricature of Bilbao in several years. Of course, such architecture can be enjoyed, and baroque-Disney ideas can give an interesting effect, but the area at the foot of the Palace of Culture and Science needs something more than just a trinket.

Filip Springer, stigmatizing a Polish lack of taste and knowledge in the field of architecture in the context of Kerez's project, wrote:

> Such an architecture requires, however, a reflection from the recipient, and this is not something in Poland with which we tend to approach buildings. The basic determinant of *good architecture* is its spectacular character. If it is not something to be seen, it will not gain favour with us.
> (Springer 2017, emphasis as in original)

In Warsaw, after a long period of meandering, "architecture that requires reflection" prevailed, and public opinion seems to be reconciled with the fact that sculpture will not occupy Defilad Square. One may wonder what role fatigue played in prolonging the efforts for a new building.

The situation in Budapest is about not only a prestigious location, but also a much larger scale project in terms of surface area, and the number of institutions and newly constructed buildings considered as architectural icons. The designs of three new buildings fit into the landscape of the park, including two that incorporate urban greenery within their precincts. The project of the Ethnographic Museum offers an extension of the public space of the park. On the one hand, it is a clear sign in space, and on the other hand, its aim is to blend into this space. The size and complexity of the Hungarian investment is unmatched. Unlike in Warsaw, the project in Budapest enjoys the support of the Ministry, which provides financial resources for the implementation of the investment and the city to which the land belongs – but it was necessary to fight for public support. In Warsaw, the support of the city authorities is primarily declarative.

It remains to revisit the question posed at the beginning of the chapter: is a Central European Bilbao possible? Despite the unsuccessful attempts, there is no reason to answer in the negative. The spectacular building of the

Guggenheim Museum was not an end in itself. Its shape was part of a large-scale, integrated project of urban revitalization (taking into account the development of transport infrastructure, rehabilitation of the river, relocation of the port, development of the wharf). Its important goals were to connect the new city with the riverbank, which was previously unavailable for use due to the difference in topography. Authors who often refer critically to the form of a museum as a place for the presentation of art, however, agree on the importance of the building for the city's cultural policy. This "jewel in the crown of world architecture" (Azua 2005: 80) has been used in the city's marketing to this point. Bilbao began to be identified with its museum and has become a global destination. In the same way, the museum has been identified with architecture, leaving the collection in the background. It seems that this is the similarity between Warsaw and Bilbao. It is difficult to compare the collection of international art of the Guggenheim Foundation to a largely local art collection created by MSN. But the situation is similar in the sense that the collection itself does not have the power to attract crowds of tourists, in contrast to the Gehry's packaging. In Warsaw, the collection is just being born, and thus attention has been focused on the building. Finally, the Warsaw museum focused on the program (appreciated by art critics and popular with the audience) from which the form of the building organically began to grow.

In Central Europe, such comprehensive, large-scale projects based on culture are rare. The project whose center was to be located in the SSS, Łódź was similar to the investment in Bilbao in this respect, but it was never implemented. The heat and power plant was revitalized; however, even when the building was completed, only some of its functions and tenants had been determined. The Budapest investment also has a comprehensive character – it combines the construction of museums, the adaptation and renovation of existing buildings, and the revitalization of the park. The project has just begun; its completion is planned for 2121, and it will be possible to evaluate it at that point in time.

Austria may be an apt point of reference for the discussion of icons, but representing two opposing tendencies – spectacular and minimalist – where two institutions of the Kunsthalle type have opened in the space of six years, the Kunsthaus Bregenz designed by Peter Zumthor (opened in 1997), and Kunsthaus Graz (2003), the work of Peter Cook and Colin Fournier. Zumthor designed his building as a translucent cuboid whose silhouette blends into the surrounding buildings and almost reflects in the waters of Lake Constance. This effect of merging with the landscape arises from the etched glass envelope. While the vanishing architecture of Bregenz rose, the Friendly Alien (as baptized by architects) landed in Graz – a blue biomorphic blob distinct from everything else there. Its round design resembles a baby hippo, a sea slug, a porcupine, a whale (Bogner 2004: 114), "a heart removed from the bloodstream with upward arteries, a cow's udder thrown on the asphalt" (Jarecka 2006b: 16), a gently falling cloud, a big balloon caught in the trees (which can be seen especially from the castle hill). Such "human scale" projects are possible to achieve in Central Europe.

Notes

1 In 2005, Warsaw was not the only European capital which did not have a museum of modern (or contemporary) art; neither did Bratislava. After 1938, a museum building dedicated to art, the Centre of Japanese Art and Technology, opened in 1994 (since 2007, the Museum).
2 It is puzzling that a serious critic of such architecture, Deyan Sudjic, was appointed to the jury of the competition, as Warsaw awaited an architectural icon.

4   Adaptive reuse for museums

The architectural icons to which the previous chapter was devoted were meant to stand out in space, to literally and figuratively stick out from what is around them. Almost all museums in Central Europe that can be described as icons (or in relation to which such ambitions are reported) represent the new architecture (with the exception of the Elektrownia Mazovian Center for Contemporary Art in Radom, which combines old and new architecture, and the MOCAK Museum of Contemporary Art in Krakow, which "absorbed" the block of old factory halls). The opposite tendency is to reintroduce the existing architecture and adapt it to museum and exhibition functions.

Apartments, offices, hotels, restaurants, and cultural facilities have been created in buildings that served other purposes in the past. Such buildings gain a second life, often revitalizing a whole neighborhood. Post-industrial architecture in particular is often used for the needs of museums and centers of modern art, although other types of buildings such as residences, tenements, synagogues, and barracks are adapted to such requirements, as well. The fashion for museums in post-industrial spaces in Central Europe may be combined with the successes of museums in the West since the 1980s, while the tradition of using buildings of a different character, especially residential, dates back to the origins of museums.

The issue of repurposing architecture for museums can be examined from many angles: the revitalization of neglected urban areas, the historical context of existing architecture for the reception of art, the symbolism of the architecture that has been co-opted, location factors, and space in the urban milieu. The issues of location and site will be the subject of this chapter. The number of investments located in repurposed buildings indicates the almost mass nature of the trend.

The tradition of adaptive reuse

The end of the twentieth century and the beginning of the twenty-first ushered in a series of adaptations, some more historical than others, for the performance of new functions. Often the spectacular nature of these projects is combined with a dramatic change in function. The point of departure for the proceeding reflections on the phenomenon of adaptive reuse is the emergence in the mid-eighteenth century of the concept of "monument" and the need for its protection, as well as the concept of cultural heritage, coined in the second half of the twentieth century that encompassed the meaning of "monument". Changing a building's function is a way to preserve and protect it. The ground for the emergence of the cult of monuments was laid by the French Revolution, one of the fruits of which was the creation of the Louvre Museum, the archaeological discoveries of Johann Joachim Winckelmann, and the dissemination of knowledge about monuments. The popularity of historical novels and history painting in the nineteenth century, as well as the creation of nation-states in which the sense of responsibility for monuments resulted in the creation of systems for their protection, were also important sources. It should be borne in mind that the reuse of buildings for other purposes has a centuries-old tradition, but significantly, the desire to protect them was not a motivation.

The concept of a monument is inherently connected with conservation. The French explorer and restorer of medieval architecture Eugène Emmanuel Viollet-le-Duc advocated for stylistic unity of a given object, in the name of which he permitted the removal of interventions from subsequent epochs and the addition of new elements in the original style. He also spoke about the historical functions of buildings, writing: "the best of all ways of preserving a building is to find a use for it, and then to satisfy so well the needs dictated by that use that there will never be any further need to make any further changes in the building" (quoted from Eugène Viollet-le-Duc [1990 {1854}] *The Foundations of Architecture. Selections from the Dictionnaire raisonné* [New York: George Braziller]: 222, from: Plevoets and Van Cleempoel 2011: 156). Working at the same time, John Ruskin recognized restoration as a form of destruction and advocated only those actions aimed at preserving and maintaining the object. Alois Riegl formulated the theoretical basis of the twentieth-century theory of conservation. He ascribed special meaning to so-called "age value", which is created with the passage of time, the physical consumption of material, and in the intangible – that is, the imagination of time that has elapsed since a work's creation (Szmygin 2003: 150). In his view, the guiding principle of conservation was respect for the historical form and substance of the monument (Szmygin 2003: 152). The first document devoted to the protection of monuments on international grounds is The Athens Charter for the Restoration of Historic Monuments adopted at the First International Congress of Architects and Technicians of Historic Monuments in Athens, 1931. Already in the first article there appears a reference to the historical function of a building: "The Conference recommends that the occupation of buildings, which ensures the continuity of their life, should be maintained but that they should be used for a purpose which respects their historic or artistic character" (The Athens Charter for the Restoration of Historic Monuments 1931). The Second Athens Charter from 1964 introduced the concept of the social utility of the object, whose reuse would be contingent upon maintaining the current shape and appearance of the building:

> The conservation of monuments is always facilitated by making use of them for some socially useful purpose. Such use is therefore desirable but it must not change the layout or decoration of the building. It is within these limits only that modifications demanded by a change of function should be envisaged and may be permitted.
>
> (International Charter for the Conservation and
> Restoration of Monuments and Sites 1964: article 5)

The adaptation of historical buildings as museums does not always go hand in hand with conservation guidelines, because changes in function often involve not only the interiors, but also the exterior appearance of the building – from discreetly marking the presence of a new institution to establishing a dialogue between the new and pre-existing architecture.

Extensive writings on the adaptive reuse of buildings accompanied the investments. Bie Plevoets and Koenraad Van Cleempoel (2011: 155–164) reviewed many of these titles in an article on the subject. A voluminous publication by Sherban Cantacuzino, *New Uses for Old Buildings* (London, 1975) considered selected structures according to their original functions: churches and chapels; monasteries and other religious premises; fortifications, gates, and barracks; town houses, country houses, outbuildings, and ancillary buildings; schools; grain exchanges; mills and granaries; malting plants and breweries; warehouses and other industrial buildings; and pump stations. In 1989, the same author published *Re-Architecture. Old Buildings/ New Uses* on a similar subject, adopting a more descriptive character compared to the catalog format of the earlier publication, and representing a different set of institutions. Both books present objects from various European countries and the United States, whereas many other publications treat only national heritage (e.g., a volume published in Paris under the title, *Bâtiments anciens . . . Usages nouveaux. Images du possible* [1978], which presents in catalog form only French examples).

The adaptation of existing facilities to perform cultural functions (museums, galleries, libraries, theaters, concert halls) has become more and more common over the years; however, this is numerically subordinate to commercial investments. Most examples of the adaptation of industrial and historic buildings described in the literature come from the United Kingdom, followed by the United States and France. As Michael Stratton writes:

> Britain was the world's first industrial nation. It was also one of the earliest to experience the full trauma of decline in traditional manufacturing and dock handling, and has pioneered the conservation and re-use of redundant factories and warehouses.
>
> (2000: 8)

The oil crisis of 1973 put an end to post-war economic growth, which affected not only the economy but also the social and urban fabric of cities. The revitalization of cities such as Manchester, Liverpool, Newcastle, and Bilbao, which began in the 1990s, has become a model example for depressed cities and districts around the world.

The character and typology of buildings adapted for museums

From the beginning of its status as an independent architectural type (i.e. the eighteenth century), museum planners have sought the most prestigious location, and an architectural form that underlined that prestige. Although many newly built museums focus on the prestige of location, it need not always be central. While the site for the Museum of Modern Art in Warsaw was chosen in the very center of the city, on the monumental Defilad Square, the Guggenheim Museum in Bilbao, together with other spectacular buildings, was erected in the revitalized port district of Abandoibarra, designating the birth of a new city. However, it is not always possible to build from scratch. The limitations include not only financial resources for construction, but also the site itself, especially in city centers. In many cases, the use of a pre-existing building and its adaptation for museum or exhibition purposes is a necessity; in others, it may represent a conscious choice.

The typology of buildings adapted for the needs of art is broad and not at all restrictive. The two largest groups are post-industrial buildings and residential buildings. Castles, palaces, and residential structures are a natural place for art. Museums originate from royal, princely, or magnate collections assembled in private residences and, over time, made available to narrower or wider audiences. An archetypal museum of this kind is the Múseum Central des Arts in Paris, opened at the Louvre Palace on 10 August 1793, the first anniversary of the fall of the monarchy in France. Residential spaces, as opposed to factories, power plants, railway stations, or anti-aircraft shelters, were filled with works of art. Filling the latter with art constituted a real revolution at that time.

Since then, there has been an interest in post-industrial architecture, the spaces of which have been used for art institutions, first in the United States and then in Europe. Independent art galleries founded in spaces far from the elegance and seriousness of the museum hall, and more in the character of the artist's studio, gave rise to great museums. Initially, the alternative type acquired a mainstream character. The placement of the art gallery within post-industrial architecture began in the Manhattan district of SoHo, now an artists' mecca. It was a jungle of cast-iron, Victorian-era warehouses whose rental in the 1960s was inexpensive and offered an enormous amount of space to the world's largest artist population (Lorente 1998). Following the artists, art dealers flooded into the district; art cafes, restaurants, fashionable music stores, clubs, and boutiques began to emerge. The artistic atmosphere attracted crowds of young professionals to the lofts; ultimately, museums emerged here. In 1977, the New Museum of Contemporary Art began to operate on the premises of an adapted warehouse, and in 1992, also in such a space, a branch of the Guggenheim Museum opened (Lorente 1998: 253–254). In the 1980s, museum creators on a broad scale – city authorities, investors, and museum workers – became interested in the past industrial functions these buildings served. The structures offered spatial dimensions suitable for contemporary art and provided momentum to the works created within them. Their austere walls presented an attractive industrial context for the art.

Museums and art centers created in post-industrial buildings have a diverse character. These are both alternative galleries and large public museums; places hidden from the gaze of passers-by, as well as those that strongly announce their presence; buildings located in city centers as well as on their periphery; buildings that have become an integral part of the revitalization processes through their adaptation, located both in still-functioning and waning industrial areas.

With respect to architectural form, museums created in adapted buildings can be divided into two main categories. The first is signature buildings, where an act of adaptation becomes a display of the architect's virtuosity. In some cases, these are buildings that gain iconic status. The Tate Modern (Jacques Herzog and Pierre de Meuron, 2000) is a museum icon created at the disused power plant designed by Sir Giles Gilbert Scott in London's Southwark district. Outside, the intervention in the red brick building is minimalist in nature; its only recognizable element is the glass tank discreetly lit after dark. By contrast, the architects gutted its interior, once filled with machinery, to accommodate gallery space. The main entrance to the museum features a ramp located on the short axis leading to the basement level. The entrance hall stretches to the height of five stories. On the ground level is also the so-called Turbine Hall for special exhibitions. Escalators and elevators provide circulation between floors. The London power plant is not the only typological model (e.g. in 1988 in Malmö, the center of modern Rooseum was established in the former 1900 power plant),[1] but no other institution has won such recognition or popularity. The architect's signature is also visible on another British edifice, created as part of the revitalization project of the Newcastle and Gateshead quays, the Center for Contemporary Art BALTIC, for which the mill compound was adapted (Dominic Williams, 2002).

There is also a sizeable group of museums that the "signature" category does not fully encompass, but new construction solutions are evident and the architect is not anonymous. One of the first large museums of contemporary art in the United States to take over a warehouse is the MoCA LA (Museum of Contemporary Art in Los Angeles). In 1983, Frank Gehry adapted the buildings that previously housed a police car warehouse, creating Temporary Contemporary, the museum unit named after its temporary nature (since 1996, the Geffen Contemporary). This group of museums also includes the Tate Liverpool located in the dock warehouse (James Stirling, Michael Wilford and Associates, 1988) and the Museum of Contemporary Art in Berlin at the Hamburger Bahnhof (Josef Paul Kleihues, 1996).

In contrast with such visually strong adaptations are "non-architectural" adaptations (McClellan 2008: 98). Architects "without a name" in this case create the museum buildings; they are characterized by formal simplicity and flexibility, and adaptation is basic. McClellan (2008: 97–8) calls museums created in this spirit "loft museums" and includes the Andy Warhol Museum in Pittsburgh (1994), the Massachusetts Museum of Contemporary Art in North Adams (MASS MoCA, 1999) and Dia:Beacon (2003).

Post-industrial architecture for museums in Central Europe

The Central European fashion for locating art institutions in post-industrial provincial buildings is the result of the success and popularity of this type in Western Europe; this does not mean that before 1989, Central European artists did not utilize abandoned (in some cases industrial) buildings, but the practice was more incidental. Grzegorz Klaman started his artistic and exhibition activity in Gdańsk in this way. He created two art institutions in the 1990s and after 2000 in adapted buildings – the first in a former bathhouse, the other in the former shipyard. The choice of buildings for adaptation on which the philosophy of the institution was based was rooted in Klaman's earlier activities. Even in his student days, writes Aneta Szyłak (1995: 10), he was looking for new areas for art, annexing unwanted and forgotten places. Together with a group of artists, he created and presented his works on the Gdańsk Island of Granaries – first in bars, and then in one of the burnt-out cereal warehouses, which operated as Wyspa Gallery from 1988. According to Szyłak, this place had "only brick, soot-covered walls, [. . .] the roof was sky, the floor was covered with sod, and the windows overlooked the river channel" (Szyłak 1995: 12).

After 1989, the Czech Republic and Poland in particular undertook adaptive reuse on a large scale while trying to preserve the character of the pre-existing condition, absorbed by the picturesque, visually attractive adaptations carried out in the Western countries. In each case, the approach to a post-industrial object is different – at times it is treated like a husk, a shell, simply "romantic" packaging that only evokes old functions on the exterior; at other times, it is a minor intervention into the existing fabric, whose only goal is to adapt the building to new functions.

All manner of buildings undergo adaptations for the needs of museums and art centers, and the parallels with Western European or American institutions are easy to see. In Central Europe, I have identified fourteen such types: 1) the power plant, heating plant, transformer; 2) the factory/plant; 3) the mine; 4) buildings related to transportation; 5) the mill; 6) the shipyard; 7) the brewery; 8) the exhibition pavilion; 9) the palace, castle, and residence; 10) the tenement house and villa; 11) defensive and military architecture; 12) religious architecture; 13) the bath; and 14) the swimming pool. Typology facilitates the organization of the institutions and their comparisons between individual Central European countries, but in my view, the Western inspiration for the adaptive reuse of post-industrial buildings for art is not restricted to parity with a concrete type (in the sense of a museum in a factory being inspired by another museum in a factory, and so on); rather, it is of a more general character and concerns spatial, visual, and atmospheric attractiveness. The key to discussing museums in repurposed buildings will be typology.

The power plant/heating plant/transformer

The power plants used as museums and modern art centers in Central Europe are not among the largest, but it is the power plant type that was most commonly repurposed. The transformation of the power plant in London's Southwark district at the Tate Modern, one of the most visited museums of contemporary art in the world, is the direct parallel for institutions such as the Elektrownia Mazovian Center for Contemporary Art in Radom, the Cricoteka Center for the Documentation of the Art of Tadeusz Kantor in Krakow, TRAFO Trafostacja Sztuki in Szczecin, the Tatra Gallery in Poprad, and Trafó House of Contemporary Arts in Budapest, as well as the plans for adapting the heating plant in Bratislava. The Tate Modern should be considered not only as a typological example, but also much more broadly as a prototype for the transformation of industrial buildings for cultural purposes. The visual appeal of the brick building certainly played a major role here. Giles Gilbert Scott designed the power plant (built in 1947–1963) as a rectangular brick building with a chimney in the middle of the façade facing the Thames. His architectural style is described as a combination of historicism and art déco. The façade has been divided into six large, cathedral-type windows extending over almost the entire height of the mass. In the architectural competition for the building's adaptation, this project was chosen for the high degree to which it respected the original architecture. One of the jurors, Michael Craig-Martin (2008: 47) noted that,

> All other proposals treated the existing building as a shell within which their new structure would stand. Herzog & de Meuron's was the only proposal that completely accepted the existing building – its form, its materials and its industrial characteristics – and saw the solution to be the transformation of the building itself into an art gallery.

The role of Tate Modern can be compared to that of the Guggenheim Museum in Bilbao, which entailed a constellation of new, spectacular buildings. Importantly, both the Tate Modern and the Guggenheim Museum were part of the revitalization processes of neglected districts – the former as the trigger for the process of district revitalization, and the latter as part of a large integrated investment.

One of the largest buildings emerging from the power plant type in Poland includes the Elektrownia Mazovian Center for Contemporary Art in Radom (MCSW; see Atlas 3.12). The creation of the MCSW is linked with the Museum of Contemporary Art established in 1990 as a part of the Jacek Malczewski Museum in Radom (see Atlas 3.13), but without the exhibition space enabling the presentation of the collection. The idea of creating an art center for the Radom collection arose only in 2004, whereupon a public debate about the need for its creation and possible location flared up in the city. Kaja Koziarska, a graduate student in architecture at the Warsaw Academy of Fine Arts, drew attention to the potential of an abandoned power plant building from 1901, which she adapted into a student center for her thesis project. The location seemed attractive and the acquisition procedures for the building began. The MCSW was established in 2005, and the exhibition activity within its severe walls started the following year. Andrzej Kikowski and the Biuro Usług Projektowych from Warsaw won the competition for a concept that employed a contrast of red (the old building of a brick power plant) and black (the new cubic forms covered with sheet metal), with the addition of white at the first level. Black, minimalistic forms pierced by a series of windows create a kind of superstructure and addition. Construction and modernization were completed in 2014. From a visual point of view, the Tate Modern and MCSW are completely different. In London, the modern architecture of the façades is discreetly marked, while in Radom, colored blocks are strong accents competing with the brick walls of the old power plant.

An echo of the Tate Modern, although on a much smaller scale, is the headquarters of the Cricoteka Center for the Documentation of the Art of Tadeusz Kantor in Krakow (see Atlas 3.7), opened in 2014. Established in the building of the former power plant (erected in 1899–1900), it is located on the banks of the Vistula River in the district of Podgórze, in close proximity to the MOCAK Museum of Contemporary Art opened three years earlier. Cricoteka struggled with space issues from the beginning of its existence in 1980. Due to the shortage of exhibition possibilities, its collection has never been shown in its entirety. In the architecture competition held in 2006, a project was created jointly by two offices: Vision, Stanisław Deńko's firm, and Piotr Nawara and Agnieszka Szultk's nsMoonStudio, Krakow. The museum they designed takes the shape of a bridge span over the historic power plant, whose form directly refers to Kantor's art – the idea of *emballage* and the art of conflict, clashes, breaking stereotypes, and conducting unusual collisions of forms and content (Budowa Muzeum Tadeusza Kantora i nowej siedziby CRICOTEKI). The point of departure for the building's form was a drawing Kantor made depicting a man carrying a table. The shape of the building and the content it communicates predetermined the museum's iconic status; it is a prop for its contents. New and old architecture have not been structurally integrated but arranged, so that the new architecture burrows into the old one. A literal reference to Tate Modern's renowned ramp is a staircase on the side of the building that descends into the underground space, where the ticket office, cloakroom, and shop are located.

In the 1990s in Szczecin, efforts were made to transform the historic power plant to house contemporary art. After a project was drawn up to locate the BWA Art Center here, the Association for the Encouragement of Contemporary Art (created in 2004) attempted to adapt it under the name TRAFO Trafostacja Sztuki (see Atlas 3.14). The so-called transformer house was built in 1911–1913 as the first power plant in Szczecin (expanded in 1926 and 1933). After the Second World War, a red brick building housed an energy plant. In 1976, the building was slated for demolition, which was prevented by its entry into the register of monuments in 1984. After several changes in ownership, in 2008 the building was taken over by the city in a state of ruin, which in turn enabled efforts to create an art center there (Soćko 2009). The resulting adaptation created a space of over 600 square meters with a main hall with a main hall of 19 meters high, conceived as a place for exhibitions, the organization of concerts, film screenings, and alternative theater performances and happenings. The hall also draws inspiration from the Turbine Hall at the Tate Modern. TRAFO began operations in 2013.

In 2005, the Silesian power plant was transformed into an art space. The Association of Cultural Initiatives established the Elektrownia Contemporary Art Gallery on the space of the nineteenth-century "Saturn" mine in Czeladź (which since 2016 has been managed by the Saturn Museum in Czeladź). The interior is still filled with original fixtures and objects from the power plant (a flywheel, chains, a gantry, a control panel, and devices producing electricity) and serves as a backdrop for the contemporary art exhibited here. According to the creators of the gallery, "After a century, almost nothing has changed. This is a magical place cloaked in the aura of European industrial power at the turn of the nineteenth and twentieth century" (Konopelska n.d.).

The only example of adaptation of a post-industrial building for modern art in Slovakia is the Tatra Gallery in Poprad, which has been located in the former Secessionist-style steam power plant since 1993. The block consists of two connected halls with pitched roofs and a tower. The power plant built by Siemens Schuckert, Budapest-Pressburg, operated in the years 1912–1956 supplying electricity for the tram; later, it was used for industry. In the years 2000–2009, the building underwent a major renovation, during which it was added to the Slovak list of cultural heritage in 2003 (Ondrušeková 2008: 141).

In Bratislava at the turn of the new century, Peter Žalman, the Slovak architect behind the Danubiana project, proposed the repurposing of the municipal heating plant as a contemporary art gallery that would compensate for the absence of such an institution in the capital. The heating plant is located in the former industrial district of Čulenova, whose character had begun to change with the introduction of residential and office spaces. In 2009, part of the greenhouse – a boiler room and a turbine hall – was entered in the monuments registry as exemplary of Dušan Jurkovič's architecture. The brick structure has a compact cubic massing, and the main hall with its rows of narrow windows reaches a height of 25 meters. Žalman's adaptation involved obtaining between 2,000 and 8,000 square meters of exhibition space, which was dependent on the funds allocated for investment. Press reports made frequent comparisons with the transformation of the London power plant (e.g. Kráková and Gurová 2009; Minca 2009). In 2010, the architectural competition for the development of this area was resolved with the adaptation of the power plant and the construction of three high-rise residences. Zaha Hadid's studio won the commission. The developer of the Sky Park complex announced the reconstruction of the heat plant (Jurkovičova tepláreň 2017); as of 2018, the decision regarding its function still had not been made.

Locating cultural institutions in post-industrial facilities is not a dominant trend in Hungary; adaptations were carried out more often on residential building terrain. The first institution that employed post-industrial architecture is the Trafó House of Contemporary Arts in Budapest, opened in 1998. It was built in the former transformer station dating from 1909. At the beginning of the 1990s, a French anarchist artistic group functioned there, after which Trafó House started its activity in various areas of contemporary art: dance, theater, art (Trafó Gallery), literature, and music.

The factory/plant

Various types of factories and plants often serve as spaces for museums, art centers and galleries. Their square footage and architecture vary widely depending on the profile and scope of activity for which they were originally created. MASS MoCA in North Adams in the United States is one of the largest. The museum was founded in a complex of twenty-five buildings from the second half of the nineteenth century belonging to the O. Arnold and Company textile printers. The plant was closed in 1942 during the economic downturn, and purchased by the Sprague Electric Company in the same year. A company employed half of the local population, and its closure in 1985 had catastrophic consequences for the city. In the following year, local authorities began to look for development opportunities. Thomas Krens, director of the Guggenheim Foundation since 1988 and at that time director of the Williams College Museum of Art in neighboring Williamstown, had been seeking a new location for the display of contemporary art because the collegiate museum was not suited to the presentation of large-format works. The spatial arrangements and character of the buildings appeared to be perfect for contemporary art. The individual brick buildings of MASS MoCA are connected with each other by bridges, viaducts, and footbridges, accompanied by overlapping court-yards (Dobrzynski 1999). This complex adaptation and the social aspect of the investment constitute a reference to many Central European revitalization projects.

Multiple examples of the adaptation of factory buildings to museums of art in the West may be added: the Museum für Gegenwartskunst in Basel (today Kunstmuseum Basel) was opened in 1980 on the premises of a nineteenth-century paper mill; in Schaffhausen, Switzerland, the Hallen für Neue Kunst was created in a converted textile factory building in 1983; the Saatchi Collection Gallery in London was started two years later in the building of the former paint factory; in 2002, part of the giant factory Fiat Lingotto in Turin was adapted by Renzo Piano for the Pinacoteca Giovanni e Marella Agnelli; in the early 1990s in Berlin, the Institute of Contemporary Art KW – Kunstwerke was created in an abandoned eighteenth- and nineteenth-century margarine factory in the Mitte district.

Former factories have been used for the headquarters of two contemporary art museums in Poland and several art centers in the Czech Republic and Hungary. MOCAK in Krakow and ms^2 in Łódź are the largest and represent two different types of adaptation – a combination of old and new architecture in the first case, and the desire to showcase the original shape of the building as much as possible in the second. The Hungarian Gallery of Paks represents the approach used at MOCAK on a much smaller scale, while the DOX in Prague, the Wannieck Gallery in Brno, and the MEO in Budapest recall Łódź in their approach to old buildings. In contrast, FUTURA in Prague and 320fok in Siófok represent a basic, minimalist model of adaptation.

The largest intervention in the existing architectural fabric among the museums took place in connection with the adaptation of the halls of Oskar Schindler's German Enamelware Factory to MOCAK (see Atlas 3.8). The decision to locate a museum dedicated to contemporary art at the factory was made in 2006. For a long while, no agreement had been reached regarding the implementation of exhibition activities for contemporary art in a building so strongly marked by history. The Factory of Enamelware and Tin Products "Record" by Izrael Kohn, Wolf Luzer Glajtman, and Michał Gutman was established on this site in 1937, and then in 1939–1944, the Schindler Factory operated there. It produced mainly kitchen pots, pans, buckets, and mess tins for the Wehrmacht. From 1941, it also served as an armaments factory, and in 1943–1944 as a sub-camp of the forced labor camp in Płaszów. After the war (in 1947), the factory was nationalized. Until the 1990s, the Telpod Telecommunications Equipment Manufacturing Plant and Spółdzielnia Spożywców were active here, with the Suprema Record Factory functioning in the former labor camp. In 2007, an international architectural competition took place, won by Claudio Nardi from Florence. The creation of the new museum entailed the adaptation of six factory halls and the erection of the main building. The finished museum complex was opened to the public at the end of 2010; however, the exhibition program began only in mid-2011.

The architecture of MOCAK is a legible signature of its creator. The new architecture covered the factory halls; only in one place its original brick wall is exposed. Today's shed roof reproduces the shape of the original roof and complements the remaining factory buildings. Two floors of exhibition halls have been partially hidden underground, so as to not overwhelm the industrial landscape of the area. The architects also used a system of stone partitions several meters tall. These separate the MOCAK building from the street; they also create the cozy atmosphere for the courtyard between the main and auxiliary buildings, and the front building of the factory (which houses the historical museum).

The impulse for the creation of MOCAK was launched in 2004 by the Ministry of Culture's program "Znaki Czasu" (discussed in Chapter 8). The desire to create the institution had been expressed independently by the Mayor of Krakow, Jacek Majchrowski and the Marshal of Małopolska, Janusz Sepioł but with each imagined in a different location. The dispute regarding not whether the museum was needed and whether it would be built, but where it should be situated, continued through 2006. Even after the results of the architectural competition were announced, a group lobbied to change the museum's location. Schindler's Factory was chosen by the mayor, who in an interview stated that "locating everything on the Main Square and the surrounding area is not a good solution" (Urok zamkniętego zaułka 2005). In turn, the Marshal argued that the project of locating the museum in the Schindler's Factory was "one bridge too far away" (Sepioł 2005: 2), and proposed two other places: a historic railway station building, next to which a shopping center, hotel, and apartments were built; and close to this, the building of the former Peterseim factory (near the opera house, then under construction) which would create the so-called New Town. Two concepts – one central and one more peripheral – clashed in the discussions about the museum. The second one prevailed; however, it must be emphasized that its aim was not to create distance from the center, but to establish another hotspot for cultural life in the city. The Mayor of Krakow, expressing himself on the subject of the location, directly stated that the museum in the factory is part of the current "fashion for locating this type of institution in post-industrial facilities" (Hajok 2005). The role that the museum can play in the revitalization of a neglected district was also pointed out. In a 2010 interview, just after the opening of the building, the director of MOCAK, Maria Anna Potocka, expressed her conviction: "I believe that MOCAK will affect Zabłocie like a respirator. This deep breath, so necessary for the development of the district, cannot mean only a joyful commercialism that kills the 'romantic provincialism' of the place" (Hajok 2010: 6).

With the initiation of large-scale investments (from the opening of the university in 2000, the Kotlarski bridge in 2002, and the blocks of flats and office buildings that from the end of the decade systematically displaced post-industrial architecture) the district quickly began to change its character. The progressive industrialization of this area, which in the 1920s had become one of the most important industrial districts of Krakow, dates to the beginning of the twentieth century (Salwiński 2011: 17); after 1989, as Jacek Salwiński points out, "the industrial part of Krakow fell into a period of malaise" (Salwiński 2011: 22). The documentary film *Zabłocie zastane* [Zabłocie Found] was one of the museum's first projects. Potocka indicated the importance of the museum for the new face of the district:

> A lot of chaotic factory buildings and buildings here, like in a small town. We wanted to capture all that in the film in the eleventh hour, because it will change immediately. The district has gone under the tender knife of capitalism and will soon become snobbish. In a sense, our task is to give this place a more sophisticated character.
>
> (Muzeum bez kuratorów 2010)

Industrial Zabłocie in the early twentieth century, with its waning activity, had been labeled a bad district. It largely resembled Southwark, where the Tate Modern was created. City authorities deciding to locate the museums at the Schindler's Factory evidently counted on their similar impact on the surrounding area, as had been the case in London. Although Southwark is located in the center of London, it could be circumvented by a wide berth, particularly since it was devoid of tourist attractions. Andrew Marr (2008: 17) stated, "It was a place people moved out of when they could. The good life was elsewhere". The opening of the museum helped attract developers who in turn began transforming warehouse buildings into expensive lofts. Restaurants and cafes were opened in the district, the boulevard on the Thames became a popular place for walks, and the riverbank was joined by a footbridge, making the district fashionable. The Tate Modern was at the same time at the center of a major city revitalization project called "South Central", whose aim was to extend the so-called "Tate effect" beyond its initial impact on the surrounding area (Travers 2005: 26–27). Karsten Schubert (2002: 109) noted that the revitalization of Bankside was not the result of a political plan developed by the city authorities, but rather was the result of a museum intervention. To a greater or lesser extent, almost all adaptive initiatives, not only Krakow, counted on the Tate effect.

In terms of combining old and new architecture and concealing old materials with new ones, as at MOCAK, a much smaller example is the Gallery of Paks (see Atlas 2.6), a modern and contemporary art gallery in the town of Paks in central Hungary. Part of the vegetable processing plant located among the apartment blocks was adapted in 2007 for the gallery. The new façade cladding and metal and glass construction materials distinguish the building from the backdrop of the factory and residential neighborhood.

On the other hand, similar to the museum in Krakow in terms of the nature of the location and the character of the exhibition halls, the DOX

Centre for Contemporary Art (see Atlas 1.6) opened in Prague in 2008. It was established in the former industrial district of Holešovice, whose character changed at the turn of the new century to become more residential and business-oriented. The founder of DOX, Leoš Válka, originally planned a completely different use for its buildings:

> I was looking for a space that could be converted for a commercial purpose, which was a residential, loft kind of building. These industrial buildings were ideal candidate[s] for such a project. But when I saw the potential of the buildings I realized that it would be an ideal contemporary art space. So I decided to go against my commercial motives and I decided to go for art, basically.
>
> (Willoughby 2008)

The then artistic director at the DOX stated that "The DOX is a symbol of the district's rebirth" (Anděl 2008, 17). Válka is familiar with Western revitalization projects and deliberately refers to them. The name DOX itself is intended as an echo of the transformation of the London and Amsterdam Docklands port districts into centers of business, trade, and social life (Skřivánek 2008: 38–41). DOX was created in a former metal factory from the turn of the nineteenth and twentieth centuries, and stands as an example of conjoining old and new architecture. It consists in the connection of two industrial facilities that were then expanded. The building's severe, industrial character has been preserved. Both parts correspond well to one another, and it is difficult to distinguish between the added and original elements.

The new headquarters of the Muzeum Sztuki in Łódź (see Atlas 3.10) was established on the grounds of a textile factory in a former weaving mill, quite by accident. Having been housed since 1946 in the former palace of the Maurycy Poznański, for several dozen years the museum waited for a proper building, which it eventually received. In 1973, a competition for the conceptual design of a modern building in the Park of Culture and Recreation in Zdrowie (a district of Łódź) was held; Jan Fiszer's project won first prize, but the investment did not come to fruition due to funding cuts. The museum's salvation turned out to be an investment undertaken in the nineteenth-century textile factory of the Towarzystwo Akcyjne Wyrobów Bawełnianych that belonged to Izrael Kalmanowicz Poznański, which in 1999–2006 was transformed into a new shopping, entertainment, and cultural district called Manufaktura. The French firm Apsys decided to transfer one of the buildings to the museum free of charge. The Museum's new exhibition space, called ms², was opened here in 2008. The commercial nature of the museum's neighborhood frequently induced the media to raise concerns about shallowing the exhibition program (on the challenges of this neighborhood, see Chapter 5). The typological parallel for Łódź is the powerful MASS MoCA. Even if it is difficult to talk about transplanting this particular American model to Łódź, North Adams is certainly one of the best-known and widely described examples of the adaptation of a post-industrial building for a museum. What is more, North Adams presents a successful example of revitalization through culture. As the leading American dailies proclaimed, thanks to the museum the city returned to life; they referred to it as a nascent SoHo (Kifner 2000). The adaptation of the building of the Łódź weaving mill respected the original architectural fabric. The presence of the museum outside is announced only by the inscription placed on the roof, the neon in the windows and the ramp running from the level of the car park to the first floor, where the cafe and first exhibition rooms are situated. In the interior, the original division into stories has been preserved, hence there is no space high enough for the presentation of large-scale works.

MOCAK and DOX are located in post-industrial districts outside the city center, the revitalization of which had just begun when they were created. The ms^2 branch has become part of the entire revitalized complex that, in line with the objectives, has become a new urban center. Similar in character to the complex in Łódź, engineer Friedrich Wannieck's machine factory "Vaňkovka" in Brno contains the gallery space, since 2006 occupied by the Wannieck Gallery (2013–2015 as the Richard Adam Gallery; see Atlas 1.1), then since 2016 the Fait Gallery operates in the space. At the time of its establishment in 1865, the factory was located outside the city walls. In the twentieth century, however, the city grew considerably. Today, the post-industrial area occupies a large plot in Brno's city center. The factory complex, expanded several times, consisted of several buildings housing separate functions. The period of its prosperity ended after the First World War, and it was closed for the first time in 1930. From 1937, it functioned as a weapons factory; at the end of the 1960s, it was intended for demolition, and in 1988, it was finally closed but not razed to the ground. In the 1990s, a group of historic industrial architecture enthusiasts began to lobby for the revitalization of the factory, citing French, Italian, German, and British designs. In the years 1996–2002, a number of cultural events were organized in the complex – exhibitions, concerts, festivals, and workshops.

A similar form of artists' "take-overs" occurred elsewhere, for example at the Amsterdam docks and ufaFabrik in Berlin. In the first case, a large-scale construction project was carried out in the port, and in the second, a group of artists and activists reached an agreement with municipal authorities who legalized their presence in the complex. The Brno authorities decided not to abandon the cultural presence at the Wannieck factory and instead divided the complex into two parts: one was created as a shopping center, and the other was slated for a contemporary art gallery. Adaptation works that interfered least with the original structure of buildings were carried out in 2004–2005. The art gallery is a huge hall with an area of 3,800 square meters; the main entrance leads directly to the exhibition hall. In terms of building typology, the Wannieck Gallery should be grouped with MASS MoCA in North Adams. Both factories had created powerful complexes of specialized buildings in the past. In Brno, only one building was designated for a gallery, squeezed into a commercial neighborhood. In North Adams, however, all buildings in the post-industrial complex serve contemporary art.

In Hungary, the center of contemporary art MEO (see Atlas 2.3) in Budapest was maintained in a similar spirit. It operated in the years 2001–2006 in a tannery in the former industrial district of Újpest. The art complex consists of two adapted factory buildings intended for exhibition purposes and a new front reception building. Located far from the center of Budapest, the complex is adjacent to the great slabs of the tenements and block apartments. MEO was created as the initiative of Hungarian businessman and art collector Lajos Kováts and Márton Winkler, a leather trader and art collector who donated two buildings belonging to the nineteenth-century tannery in order to transform them into a place where works from their collections could be presented permanently. The MEO model of operation was to be a Western one (Kováts pointed primarily to the inspiration of London's Saatchi Gallery). It is often described as a museum (as it presented a collection), but the nature of the operation was more like an art center or gallery. The factory buildings were adapted in a simple manner; most of the interior walls have been plastered and painted white, and modern communication arteries have been introduced in the form of platforms, stairs, and footbridges. The front building is an example of contemporary architecture – the milky color of the façade did not stand out during the day, while at night it glowed with colored lights hidden under the outer panels.

The 320fok Centre for Contemporary Art began its activity in a building of former bakery at the holiday resort of Siófok, in 2007. It was located within a district of single-family houses. In 2010, the results of the architectural competition for the reconstruction and modernization of the brick building were announced. The result was to be a "world-class contemporary center of culture, education and technology with remarkable architectural expression" (Winner Announced for 320fok Cultural Center 2010). Tamás Attila Tarnóczky's project won, but it will not be implemented due to the lack of funding.

In Prague in 2002, the Italian architect Alberto Di Stefano and a group of immigrant friends began searching for a place suitable for a contemporary art gallery. The choice fell on a small factory in Smíchov, until recently a working-class district of the city that since the 1990s has seen a steady stream of new, mainly residential and commercial investments. The FUTURA Center of Contemporary Art (see Atlas 1.7) they established found itself on a less-frequented street built up with tenement houses and low-rise apartment buildings from the beginning of the twenty-first century. The gallery's headquarters is hidden from view; only the sign on the tenement house façade announces its existence. To get to it, one passes through a gate and takes a staircase leading to the yard fronted by the factory façade. Due to limited finances, the adaptations were restricted to those necessary only for the building's exhibition function. This minimal interference meant that the original character of the interior has been preserved. As for the character of the investment, FUTURA is reminiscent of MASS MoCA, where the austere industrial walls are combined with the white cube. However, the scale of these investments is incomparable as are the financial outlays allocated to each. Of course, both this investment and many others described here echo the transformed power plant at the Tate Modern with its raw, brick walls and white exhibition halls. The London museum, despite having cost a fortune, has a minimalist character. In the Czech example, the economic calculations forced this character on the institution.

Another reminiscent of the American institution in terms of the type of the building is 8smička (see Atlas 1.3) located in the Czech town of Humpolec. The building was a former textile factory owned by Karel Trnka that specialized in production of broadcloth. It was built in the end of the nineteenth century. In 1948, the factory was nationalized and became part of the enterprise *Sukno*. Branches that formed *Sukno* were given numbers from 0–18. The Humpolec branch was named No. 8, hence the present name of the center of contemporary art. The factory operated there until 1989. The building went through a three-stage revitalization in 1995, 2010, and 2016, leading to the opening of the art center in 2018.

The mine

The cultural institutions in the revitalized Ruhr area, specifically the mid-nineteenth-century Zollverein in Essen (the largest coal mine in Europe) are the point of reference for museums located in mining buildings. In 1997, Norman Foster created the Design Zentrum Nordrhein Westfalen in the boiler room and in 2007 Rem Koolhaas's OMA (Office for Metropolitan Architecture) adapted the coal cleaning building for the Ruhr Museum. Also, in the Province of Hainaut, Belgium, a coal mine was transformed for artistic purposes; in 2002, MAC's (Museum of Contemporary Arts) opened in the nineteenth-century Grand-Hornu complex.

In 2014, the Muzeum Śląskie in Katowice (see Atlas 3.6) began its activity in new headquarters. The original concept for an underground museum located on the site of a former coal mine – the only investment of this kind in Central Europe – refers to the best models that combine new architecture with the history and identity of the place. Here it enters into a dialogue with the *genius loci*, creating clear symbolism by changing the site function from industrial to cultural production, transcribed onto the existing historic fabric. The museum has been waiting for a proper building since its inception in 1929. In that same year, the first architectural competition for its design was announced, but none of the projects submitted were selected for implementation. Then in 1936, the Silesian Voivode commissioned Karol Schayer to design the museum. Construction ended in 1939, but due to the outbreak of war, the museum did not move into the new headquarters. The Nazis ordered the demolition of the building, and the museum itself was liquidated. The revival of the institution took place in the 1980s. In 1984, the city of Katowice transferred a hotel building in the city center to temporary headquarters, and in 1986, the results of the second architectural competition for the new building were announced. Jan Fischer produced the winning design. Although design work was underway until 1990, construction was not begun, as the funds reserved for the museum were redirected to the construction of the Silesian Library. In 2003, the idea to adapt the centrally located buildings of the coal mine "Katowice" (closed four years earlier) for museum purposes arose. In 2007, the team Riegler Riewe Architekten from Graz won the architectural competition (no second prize was awarded). The area for the museum encompassed one-third the size of the complex, in which a number of historic mine buildings and structures there were also included in the museum (the mine shaft hoisting tower "Warszawa II", a symbol of the new museum, has served as a viewing platform since the museum's inception; in 2017, the carpentry and bathhouse buildings were adapted. The remaining nine buildings are still in the process of revitalization). The new museum building is hidden underground, its presence on the surface signaled by light towers (also called glass boxes) reaching several meters in height that illuminate the exhibition halls.

The revitalization of the mine site included recreational areas for residents (including the possibility of going up the observation tower) in a manner reminiscent of activities and investments in the Ruhr. The revitalization of degraded areas was comprehensive, and the scale of the project was incomparably greater; the existing infrastructure was repurposed for new functions, including cultural ones. The very idea of introducing underground exhibition halls naturally brings to mind Tadao Andō and his Chichu Art Museum on the Japanese island of Naoshima (opened in 2004). That underground museum is based on the relationship between art, architecture, landscape, and local history, and its construction is reminiscent of land art. Hiroyuki Suzuki (2005: 111) writes in the monograph on the museum that "the gesture of burying buildings underground represents not only the process of architecture's disappearance, but also the process of its purification". The design of the Muzeum Śląskie is similar to the Ando museum, not only in the exhibition halls' descent underground, but also in the deep connection to place. An even more direct inspiration for the Katowice Museum project is the new wing of The Nelson-Atkins Museum of Art, the so-called Bloch Building (Steven Holl, 1999, completed in 2007) in Kansas City. It is a 256-meter-long, terraced-shaped building, whose foundation has been embedded in the landscape, and whose plan articulates five irregular wings of various sizes. Their character changes depending on the intensity of exterior light: during the day, the coating on the translucent glass absorbs light, while at night, the pavilions' forms glow against the landscape (Sachs 2008: 201). The similarity of the museum in

Katowice consists on the one hand in the integration of the new mass with the existing historical buildings, and on the other, in the use of an element that plays the role of a trademark: the light tower in Katowice, and the so-called lantern in Kansas City. Despite the similarities, these structures serve different functions: in Katowice, they illuminate the exhibition space which is entirely hidden underground, while in Kansas City, they fulfill the function of exhibition and entry spaces.

The context for the Muzeum Śląskie is the private Szyb Wilson Gallery (see Atlas 3.5), located in the "Wieczorek" coal mine. Focused on promoting young artists, it was created in 1998 by entrepreneur Johann Bros and consists of three rooms with a total area of 2,500 square meters. It occupies the buildings of the guildhall and mine baths whose origins date back to the 1930s. Bros, who left Poland for Germany in the 1970s, recalls: "I saw that many old factories or halls create offices, galleries and even luxury apartments. When I returned to Silesia in 1989, I decided to buy a disused factory and do something similar" (Malkowski 2006: 10). While the Muzeum Śląskie occupies a strictly central position in the city, the Szyb Wilson Gallery is located off the beaten track.

Buildings related to transportation

Two large railway stations transformed into museums serve as the inspiration for the type: Gare d'Orsay in Paris, adapted to the Musée d'Orsay, and the Hamburger Bahnhof in Berlin adapted to the Museum of Contemporary Art. The first museum was opened in 1986, and the second exactly ten years later. The Paris adaptation especially has stimulated the imagination of museum creators around the world. The station designed by Victor Laloux was built for the Exposition Universelle in 1900. After its inauguration, the French painter Édouard Detaille said: "The station is magnificent and has the atmosphere of a palace of art" (House 1987: 67). Until 1939, it functioned as one of the main stations in Paris; once it was taken out of service, it performed a number of temporary functions. Various possibilities for the building's intended use were considered: the creation of an air terminal, Air France offices, ministry headquarters, a school of architecture, and even its demolition to build a hotel in its place. However, in 1973, the building was designated an historic monument, and four years later the decision was made to create a museum within it. According to Andrea Kupfer Schneider (1998: 12–13), the plans to create a hotel or a school of architecture were not monumental enough to meet Parisians' expectations for the city center. The creation of a transport museum here would be logical, but not sufficiently elegant. They therefore embarked on the creation of an art museum that would combine nineteenth-century collections overflowing from other museums.

In Central Europe, smaller stations were used for art, though they were not always dedicated to this singular function. Such was the case in the towns of Tarnów, Žilina, Banská Štiavnica, and Częstochowa. In Krakow and Katowice, plans to adapt railway stations to this end have not been implemented. In Prague, one of the railway buildings (although not a station) served as an art space.

At the end of 2010 and for almost the next three years, the BWA Tarnów (see Atlas 3.15) was moved to the railway station in Tarnów. In anticipation of the adaptation of the Marksmen's Brotherhood building for exhibition purposes, the gallery took advantage of the waiting room throughout the whole functioning railway station to display art. In 2013, the gallery moved to its intended headquarters, yet the exhibitions from the collections of the Małopolska Foundation of the Museum of Contemporary Art continue to be presented here. The success of the gallery in the station space has in turn sparked plans to use its empty, western pavilion as an exhibition hall, library, workshop space and residency rooms (Cymer 2015: 24).

Both Polish Tarnów and Slovak Žilina railway stations are still in use. Zilina railway station scale, however, is much smaller. In this building, Stanica operates as a multidisciplinary cultural center. In 2003, its activity was inaugurated by the non-governmental organization Truc Sphérique. This 1945 building is located in the middle of a large roundabout operating on two levels. It was leased for a period of thirty years for cultural purposes. The partially renovated building contains a gallery, ateliers, and workshops, an internet cafe, a waiting room, and a multi-purpose room used designated for theater, dance, concerts, discussions and screenings, and a bar. Trains traveling in the direction of Rajec also continue from here, enabling travelers to interact with the cultural offerings in the building. As the co-founder of Stanica, Marek Adamov, has stated:

> The claim that all travellers will automatically become participants in culture, let alone lovers of contemporary art, is extremely naïve, although one cannot disagree that their daily presence creates an atmosphere that an ordinary cultural institution cannot boast of so easily. In other words: a community is created in which everyone (artist, viewer, volunteer, traveller or passers-by) has a specific role.
>
> (Adamov 2012: 187)

Another Slovak space, Banská St á nica (see Atlas 4.1), also started operating in a functioning station in Banská Štiavnica in 2001. The building houses artists' studios, and in the waiting room projects are being implemented. Artists create a monumental work there once a year.

The station in Częstochowa was adapted for a modern art context by the Regional Society for the Encouragement of the Fine Arts, which acquired in 2007 a remnant of the station serving the Vienna-Warsaw line. The building was renovated and adapted for exhibition purposes, as well as for concert activities organized by the society. As the space for artistic activity occupied a mere 200 square meters, a project for the extension of the building followed to add a cinema, a concert and theater hall, and a hotel. The new functions were intended to provide the institution with self-financing, but the growing conflict between the management of the Society and the city meant that the project was not implemented.

The Czech MeetFactory (see Atlas 1.8) center, founded in 2003 in the Holešovice district's former slaughterhouse in Prague, since 2007 has operated in the railway building leased from the city. It stands on a plot between a multi-track railway, a busy town beltway, and a viaduct, next to undeveloped post-industrial buildings and the scrapyard in the Smíchov district. The building, as well as the organization located in it, is of an alternative character. Just like FUTURA, it is raw, adapted to its artistic functions in the most cost-effective manner possible. The hallmark of the elongated façade, visible from the roadway and tram line running alongside the road, are two red, life-size cars suspended vertically on huge hooks sticking out of the façade (created by the founder of the center, David Černy). The center is focused on a wide spectrum of visual arts – fine arts, theater, music, film. A gallery of contemporary art, a theater stage and a multi-functional stage occupy the ground floor; on the first floor, there are artists' residential studios, and on the second floor, studios and offices. The MeetFactory's genealogy reaches back to Andy Warhol's famous Factory in New York from the 1960s, as well as residency and exhibition programs that preceded the project in Prague: Künstlerhaus Bethanien and DAAD in Berlin, IASPIS in Stockholm, PS1 in New York, and Rote Fabrik in Zurich. The MeetFactory's activity should also be included in the category of factories of art and culture; they all duplicate a similar model that emphasizes inter-disciplinarity, the avant-garde, and independence. Embracing a post-industrial guise, they each emphasize their alternative character.

The Musée d'Orsay has already been mentioned in reference to the idea of locating MOCAK in Krakow in the main building of the train station. Lobbying for this location, the Marshal of Małopolska counted on a Polish d'Orsay. Collector and owner of a gallery Andrzej Starmach, however, drew attention to the inappropriateness of such a comparison:

> It must be remembered that the train station d'Orsay had been adapted to a ready, finite collection. It was already known which, how many, and where the works would be found: where the paintings would hang, and where works on paper would go. The present museum as it had been created requires quite different spaces than those at the Krakow railway station.
>
> (Starmach 2005: 10)

In addition to the issues of location and disposition, he also noted the high cost of purchasing a railway property, which proved to be key. Likewise, the implementation of the center of contemporary art under the program "Znaki Czasu" in Katowice's historic train station did not come to fruition.

The mill

The mill as a building type is adapted for the purposes of art only relatively rarely. The most extensive example is BALTIC, which, on account of scale, is difficult to compare with any other institution. In 1999 in Duisburg, the Herzog & de Meuron studio transformed an unused mill and warehouse from the grain port into a multi-functional complex housing the MKM Museum Küppersmühle für Moderne Kunst. In Prague, a mill was used for the creation of the Kampa Museum, and in Bydgoszcz, it was adapted to the contemporary art branch of the local Leon Wyczółkowski District Museum.

In 1998, preparatory work began in Prague to create a museum of modern art (see Atlas 1.9) within the historic buildings of a mill located on the island of Vltava, in the city center district of Kampa. The creator of the project was Meda Mládek, who emigrated from Czechoslovakia during the communist takeover. The collection she and her husband assembled represents a cross-section of works created by artists in Central Europe during the communist period. After the Velvet Revolution, she decided to give part of the collection to in the city of Prague. It then became necessary to find a place for a permanent installation. The choice settled on the run-down buildings of the mill. The Sova's mill complex is located in the prominent part of the city in Malá Strana, and is perfectly visible from the frequently traversed Charles Bridge. Of medieval provenance, it was rebuilt from stone during the Renaissance; in the nineteenth century, it underwent a thorough reconstruction. In the 1990s, it was in a deplorable state as a result of numerous natural disasters endured over the centuries. In 1998, the architectural competition for the building's adaptation took place; Helena Bukovanska's project was selected for implementation. Václav Cigler, Marian Karel, and Dana Zámečníkova designed a glass footbridge forming an observation deck and a glass and steel tower whose shape became the subject of a dispute with the monuments protection authorities. This took place in the context of the discussions on the role and scope of the protection of historical monuments in the center of Prague triggered by the construction work in the Czech Republic (Fialová and Tichá 2008: 53; Pučerová 2008: 50). The museum was opened in 2001.

Typologically, the Kampa building should be related to that of the Centre for Contemporary Art BALTIC. Both mills obviously operated on completely different principles and their scale and style are also incomparable (the mill in Gateshead, operating in 1950–1981, had a grain elevator with a silo with a capacity of 22,000 tons and a total of 148 concrete silos). Nevertheless, they are joined by the introduction of glass into the construction (in BALTIC with the glazing of side elevations, and in Kampa, the glazing of the tower housing the staircase and terrace). In addition, the Kampa terrace should be related to that of the Castello di Rivoli Museo d'Arte Contemporanea near Turin. Opened in 1984, the museum operates in the fortified fourteenth-century castle of the Savoy family (expanded in the seventeenth century and rebuilt in the eighteenth century). Part of the adaptation project entailed the creation of a steel and glass belvedere on the top floor protruding beyond the roof structure, overlooking the Alps (Cantacuzino 1989: 60–62).

In Bydgoszcz, four historic buildings on the so-called Mill Island have been transformed for the needs of the branches of the Leon Wyczółkowski District Museum. The island is an isolated whole located in the immediate vicinity of the old town and the symbol of the new city: the opera. In 2007–2009, a major renovation was carried out in the 1851 Camphaus Mill, or Red Granary building (so-called for its red brick façades), for the needs of the permanent and temporary exhibitions of the Gallery of Modern Art. In 1945, the building was taken over by the state treasury and leased by state-owned grain factories until 1974. Five years later, the District Museum began to operate there, taking over the building in 1997. Its poor technical condition meant that only seasonal exhibitions of contemporary art were held; the permanent presentation of the collection would be possible only after the renovation. A staircase and a panoramic elevator located in a glazed structure were added to the brick block.

The shipyard

In Western countries, a number of port buildings can be cited – in particular, warehouses that have been adapted to the needs of art such as Magasin 3 Stockholm Konsthall (opened in 1987) and Tate Liverpool (1988). Harbor buildings have not been a popular place for the presentation of art in Poland, where only one institution, the Wyspa Institute of Art (see Atlas 3.3), has taken advantage of the type (2004–2016). In this case, it adapted the former Naval Shipbuilding School dating from 1940 on the site of the former Gdańsk Shipyard. At the beginning of the twenty-first century, the process of revitalization of the shipyard's area began and included the construction of residential buildings, the adaptation of selected historical buildings for service and cultural purposes, the placement of an avenue of communication, and the setting of a seaside promenade. Although some parallels may be drawn to the Tate Modern opened four years earlier, in terms of the role that the museum played to raise the status of the district, in Gdańsk, the process appears to be different. There, the project was not about the architecture and volume of the building, or well-known architects as in London, but rather the program of civic engagement. The creators stated that its character and program concept:

> grows directly from the specificity of the place where it is located, its history and tradition on the one hand and the future that is planned on the other. Keeping in mind many failed revitalization projects in Europe,

the Institute's creators are applying critical theoretical tools to assess the phenomena around them.

(Wyspa n.d.)

Like FUTURA and MeetFactory in Prague, the Wyspa's building was subjected only to a basic adaptation restricted to the requirements for the presentation of art and the implementation of the artistic and social program. A visualization of an extension comprised of two massive cuboids, one horizontal and one vertical, was also prepared, but Grzegorz Klaman said that it was not meant to be implemented:

> This is a hypothesis. We needed a clear vision to start talking with the developer. However, in practice we gradually saw that there was no need to expand this facility, that it is enough to secure it in its block and make necessary repairs in order to meet heating or safety standards. This is not Paris or New York, we do not need 15,000 square meters here. Rather, one must focus more on the quality of these activities than on scaling up.
>
> (Interview with Grzegorz Klaman 2011)

In 2016, Wyspa was closed at this location, and the building was intended for the temporary headquarters of the NOMUS New Museum of Art in Gdańsk, the new branch of the National Museum (scheduled to move in in 2018; see Atlas 3.4).

The brewery

The earliest European examples of adaptive post-industrial museum projects include the Museum of Modern Art, Oxford (from 2002, the Modern Art Oxford), opened in 1966 in the old brewery. The brewery is a building type modernized in the Czech Republic with particular frequency. Many are adapted to new functions; however, these have not been popular places for art. The exception is the brewery in Český Krumlov, adapted as the Egon Schiele Art Center (see Atlas 1.2) and opened in 1993 through a private initiative. It was to present the figure of Egon Schiele, the art associated with the city, and show a context for the work of an Austrian expressionist in the form of temporary exhibitions of modern and contemporary art (especially Czech). Located in the old town in the Vltava bend, the history of the brewery dates back to 1503, when it opened on the site of four municipal tenement houses. Expanded many times, it operated there until 1949. After its closure, the complex of buildings was transformed into craft workshops, municipal offices, a locksmith's workshop, a laundry, a canteen, and the administration office of the municipal baths and archives. The renovation of the building, consisting of a modern, white painted space with exposed wooden ceilings and floors hidden behind the Renaissance façade, was carried out in less than a year.

The exhibition pavilion

Exhibition pavilions are significantly different from post-industrial facilities in that they were designed expressly for receiving the public and for presenting objects. In character, they resemble museums. Trade Fair Palace in Prague and the Four Domes Pavilion in Wrocław are examples of two large buildings of this type that have been repurposed as museums. The shop pavilion also makes reference to this formula, serving as a temporary exhibition space for the Museum of Modern Art in Warsaw (MSN).

The Trade Fair Palace in Prague (see Atlas 1.10) was erected for the glory of industry, although it was not directly engaged in industrial production. It was established in 1925–1928 as the seat of international technical fairs. Designed by Czech architects Oldřich Tyl and Josef Fuchs in the Functionalist style, today it is one of the finest examples of its kind in the Czech Republic. The rectangular building is 140 meters long and 75 meters wide, and consists of nine floors. After the fair had been moved to Brno, it served as an office building, and in 1974 it was destroyed by a fire. A discussion about what to do with the vast, burnt-down construction took place over four years. One option was to demolish it; another, to subdivide it into smaller buildings. Surprisingly, it was not the most commercial solution that eventually triumphed, but a cultural one: in 1978, the building was donated to the National Gallery (see Atlas 1.10) as a location for a branch devoted to art from nineteenth century to the present day. Reconstruction plans were drawn up in 1984–1989, and in 1995 the museum opened its 20,000 square meters of exhibition space to the public. Victoria Newhouse compared it to the adapted Lingotto factory in Turin. In a building with an area of almost 1 million square meters transformed by Renzo Piano, there was a shopping center, conference rooms, offices, hotel, restaurants, polytechnic, university, cinema, auditorium, and exhibition spaces. Prague is for Newhouse a negative example which "fails without the enlivening factor of commercial activities. [. . .] [the] reservation of the large industrial structure for art alone leaves unoccupied areas that contribute to the museum's moribund atmosphere" (2006: 202). It is located outside the city center, which is not conducive to public access. However, the Veletržní palác problem was not its location, but the program activity that for many years was criticized by the art community (see Chapter 7). In 2015, the building began to transform: part of the ground floor, thus far used by other artistic organizations, became a spacious, glass café – a lively, fashionable meeting place, and buffer space between the street level and entrance hall. In 2018, an architectural competition was organized for the remodeling of the interior.

The Four Domes Pavilion in Wrocław (see Atlas 3.20) has a similar character. The Museum of Contemporary Art, a branch of the National Museum in Wrocław, was opened there in 2016. The pavilion, designed by Hans Poelzig, is part of the Exhibition Grounds for the purposes of the 1913 Centennial

Exhibition organized on the occasion of the one hundreth anniversary of the Prussian victory over Napoleon. Until the end of the Second World War, it housed art exhibitions; in 1948, it was one of the venues in the Regained Territories Exhibition. Later, the Documentary and Feature Film Studios was active there. The museum is outside historical city center, but is just next to the Centennial Hall. Along with the Pavilion and the Exhibition Grounds, the Hall was included on the UNESCO World Heritage List in 2004, providing the newly created museum with an additional context and an influx of visitors.

The exhibition building is also a shop pavilion. In 2012, MSN was set up in the furniture pavilion "Emilia" (see Atlas 3.17), in anticipation of its headquarters. The glass building, located opposite the Palace of Culture and Science, made it possible to establish a relationship with the place in which the future headquarters will be erected. The form of the building was most reminiscent of the New National Gallery in Berlin, where the exhibitions were visible both from within and without. The museum carried out activities here until 2016, after which the pavilion was demolished for the construction of an office building.

The palace, castle, and residence

Contemporary art naturally belongs to palaces and castles. Even when we are dealing with the adaptation of such a building to a museum of contemporary art, the change in function is of an evolutionary nature. The points of reference are the Louvre and the Luxembourg Palace in Paris, and a series of castles and palaces in various parts of Europe; for example, the aforementioned Castello di Rivoli; Palazzo Venier dei Leoni in Venice, which holds Peggy Guggenheim's collection (since the collector's death in 1979, it has functioned as a museum); and Palazzo Grassi, bought in 1983 by the Fiat group for exhibition purposes, and serving since 2006 as a museum of contemporary art belonging to the collector François Pinault. This kind of adaptation did not appear in Central Europe for the first time after the change of regime, but was undertaken much earlier. Today, however, together with museums created in other types of buildings, they are an important component of the museum boom. In Poland, earlier examples of such adaptations include the aforementioned Maurycy Poznański's palace at Więckowskiego Street in Łódź, in which the Muzeum Sztuki was opened in 1946. The palace was erected by one of Izrael Poznański's sons in 1900. The art of earlier periods was also presented alongside the collection of contemporary art (for which the museum earned its reputation) in the three-story, Neo-Renaissance edifice. The Ujazdowski Castle in Warsaw, which was granted to the Centre for Contemporary Art in 1985, belongs to this same type. This is a special case, however, because it is not the original baroque building one visits, but rather its 1970s-era reconstruction.

Palace interiors served as the context for the contemporary art museum in Budapest, as well. Since 1975, the Hungarian National Gallery (Magyar Nemzeti Galeria) has been operating in the former Royal Castle. A collection of modern art was also installed there in 1989, transferred to the Hungarian government by Irene and Peter Ludwig and forming the beginnings of the Museum of Contemporary Art. The edifice towering over the city on the Buda hill has a rich and dramatic history. Its origins date back to the medieval period (1247–1265), but over the centuries, it was repeatedly demolished, burned, and reconstructed. In the years 1875–1912, the castle was rebuilt according to the designs of Alajos Hauszmann with the objective that the result would equal the finest European residences. The castle suffered severely during the Second World War, and reconstruction continued for decades. At that time, it was also to be used for cultural purposes: the Budapest History Museum, the Hungarian Museum of the Working Class Movement, and the Hungarian National Gallery, as well as the Széchényi National Library, were located there.

Initially, the Ludwig collection was presented in the centrally located building "C", where it functioned alongside the art collection of the Hungarian National Gallery, after which it was moved to building "A" in the eastern wing in 1991. The context for the contemporary works was Neo-Baroque interior excess and the monumentalism of the entire building. The castle complex, which is also in the immediate vicinity of the cathedral, is one of Budapest's main tourist attractions. The location of the contemporary art collection in a building that served as a symbol for the city along the main tourist route both confirmed the high status of the new art and made it more accessible.

In Prague, the palace became a place for the presentation of contemporary art at the Artbanka Museum of Young Art (AMoYA; see Atlas 1.5). Its location was just as prestigious as the Ludwig Museum in Buda – in the old town, on the main tourist street leading to the Charles Bridge. In 2011, Petr Šec and Olga Dvořák, owners of the commercial gallery Dvorak Sec Contemporary, created the Artbanka organization that searches for promising artists and purchases their work for the collection. In the same year, they founded a museum that they opened in record time – preparations took only four weeks – in the baroque Colloredo-Mansfeld palace. The building (over 4,000 square meters) is managed by the Prague City Gallery, which had not used it due to its poor condition. Until the period of renovation, the building was lent to AMoYA and adapted on the most basic level to perform in this new capacity. A reception space and a museum store were created, while works in rooms, staircases, and halls were placed without any prior intervention into the existing space. Despite its success (it received eighty thousand visitors over a year and a half, not including the free open area), the museum was closed at the beginning of 2013.

In Veszprém, the Baroque Dubniczay Palace was adapted for the presentation of the twentieth-century art collection amassed by Károly László. In Pécs, the building used by the regional authorities was used as the site for the Modern Gallery of Hungary (Modern Magyar Képtár) where since 2001 a collection of art from the second half of the twentieth century has been displayed (see Chapter 5).

The tenement house and villa

An extension of aristocratic residential architecture – albeit on a smaller scale – is the tenement house and villa, where usually smaller private museums are created. The two Picasso museums provide context, one located in the Baroque Hôtel Salé in Paris (Roland Simounet, 1976–1984) and the other in a Renaissance building in Barcelona (Jordi Garcés and Enric Sòria, 1981–1986).

In Bratislava in 2001, the Milan Dobeš Museum (see Atlas 4.3) was opened in a tenement house in the old town on the initiative of the Slovak collector Peter Sokol. The passion for Dobeš's art, whose work aligns entirely with the constructivist trend, led to the creation of a museum devoted not only to one of the most important Slovak contemporary artists, but also to international constructivism in the historical center of Bratislava. A two-story tenement house was selected for the institution's headquarters; the permanent collection appeared on the first three levels, and temporary exhibitions occupied the attic level. The origins of this tenement house are medieval; however, in the eighteenth century, it was rebuilt in the Baroque style. As part of the renovations of the building for museum purposes, architects combined historical architecture with new glass and metal elements, making of the top floor a skylight that illuminates the other levels. The museum closed in 2016.

Another historical tenement dating from the first half of the fifteenth century in Bratislava became the headquarters of Nedbalka Gallery (see Atlas 4.4) in 2012. A new wing was built in 1995 according to the design of Viktória Cvengrošová and Virgil Droppa, when the building was the headquarters of the bank. Four floors, adapted for galleries, are lined with an oval well echoing the architecture of the New York Guggenheim Museum.

In Veszprém, this type of building served as the site of Gallery of Modern Art – Collection of László Vass. For the permanent presentation of the Hungarian collection and international constructivism, the city had allocated three uninhabited, dilapidated tenements on the main historical street. The restoration was completed in 2003. As a result of construction works, all tenement houses were connected together, resulting in the creation of nine exhibition rooms and a library of contemporary art.

The tenement houses located in the old town of Győr, known as the Esterhazy palace, in 1997 became part of the Municipal Museum of Art and at the same time the seat of the Hungarian art collection from the first half of the twentieth century, assembled by Béla Radnai.

The site for the then Central Bohemian Gallery in Prague was similar in nature. In 1973, three adapted medieval tenement houses were opened as the new seat (office spaces and exhibition venue) of the Central Bohemian Gallery, which in 1993 changed its name to the Czech Museum of Fine Arts. The location in the heart of historical Prague, in close proximity to the Old Town Square, made it impossible to display the collection permanently; it was also inadequate for the needs of larger temporary exhibitions. Following the return of Nelahozeves Castle to its pre-communist owners, the Lobkowicz family, in 1993, the solution to these problems was the transfer of these activities to Kutná Hora (see Atlas 1.4).

Defensive and military architecture

Museums created in anti-aircraft bunkers are among the most unexpected and therefore most visually attractive types of objects to undergo adaptation for artistic purposes. In 2011, a civil shelter from 1942 located at Strzegomski Square in Wrocław was used as the temporary seat of the Wrocław Contemporary Museum (see Atlas 3.19). The building was built on a circular plan, with six floors and walls over one meter thick. In 2010, it was occupied by the eighth edition of the Survival Art Review. Earlier, Stanisław Dróżdż created a mural on the façade and Andrzej Jarodzki's installation *Train to Heaven* was installed in front of the building. A locomotive 20 meters long, produced in 1942 at Linke-Hofmann-Werke in Wrocław, was set vertically. According to the original idea, after the opening of the museum building proper, the shelter was to remain in use as studio warehouses and a site for intimate exhibitions (Czernichowska 2009). The individual stories of the shelter serve as a display space; the roof holds a café with a terrace offering a panoramic view of the city. Typologically and formally, the Wrocław museum nods to the contemporary art department of the Vienna MAK (Museum of Applied Arts) located on the Second World War-era Flak anti-aircraft tower, as well as to the anti-aircraft shelter in Berlin of the same era, adapted for the private collections of Christian Boros and Karen Lohmann (Sammlung Boros), whose private flat is also in the building.

In Košice, barracks were used for art. In 2013, the city took advantage of its position as European Capital of Culture to create very necessary infrastructure for contemporary art there. One of the investments was the interdisciplinary center of culture and art Kasárne/Kulturpark, located in the nineteenth-century military barracks. Peter Radkoff, a project consultant for the ECoC initiative, said that winning the competition probably saved the building from developers' plans to transform it for other purposes (A Person Working in Independent Culture 2013: 20). In addition to the exhibition space, there is also a Centre for the Support of Culture and Creativity.

In turn, the eighteenth-century edifice of the arsenal in Białystok, which after the Second World War served as a high school dormitory, was adapted for the needs of the Bureau of Art Exhibitions. Activity of BWA Gallery in the renovated building began in 1975. After the political transition it has been known as the Arsenal Gallery (see Atlas 3.1).

Religious architecture

Former religious buildings are much less frequently used for exhibition purposes than residential buildings. One of the best-known examples is the Met Cloisters, a branch of the Metropolitan Museum of Art in New York, opened in 1938. The museum building was composed of elements assembled from several medieval French monasteries. In 2003–2007, Peter Zumthor designed the building for the Columbus Museum in Cologne, of which the ruins of a Gothic church and the chapel built on the site in 1950 are an integral part. The museum was established to accommodate a collection of sacred art from late antiquity to modern times. In both cases, the change in function was closely related to the original character of the adapted building. In Central Europe in particular, synagogues served as places for art, as was the case in Hungary in Győr, in Slovakia in Trnava and Žilina, and in Poland, where Jewish prayer houses in Krakow and Łódź were transformed into contemporary art galleries.

The synagogue in Győr, a branch of the Municipal Museum of Art, displays János Vasilescu's paintings collection. The synagogue was erected in the years 1868–1870 by the city's Jewish minority. The building suffered serious damage during the Second World War, and as the number of Jews in the city dropped drastically, an expensive reconstruction was not possible. It was the city council that took this up at the beginning of the new century. The building was put into use in 2006, no longer as a place of worship, but for a museum and the music department of the University of István Széchenyi, which uses it as a concert hall.

In Slovakia, Jan Koniarek Gallery in Trnava opened in 1994, presenting the collection of twentieth century Slovak art opened its branch, Centre for Contemporary Art, in the historic synagogue (erected in 1891–1897).

In 2011, the historic synagogue in Žilina (see Atlas 4.9), erected in 1928–1931 according to the design of Peter Behrens, was marked for cultural activities carried out by a group of enthusiasts working earlier on the Stanica project. Since after the war the edifice was no longer used according to its original function, its interior was adapted to accommodate a theater, concert hall, university auditorium, and cinema. When the Jewish kehilla allocated the building to the Kunsthalle, it turned out that comprehensive reconstruction efforts were necessary in order to remove the interventions dating from the second half of the twentieth century. The exhibition activity in the synagogue building under the name Nová synagóga/Kunsthalle Žilina began in 2013 before the restorations were completed. In 2017, most of the construction work was finished and Nová synagóga ("kunsthalle" in the name was dropped) was opened to the public.

In Krakow's Podgórze district, the Zucher Jewish House of Prayer, erected in 1879–1881, was adapted in 1997 to house the Starmach Gallery. Similarly in Łódź, the historic building of the market hall at Piotrkowska Street dating from the second half of the nineteenth century – used in the 1940s as a prayer house, and then a production and service facility as well as a publishing house – was repurposed for the private gallery of contemporary art, Atlas Sztuki [Atlas of Art] (2003–2017).

Another type of building, the historic Jesuit College in Kutná Hora, a town included in the UNESCO World Heritage List located about 70 kilometers from Prague, serves as the seat of the Gallery of the Central Bohemian Region which is the direct successor of the Czech Museum of Fine Arts. The Baroque complex from the seventeenth and eighteenth centuries was built on a hill just next to the Gothic St Barbara's Cathedral. From 1776, after the dissolution of the Jesuit order (1773) until 1997, it was used by the army. The vision of developing a large building was the subject of a dispute in 2008–2009 between the museum management and the regional authority. The original aim was to create the Kutná Hora Arts Center as a "branch" of the Prague museum and present its permanent collection. As a result of the change of director and related staff changes, the institution changed its name to GASK – Gallery of the Central Bohemian Region, and the headquarters were transferred to Kutná Hora. Architect Jiří Krejčík's plans for adaptation were carried out between 2004 and 2009 with attention to the historical form of the building. Its ground plan resembles the letter "F" and the elongated façade, flanked by two towers, is lined on the other side of a narrow road by a Baroque "gallery" of Jesuit saints. The Jesuit College, symbolically situated between St Barbara's Cathedral and the town, stands over a south-facing slope.

The bath

In Gdańsk, the LAZNIA Centre for Contemporary Art (see Atlas 3.2) was founded in 1998 in the historic building of the municipal bathhouse. The building has been used by artists since 1992. There were then three art groups: Galeria C14, Galeria Wyspa, and Formacja Totart, which established the Atelier Open Foundation, whose aim was to create art studios and exhibition spaces. After misunderstandings among the artists, a new foundation by the name of Wyspa Progress by Grzegorz Klaman was established in LAZNIA from 1995, which then led to the creation of the Center for Contemporary Art. Architecturally, the bathhouse is Neo-Romanesque in style. It contains three staircases, thanks to which it was possible to separate the movement of women, men, and children. The building was renovated by the artists themselves until 1997, when a general renovation was carried out before the exhibition organized for the celebration of the millennium of Gdańsk (it paved the way for the creation of a public institution). Previously, the artists considered other options for locating their headquarters – they considered the barracks and the so-called Small Armory – located in the immediate vicinity, in the notorious Lower Town district, characterized by high unemployment and high crime rates. The causes of these problems in this part of Gdańsk were the development of the city in contrary directions, the separation of the city center by a transit road, and a shifting of industrial production to the suburbs. Due to the difficulty of the neighbor hood, the center's goal was simply to undertake purely artistic activity, but also to be a driving force of social and cultural development in the district. In 2008, LAZNIA acquired a second building, located in the New Port district, another city bath also in the Neo-Romanesque style, built from 1907–1909. The new headquarters was opened at the end of 2012 under the name LAZNIA 2 Art Education Center. The project featured an exhibition hall, a cinema studio, workshops for the organization of activities serving children and youth, an urban public library with a reading room, and guest rooms.

The swimming pool

The most original site to be adapted, which has no counterpart, is the Kunsthalle Košice (see Atlas 4.6), opened in a historic building of an indoor swimming pool built in 1957–1962 by the local architect Ladislav Greč. The whole space is used for exhibition purposes, including the pool. The Kunsthalle was implemented on the back of the European Capital of Culture program in 2013. The umbrella institution k13, the Košice Cultural Centers, which also manages Kasárne / Kulturpark, Výmenníky / SPOTs and Amfiteátr.

Summary

In reaching toward the museum solutions worked out in the West, Central Europe has become a virtual basin for institutions located in post-industrial buildings. It is not only the fascination with simple, often rapid, and relatively inexpensive options, but also a fashion that becomes the determining factor for thinking about a city's culture. In Poland particularly, every major city has implemented or at least planned a museum or center of contemporary art in a building originally used in heavy or light industry, but Prague is the leader in this area. In many cases, there is a misconception that the recipe for success, be it on the cultural, tourist, or image fronts, is to transform an existing building into a museum. The question of what will be shown in it is relegated to the background. However, there is a small chance that the building itself will become an audience magnet, if not on the scale of a Guggenheim Museum in Bilbao, then a Kunsthaus Graz. The Tate Modern, which served as a model for so many sites, has after all a world-class collection in addition to its architecture. Of course, there are buildings that succeed more on account of their architecture than on what they present inside; for example, the BALTIC Center for Contemporary Art in Gateshead, or Le Magasin in Grenoble. Nevertheless, a venue's success depends on many factors. Certainly, the Muzeum Śląskie stands an excellent chance of becoming a symbol of Silesia for the way it combines new and old architecture. By exploiting a disused mine and locating the exhibition rooms underground, revitalizing this post-industrial area in the heart of the city, it consistently is overcoming the industrial image of the region through a focus on culture, knowledge, and technology. Also in Krakow, two museums open at the Schindler's Factory for modern and historical art will certainly play an important role in the cultural "exit" of the city from the very center to the opposite bank of the river. The magnetism of this place is connected not necessarily with the uniqueness of the building's architecture, but with its historical symbolism.

Residential edifices have always accompanied art that was often contemporary for a given era. The position, nature of development, and financial considerations are among the local factors taken into account for adaptation of an existing building. The cost of adaptation when the building is subjected only to minimally invasive changes, such as heating installation, toilet construction, or the assembly of lifts, will be significantly lower than the cost of erecting something completely new. In cases of more complex transformations, the economic calculation does not necessarily have to tilt the scales in favor of historic buildings. Implicit in an existing building is the possibility of engaging the symbolism of the place, as in the case of the Ludwig Museum's first location in Budapest or MOCAK in Krakow. Irrespective of the architect's efficiency, however, it is never possible to create the same exhibition conditions as in new structures, given the limitations (story height, warehouse space, communication between levels, the location of the entrance, the size of the exhibition halls and their articulation). On the other hand, this does not always mean that a new building presents a solution to all problems, and the deficiencies will emerge sooner rather than later. Adapted buildings may also limit the possibilities for architectural iconicity It is not impossible, as the Tate Modern in London with its glass "aquarium" superimposed on the brick body of the former power plant demonstrates, but it is not always possible to interfere to such an extent in the fabric of historic buildings. Despite these obvious limitations, the advantage of the historical edifice as a place for contemporary art is to a large extent in keeping the gigantomania of the genre in check, which sometimes simply is not compatible with the museum's interiors or – especially in the context of residential facilities – the relationship between art and everyday life.

A historical building also often provides a location that would not be possible for a new building. Repurposing a building for exhibition use may be the only opportunity for an institution to procure real estate in the city center, and even then, it is not always possible to build in the very center, as was the case with the Museum of Modern Art in Warsaw. Having a building with convenient access to and from the city center usually translates into better attendance numbers. Almost all the adapted residential structures described here are located in city centers, with religious buildings in close proximity. The situation is different with museums built in industrial buildings; many of them are located in city centers, but usually a distance must be traversed in order to reach them. Two kilometers is a conventional distance, often the maximum distance that is traveled on foot to each a museum; greater distances often assume the use of transport, which can sometimes result in the creation of barriers between places.

Table 4.1 presents the institutions ranked in order of their distance from central points within a given city. This division is not strict, because a greater

Museums and art centers in adapted buildings used in the past in industry, transport, defense, and recreation	Distance from the market / central square / main street (on foot) in km
Białystok: Arsenal Gallery Bratysława: Milan Dobeš Museum Bratysława: Nedbalka Gallery Bydgoszcz: Gallery of Modern Art (branch of the Leon Wyczółkowski District Museum of Art) Český Krumlov: Egon Schiele Art Centrum Győr: Synagogue (branch of the Municipal Museum of Art) Košice: Kunsthalle Kutná Hora: GASK – Gallery of the Central Bohemian Region Łódź: Atlas Sztuki Poprad: Tatra Gallery Prague: Artbanka Museum of Young Art (AMoYA) Prague: Czech Museum of Fine Arts Szczecin: TRAFO Trafostacja Sztuki Veszprém: Gallery of Modern Art – Collection of László Vass Warsaw: Emilia pavilion (Museum of Modern Art) Žilina: Nová synagóga	"< 1 km
Brno: Wannieck Gallery/Fait Gallery Czeladź: Elektrownia Contemporary Art Gallery Gdańsk: LAZNIA Centre for Contemporary Art Gdańsk: Wyspa Institute of Art Katowice: Muzeum Śląskie Košice: Kasárne/Kulturpark Paks: Paksi Képtár Prague: Kampa Museum Radom: Elektrownia Mazovian Center for Contemporary Art Siófok: 320fok Centre for Contemporary Art Tarnów: BWA Tarnów in the railway station Žilina: Stanica	1 km – ≥ 2 km
Budapest: KOGART Budapest: Trafó House of Contemporary Arts Krakow: MOCAK Museum of Contemporary Art in Krakow Krakow: Cricoteka Center for the Documentation of the Art of Tadeusz Kantor Łódź: Muzeum Sztuki ms^2 Prague: FUTURA Contemporary Art Center Prague: Trade Fair Palace (Galeria Narodowa) Wrocław: Wrocław Contemporary Museum in civil shelter	2 km – ≥ 3 km

(*Continued*)

(Continued)

Museums and art centers in adapted buildings used in the past in industry, transport, defense, and recreation	*Distance from the market / central square / main street (on foot) in km*
Prague: DOX Centre for Contemporary Art Wrocław: Four Domes Pavilion, Museum of Contemporary Art (branch of the National Museum in Wrocław)	3 km – ≥ 4 km
Katowice: Szyb Wilson Gallery Prague: MeetFactory	5 km – ≥ 7 km
Budapest: MEO Contemporary Art Collection Gdańsk: LAZNIA 2 Art Education Center	"> 7 km

distance from the city center may mean closer proximity to points of interest, but it sheds light on information about their location in urban space. Most institutions are located within 2 kilometers of the city center. The Four Domes Pavilion in Wrocław, however, is located more than 3 kilometers from the city center, but is close to other places of interest (Centennial Hall and the zoo); similarly, DOX in Prague is conveniently connected with the center by tram. The MeetFactory in Prague is more than 5 kilometers from the city center. The proximity of railway tracks, multi-lane roads, and unattractive neighborhoods give an impression of inconvenience. The Szyb Wilson Gallery is located at a similar distance; it is far away from the center of Katowice, but is located near the Nikiszowiec district close to a historic workers' settlement, one of the city's major tourist attractions. The now-closed MEO was the most distant from the center at over seven kilometers, but it should be noted that the metro line provided convenient access from the center of Budapest.

Only a few of these institutions operate in post-industrial districts or are a part of larger post-industrial complexes (Wannieck Gallery/Fait Gallery, Wyspa Institute of Art, ms², MOCAK, DOX, Szyb Wilson Gallery), while others are located in individual buildings associated in the past with industry or production. Similarly, only a few buildings are a combination of old and new architecture, announced by their elevations (Elektrownia Mazovian Center of Contemporary Art, Muzeum Śląskie, Museum Kampa, Cricoteka, MOCAK, Gallery of Paks, Gallery of Modern Art in Bydgoszcz); still others hide behind the existing walls, regardless of the extent to which they have been renovated (TRAFO Trafostacja Sztuki, Egon Schiele Art Center, Tatra Gallery, Wannieck Gallery/Fait Gallery, ms², Trade Fair Palace, Four Domes Pavilion, MEO, Nedbalka Gallery, GASK, Milan Dobeš Museum, Nová synagóga Žilina) or whether they are very basic (AMoYA, FUTURA).

It is also necessary to pay attention to the geography of adaptation projects; they are not tied exclusively to large cities or cities that are centers of culture. Most of these are in the capitals and major regional cities, but some also appear in smaller centers.

In many cases, the change in function provided a lifeline for existing buildings that were either threatened with demolition or were falling into ever-greater states of ruin. Even if the interference with the existing architectural fabric is moderately large and alters the interior layout while leaving the façade unchanged, the transformation for these buildings is fundamental, for most of them have not been publicly available or easily accessible.

Note

1 In 2006, Rooseum was closed; at the end of 2010, a branch of the Moderna Museet with its headquarters in Stockholm was opened there.

5   Museums in cultural context

A museum's context strongly influences institutional identity, programming, and visitor relationship building. Whether a museum is built within the city center surrounded by monuments, residential buildings and shops, or is isolated among the greenery on the outskirts, influences perception; still other museums exist in the immediate vicinity of other museums, cultural institutions, and spaces for entertainment and recreation.

The cultural districts and complexes in which museums operate are not modern inventions; they existed in ancient Greece, Rome, and Alexandria, and the idea of multi-functionality succeeded in the Renaissance. Specialized museum districts began to appear in cities in the nineteenth century, but the popularity of placing museums and other cultural institutions in close proximity to one another or even under a shared roof increased in the second half of the twentieth century. From an urbanistic point of view, cultural districts are prestigious and constitute a ready-made tourist product; they also may make it easier for museums to reach an audience.

In the current chapter, I discuss Hungarian and Polish cultural districts and complexes (in the Czech Republic and Slovakia, no such complexes containing institutions dedicated to contemporary art exist). My goal is primarily to show the diverse nature of these undertakings and to draw attention to the importance of context for a museum's identity.

The tradition of museum complexes

The tradition of joining a museum, library, and academy under one roof dates back to antiquity. Undoubtedly, it was the first public museums – the Louvre, the British Museum – which served as the model for a number of subsequent complexes in Europe and beyond. Over time, the number and variety of such institutions began to increase. More and more frequently, museum districts began to evolve over the years. The Kunstareal in Munich, Museumsinsel and Kulturforum in Berlin, Museumsufer in Frankfurt am Main, Museum Mile in New York, National Mall in Washington, and MuseumsQuartier in Vienna are selected examples of this phenomenon, each well-promoted under a common brand.

With museums in mind, Josep M. Montaner (1990: 7–11) created a typology of great cultural complexes. He distinguished four types, depending on their degree of functional integration and spatial disposition. In the first type, the interiors have the most homogeneous character. The Centre Pompidou and the Carré d'art modeled on it, the Museum of Contemporary Art in Nîmes (Norman Foster 1993) are examples. The second type is based on a clearer distinction between components within the whole complex, e.g. the complex created in 1975–1986 in Cologne that includes the Wallraf-Richartz-Museum, the Ludwig Museum and Philharmonic (functioning together until 2001). In the third type, historical buildings within the old city are repurposed as a system of museums, libraries, galleries, and other cultural institutions. An example is the Center de Cultura Contemporània de Barcelona (1994), opened in the eighteenth-century Casa de la Caritat in Barcelona, next to which the Museu d'Art Contemporani de Barcelona (MACBA, Richard Meier) opened a year later. This last type includes historic buildings situated in the natural landscape that are adapted for new functions. Montaner offers Saline Royale in Art-et-Senans as an example. Because Montaner's typology refers to museums created in the 1980s, it does not include a series of later examples (e.g. the Lowry in Salford, by Michael Wilford, opened in 2000) and it omits cases in which the cultural complex consists only of newly erected buildings, as exemplified by Cidade da Cultura de Galicia in Santiago de Compostela (Peter Eisenman; its first section opened in 2011).

In Central Europe, there are several complexes and cultural districts that contain a museum or exhibition space for contemporary art. Two substantial examples emerged in Hungary in the 1970s: the cultural institutions located in the Royal Palace in Budapest, and the museum street in Pécs, while the rest arose in the new century. These may be ranked using Montaner's categories. It is difficult to find an example of the first type in Central Europe, while the district type in which new buildings accommodate various institutions is relevant. Complexes and districts in which space for art complements the main functions of trade and entertainment are also popular. I have placed Hungarian and Polish cultural districts and complexes within three groups: 1) those operating under one roof, 2) museum districts, and 3) art/trade/entertainment complexes.

Complexes combined under a shared roof

The Buda Castle in Budapest, located above the city, was designated for culture after the 1956 revolution. There were three museums in its individual wings, a library, and in the years 1989–2004, the Ludwig collection as well, which gave rise to the Museum of Contemporary Art. These cultural institutions are not connected in any way; only one tour operator created a brand of Buda Castle Budapest for its tourist services.

A new investment in the new Millennium City Centre – the Palace of Arts and the neighboring National Theatre building also located on the banks of the Danube – can compete with the Royal Castle in terms of scale, but it is outside the city center. The district was created in the area intended for the World Expo fair planned for 1995 on the Pest side of the river. As reported by *The New York Times*:

> Back in 1987, when East was East and West was West, the Austrians and the Hungarians decided to hold a joint world's fair in Budapest and Vienna in 1995 and offer the event as a symbol that would arch over the Iron Curtain and restore one of central Europe's most historic links.
>
> (Bohlen 1991)

First, in 1991, Budapest expressed doubts about the organization of the event; then Vienna withdrew. In 1996, Budapest declared its intention to carry out the Expo independently, but this never came to fruition. Traces of preparations left their mark on the cityscape – the area for the project was cleared of buildings and a bridge over the Danube was built. In the year 2000, new investments were started here, some of which became part of a prestigious cultural district.

The nascence of the cultural district on the Danube was the building of the National Theatre, which was originally intended for the city center on Erzsébet Square; construction began there (the so-called "national hole" became the target of jokes and ridicule). The then right-wing government decided, however, to transfer the theater to the Danube, while the left-wing government of the following term decided to supplement it with other cultural institutions. The TriGránit development company undertook the implementation of the Millennium City Centre. The first phase, in 2002–2004, assumed the construction of a cultural complex, a multi-purpose building, and a congress center, with which a theater building was combined; and the second phase consisted of the construction of two hotels and two office buildings. Two residential buildings completed the entire project on the north side; ultimately the investment covered a total of 10 hectares of land. The developer's descriptions highlight the location's advantages: the proximity of the historical center, easy access to transportation, and a magnificent view of the Danube and Buda hills. However, the project did not bear fruit: the multi-purpose building for exhibitions, other sports, music, congresses, fashion shows, and entertainment programs, as well as the congress center with a plenary room for over five thousand people, were not completed. Two hotels, a water park, and a casino likewise were not finished. A plaza was planned, but in place of this and the multi-functional exhibition center were a large parking lot and paths that lacked the logic of the original plan.

The monumental Palace of Arts (Művészetek Palotája, abbreviated as Müpa) opened in 2005, the result of a partnership between the Ministry of National Cultural Heritage and a private developer. Three institutions emerged within a building with an area of 70,000 square meters: in the center, the Béla Bartók National Concert Hall (which holds 1,700 and is the seat of the National Philharmonic), to its left, the Festival Theatre (which holds 452 people and is the seat of the National Dance Theatre),[1] and to the right, the Ludwig Museum – Museum of Contemporary Art (see Atlas 2.2). The Ministry's original idea in 2001 had been to locate an institution of folk tradition, the House of Tradition, in the palace. Ultimately, the institution was founded, albeit under the changed name, Hagyományok Háza, in the historical Vigadó building.

From the beginning, numerous controversies and media turbulence accompanied the implementation of the Palace of Arts. The daily *Népszabadság* (György 2004) expressed concern that the new investment, which was supposed to be the engine of change in the industrial district, would actually affect its gentrification.

The most common objection to the Palace of Arts was that the creators were groping in the dark for something enigmatic – architects had no knowledge of the exhibition concept or the collection's nature, because the ministry had not made a decision on who would occupy the space. Those in museum and artistic circles were outraged that the establishment plans for the institution were created without the participation of specialists. Originally, the investor wanted to allocate the space to auction houses or small galleries. Then the idea of creating a new institution emerged – the Museum of Modern Hungarian Art (Modern Magyar Művészeti Múzeum, 4M), but without a specific vision regarding its collection and exhibition program.

In 2002, the elites of the Hungarian museum and art worlds took the floor online in the forum of the modern art journal, *Exindex*.[2] The nature of this discussion resembled on many levels the subsequent debate surrounding the Museum of Modern Art in Warsaw. László Beke stated that the project lacked a "responsibly taken and acceptable museological concept". In terms of defining the profile of the new museum, József Mélyi, Katalin Timár, and Edit Sasvári stressed the need to re-evaluate and redefine the role of already-existing institutions. Many people postulated the creation of a new institution; for example, a museum of the twenty-first century (Erzsébet Tatai, Katalin Bakos, Judit Angel) or a Hungarian Museum of Contemporary Visual Arts (Júlia N. Mészáros), which would operate independently or in cooperation with the Ludwig Museum. Another idea was to create an exhibition space with the character of the Kunsthalle, already functioning in Budapest, from which a museum of contemporary art would gradually emerge (Márta Kovalovszky, Péter Kovács). Other proposals included the creation of a Museum of Collectors (Julia Fabényi). But there were also opposing voices which stated that the museum by no means should be created on the basis of private collections (Éva Forgács). There were also discussions (similar to those in Warsaw and the MSN) about the interim definition of the collection. Its temporal beginning boundaries were proposed as: the 1990s, the end of the 1980s, and the end of the Second World War. Many were in favor of creating international collection.

This dynamic discussion provoked János Vasilescu, a Romanian collector living in Hungary, to donate a collection of four hundred works of twentieth-century Hungarian art to the state. There were even plans to house it in 4M and narrow the museum's exhibition program to painting. The Vasilescu Foundation was established (its chairman, Sándor Dejman, was the owner of the development company working on the Palace of the Arts), whose aim was to transfer the collection of art to this museum (Szanto 2001); however, competition was announced and it was moved to Győr. At that time, the idea of separating the modern art department from the Hungarian National Gallery and transferring it to the Palace of Arts also arose, but in the end, the building was too small to accommodate the whole collection (Interview with Krisztina Szipőcs 2007). Other ideas included obtaining collections from Pécs and Székesfehérvár, and works from Vasilescu, Kolozsváry, Kieselbach, and Károly László collections. But no one was able to articulate how to accomplish this (Szentpéteri 2005).

After the change of the regime in Hungary, a decision was made to transfer the Ludwig Museum to the Palace of Arts, which meant that the Hungarian National Gallery would be able to take over building "A" of the Royal Castle from the museum. Due to the fact that the building initially was not designed for the Ludwig Museum and its collection (since the presentation of the initial idea, architects repeatedly have redesigned it), it has numerous shortcomings, e.g. insufficient storage space. While the move deprived the museum of the Hungarian National Gallery context as well as proximate tourist routes, the museum gained a much larger, modern exhibition space located in an area of increasing cultural activity in the capital. The first exhibition in the new location opened in 2005.

The architectural form of the Palace of Arts was not widely discussed, in contrast to the kitsch project of the National Theatre opened in 2002 (designed by Mária Siklós), whose shape resembles a ship drowning in the Danube's current. This narrative continues with the sculpture garden that surrounds it. Despite the physically open character of the district (there are no fences or gates), its exclusivity creates a psychological barrier; there is no place for popular events. All of its cultural institutions represent high culture, placed in two monumental buildings. The social barrier is only enhanced by the weak integration of buildings. According to Krisztina Szipőcs, this space should function as an agora for both institutions; on the contrary, the location of the buildings hinders this – the theatre's entrance is turned away from the Palace of Arts, and the area between both is used as the car park and for auxiliary functions (Interview with Krisztina Szipőcs 2008).

Dejman had stated several times during the opening ceremony that the Palace of Arts is the first of its kind, a three-pronged cultural center housing a concert hall, theater and museum (Metz 2005). Similarly, the director Imre

Kiss, when asked in an interview with what the Palace could be compared, replied:

> Considering content, complexity, there is no comparison. In this case we can talk about a one-of-a-kind building, as I do not know of anything similar either here or abroad. Speaking frankly, it is cultural multiplex; putting it nicely, a Palace of Arts. After all, many branches of the best Hungarian and foreign art appear here.
>
> (Szále 2005)

It is hard to believe that the creators of the institution were not familiar with foreign cultural complexes. The genealogy of the Palace of Fine Arts begins at the Pompidou Center in Paris. The exhibition in 2005 of works from the National Museum of Modern Art located in Pompidou – *The Enigma of Modernity* – inaugurated the work of the Ludwig Museum in its new location. In terms of its connection at the planning stage to conference, office, and residential functions, the investment should also be mentioned alongside the London Barbican. The Barbican Centre, with three theater halls, two art galleries, seven conference rooms, a library, and three cinemas, was to meet the cultural needs of the four thousand people living in the self-sustaining housing estate established in the area. The basic difference between these investments is that in Budapest, the focus was on the importance of cultural offerings for congress guests, but ultimately this function was not implemented.

Despite the seemingly good communication with the city center, the museum is off the beaten track; it is a destination. Krisztina Szipőcs admits: "It is not difficult to get here, tram No. 2 is the easiest way, but as it is not the inner city, not [in] the walking area of Budapest, you have to plan your trip, you cannot enter here 'accidentally'" (Interview with Krisztina Szipőcs 2017).

Of course, there are many examples of modern art museums that were intentionally located away from the hustle and bustle of the city – e.g. the Essl Museum in Klosterneuburg near Vienna (closed in 2016), the Menil Collection in Houston, Fondation Beyeler in Basel, the Goetz Collection in Munich, the Louisiana Museum of Modern Art in Humlebæk near Copenhagen, the great National Museum of Twenty First Century Arts in Rome (MAXXI), and the Danubiana Meulensteen Art Museum in Čunovo. The Ludwig Museum, however, did not choose this location, nor did it have any influence on the building's form. As the institution initially functioned in a tourist attraction, it also had a better, more frequented context for its contemporary art collection. Culture Minister Zoltán Rockenbauer stated that, "the whole project was faltering because the conference center was to be the heart of the concept, thanks to which the entire investment would become profitable" (Szentpéteri 2005). However, it is difficult to say whether conference and congress participants would significantly increase the consumption of culture on offer in the adjacent building, especially at the Ludwig Museum.

Another flagship project of Hungarian cultural policy at the turn of the century, albeit only somewhat related to the visual arts, was the creation of the Millennium Park located in the nineteenth-century factory of Ábrahám Ganz in Buda (initially it had served as a foundry; later it produced machines, including locomotives). In this case, the artistic component consists only of a small gallery. The fully funded project, which occupied a central place in the Hungarian Millennium celebrations, was dedicated to Hungarian inventors and the history of their inventions; it made reference to the La Villette science and technology park in Paris. Opened in the summer of 2001, the complex constituted an important element in the revitalization of one of the largest communication hubs in Budapest, Moszkva tér (Keresztély 2005: 455). A Palace of Wonders in five buildings houses concerts, theater performances, exhibitions, programs for children, and a small gallery of media art.

Likewise in Košice, cultural activity rescued a complex of historic buildings in connection with the title of ECoC, which the city carried in 2013. A number of investments took place, the largest of which was the transformation of a historic nineteenth-century military barracks into the center of contemporary art and creativity under the name Kasárne/Kulturpark (already mentioned in Chapter 4). The original project included the creation of an independent cultural center inhabited by different arts. One of the larger buildings was to be transformed into the so-called Incubator, and the other into the department of art for the university. Also planned were a dormitory, spaces for creative work, and design rooms. The Incubator was eventually created in the Kulturpark space, but without the university component (A Person Working in Independent Culture 2013: 20). Of the original buildings, three main buildings remained and eight new pavilions were added. In the main building "Alfa", there were two multi-purpose rooms for concerts, theater performances, lectures, and conferences, two smaller multi-purpose rooms, audio and video studios, and an art gallery.

An investment in the center of Warsaw was to be a complex integrating multiple cultural functions under one roof (see Chapter 4). Christian Kerez, the creator behind the winning project at the Museum of Modern Art (see Atlas 3.18) which is to stand at the foot of the Palace of Culture and Science, was asked in 2008 to make fundamental changes to the project in order to make way for another institution, the Rozmaitości Theater. At that time, even the idea of changing the name of the complex to the Centre for Modern Art was floated. In the end, it was determined that the building of the Museum of Modern Art would be created; a theater room and its back office constituting about 30 percent of the total area of the building would be integrated into its plan. Kerez's multi-functional plan ultimately was not realized. In the third architectural competition, guidelines called for two buildings adjacent to one another.

Museum districts

The "museum street" in the Hungarian city of Pécs is considered to be the earliest museum district in Central Europe. Typologically, it refers to the Berlin Museum Island or the Munich Art District, although on a much smaller scale. In the 1970s, the development of museums in Pécs came to life: museums were newly made or acquired, and a large number of these were located on and in the immediate vicinity of Káptalan Street, nowadays referred to as "museum street". Most of these institutions – the Victor Vasarely Museum, the Amerigo Tot Museum, the Modern Hungarian Gallery, the Renaissance Lapidarium, and the Ferenc Martyn Museum – function as part of the larger Janus Pannonius Museum. A cultural investment plan emerged in connection with Pécs' candidacy for the title of ECoC in 2010, which in its key points also included museums for this area. The city planned the construction of the so-called Great Exhibition Space adjacent to the Baroque building of the region's authorities where in 2001 the Modern Hungarian Gallery opened on the first floor, featuring an exhibition of Hungarian art from 1955. It was assumed that the new building would house various halls for temporary exhibitions. In addition, the collection of art from the first half of the twentieth century, located at the time in another building on "museum street" was to be located there following the restoration work (Takáts 2005: 64–65).

Despite Pécs having won the competition for the title of ECoC, the project was not fully implemented. Financial and technical considerations hindered progress. It turned out that the area planned for construction had functioned in the Middle Ages as a quarry, and for the purpose of the investment, it would have to be emptied. Due to the difficulties encountered, the design was changed: instead of the Great Exhibition Space, a fully glazed reception space was created, along with a relatively small, temporary exhibition space hidden underground.

The exhibition space proposed in the competition documentation has been included in the Zsolnay Cultural Quarter project.[3] The district was established on the premises of the Zsolnay porcelain and ceramics factory occupying a vast area east of the Pécs city center. The Zsolnay factory itself has been a city symbol since the second half of the nineteenth century. The cultural district of 41,000 square meters was planned as a reference to the Western European creative districts conducive to cultural revival. The eastern part of the complex was designed using a number of historic buildings. In 2008, a competition for the architectural concept was carried out, and construction works took place from 2009–2012. The complex consists of four parts: the Craft District, the Creative District (where spaces for contemporary art exhibitions were open in 2010 in the new building, Pécsi Galéria, as well as workshops and rooms for various events directed at young people), the District for Families and Children, and the University Quarter. In addition to the art gallery, the district includes: the

Bóbita Puppet Theatre, a scientific and technical exhibition, a concert and theater hall, auditoriums, the Zsolnay collections belonging to László Gyugyi, lecture rooms and offices of the University of Pécs, the library of the Department of Music and Visual Arts, craft workshops, and the Zsolnay Mausoleum. It is assumed that the Zsolnay Quarter is to become the center of the city's cultural life. In its immediate vicinity, a new Kodály Centre for conferences and concerts and a library have opened. The complex's layout and character resembles the Vienna MuseumsQuartier – also built within the historical walls, with activity carried out both in historic and modern buildings. A service wing with pubs, bars, cafes, and restaurants was planned for the complex; but these were only partially realized, and operations are limited to the opening hours of the accompanying attractions to the exclusion of night life (with the exception of special events). By contrast, in Vienna, the public space created within the courtyard is teeming with life both during the day and in the late evening; it is one of the most popular leisure and entertainment areas in the city.

Museum specialist Gábor Ébli is of the opinion that the Modern Hungarian Gallery "paid the price for it [Zsolnay Cultural Quarter], being moved into the background" (Interview with Gábor Ébli 2018). Before 1989, it was one of the most important art museums in Hungary, regularly attracting visitors from the capital. After the transformation, "Funding ran out soon and instead of being an institution of national significance, a status the Modern Hungarian Gallery had acquired by the late 1970s, the museum has been turning more and more local, receiving less and less attention and funding by the municipality".

The beginning of the second decade of the twenty-first century brought with it another project for a cultural district in Budapest, this time encompassing the City Park and its nearest vicinity. The 100-plus-acre park is a major tourist attraction; at the same time, it also serves as one of the most important leisure spaces for city residents. The National Exhibition was held there in 1885, and in 1896, the Millennium Exhibition. Important historical events took place at Heroes' Square, and the nearby Ötvenhatosok Square had been the site of the 1956 revolution. Until the 1970s, the Budapest International Fair was held in the park. In 2002, the Andrássy Boulevard reaching Heroes' Square along with the adjacent buildings were included on the UNESCO World Heritage List (Liget Budapest Competition Program 2014: 32). The museum district concept has evolved from an idea that would hide some of the buildings underground, to one that would create iconic edifices filling the park (on this topic, see Chapter 4). The point of reference for the concept are the Museum of Fine Arts, which is the heart of the entire project, and the Műcsarnok opposite, both symbolically located at the entrance to the park (although not formally part of the project).

The implementation of the new investment commenced in 2011, with the establishment of the office of the Hungarian commissioner for the construction of the museum district. In 2012, Péter Inkei, director of The Budapest

Observatory – the Regional Observatory on Culture in East-Central Europe, emphasized that the project "is utopian in relation to the government's real economic difficulties" (Jagodzińska 2012: 151). However, its implementation continued. First, a competition in 2013 for the idea and spatial parameters of the museum district under the name Liget Budapest Project was held. After site was selected for particular institutions, the architectural competitions for the individual buildings was announced. During the implementation of the project, there were changes in the plans for the intended institutions. Ultimately, from the four planned museum buildings, it was decided that two would be created – the New National Gallery and the Ethnographic Museum, as well as the House of Hungarian Music, which will combine performance and exhibition functions. As part of the Liget Budapest Project, the Museum of Fine Arts was modernized (2015–2018), and the historic Hungarian Museum of Transport will be modernized, which will act as the House of Hungarian Innovation. The small, historic Olof Palme House building will hold events organized by the district authorities. The City Park Theatre in the park will be rebuilt; the zoological garden will undergo modernization and extension. The National Conservation and Collections Centre erected in the immediate vicinity of the park will serve art museums and the Ethnographic Museum. New leisure spaces will be created, as well as a network of promenades, walking paths, and bicycle paths. The investor is the state-owned Városliget Zrt (comprised of three shareholders: the state treasury, the city of Budapest, and the 14th District of Budapest).

The scope of the idea, the momentum of the original plans, and the concentration of large museum buildings in one area suggest affinities with the largest projects in Western Europe. The ultimate point of reference is Museum Island in Berlin, where the construction project is also underway (its concept was developed in 1999, and completion of construction works is forecast for 2025/2026). There, four museums will be connected by an underground promenade, and a reception building for the entire complex (James-Simon-Galerie) will be built. The Humboldt Forum is already adjacent to Museum Island (on the site of the non-existent Stadtschloss), to which two museums will be transferred from the museum complex in the Dahlem district, away from the Berlin city center. The Hungarian and German projects combine the improvement of communication and organization, and the construction of new buildings to which museums will be transferred from existing locations. The Városliget project also resembles Kulturforum; the equivalent of Museum Island was created in West Berlin (the first building opened in the 1960s, the greater part was carried out in the 1980s, and the last – the Gemäldegalerie – in 1998). The similarity consists in combining museums and buildings performing other cultural functions in the district – in the case of Berlin, a philharmonic, the Chamber Music hall, and a library. The proximity of individual buildings on Museum Island and the management of space between them – in contrast to Kulturforum – promotes leisure (which will be an important element of the Budapest project, as well). Among the points of reference for the Budapest project were also Millennium Park in Chicago, the park next to the Prado Museum in Madrid, and Zoo-Museum District in St Louis.

Városliget Ltd.'s goal is to create the Liget Budapest brand especially abroad, as Balázs Jelinek, Project Director explains, "the potential is mostly abroad, because in Hungary everyone knows it as the City Park. It is a very well-known part of the city and we think it is impossible to reshape the brand that is already in everybody's heads" (Interview with Balázs Jelinek 2017). The museum district was designed primarily to strengthen the tourist attractiveness of Budapest (see the interview with László Baán, Chapter 2). Studies have shown that the project will greatly increase night guests to Budapest. Returns on the modernization investment are expected after fifteen years of operation. The project is financed from budgetary funds, although an application for EU funds was originally planned (Jelinek 2017).

The Bydgoszcz Museum Island also contains a museum district. Several buildings on the Mill Island were adapted for the Leon Wyczółkowski District Museum, and the area was further enlivened by the creation of leisure spaces. What distinguishes the aforementioned Western investments from the one in Bydgoszcz is that all the buildings in the latter have been adapted for exhibition purposes. The investment is therefore part of the third type identified by Montaner. From the end of the sixteenth century to the second half of the eighteenth century, the island had a mint, and after its closure, a mill complex that was still active in the first half of the twentieth century. In the years 2006–2010, the island was revitalized. First, three footbridges were created, ensuring access between the island and various parts of the city. Then, five ruined buildings were adapted for the District Museum's exhibitions: the two-story White Granary was designated for collections and studios of the Department of Archeology in a tenement house where coins were probably minted; the European Money Center was created; a Red Granary built in 1861, and an adjoining Millers House, were transformed into the Gallery of Modern Art. A nineteenth-century residential house built for the Rother Mills employees in the southwestern part of the island reopened as the Leon Wyczółkowski House (Szybowicz, Ślusarczyk and Woźniak 2009: 104–115). Some of these buildings have been in the possession of the museum since 1975; they were acquired for storage purposes and scientific labs. The cultural-recreational-entertainment complex – which also includes a concert amphitheater, green areas with walking paths, and the revived Rother Mill (in which a multi-functional service facility is to be built, under construction from 2015–2019) – should be considered in a broader context, including the site of the Opera Nova on the Brda's opposite shore. The Bydgoszcz district was well connected with the urban fabric and is conducive to leisure.

In Krakow, the districts of Zabłocie and Stare Podgórze began to grow into a new cultural enclave. Podgórze, where the Jewish ghetto was situated during the war, was still one of the most neglected parts of the city at the beginning of the twenty-first century. The first symptom of the changes was the construction of the Andrzej Frycz Modrzewski Krakow University (opened in 2000), the largest private university in Krakow. Soon after, the dynamic changes have occurred, namely the demolition of industrial buildings and the construction of housing estates in their place. The exhibition presenting Krakow during the Second World War in the Schindler's Factory (a branch of the Historical Museum of the City of Krakow) and MOCAK (see Atlas 3.8) were opened in 2010, and four years later, in the old power plant building, Cricoteka also opened. In 2018, the Podgórze Museum (another branch of the Historical Museum of the City of Krakow) was founded on the initiative of the district's residents. Monika Murzyn-Kupisz referred to Podgórze as a "rising" quarter of culture. Pointing to its development, which she analyzes together with the Jewish district of Kazimierz, she did not fail to notice that "the positive cultural impulses visible in Zabłocie in previous years are weakening due to the dominance of commercial actors and the lack of sufficient support from city authorities, including large urban cultural institutions", and as a result, "instead of a cultural district, Podgórze may become an enclave of luxury housing and Class A office space rentals" (Murzyn-Kupisz 2013: 119–120). The role of MOCAK as a catalyst for change in the district is smaller than expected, and the potential of the institution has not been taken advantage of.

Art/trade/entertainment

The borders of trade, entertainment, and art, in that order, became the domain of Łódź and Poznań. In the centers of both cities, and in a short period of time, commercial complexes took shape (making use of the existing post-industrial architecture in both cases) within which a number of outlets for entertainment and contemporary art also emerged.

In Łódź in 2006, within the revitalized nineteenth-century textile factory complex, the center of trade, entertainment, and culture was opened under the name "Manufaktura". Part of this became a branch of the Muzeum Sztuki ms^2 (see Atlas 3.10). The history of Manufaktura begins in 1999, when Apsys Company became the owner of the land and property of the former Izrael Kalmanowicz Poznański Cotton Goods Joint-Stock Company, and began preparatory work for the revitalization of historical buildings. The importance of this investment is directly related to the scale and role played for decades by the plant as a symbol of Łódź's industrial might. The origins of the factory date back to 1871–1873, when Izrael Kalmanowicz Poznański bought the area for the planned investment. In 1889, the plant was transformed into I.K. Poznański Cotton Goods Joint-Stock Company, and Poznański himself became owner of the second largest enterprise in the city (it occupied an area of 270,000 square meters). Through the beginning of the twentieth century, the main part of the factory was established, which included the high weaving mill in 1895, later adapted to the museum (Kusiński, Bonisławski and Janik 2009). After the Second World War, the enterprise was nationalized as the Zakłady Przemysłu Bawełnianego Juliana Marchlewskiego. The gradual decline in employment and production in the 1980s resulted in a bankruptcy petition, filed in 1991.

The creation of Manufaktura in this area saved the historical walls from demolition and opened them in a symbolic way for local residents. The construction works at the factory took place in 2003–2009; the shopping and entertainment center opened in 2006, and the museum in 2008. The complex contains shops, cafes, pubs, restaurants, a bowling alley, a cinema, an entertainment center, a climbing wall, the Factory Museum, a theater, experimentarium science center (whose offerings change), and a public space with a fountain, benches, and lanterns. The interior "market" may be entered through the historic gate, as well as through a series of intersections between the buildings. The structure of the complex creates an enclosed space that is accessible twenty-four hours a day.

Manufaktura was the first major revitalization project in Poland, and its image of success and popularity attracted new projects both in Łódź and in other Polish cities. Not only the size of the complex, but also the presence of the Muzeum Sztuki, render Manufaktura different from many other shopping malls, which rose *en masse* in Central Europe. The museum's location was an initiative of the Manufaktura investor who donated the building. As noted by a journalist in *Gazeta Wyborcza*:

> Traditional shopping centers have no future. Fewer and fewer people are coming to the openings of these malls, and all of them are similar. A French investor who brings culture to Manufaktura does not do it out of pure philanthropy. He is looking for a way to attract customers and he has found the perfect one.
>
> (Michałowicz 2004)

The building on the site of Manufaktura is the salvation of the museum, but it has often faced criticism for the commercial nature of the neighborhood. Even before the opening of ms², Jarosław Suchan repeatedly refuted the allegations and explained that the commercial neighborhood does not have to reduce the level of or even determine the program:

> For some, the location of the museum in the vicinity of a commercial center may seem controversial. In my opinion, however, it is a chance to abolish the artificial boundaries of the so-called high culture one lives with on a daily basis. These are borders that intimidate many, excluding many museums excluded by their high arc.
>
> (Kowalewicz 2008: 2)

Repeated questions from journalists regarding the museum's commercial context show how controversial an issue the clash of art with trade and entertainment was. And yet museums in large cities often adjoin commercial spaces. A commercial neighborhood is a challenge for the museum, which is measured by the program of exhibitions and the method of working with the collection. Suchan himself admits at the same time that,

> the location of ms² in one of the most visited places in Łódź is an undoubted advantage. These thousands do not run to see works by Kobro or Robakowski right after shopping in the museum's boutiques; nevertheless, they want to see the building, to see the name, to see the banners with exhibition titles – it somehow stands out to the mind, arouses curiosity which, at least for some, finally prompts a look into this strange building.
>
> (Interview with Jarosław Suchan 2018)

Examples of the co-existence of commercial and museum space are the Fiat Lingotto factory in Turin and the Mori Tower skyscraper in Tokyo, where offices, hotels, cinemas, theaters, shops, banks, and the Mori Art Museum (opened in 2003) operate. Formally, the closest concept to Manufaktura is the MuseumsQuartier. While it is the case that the commercial aspect is not extensive in the latter (being limited to museum shops and one central store selling art-related merchandise), there are more museums and exhibition spaces. But in both cases, the heart of the investment is the public space, the heart of residential city life.

In Poland, Manufaktura is most often compared to "Stary Browar" [Old Brewery] in Poznań, the center of trade, art, and entertainment of a similar character – the difference being that in the latter, the artistic element, like the entire institution, was associated with private capital. With this project, creator Grażyna Kulczyk formed a new kind of commercial space on Polish soil that placed commercial and high culture under one roof. The accomplishment would not be so spectacular if it were not for the revitalized historic brewery walls from the late nineteenth century that encompass it.

Julius and Alfons Hugger, sons of the German brewer Ambrosius Hugger, erected the brewery in the 1870s–1890s. After the First World War, the Huggers moved to Germany, and in 1926 the brewery was taken over by doctor Roman May's Chemical Company, followed by the Union Brewery of the Association of Restaurateurs, and after the Second World War, the Brewing Plant. In 1980, it was closed, and until 1997 it housed a water bottling plant. Kulczyk Fortis LLC then bought the brewery buildings and started the investment. The construction works were carried out from 2002–2007, and the Old Brewery was opened in stages.

The complex is a closed space made accessible by its location in the city center, next to the park and a short distance from the Old Town. The area in the immediate vicinity of the complex was revived, and over the years the more frequently used East-West axis gave way to the north-south one that connects the complex with the Old Market (Głaz 2005). Following the extension, the resulting complex covers 122,000 square meters of space and six floors. In addition to shops and service outlets, there is a cinema, clock tower, gallery, and space for cultural events, e.g. film projections, concerts, and theater performances. The Art Stations Foundation implements the cultural program. The Art Stations Gallery (in operation from 2009 to 2016; see Atlas 3.11) opened in the new building. Art in the "Old Brewery" occupies not only gallery spaces, but also exists in various forms (sculptures, installations, video) introduced into the commercial space. As part of the investment, Kulczyk planned to open a private museum of modern art to house her own collection, but she abandoned the project due to the lack of support from the state.

As the owner of the entire private enterprise, Kulczyk did not have to answer to allegations or questions related to the co-existence of low and high culture within a single complex as the director of the Muzeum Sztuki in Łódź Similarly, an underground museum was planned as a private investment, although in this case the collector sought European funding.

Summary

The location of museums is of great importance for their identity, program activity, and building relationships with the public. Co-existence with other cultural institutions – both museums and institutions of a different nature – also creates a specific context. In many historical cities, with their accumulation of museums, theaters, philharmonics, and other cultural institutions, the inner core itself can be regarded as a museum or cultural district. This is the case in Krakow, Prague, and Bratislava, for example. The term "city as museum" has even been coined, capturing this character. A separate, contained museum district or a cultural complex located outside the main city square, which for other reasons is teeming with life, is different in nature, however.

Hungary possesses a special concentration of cultural complexes. The district of museums created in the Budapest City Park was intended to integrate almost all major Hungarian art museums – the Hungarian National Gallery will move from the Royal Castle to adjoin the Museum of Fine Arts and Kunsthalle; likewise, the Ludwig Museum, Museum of Photography, and Museum of Architecture, but these will ultimately not move to the district. All buildings will be opened more or less simultaneously, which will also determine how they function. City Park is already a popular place for leisure for Budapest residents and visitors alike, and the accumulation of museums and other cultural functions combined with its revitalization will only increase this potential.

The museum complex in the Royal Castle building is prestigious. The castle hill is an obligatory destination for sightseeing in Budapest, with its presidential palace, cathedral, and wonderful panorama of the city. The location of the Ludwig Museum here emphasized the importance of collections from the start. The Palace of Arts is also picturesquely situated on the

Danube, but it is not easily accessible for tourists. Its location in the new office and residential district, next to the developing post-industrial district, set up the challenge for the institutions located here. This was especially the case for the area in front of the Ludwig Museum, the only institution open during the day, while the others are concentrated around night life. In many respects, the neighborhood is reminiscent of Krakow Zabłocie. In both cases, museums have neighbors who arrived at the same time as museums. Establishing a relationship with the immediate surroundings seems to be a priority, although this has not yet been accomplished. The Zsolnay Cultural Quarter in Pécs refers to the fashionable neighborhoods of the Western cultural districts, and visitor statistics show that it is much more popular among tourists than residents of the city. The reason for this is an awkward relationship to the city; the district is about a twenty-minute walk from the city center. In spite of the rich cultural offerings and educational institutions, there is nowhere to go after dark (bars, pubs, or restaurants), and the student community spends its time in the city center. All-night festivals organized in the district provide links to the community, but these are infrequent and individual events. District managers cite a relatively high crime rate as one of the reasons for the district's impoverishment after dark, noting that the route from the city center to the district is not safe (Interview with István Márta 2014).

Commercial complexes such as Manufaktura and "Stary Browar" provide yet another context for art. In these cases, the neighborhood does not encourage leisure, as elsewhere, but rather entertainment and consumption. Art is just one of the elements on offer. Within the museums themselves, not only those located in or adjacent to commercial complexes, there are also commercial spaces (bookstores, cafés) which in extreme cases approach the character of department stores. As a global trend, in order to meet visitor demands, larger and better-equipped reception areas are being created (the most spectacular examples include the glazed courtyard at the British Museum, Le Grand Louvre, and the aforementioned new building on the Museum Island in Berlin). A well-stocked bookshop in ms^2 and a cozy upstairs café are nothing extraordinary, and do not constitute an extension of the commercial neighborhood.

Locating museums in close proximity to each other is not a new phenomenon in Central Europe, but before they had not adopted more structured formulae and were rather organic in nature. In many instances, cultural districts and complexes should be combined with the desire to revitalize a given area, especially if the city itself is an investor. All of these investments were accompanied by media attention and public discussions. The most extreme case flared up around the Liget Budapest Project: it is the largest; it involves the forced relocation of the largest art museum in Hungary; and it involves a historical place of recreation, the city park. One of the arguments raised against it is the destruction of green spaces (which the developer refutes with numbers indicating the investment actually will create more green space).

Miklós Székely also points to another issue accompanying cultural districts; namely, that "the concentration of immense cultural energies in one part of the city is not a good solution while various subcenters in the city need development". He believes that enormous financial resources targeted toward one investment should be used "to develop all those subcenters within the city which need to attract people and become smaller agoras in the city" (Interview with Miklós Székely 2018). This is an important point in the discussion on the role of districts and their influence not just on the economy (in the case of Liget Budapest, economic influence has been estimated) and the image of the city, but also on its urban and social development.

Notes

1 Both institutions are guaranteed a number of free performances in the rooms of the Palace of Arts (one hundred each). The halls are managed by the Palace of Arts, which makes decisions regarding their use on the days for which there are no scheduled performances.
2 Comments and opinions quoted after the summary of the debate, held on the Internet forum at www.exindex.c3.hu within 19.03–7.05.2002: Summary of the Debate, 2002.
3 Investments related to the title of the ECoC have accelerated (not generated) the implementation of the earlier revitalization project.

6 Private museums, art centers, and collectors

The ancestry of the museum reaches back to the era of royal, princely, and magnate collections. The formation of the modern public museum type, independently managed and financed, by no means curtailed cooperation among museums, collectors, and private collections. On the contrary, it paved the way for a different framework. From that point forward, urban public and private museums have successfully co-existed. In 2016, Larry's List, a Hong Kong-based art market research company, published the *Private Art Museum Report* identifying 317 museums of contemporary art around the world and studying collectors who have opted to make their collections available to the public. Its authors report that the number of private museums engaging with contemporary art has grown significantly with the advent of the new century – more than half (53 percent) of all private museums emerged between 2000 and 2010, and nearly one-fifth of them (18 percent) were built between 2010 and 2015 (Larry's List Ltd. and AMMA 2016: 25). The museum boom currently underway also encompasses the creation of private museums from private art collections. It is worth recalling that for several decades, the Central European custom of private art collecting had been interrupted as private property was nationalized. It was only after 1989 that private museums could reappear, and private collections could be presented publicly and join the repositories of public museums. However, not everyone has benefitted from these possibilities, and for various reasons (including fear of theft), some collections remain publicly unknown. There are in fact not many private art museums in Central Europe. In a few cases, a private collection initiated the creation of a public institution. Private art centers or large galleries presenting private collections number only about a dozen. The *Private Art Museum Report* has taken into account individual museums from the Czech Republic, Poland, and Slovakia (none from Hungary), but the data is modest in contrast with that for other countries; nine such museums have been identified in Berlin itself, for example.

In this chapter, I present private museums and other private initiatives in the field of contemporary art – galleries grounded in collections, or galleries and art centers that operate alongside private collections. I discuss their creators' motivations and refer to the geographic context of these institutions. I am also asking whether these establishments are numerous enough and whether they sufficiently complement the landscape of public institutions.

Private museums for private collections

The construction of a private art collection and a museum that can accommodate it is a financial commitment that few collectors are making. A museum building is not a one-time financial investment; it also requires continuous resources for its maintenance and development. This is the main reason why in Central Europe private art museums presenting art collections of the twentieth or twenty-first century number only six, some of which were created with a significant share of public money. These museums vary in size, housed both in large buildings and intimate ones. Their legal status and funding models are different from one another. Unlike many private museums created in Western European countries and the United States, these are not usually the fruits of great personal fortune with which the benefactor is able to build in style.

Three private museums of modern and contemporary art were created in Slovakia. Given the size of the country, this is phenomenal. The only example of a private collector-philanthropist museum realized with panache in Central Europe is the Danubiana Meulensteen Art Museum in Čunovo near Bratislava (see Chapter 3 and Atlas 4.5). The museum was created through the initiative of the lawyer Vincent Polakovič, who after traveling to France in the early 1990s, inspired by Vincent van Gogh's house in Arles, decided in 1993 to establish a private gallery in Poprad – the Žltý house (the Yellow House) of Vincent van Gogh. After a year of operation, the gallery faced an uncertain financial future; hence, Polakovič traveled to the Netherlands in search of support. There, he managed to convince Gerard Meulensteen, a Dutch entrepreneur in the electronics industry, to back his investment of building a museum. According to the original plan, the whole floor of the museum (opened in 2000) was intended for the permanent presentation of his international art collection. From the beginning, the exhibitions were temporary. Only the new wing was added (2013–2014) to accommodate Meulensteen's and the Danubiana's collections. In 2014, Danubiana obtained non-profit status and is now financed primarily by the Ministry of Culture. Vincent Polakovič explained,

> I began to wonder what would happen to the museum when he [Meulensteen] was no longer around. After all, he had reached a certain age. I asked him if he could imagine donating Danubiana to Slovakia and its artists. He agreed with this idea and then it was only up to the Slovak government. The government decided to accept the offer.
>
> (Interview with Vincent Polakovič 2017)

The second private museum established in Slovakia was the Milan Dobeš Museum (see Atlas 4.3), which operated from 2001–2016 in Bratislava. It was both much smaller and more frequently profiled. The collector Peter Sokol founded it; since 1992, he has been collecting the work of Milan Dobeš (b. 1929), an outstanding Czechoslovakian artist known for his adherence to geometric abstraction. Sokol began collecting art two or three years before he met Dobeš; later, his work dominated the collection, becoming so extensive that it warranted its own exhibition. At that point, Sokol convinced Dobeš to create something more – a museum (the artist himself did not take part in its formation), in collaboration with the Foundation of the European Cultural Society. It was referred to as the first private museum of modern art in Eastern Europe, though the opening of the Danubiana had taken place earlier. This said, it was the first fully Slovak private museum of art. Dobeš's work was shown with that of other constructivist artists – both at the permanent exhibition and in the program of rotating exhibitions. Sokol simultaneously ran the Komart Gallery located opposite in a tenement house. He accepted the assumption that the museum would present geometric abstraction created by deceased artists, while the gallery would promote living artists through exhibitions and sales. The owner's financial problems, however, forced the closure of the museum.

The third private museum in Slovakia, the ZOYA Museum (see Atlas 4.7), was established in 2009 in the village of Modra at the ELESCO winery. The museum is an extension of the ZOYA Gallery opened four years earlier in Bratislava. While the gallery is located in the Baroque Palace of Erdődy, in Modra, the museum occupies the modernist wing of a large wine production complex. The ZOYA collection, one of the largest private collections in Slovakia, includes works by twentieth- and twenty-first century Slovak artists, as well as Andy Warhol, whose parents came from the village of Mikova in eastern Slovakia. The Slovak collection is presented in the gallery in the form of a permanent exhibition, while the Warhol collection is in the museum. Temporary exhibitions are also organized in both places.

In 2002, the Museum Kampa (see Atlas 1.9) was established in Prague, but in this case the city authorities concluded an agreement regarding the collection's ownership and financing. The museum collection represents art collected by Meda and Jan Mládek after emigration. In 1946, Meda went to Geneva to study economics. When the communists seized power two years later, she decided to stay in exile. After completing her doctorate in Switzerland in 1955, she went to Paris, where she studied art history. There, she met her future husband Jan Mládek, who participated in the shaping of Czech economic reform for the government in exile (Vlastník 2001: 36). The beginning of the collection is marked by the acquisition of one of František Kupka's paintings, donated to Mládek as a gift by a Parisian antiquarian. Meda recalled in an interview saying, "It's nothing special, I bought it at an auction for fifty dollars, but this artist of yours will be famous one day" (Vlastník 2001: 37). Shortly after this incident, she went in person to meet Kupka, who worked in the village of Puteux near Paris. Enthralled by the artist, she amassed the largest private collection of his works, consisting of 225 paintings, graphics, and drawings. After the artist's death, the prices of his work began to rise rapidly. In 1960, the couple moved to Washington, where Mládek developed a collector's passion. In addition to works by Kupka and Otto Gutfreund, Meda bought art by contemporary Czech and Slovak artists, many of whom had no possibility of exhibiting in communist Czechoslovakia (Volf 2003: 31). In 1967, she returned to the country where – with the help of the National Gallery director, Jiří Kotalík (whose doors were opened to her by the director of the Guggenheim Museum in New York) – she reached the studios of local artists, and presented the works she purchased at exhibitions in the United States. In 1983, the Mládeks wrote a will that recorded the works of Kupka and Gutfreund at the National Gallery in Washington, and the contemporary works at the National Gallery in Prague. Mládek changed these records after arriving in Prague in 1989 during the Velvet Revolution (already without her husband, who died two months earlier, without living to see the free Czechoslovakia he was fighting for) (Bulkacz 2004).

In 1993, she offered to donate the collection to the authorities of Prague and began to search for a suitable building for the museum. Initially, she was interested in the former Karlov monastery in Prague, which housed the Police Museum. The place seemed ideal as a metaphor for the fact that during the totalitarian era, Czech art had been largely cut off from the world (Volf 2003: 32). The idea did not come to fruition, however. With the agreement of city authorities, Mládek then developed the vision of locating the museum in the abandoned Šova's mill buildings on the banks of the Vltava River (see Chapter 4). In 1999, a contract was signed between Mládek representing the Jan and Meda Mládek Foundation and the City of Prague, which states that a part of the collection would be donated to the city (specifically, 215 of Kupka's pieces, 240 collages and objects by Jiří Kolář, and 279 works by Czech and Slovak artists dating from 1965–1985), and that the city as owner would loan these works to the foundation at no charge (The Jan and Meda Mládek Foundation). Municipal funds covered 80 percent of the costs of the building renovation, while the remainder was financed by the foundation and private sponsors (Bulkacz 2004). The building remains the property of the city and is rented by the foundation.

The collection was presented as a permanent exhibition for a considerable time, while temporary exhibitions occupied a smaller area. In 2015, the museum decided to invert this such that only a small exhibition representing the achievements of František Kupka and selected works created during the Second World War appear at the headquarters. At that time, the museum started a cooperation with the town of Moravský Krumlov, whose castle exhibited works from the Mládek collection. Chief curator of the Museum Kampa, Helena Musilová, said that:

> For the past fifty years in this castle there was exhibited the *Slav Epic* by Alfons Mucha, so the castle is quite popular. It is present in every guide on the Czech Republic. The owner of the *Slav Epic* is the City of

Prague and in 2012 the series was transferred from Moravský Krumlov to Veletržní Palace. The castle in Moravský Krumlov was left without interesting programming for its big space. That is why they invited us to prepare an exhibition for people coming to the town from all over the world to see Mucha.

(Interview with Jiří Pospíšil, Helena Musilová
and Sandra Průša 2015)

Thus the Mládek collection, sometimes referred to as the Czech Peggy Guggenheim, became a consolation prize for those who came to this sleepy town to see the great painting cycle of the master of Art Nouveau.

The lifespan of another Prague museum, the Artbanka Museum of Young Art (see Atlas 1.5) located in the palace on the Royal Route was very short. The museum was conceived as a living space for art.

The head curator of AMOYA, Vlado Beskid (2011: 10), wrote in the catalog for the first exhibition:

We didn't simply want to create another "museum" show, but also to define a new laboratory environment for visual art, another communication channel for the necessary direct comparison between the Czech and international scenes, for the exchange of ideas and improvement of the cultural "metabolism" in Central Europe.

The museum did not show the collection in the form of a permanent exhibition; rather, it aired both established and debuting artists, with the local art scene providing an international context. The courtyard, open to the public, featured David Černy's monumental work *Guns* (1994), and in the basement, his famous *Shark* (2005) installation. In contrast, in the section B staircase, it was possible to view the well-known work of the Czech group Kamera skura and the Slovak Kunst-Fu *Superstart* (2003). The museum was closed due to the high operating costs.

Additional private art institutions are being planned in Prague. The opening of the Kunsthalle Praha, sponsored by the Pudil Family Foundation, has been announced for 2020. This institution is being built in the city center, below the castle hill in the converted Zenger Electrical substation. It is intended to be "a new center for modern and contemporary art" (Kunsthalle Praha), which is a space not only for temporary exhibitions, but also for the presentation of Czech art from the early twentieth century to the present.

In contrast to Prague, in Poznań and Warsaw it was not possible for a collector and the city authorities to collaborate on the construction of the museum. A private museum of contemporary art has been planned in Poland since at least 2008. Grażyna Kulczyk, the creator of "Stary Browar" in Poznań and the Art Stations Gallery (see Atlas 3.11) operating there until 2016, wishes to build it. Kulczyk began collecting art in the 1970s; in the

1990s, she ran a gallery out of a car dealership. A selection of works from her collection was presented at the *GK Collection # 1* exhibition at "Stary Browar" in 2007. Part of this collection is also on permanent public view in the market and service space of "Stary Browar". The collection was also the starting point for the private project Art Stations Museum of Contemporary Art, planned as part of the "Stary Browar" complex. The collection was meant to be presented in the form of temporary exhibitions; there was to be a space for contemporary dance, as well. Kulczyk engaged world-renowned architect Tadao Andō to implement the project. However, the lack of state support proved a hindrance to the implementation of a private enterprise. Kulczyk said in 2009: "I would build a museum with my own resources, although my successors would probably have been cursing me for several generations. But after consultations with specialists, it turned out that financing the everyday functioning of this institution without external help would be impossible" (Torbicka 2009).

The failed investment in Poznań took Kulczyk to Warsaw, where in 2015 she approached the city authorities with a proposal to collaborate in the creation of a Museum of Contemporary Art and Performance. She chose a plot on the Vistula River for its location, near the University of Warsaw Library and campus, the Copernicus Science Center, and the Academy of Fine Arts. Her plan for the building was to create a collection room, space for temporary exhibitions, and space for performance art. She referred to the project as an "interactive cultural center" (Bartoszewicz 2016), and wanted to engage one of the best-known architectural studios (Peter Zumthor's proposals, Herzog & de Meuron, and Snøhetta's studio). The construction was to be completed in the record time of two years. The proposal she put forth to the Warsaw authorities included the purchase of a plot of land and the cost of erecting the building, in exchange for the city's maintaining the museum. After twenty years, the plot, building, and part of the collection would become public property. The city, however, decided not to get involved financially. The contentious issue was the impact the selection of the director and the program board could have on program decisions. Kulczyk did not hide her resentment, saying in a media statement: "This is how similar partnerships are organized around the world. I believe that we had the opportunity to create a world-class museum in Warsaw, attracting thousands of people" (Bartoszewicz 2016).

At the same time, Kulczyk began building a museum of contemporary art in the Swiss village of Susch, located near the border with Italy, Austria, and Liechtenstein. Its opening is planned for 2019. Kulczyk's plan was to create two museums; the one in Switzerland is not meant as a substitute for the one in Poland.

Another abroad private museum, Museum Jerke (see Atlas 3.21), was opened in 2016 in German Ruhr region, in Recklinghausen. It is a small museum of Polish avant-garde art established by German art collector with Polish roots, Werner Jerke.

The only private museum of modern art in Poland was created in 2010 in Konstancin-Jeziorna near Warsaw. Villa La Fleur was founded by Marek Roefler, co-owner of a real estate development company and collector of art of the School of Paris. The collection, featuring painting, sculpture, and graphic art by Polish and Jewish artists from the first half of the twentieth century in France, is presented in a stylish villa dating from 1906, which was purchased with a view to building a museum within it. According to the collector's intentions, the museum has the character of a residential house, where works of art are presented among period interior furnishings. Roefler's inspiration in creating the museum was the Petit Palais in Geneva, in which the industrialist Oscar Ghez arranged a museum presenting his own collection of artists from the School of Paris.

Private collections as the seed for public museums

Like the Danubiana, the Museum Kampa, and Kulczyk's plans for a Warsaw museum, private museums are often connected with the public sphere – they are co-financed, or after some period are transferred to public authorities by the owner. Often, the private collection immediately becomes the leaven of the public museum. Of utmost importance for museology in Central Europe was the gift of the German collectors Irene and Peter Ludwig to Hungary, which led to the creation of the first museum of contemporary art in the region.

The Ludwigs' mission was to expand their constantly growing collections of art, filling gaps in museum collections in Germany and abroad through donations and long-term loans, or initiating the creation of new museums. A selection of works from their collections was presented for the first time in Budapest in 1983; this was an exhibition of works from a museum of modern art opened in Vienna four years earlier, whose collection consisted of a donation from the Ludwig collection. At that time, Peter Ludwig also began discussions with the Hungarian authorities regarding the possible establishment of a foundation in Budapest, the organization of an exhibition of Hungarian art in Aachen, and the creation of a museum in Hungary. The second exhibition from their collection was organized in the Hungarian National Gallery in 1987, enthusiastically received by the public.

The contract establishing the Ludwig Foundation in Budapest was signed in 1988. In the next year in Aachen, an exhibition of Hungarian art took place at the National Gallery, from which thirty-four works were purchased for the Ludwig collection. In 1989, it was also agreed that within a five-year period, the Ludwig Museum (see Atlas 2.2) would be built in Budapest. The Foundation has donated seventy works to the Hungarian state that formed the basis of the museum's collections, which until the opening of the new institution were managed by the National Gallery. Katalin Néray, the first and long-standing director of the succeeding museum, wondered why the Ludwigs' choice had fallen to Budapest. She wrote that:

the last government, representing the so-called gentle dictatorship, wanted to show its openness, and this in turn became the long-standing obsession of Peter Ludwig, who wanted to do something behind the Iron Curtain. When you look at the political situation of the early and mid-eighties, it turns out that Hungary was its only possible option in the region.

(Néray 2006)

The Ludwig collection, which includes works by artists from the West and from Eastern Europe, created a context within the Hungarian National Gallery for Hungarian modern and contemporary art. At that time, all the works submitted from the Ludwig collection and 108 works by contemporary Hungarian artists from the National Gallery were shown. The first permanent exhibition in a separate building was opened in 1991, on the first floor of the Royal Castle Building A. There were another ninety-one works placed on long-term loan from the Ludwig Foundation. In 1993, the Ministry of Culture and Education issued a permit to operate a museum. Since 1995, the museum has been functioning as an independent, specialized institution within the National Gallery; in 1996 the ministry officially created a new museum as an autonomous institution – the Museum of Contemporary Art – Ludwig Múzeum Budapest – occupying three floors of Building A with an exhibition extended to include important works of Hungarian art.

The opening of the museum was a great success but, as Néray wrote, it was not lacking for critics. Some opinions held that the museum should not be restricted to contemporary art, since there was no modern art museum in Hungary, and modern art is dispersed across various collections. Some criticized the fact that the museum represented the taste of a private collector. However, according to Néray (1998), "big collections are based on private initiatives of kings, bishops, aristocrats, etc. Our mission is to create a context for those collections that we are trying to create in Budapest, which is also my personal obsession".

In Győr, two collections of modern art that were donated to the Municipal Museum of Art became the basis for establishing separate branches dedicated to them. In 1992, the museum guaranteed the takeover of the Béla Radnai collection, comprised of more than a thousand objects of Hungarian, and in particular, interwar art. It is considered one of the most important private collections created in the interwar period, and at the same time it is the only collection that has survived to the present day as a coherent and representative whole (Várkonyi 2005: 56). The owner of the collection, a psychologist, collected contemporary art with a special emphasis on the so-called Gresham Circle. After his death in 1962, his wife maintained the integrity of the collection. To this end, she rejected offers of purchase by Hungarian cities: Szeged, Szombathely, and Pécs, as well as Peter Ludwig, and decided to bequeath the collection to the city of Győr. The city council adopted a resolution that the collection would remain under the widow's care; that she would receive a life annuity; and that the buildings of the so-called Esterhazy Palace would be renovated and designated for the museum. The construction and restoration works were completed in 1997, followed by the opening exhibition of the Radnai collection. After the death of the collector's wife in 2005 the art became museum property (Kolozsváry 2005: 49–53).

Győr then won the "competition" of cities to take over János Vasilescu's collection. Originally from Romania, he decided in 1946 to settle in Hungary to become an entrepreneur. He amassed a large fortune that enabled him to pursue his passion for collecting – mainly paintings, but also sculptures by Hungarian artists from the 1960s and 1970s; Lili Ország's work occupies a central place. Vasilescu's collection became famous for the family quarrel concerning its future. Vasilescu wished that the entire collection would be publicly available. As the collector's son demanded that half be given to him, Vasilescu decided to repay him directly. To this end, he decided to sell works that he considered less critical to the integrity of the collection. During his lifetime, he decided to transfer the collection to a public institution. After an international application procedure, the Vasilescu Foundation chose Győr as the place for their permanent location, and in 2006, an exhibition opened in the renovated building of the historic synagogue as a branch of the Municipal Museum of Art. The reasons for this decision were on the one hand the growing importance of the city as an artistic center in Hungary (earlier collections of Péter Váczy, Imre Patkó, Radnai, and Ernő Kolozsváry were found here), and on the other, the link with the Jewish origins of Vasilescu's favorite artist, represented by the selection of the synagogue. The deceased collector's son sued the city for the return of his father's art.

In Dunaújváros, the private collection belonging to Lajos Takács, a Hungarian living in Sweden, gave impetus to the creation of a new art institution. In 1989, an exhibition of Salvador Dalí's works from his collection took place in the town, and met with great interest. The collector offered to loan the collection to the city authorities, provided that it was displayed in an appropriate exhibition venue. In 1990, therefore, the City Council established the Modern Art Foundation, whose aim was to create a Museum of Modern Art and to build a collection of contemporary art. Works loaned by Takács would provide its foundations. In 1997, the institution under the name Institute of Contemporary Art (ICA-D, see Atlas 2.5) opened in a new building. Takács ended cooperation with the foundation the following year.

Private galleries for collections

Private galleries for private collections are created much more frequently than private museums. A few non-commercial galleries (or those in which the commercial element is not dominant) that serve as permanent exhibitions for collections of contemporary art can be identified in Central Europe.

Two such venues were created in Veszprém. In 2003, the Modern Art Gallery – Vass László Collection opened. Its beginnings date back to the second half of the 1970s. Vass worked as a designer at the Hungarian Fashion Institute, and after a few years, opened his own shoe store in the center of Budapest. At that time, he became interested in Hungarian contemporary art. He collected mainly works representing constructivism – paintings, drawings, sculptures, photographs. This is considered to be the best collection of constructivism in Hungary. It was initially Hungarian, but since the 1990s, the collection included foreign works that provide Hungarian art with an important international context. In 1999, the House of Arts in Veszprém organized an exhibition of selected works from the Budapest Vass collection in its Csikász Gallery, as part of an exhibition cycle presenting Hungarian collections. During the preparations for the exhibition, the collector mentioned that he would like to make the work permanently available to visitors. This gave way to the initial idea of transferring the collections to Balatonfüred, where Vass planned to open a private gallery; but ultimately, the city of Veszprém put forth a proposal to donate three tenements in the historic city center for this purpose.

Shortly after the Vass collection was made available to visitors, another collection arrived to Veszprém in 2006 at the House of Arts in restored Dubniczay palace. The Károly László (known internationally as Carl Laszlo) collection includes art from the eighteenth to twentieth centuries, and also includes industrial design, Asian art, design, and photography. During the Second World War, the collector was deported to Auschwitz. Following the war, he completed his medical studies in Switzerland and became interested in culture: he wrote plays, founded his own theater company, dealt art, and created his own collection. For the exhibition in Veszprém, he chose only twentieth-century works – namely, the avant-garde from the early part of the century, works from the interwar period, and works by artists (both Hungarian and foreign) who entered the scene in the 1950s. The long-term loan ended in 2017, four years after collector died, and his heir – who did not manage to reach a compromise with various Hungarian institutions on the future of the collection – withdrew the works from Hungary. Its place was taken in 2018 by another private collection – Irokéz Collection – with intention to show it as a long-term exhibition lasting at least a year and a half.

One of the largest and most respected collections of contemporary art in the Czech Republic was created by Vladimír Železný, former director and co-owner of the first private television company, Nova TV, and later a politician. He focused his collecting activities on classical modernism and post-war art from the 1970s. Železný began to collect in 1997, buying at auctions and also directly from artists. At the beginning of the new century, his collection had grown to about 1,500 works. The collections are shown in the Galerie Zlatá husa in Prague, which he founded in 2002.

Another substantial collection of Czech art that included works from the 1980s to the present was created by Richard Adam. In 2006, Adam opened the Wannieck Gallery (renamed the Richard Adam Gallery in 2013) with an exhibition from his collection in the restored historic Friedrich Wannieck factory in Brno which he ran until 2015. His collections occupied the main exhibition space in the post-industrial building, which Fait Gallery took over when the Richard Adam Gallery closed.

In Slovakia, the painter, graphic artist and illustrator Ernest Zmeták was also one of the most well-known collectors. Together with his wife Danica, an art historian and curator of the Slovak National Gallery, they donated 2,145 works of art in 1979 to his native town of Nové Zámky. The gift became the core of the gallery that was created at that time (twentieth-century art formed only a portion of the whole collection).

Private collections within private galleries

The MEO (see Atlas 2.3) in Budapest is an example of a fully private enterprise in the field of contemporary art, consisting of a building, a collection, an exhibition program, and financing, following the fashionable Western trend of adapting a post-industrial building in an undistinguished neighborhood. It did not stand the test of time. Its founder, Lajos Kováts, created two collections. The first was the IPARTERV group's 1960s art, which exhibited at the MEO only once in 2001. The second, which he started specifically with the MEO in mind, took up the most contemporary art. Kováts, who also owned the commercial Blitz gallery (founded in 1991, operating at the MEO headquarters from 2001) was critical of the Hungarian art market and the lack of financial facilities for collectors of contemporary art following the closure of the institution.

In 2004, another Hungarian collector, Gábor Kovács – first and foremost a businessman and economist – created KOGART (see Atlas 2.1). The KOGART gallery exhibits mainly nineteenth- and twentieth-century art; however contemporary art, which it has been collecting systematically since 2008, is the most important from the point of view of patronage. KOGART was created in the context of the "Arts & Business" program and is the first Hungarian manifestation of the concept whose origins are in Great Britain. The ambition of the Gábor Kovács Art Foundation was to persuade approximately a hundred companies registered in Hungary to join the initiative of building art collections. For this purpose, it was seeking to transfer 1 million tax-deductible forints (about 4,000 euros) yearly, over five years. The Ministry of Education and Culture also joined the program, committing to contribute 1 million forints (up to 50 million annually) for each 2 million obtained in this way (Fertőszögi 2008: 2). A five-member jury recommended approximately a hundred works for purchase each year. The program functioned only for three years. In 2015, on the basis of an agreement with the Ministry of Human Resources, KOGART organized thirteen exhibitions annually between 2015 and 2018, with resources provided by the government, in Budapest, in the provinces and abroad.

The collection of Hungarian contemporary art known as Irokéz, created by local entrepreneurs Gábor Pados and Zsolt Pajor, was located in Szombathely. The first works entered their collections in the early 1990s, and in 2001 they were presented for the first time to the public in the Irokéz Galéria. Works by artists formerly associated with the artistic group Újlak, which at the turn of the 1980s and 1990s belonged to the circle of Budapest subcultures, form the center of the collection. They understood the collector's task as to support artists – often young, whose work had not yet entered the institutional circulation and which was less well known to the public, particularly as the founders did not conceive of creating a collection at all (Szoboszlai n.d.). The Irokéz Gallery and co-hosted by the collectors the acb Gallery in Budapest are rather sites where Hungarian contemporary artists' work may be presented other than collections per se. In 2008, the collection was exhibited in a large group show at the Hungarian National Gallery and later in Műcsarnok, MODEM and House of Arts in Veszprém. The acb Gallery in turn gained the leading position in the Hungarian gallery scene, with a ResearchLab opened in 2015 strengthening its critical role as a counterbalance to publicly funded institutions.

In Poland, several collectors of modern and contemporary art display their works publicly, and sometimes also run commercial galleries. The biggest collectors, apart from Kulczyk, are Teresa and Andrzej Starmach, who established the Starmach Gallery in 1989. For ten years, it operated on the Main Market Square in Krakow, and later was moved to the Podgórze district. For many years, it was an important place for putting Polish exhibitions on the map, especially for those artists associated with the Krakow Group, artists working in geometrical abstraction, and international artists. The collection was presented comprehensively for the first time in 2009 at the major exhibition at the National Museum in Krakow, *Collection. Twenty Years of The Starmach Gallery*. Among collector-gallerists, Marta Tarabuła and Jan Michalski, who ran who ran Galeria Zderzak in Krakow, also created an important collection of contemporary art. The gallery was established in 1985 in a private home, and since 1989 is a commercial gallery. In 2006 the aTAK Gallery opened under the auspices of the Polish Modern Art Foundation, and financed by the collector Krzysztof Musiał. The gallery promotes contemporary Polish artists, but also shows the Musiał collection. Its largest presentation took the form of a traveling exhibition, *Records of Changes. Polish art in Krzysztof Musiał's collection* in 2007–2008 at the National Museums in Wrocław, Poznań, and Krakow, and in the Zachęta Gallery in Warsaw and the Pomeranian Dukes' Castle in Szczecin.

Private art centers

Private art centers, which are not connected to collections, are much fewer in number. The gallery of contemporary art Atlas Sztuki (see Atlas 3.9), in fact a small art center, was the fruit of private capital in Łódź. It was founded in

2003 by Andrzej Walczak, one of the then-presidents and co-owner of the Atlas company (which produces adhesives and mortars). The private gallery, being a place for temporary exhibitions of contemporary art, has operated using an organizational model rarely used in Central Europe: it was not run by a foundation, association or private person, but a commercial law firm, Atlas Sztuki LLC. Neither the gallery nor its founder collected art. As Jacek Michalak, the gallery's manager, says: "Andrzej Walczak wanted this place to be a living place, so that a lot would happen, so that many people would come to see big events take place. That's what he spent the money on and that pleased him – creating a positive atmosphere. The issue of collecting was totally irrelevant" (Interview with Jacek Michalak 2017). Regardless of its highly praised exhibitions program, Atlas Sztuki closed in 2017.

The Czech Republic created the most art centers (all of which are presented in Chapter 4), the oldest being the Egon Schiele Art Center in Český Krumlov started by the foundation in 1992 in an adapted brewery. In 2003, the FUTURA Contemporary Art Center was established in Prague, and since 2005, the Karlín Studios have been part of the same project. Since 2007, MeetFactory has been operating in its second location. In 2008, the long-awaited DOX Centre for Contemporary Art was launched, a private space for contemporary art exhibitions located in a converted factory building.

Private collections in public museums

Private collections are often conveyed to public museums in the form of gifts or loans, which usually does not result in the creation of a new facility or even rooms specifically for their presentation. Shortly after opening, MOCAK included first director, Maria Anna Potocka's contemporary art collection. The collection, begun in 1973, consists of about a thousand works. As Potocka states,

> The starting point was performance art and conceptualism, but there was also a lot of painting by among others, artists from the Krakow Group and the Ładnie Group; there were also sculptures and video. The collection was given unconditionally and encompasses a whole. At the display there is no information indicating that the object comes from my collection. That would be indecent.
>
> (Interview with Maria Anna Potocka 2017)

The collection of art that forms the basis of the MODEM Modern and Contemporary Arts Center in Debrecen (see Atlas 2.4) was founded at the beginning of the twentieth century by Sámuel Lusztig. His collector's passion was continued by his grandson Péter Antal, a lawyer by profession. The collection surveys the entire twentieth century, as well as the beginning of the twenty-first, and includes nearly all of the most important tendencies in Hungarian art. Antal loaned his collection for a ten-year period to the city authorities, who in turn made the newly created MODEM the custodian of the collection. At MODEM's inaugural exhibition in 2006, more than four hundred works from the collection were shown. The exhibition occupied three floors in the building; one work – Antal Lakner's *Iceland army* – was also shown outside, in a window attached to the façade. The organizational model for MODEM changed three times (the center was established as an autonomous institution; in 2015 it was incorporated into the structure of Déri Múzeum; it again became an independent institution in 2018). The collector, not always supportive of the museum's program decisions, decided to withdraw the loan after ten years and make the collection available only for the purpose of exhibitions.

Summary

Institutions dealing with contemporary art in Central Europe – museums, art centers, non-commercial galleries – are numerous, but they occupy only a small segment of the landscape, which is still dominated by public institutions. In particular, museums and art centers are scarce, as these require substantial financial resources for both their creation and subsequent maintenance. In many cases, collectors try to cooperate with local authorities, which takes the form of cost sharing. Two unsuccessful approaches to the construction of the Grażyna Kulczyk museum show that the construction of a private museum is not straightforward. Often the key to success is investments from the public domain, which are not easy to procure. In Poland, this was successfully carried out only in relation to the Museum of the History of Polish Jews in Warsaw, which was established on the basis of public-private partnership. Many private initiatives cannot stand the test of time: AMoYA closed after not even two years of operation, MEOs after six; Wannieck Gallery/Richard Adam Gallery, nine; Art Stations Gallery, twelve; Atlas Sztuki, thirteen, and the Milan Dobeš Museum, fifteen.

The Czech Republic and Slovakia contain the largest number of private galleries and art centers. Furthermore, openings are being planned in the Czech Republic on a constant basis. Jiří Fajt, General Director of the National Gallery in Prague, sees the rise in the number of private collections in relation to the enrichment of society. He says:

> It is very much based on the individual situation of these persons. They have become rich and invested a lot of money into art collecting, so they have quite important art collections of modern and contemporary art, mostly of Czech twentieth-century art. Those collectors are now thinking about how to present it to the public.
>
> (Interview with Jiří Fajt 2018)

It is symptomatic that there are almost no such initiatives in the largest country in the region, Poland. Stanisław Ruksza, director of the TRAFO in

Szczecin, pointed to a reverse situation in Poland as compared to that in the Czech Republic:

> Social stratification, which affects the whole world, means that there are many rich people who have the financial capital to, for example, invest in art, but they do not. It is a small number of people. This also translates into a functioning art market, which in fact does not exist in Poland.
>
> (Interview with Stanisław Ruksza 2017)

Kulczyk's example shows that a museum based on a private collection would have to be fully private, as public entities are not interested in cooperating in their undertaking. The model closest to that idea in Central Europe is implemented in the Museum Kampa.

Gábor Ébli (2016b), looking at private collections throughout Eastern Europe, indicates that private collectors offer a platform for the discussion of contemporary culture:

> with the economic and other reasons in public life pushing politics and official cultural representation in quite a few East European countries towards conservative, nationalistic values, the responsibility of private actors has grown to help articulate universal and critical messages of contemporary art; more and more private museums, awards, schemes of patronage are taking over functions of public discourse, and act on behalf of civil society.

In Central Europe, primarily DOX and the former Atlas Sztuki and Art Stations Gallery – so, non-collecting institutions (not counting the smaller, non-commercial galleries) – represent this critical platform.

7 Evolutions and revolutions in grand national museums
Four case studies

The situation of new museums created since the 1990s differs significantly from museums emerging from the traditions of the nineteenth century, the beginning of the twentieth century, or during the communist period. The history and tradition of the latter may in fact be ballast for many areas of activity from management to programming. All of these earlier museums stood at the threshold of necessary change with the arrival of the new century and accompanying museum boom. On the one hand, it was necessary to invest in infrastructure (modernization and development) that failed to meet modern needs with respect to security, sufficiency of warehouse and exhibition space, and audience expectations for reception areas and recreation spaces. On the other hand, it was also necessary to change management models, reformulate missions, and shift emphases. Without exception, museums in the twenty-first century confronted a new model for participation in culture.

The subject of this chapter is national museums in four Central European capitals: the National Museum in Warsaw, the National Gallery in Prague, the Slovak National Gallery in Bratislava and the Hungarian National Gallery and the Museum of Fine Arts in Budapest. From these, I have identified four fundamental problems contemporary museums face. These are the problems of criticality, management, infrastructure, and transformation. Although the given examples are not museums of modern or contemporary art, but rather those that collect and exhibit art from an historical perspective from antiquity to the present, the issue of contemporary art occupies an important place in each of the presented discussions.

Warsaw: a call for the critical museum

In 2009, Piotr Piotrowski, a well-known and respected modern art historian in Central Europe and author of canonical books, became the director of the National Museum in Warsaw (Muzeum Narodowe w Warszawie, MNW). The museum was in crisis in 2007, when as a result of a dispute between the director and his deputy, the Minister of Culture fired the director and announced a search to fill this position, which laid vacant for nearly a year and a half; the minister did not accept the proposed candidate. The Board of

Trustees was to conduct a search for another candidate in the meantime, but this ended in a failed search. Piotrowski, who had previous museum experience (in 1992–1997, he was a curator of contemporary art at the National Museum in Poznań), was invited to submit a program proposal. He then submitted his vision of the critical museum, which was first approved by the Board and later by the Minister of Culture.

Piotrowski took over the management of the museum, whose main problems were finance, internal conflict, and insufficient exhibition and storage space. In this atmosphere, he began to implement a new programming model that was revolutionary for a traditional and conservative institution. This was based on three elements:

> their activity in the public space, their self-critique, and as regards changes of artistic geography. First of all, the museum's mission must take into account the changes going on in the present world, such as democratization, the cosmopolitan politicization of culture, European integration and its limitations, the interaction of local and global factors, and the problem of social minorities, migrations and social inequalities. [. . .] Second, a new identity for the museum should be forged by the critique of the art museum's tradition and of the practices of the key encyclopedic museums. Finally, what should be recognized by this new museum is a non-traditional artistic geography, favoring the margins instead of centers of western artistic culture, and challenging the hegemony of the West, which has been legitimized both by tradition and by the contemporary global tourist industry.
>
> (Murawska-Muthesius and Piotrowski 2015: 1–2)

A museum operating on the basis of these principles was intended as an attractive counter-proposal for museums filled with canonical works of art, and Western museums in particular. The program also had to compensate for the dearth of masterpieces.

The idea of the critical museum is not new, but it was innovative to apply it to an encyclopedic historical museum with a tradition dating back to the nineteenth century whose collections ranged from ancient to modern times. The criticality that the MNW was to cultivate traditionally is associated with contemporary art museums (MoCAs). Piotrowski called for a living museum, one constituting the collections and their history which would be reread, in turn generating new questions (including those that are uncomfortable); a museum that would question the canon and its values, and would open up discussion. He said: "Modern society does not need fossils, which is what most Polish museums are, but a partner that will accompany it in reading the past" (Polityka w muzeum 2012: 97). He believed that every museum, not only those devoted to the latest works, should look critically at its past and discuss it, and not petrify it or treat it as axiom or sacred. "In my opinion, historical and artistic museums have a huge role to play in building critical knowledge about history, in overhauling and building alternative perspectives on the history of art, on the question of canon and organization of knowledge", he said in an interview (Muzeum krytyczne to nie dyskursywny ornament 2011). In the same interview he even said, "only a critical mission can save museums". The idea of the critical museum is combined with the type of museum-as-forum, which traditionally stands in opposition to the museum-as-temple, and the museum-as-entertainment.

Critical museum, according to Piotrowski, was presented in the strategy of MNW. Its implementation was *Interventions* in the permanent exhibitions and only two temporary exhibitions, *Ars Homo Erotica* and *Mediators*, which ran during Piotrowski's short tenure. The first exhibition made the broadest impact on Polish and foreign media. It was in a sense the new director's program manifesto and attracted a large audience. Its aim was to "show the repressed homoerotic tradition in the history of art and restore the works dealing with this issue, relegated to storage by museologists" (Piotrowski 2011b: 84). The exhibition deliberately coincided with EuroPride, the first LGBT parade held in post-communist Europe. In this way, the museum was supposed to return the history, culture, and social life of sexual minorities to the debate (Piotrowski 2011b: 84). This exhibition has shown that not everyone, either within or outside of the museum (trustees, a sector of the audience) were ready for a museum (at least, not one bearing the adjective, "national") which is "capable of taking a stance on key issues in Polish or East European societies, [of being] an active participant in [the] process of developing democracy" (Piotrowski 2015: 137).

Simultaneously with program reform, Piotrowski began to rationalize the institution's structure and mode of operation that included, among other things, the reduction of posts (a result of the museum's financial problems) and a reduction in the number of departments from eighteen to eight. His vision regarding the museum's substantive and organizational management met with strong employee resistance (calls for the director's resignation appeared in letters to the Trustees and the prime minister on the anonymous blog, "Phantom in the Museum" [Upiór w museum], maintained by an employee). In 2010, when for no stated reason the museum's Trustees did not accept the "Activity and development strategy" created by the management (as an extension of the institution's originating concept), Piotrowski resigned.

National media regularly reported on the dispute within and around the museum. The essence of the problem (apart from a number of other issues, such as the development plans for the building) was the opposition to the novel idea of implementing the model for the critical museum in Poland (especially by an incumbent and conservative museum) and to the change in the organizational status quo. Piotrowski admitted in an interview:

> during these twenty years since the fall of communism, nothing happened
> here, these museums are stuck in communism; they – their structure, the

whole mechanism of functioning, is a mechanism inherited from the socialist institution. This is completely neglected in discussions about the state of museology, simply because that world is uncomfortable with it. People who are against this reform have, as I say, justified fears, specific fears; they fear for their jobs. They do not raise the fact that this museum – and in general museums in Poland – has not undergone any reform since the times of the Polish People's Republic.

(Insurance Policy 2010)

A similar statement was also made in the previously mentioned "Strategy":

> The new leadership of the National Museum in Warsaw found the museum in a state of deep collapse. In the twenty years since the fall of communism, no significant changes have been made here, and especially no significant modernization projects have been undertaken to confront the historical processes taking place both in the country and in Europe and the world. [. . .] In fact, besides of course other staffing, 2009 was not much different from 1989.

(Strategia działalności i rozwoju 2010–2020, 2010)

Piotrowski's fifteen-months-long directorate caused a much-needed ferment in the museum environment, raising the issue of the goals and missions of contemporary museums, their role in society, and their place in public debate. The failure at the directorial level opened up a crucial debate within Polish culture, while in turn paving the way for other museums to follow suit. The POLIN Museum of the History of Polish Jews in Warsaw is an example of an institution that is successfully following this path. An important contribution Piotrowski made to this debate is his book, *Muzeum krytyczne* [The Critical Museum] (2011b) in which he reckons with his time at the MNW, as well as another with Katarzyna Murawska-Muthesius, deputy director of the MNW, with whom he co-authored the critical museum program, *From Museum Critique to the Critical Museum* (2015), whose great value is its diverse perspectives, Western and East-Central European.

Prague: a controversial style of management and program building

Though not reflected in its name, the branch of the National Gallery in Prague (NG) located in the Trade Fair Palace (see Atlas 1.10) is actually a museum of modern and contemporary art. For many years, it was the embodiment of bad management and the decline of contemporary culture, and a source of disrepute for the Czechs in the international arena. All ills were associated with its Director-General Milan Knížák, who occupied this position continuously from 1999 until the end of 2010. In the 1960s and 1970s, Knížák was a well-known artist, a creator of happenings, installations, and land art. As a member of Fluxus, he organized the first concert of the artists' network in Czechoslovakia in 1966. He is also a painter and sculptor; in 2007, he had a solo exhibition at the Mánes Exhibition Hall in Prague. The NG under Knížák's directorship is a case for a controversial style of management and programming.

The National Gallery in Prague has always included contemporary art, both in its collection and its exhibition program. However, until the 1990s, the museum lacked its own building. In 2018, the NG owned seven historical buildings in Prague (and two outside Prague), each housing a separate collection according to a period or theme. In addition, temporary exhibitions are held in the Waldstein Riding School building (renovated in 2000). In 1995, the Trade Fair Palace was opened up to the public, with its collection of late nineteenth-, twentieth-, and twenty-first-century art. Prior to that time, the collection of modern French art hung in the Sternberg Palace, while temporary exhibitions of modern and contemporary art took place in the Kinský Palace and the Riding School. These details illustrate the complexity and vastness of the Czech National Gallery. Currently, contemporary art is only one among many areas represented in the museum, although since acquiring its own building, it has become the most visible one. Each collection had its own director; however, the Director-General, whose office and administration are located in the Kinský Palace in the Old Town, and whose artistic interests were – in the case of Knížák – predominantly centered on contemporary art, oversees the whole.

Despite an emphasis on contemporary art, Czech artists and art critics repeatedly demanded that the Director-General be dismissed. Critical comments about Knížák abounded, not only in art magazines but also in the daily press. Noemi Smolíková, an art historian, art critic and curator, and lecturer at the University of Cologne, spoke of the "Knížák phenomenon" in the public sphere, "which [was] a disease that art suffer[ed] from and [was] spreading to other parts of Czech culture" (Chuchma 2010). A campaign was organized in Prague in order to replace the General Director. According to Vojtěch Lahoda, an art historian who for many years was the Director of the Institute of Art History at the Czech Academy of Sciences, Knížák:

> most probably continues his happening. He is uncommunicative, arrogant and egocentric. Above all he is an artist. He concentrates only on concrete issues, on which, as an artist, he should of course focus. But if one is such an artist, and if one prefers only certain issues above others, then it is very difficult to be a director of an art gallery. Three months after he took a position as Director-General he approved an acquisition of his own artwork by the National Gallery, whereas previously there had been no decision about such a purchase. Three large sculptures stand before the Trade Fair Palace – one of them was created by Knížák.
>
> (Interview with Vojtěch Lahoda 2008)

Press releases on the subject confirmed this arrogance, as Knížák's response to any criticism was to counter-attack. In 2002, negative sentiment accumulated around the gallery inspired an artistic group called "Pode Bal" to react. In their project titled *Institutionalized Art*, the group members affixed a piece of a specially cut brick to the glass surface of the façade of the Veletržní palác, which from a distance appeared to have been thrown at the glass – yet without breaking it; the other half of the brick was attached to the inner side of the glass pane. In their press release the group said:

> We want to urge the management of the National Gallery to restrain [sic!] from its arrogance and to stop ignoring the opinions of the public and especially of the professionals in the field. We appeal to the directors of the institution to promote open dialog even with those whose opinion might differ from that of Mr. Knížák. We'd like to remind everyone, that the National Gallery is a public institution, publicly funded for the benefit of all and not a house of services for a self-invited elite.
>
> (Pode Bal 1998–2008, 2008: 39)[1]

For the opening of the Center of Contemporary Art FUTURA, David Černý prepared a piece addressing the connections between the world of culture and politics. In the garden by the gallery, he placed gigantic sculptures of two men, bent over and with their buttocks protruding. In the openings between the buttocks, video screens were installed. In order to see them it was necessary to climb a ladder approximately two meters above ground and look inside the figures. The film shown on the screens depicted men wearing masks depicting the Czech President Václav Klaus and the Director-General of the NG, who fed each other with pap to the tune "We Are the Champions" by Queen. In 2008, Knížák inspired another artistic group, Guma Guar, known for subversive actions and commentaries on political and social events. The Vernon Gallery, located in the vicinity of the Trade Fair Palace, held their exhibition entitled *Milan Knížák – Podivný Kelt* (Milan Knížák: an Outlandish Celt), where the group presented paintings and objects drawing on Knížák's own output. The aim of the exhibition was to criticize the influence that the Director of the NG had on the Czech art scene, as well as to highlight the commercial aspect of art (the showcased artwork was for sale). For the duration of the exhibition, the group changed its name to Skupina Milan Knížák (Milan Knížák's Group). In an interview, the group members said that it was unacceptable for a practicing artist to be the Director of the NG, since this led to conflicts of interest, and that one of the most shocking problems was Knížák's sculpture displayed by the entrance to the museum representing the situation when "Milan Knížák buys from Milan Knížák" (Machalická 2008). A few months after the exhibition closed, Knížák took the group to court accusing them of fraud, violation of authorial rights and slander.

In 2009, on the occasion of the tenth jubilee of Knížák's position as Director, Jan Skřivánek ventured to sum up his managerial work in *Art+Antiques* magazine. He emphasized that when in 1997 Knížák left the position of dean of the Academy of Fine Arts, which he had held since the political breakthrough, he was regarded as "a brave reformer who is not afraid of conflicts and openly expresses his opinions" (Skřivánek 2009). When in 1997 the newspaper *Lidové noviny* carried out a survey among its readers about the best successor to Václav Havel as President, the majority of respondents chose Václav Klaus and Milan Knížák. Knížák also appeared in popular TV programs (as a jury member at the Miss of the Czech Republic pageant and in Do-re-mi), and took part in televised debates. In 1998, he ran for the Senate from the ODS (Občanská demokratická strana – the Civic Democratic Party) list, but lost in the second round. It was at that time that rumors started to circulate that he was to be given the position of Director-General of the National Gallery as a "consolation prize". In actuality, a competition for the post was carried out, in which according to the decision by the independent selective committee Knížák ranked third; however, he won the position in the second stage of selection organized by the officials from the Ministry of Culture.

Skřivánek stressed that Knížák's undeniable success was the opening of a new permanent exhibition in 2000; a new presentation of art from 1930 to the present was added to the two floors devoted to the art from 1800–1930. However, the director's managerial style led to the resignations of directors of the individual collections – first the director of the pre-modern art collection stepped down, followed in early 2001 by the director of the modern and contemporary art collection, Katarína Rusnáková. In an interview for the *Ateliér* biweekly, she stated:

> I have to admit that I was taken aback by the reorganization initiated in February 2000, which deprived directors of collections of some basic competences. Suddenly it became difficult to negotiate anything, especially exhibitions with partners from abroad.
>
> (After Skřivánek 2009)

In turn, Knížák stated that Rusnáková wanted the institution to function like a Kunsthalle, where temporary exhibitions are held, whereas in his opinion the purpose of a museum was above all to safeguard collections and present them to the public. Smolíková observed that the NG's operations model was still rooted in the heritage of totalitarianism, when the institution was led by Jiří Kotalík (1967–1990), and the subsequent directors failed to overcome the obsolete hierarchical structure. According to her, similar institutions did not survive long operating in this way. In her view, directors and curators of collections ought to have much more freedom but should also be responsible for their decisions (Chuchma 2010). There had been attempts to detach the Veletržní palác from the structure of the NG as a separate institution, but Knížák opposed, saying that their maintenance would be much more expensive (Interview with Milan Knížák 2008). His assumption was that the role of the NG was not to focus on the contemporary creation of local artists – for this purpose, in his view, a Kunsthalle should be established in Prague.

> We need a genuine old factory space that would have money at its disposal to present contemporary art with all its monumentalism, to realize large-scale projects. The National Gallery is not in a position to do this. First of all, we do not have such a space, and, secondly, we cannot concentrate only on what is happening at the moment. . . . Prague and the Czech Republic in general need a large number of small galleries, many exhibitions, sale of artworks, and many small artistic actions. We have enough national institutions.
>
> (Interview with Milan Knížák 2008)

Soon after this comment was made, the long-awaited DOX Centre for Contemporary Art was opened. Despite protests, controversies, accusations, and appeals for a replacement for the Director-General by organizing a competition for the post, Milan Knížák managed to keep his position for a long time, and what is more, was appreciated by the authorities, demonstrated by the fact that he was awarded the Medal of Merit by President Klaus in 2010. Knížák was to have said then: "I am a controversial figure, and as a controversial figure I received this award. And I received it from the controversial President Klaus" (Falvey 2010). The long-awaited replacement on the post of Director-General was controversial, too. From the beginning of 2011, this role was taken over by Vladimír Rösel, the former Managing Director of a bank, who had no education in the field of art history and no experience in managing a museum. He said in an interview: "It's important to recognize that executive management means above all assigning other people [sic; delegating]. If people generally expect the general manager to decide absolutely everything, that is a bad model. And that is the current model. A change of system must take place" (Šenk 2011). Rösel did not stay in this job for long; another change came in 2013. Jiří Fajt, who took over the post, aimed to intensify cooperation with foreign curators and specialists. However, in order to do this, it is necessary to change the legal status of the museum, allowing for internationally competitive pay. Fajt stated:

> When I came to the National Gallery, I indeed gave my full attention to the Trade Fair Palace. I decided to focus on this building and invite the young generation here. The building was almost empty when I took over, and now you see many young people there who visit the collections and stay in the coffee shop.
>
> (Interview with Jiří Fajt 2018)

In 2018, the process of choosing an architect for the internal reconstruction concept of the Trade Fair Palace began. According to the director, its purpose is to change the museum "into an internationally relevant, acknowledged center of modern and contemporary art".

Bratislava: struggling for contemporary art – intersections between the Slovak National Gallery and Kunsthalle

The Slovak National Gallery in Bratislava (SNG), the main art museum in Slovakia with the widest and most comprehensive collection, serves here as a case study of both the issue of infrastructure and the issue of transformation to meet the requirements of modern museums. In contrast to its counterpart in the Czech Republic, the SNG houses and presents its collection in one building (not including its specialized branches outside Bratislava); hence the twentieth- and twenty-first-century art is an element within a larger whole. Moreover, for a long time in Bratislava (and in Slovakia in general), there was no institution like a Kunsthalle devoted to the presentation of contemporary art; through its activity, the SNG filled an infrastructural lacuna. The internal changes in the museum have to do not only with the institution's need for organizational adjustment to the new socio-economic conditions, but also with the need to have adequate space for the role it would play.

The core of the museum is located in the so-called Water Barracks built in 1759–1763 on the Danube for the river police. Four wings were erected; later, owing to river regulations, the wing situated along the riverbank was torn down. In 1950–1955, the SNG adapted the three-wing building with an open courtyard for the exhibition purposes. In 1969–1977, a new wing was added on the former site of the dismantled wing according to a design by Vladimír Dedeček, which was intended visually to enclose the courtyard. In reality, however, the space remains open because the new wing is suspended, joining the buildings only from the first floor and upward. The exhibition space in the three floors of the "bridge" used to house the gallery's collection; however, in 2001, the suspended part of the building was closed down for safety reasons (inability to maintain stable climactic conditions in the interior and a cracked roof). Further, in 1990, the gallery gained the late-nineteenth century Esterházy Palace next to the barracks for exhibition purposes (the palace was renovated in 1994 and 2005). In the 1990s, the palace presented a twentieth-century art collection. When the space of the modernist wing was closed down, the museum lost the space for temporary exhibitions; therefore, it was necessary to change the arrangement. The Gothic art section had occupied two small rooms where a permanent exhibition of twentieth-century art is now placed. The gallery calls this exhibition "The Non-Permanent Exposition of Art in the 20th-century+", because in accordance with the original plan, it was meant to be installed there for a year during the renovation period. The exhibition consisted of two parts: Modernism (the 1920s and 1930s) and Late

Modernism (the 1960s and 1970s). In addition, contemporary art from the 1980s onward appears in the form of interventions into the permanent exhibitions of art from earlier periods.

After the Velvet Revolution, the gallery's new management set out to reorganize the internal structure of the museum, as well as make efforts to gain new exhibition space and renovate buildings it already owned. Zuzana Bartošová (director from 1990–1992) initiated a mass acquisition of works by censored artists, thus filling in the gaps in the art collection from the 1960s, 1970s, and 1980s; she also began organizing monographic exhibitions of artists not previously exhibited, and finally dividing the gallery's collection into three units: the Pre-Modern and Modern Art Gallery, the Contemporary Art Gallery, and the Gallery of Architecture, Applied Arts and Design. The next Director, Juraj Žáry (1992–1996), reversed these changes: he returned to a centralized plan and limited the scope of purchases of contemporary art. Instead, he established a permanent exhibition of Slovak art from the 1960s onwards. In turn, Katarína Bajcurová (1999–2009) restored the museum's three-section concept with a minor difference: she separated the pre-modern art from modern art to create a combined gallery together with contemporary art. After the planned reconstruction and expansion, each gallery is meant to have a separate building (Bajcurová 2008).

The first major discussion about the future of Dedeček's "bridge" took place in 2001. The discussants considered two possible scenarios for the closed-down wing with 1,800 square meters of exhibition space, e.g. reconstruction and improvement of its technical condition or dismantling it. Bajcurová stated, "architectural value must not be identified with poor-quality technical realization which was the case in this building". In her view, dismantling the gallery would be:

> a particular form of iconoclasm [. . .]. It is often said that this building is a symbol of socialism and that is why it should be taken down. This is mere demagogy, because there are very many symbols of socialism in the vicinity of the SNG, and yet we do not want to demolish them.
>
> (Budúcnost' premostenia 2001: 4)

The building's architecture has caused controversy among Bratislava's residents since the moment it was created, on account of its expressive, Brutalist form resembling an upside-down staircase that contrasts with the adjacent historical architecture. Stylistically, the building echoes the Whitney Museum of American Art in New York designed by Marcel Breuer and Hamilton Smith and opened in 1966. The majority of specialists engaged in the debate were in favor of reconstructing the building. In 2003, a competition was organized for a conceptual design for the rebuilding and modernization of the SNG complex (there were two winners: the KOPA team – Juraj Koban and Štefan Pacák, and the team of Ilja Skoček jr., Matúš Vallo and Oliver Sadovský). The winners of the 2005 design competition for the reconstruction and expansion of the SNG were Martin Kusy and Pavol Paňák from ARCHITEKTI BKPŠ, who, according to the jury, treated the existing structure by Dedeček with respect, while at the same time giving it a contemporary and noble character ([Slovenská národná galéria] 2005: 22). After the reconstruction, the former amphitheater is to function as a glazed multi-functional atrium, which can serve as a space for large-scale installations and events. The courtyard will be used as city public garden with summer pavilion. The newly opened SNG will have 6,000 square meters of space for its program activity. Due to the economic crisis of 2009, realization of the project was suspended, and reconstruction started only in 2015.

For years, there was a major expectation that the SNG would function as an exhibition space for contemporary art, as such a space long had been lacking in Bratislava. Alexandra Kusá, who in 2009 managed the Modern and Contemporary Art Gallery in the SNG, said:

> We try not to concentrate on contemporary art, and for this reason we are a little more conservative. A National Gallery should not be a Kunsthalle. We present for instance art from the 1960s, we organize exhibitions devoted to older artists, and as a result we are not very popular among contemporary artists.
>
> (Interview with Alexandra Kusá 2009)

Not only was there no museum of contemporary art in Bratislava, but also there were no museums devoted to architecture, design, or photography. This may give the impression that the national gallery with its cross-disciplinary holdings across all artistic periods masquerades as a substitute for these institutions. Kusá, however, already serving as director of the SNG, disagrees, saying that this is the role of the universal art survey museum:

> Since the SNG was established we have had a transdisciplinary focus and thanks to that, our projects now are more multidisciplinary. When we exhibit architecture we do it with photography, because we have both collections. We do a lot of art historical exhibitions and a lot of exhibitions where we have mixed media – old art and contemporary art, painting, photography, architecture. We are not trying to be a museum of architecture or a contemporary museum; we are trying to be a contemporary national gallery with a very wide focus.
>
> (Interview with Alexandra Kusá 2017)

This does not change the fact, however, that the SNG is not large enough even for the realization of its basic functions – since 2001 it has been limited to one building with three floors with an area of approximately 1,200 square meters; one floor is devoted to the display of the collection and two floors to temporary exhibitions. The excessive expectations are additionally exacerbated by the building's poor condition, which led in the early twenty-first century to a considerable reduction of exhibition space, as well as the virtual elimination of modern and contemporary art from Bratislava's cultural scene.

The Czech-Slovak edition of *Flash Art* (2007) stated:

> While numerous cities in Central, Eastern and Southern Europe in addition to national galleries have also museums of contemporary art or at least a *Kunsthalle*, in Bratislava today there is only the Slovak National Gallery, which only partly and unsystematically makes up for the activities of all the above mentioned institutions.
>
> (Bude v Bratislave Kunsthalle? 2007–2008: 16)

The necessity of reconstruction and redevelopments for the SNG and the need to establish a Kunsthalle in Bratislava (see Atlas 4.2) caused genuine turmoil towards the end of the first decade of the twenty-first century among art historians, museum workers, and artists concerned with the future of Slovak culture. This turmoil resulted in the social initiative formed in early 2010, Twenty Years After the Velvet Revolution Did Not Happen (Dvadsat' Rokov od Nežnej Neprebehlo), whose aim was to generate a wide discussion on the burning questions that had affected Slovak culture for many years.[2] As the well-known Slovak artist Rudolf Sikora has said, a Kunsthalle is simply indispensable in a large city: "a metropolis without a *Kunsthalle* is not a metropolis. [. . .] Without modern exhibition spaces Bratislava cannot call itself a large city" (Kizáková 2010).

Kunsthalle in Bratislava was voiced at various occasions throughout the 1990s, bit its official history began before 1997, when the representatives of Slovak artists and theoreticians proposed the creation of such an institution in the city. In early 1999 at a session of the culture and media committee of the National Council, a discussion took place about the potential transformation of the House of Art built in the 1960s for the purposes of exhibiting visual arts, located in the city center, into a Kunsthalle; two years later, the Minister of Culture, Milan Kňažko, proposed that a Kunsthalle be created within the framework of the National Educational Centre. In 2003, the representatives of the Slovak branch of the AICA appealed to the ministry to separate the authority of the House of Art from that of the Educational Centre, and to turn the latter into an independent institution with its own legal identity. In March 2004, the work began on devising a statute for an House of Art, a so-called Kunsthalle that was intended to be a non-profit organization financed by several sources – chiefly the state. Its opening was planned for the end of that year. However, the following year brought with it legal and organizational problems, for it turned out that in accordance with the law, the state cannot finance non-profit institutions. In late 2006, the next Minister of Culture, Marek Maďarič, announced that the ministry would create an independent Gallery of Contemporary Art (Dvadsat' Rokov od Nežnej Neprebehlo). In 2007, the first exhibitions were held in the House of Art, and all exhibitions came under the jurisdiction of an independent program council of the House of Art; however, it lacked institutional resources. In December 2008, the Ministry of Culture accepted a "Plan for the Creation of the Slovak Visual Arts Centre", which recommended that the new institution be established on 1 January 2010. Despite the fact that successive and increasing formal and administrative difficulties had been overcome, the planned Kunsthalle did not emerge at that time.

Richard Gregor, who was working in the Ministry of Culture before becoming chief curator in the Kunsthalle, dealt with several projects processes in the ministry. He recalls:

> I was very much opposing when one minister came and said that we need to build a new house. Everybody who was slightly rational must have understood that this would never happen. If for twenty years we could not turn an already standing house in the center into a Kunsthalle, we would never build anything like it.
>
> (Interview with Richard Gregor 2018)

The struggle for a Kunsthalle ended in early 2014 when Kunsthalle Bratislava officially opened. Its program aimed to concentrate on big art shows spanning not less than a half of the total exhibition space that was 2,000 square meters. It operated within the framework of the Slovak Centre of Visual Arts, which itself is part of the National Culture House financed by the Ministry of Culture. This successful event, however, did not mark the end of the new institution's battle. Soon after opening, it was plagued by problems of a mainly organizational character (pertaining to bureaucracy and communication with its umbrella institution). In effect, in 2016, the ministry placed it under the aegis of the SNG. Alexandra Kusá admitted:

> It was a big surprise for me. There were some problems with leadership of the institution and after its transformation we found out there was no program at all. It was really hard, everyone was watching, the budget is mostly gone and you have to perform something.
>
> (Interview with Alexandra Kusá 2017)

Initial programming prepared by the SNG served as a lifeline, Kusa explained, offering exhibitions and educational programs to compensate for the lack of planned events:

> Now after one and a half year we do not interfere with the program. I am working very hard now to find a way to make them independent. I do not think it is a good solution to keep both institutions together. It is too much power.

There is no indication, either on the SNG's or the Kunsthalle's websites, that they are formally one institution or that there is any relation between them.

Gregor sees the reason for the prolonged process of establishing the Kunsthalle in the failure of the Ministry of Finances and the Ministry of Culture to reach a mutual agreement. He also points out that the time wasted on the struggle of making a new institution paradoxically might have not been a negative thing, as it strengthened galleries in the regions. Expectations for the institution may be compared to those connected to the Museum of Modern Art in Warsaw. Gregor says: "We tried to establish it for too long, and finally when it was established everybody was expecting something else. It was destined to a non-success to a certain way" (Interview with Richard Gregor 2018).

Budapest: home of blockbusters and controversial museum mergers

The Museum of Fine Arts in Budapest also serves as a case study for the broader topic of museum infrastructural development and transformation (especially managerial). The scale of change is comparable to that in the museum in Bratislava, but its character is different.

In 2004, László Baán became the director of the Museum of Fine Arts in Budapest. In just a few years, he managed to transform a museum focused primarily on a Hungarian audience into a museum that presented blockbuster exhibitions. He achieved good financial results and reached an international audience (see interview with László Baán, Chapter 2). He was able to fulfill the hope that Hungarian museums could overcome their previous limitations, to be inaugurated into the twenty-first century. Baán said that when he took on the position, "the museum which has the greatest collection of international art in Hungary had its internet website available only in Hungarian. It did not even have separate sections for education, communication and exhibitions". His aim from the very beginning was to develop

> a completely new attitude that would enable us to catch up with the museums of the western world, which were a good 25 years ahead of us, as soon as possible. [. . .] It was evident that it would not be enough to renew just a few things, nor to do it at a steady tempo. I was convinced that the entire paradigm of behavior, the entire system, everything, had to be changed, and fast.
>
> (Unwin 2011: 26)

One of Baán's aspirations was to improve the functioning and position of Hungarian art in the international arena. He stated in an interview:

> Although the Gallery has organized several professionally outstanding exhibitions abroad during its more than half a century of existence, it

has never taken its own independent exhibition to the really significant canon-making museums of the western world. This is not a result of some Hungarian misfortune, since the best of all the other arts – theatres, orchestras, dancers, film-makers, writers and so on – have reached top European levels in their own fields.

(Interview with László Baán 2017)

The public relations and attendance success emboldened Baán to confront a much bigger challenge – that of creating a museum district in Budapest, the heart of which would be the Museum of Fine Arts conjoined with the Hungarian National Gallery (see Chapter 5). This wide-ranging project quickly met with distrust and criticism in museum and art historical circles for its associations with a loss of autonomy at one of the largest art museums in Hungary, and a series of decisions that imposed a new organizational order.

Baán believes that, in accordance with international museum practice, Hungarian and foreign works of art should not be presented in isolation from one another but as an integrated whole. This would be a return to twentieth-century traditions prior to the Hungarian National Gallery's creation (1957), when all works were presented together. He explains:

Based on the Soviet model, a two-stage process started in the 1950s, during which the Hungarian works were surgically removed from the collection of the Museum of Fine Arts and were made into the core collection of a newly established institution, the Hungarian National Gallery. This regrettably put the Hungarian fine arts at a disadvantage since it was ripped out of its international context and was more difficult to understand outside the Hungarian borders.

(Interview with László Baán 2017, fragment
unpublished in Chapter 2)

This practice is not dominant in global museology, and is in no way confined to the countries of the former Eastern Bloc. An example is London. When the Tate Gallery warehouses reached capacity, a decision was made to create new headquarters – the Tate Modern (2000). A collection of international modern and contemporary art moved there, while the existing building remained a gallery of British art from 1500 to the present. Asked in 2012 for his opinion, László Beke, professor at the Hungarian Academy of Fine Arts (as well as former chief curator of the nineteenth- and twentieth-century art collections at the Hungarian National Gallery and director of Műcsarnok) stated: "Dr. László Baán wants to create an international museum which includes Hungarian art. The idea is not bad in itself, but in this case there is not enough material to allow for setting up these two collections side by side" (Jagodzińska 2012: 148). Such an arrangement, in his opinion, would create disequilibrium.

In spite of criticism within the milieu, in 2012 the Hungarian National Gallery was placed under the aegis of the Museum of Fine Arts. In practice, this meant, among other things, the combination of administrative and financial departments, as well as redundancies. The institution would remain in its current location until the planned move to the new building. The general director of the Gallery, who learned about its "liquidation" from the newspapers, resigned from his post in December 2011 in protest.

The main reasons for this criticism included haste, the failure to consult specialists and various interest groups, and fear – justified, as the history of this project showed – that cultural institutions and museum workers would be treated as pawns. The history of building the Palace of Arts, where discussion also had been lacking, was repeated to a great extent. In effect, the Ludwig Museum (see Atlas 2.2) was introduced into a new building that was incompatible with its needs, and that was created for an enigmatic project lacking specific plans for its architectural design, construction, and art institutions (see Chapter 5). The Ludwig Museum was originally intended to be part of this major museum investment. The combination of the Hungarian National Gallery and the Museum of Fine Arts is the first step; the next is to relocate the collections from the nineteenth century to the present in a single, newly erected building in City Park (see Chapter 3). Although the Museum of Fine Arts collects international modern and contemporary art, it is the domain of the Ludwig Museum – hence the justification for placing the three collections under one roof (just as earlier, the Hungarian National Gallery and the Ludwig Museum were in the neighborhood of the Buda Castle). Finally, after the results of the architectural competition were announced, it was decided that the museum will remain in its current location, and the new building will be called the New National Gallery. The reason for this change was the negative opinion of the Ludwig Foundation. The imbalance in the presentation of the collection of modern and contemporary Hungarian and international art, which Beke previously cited, needs to be balanced by Baán's assumptions that "significant deposits in the permanent exhibition will be made by our large European partner institutions" (Interview with László Baán 2017).

Summary

Changes in museums and national galleries in Central Europe began very late. In many cases, it was easier to set up new institutions and build buildings for them than to carry out reforms aimed at modernization. Many of the problems that had and still have to be solved are common not only to these museums, but also to several other funds for regional and municipal museums financed with the central budgets of individual countries. The four case studies presented here also show how different issues are central to major art museums in individual countries. Although diverse in scope and form, interestingly, all important struggles and disputes revolved around contemporary art. The National Museum still possesses the only permanent exhibition of modern and contemporary art in Warsaw. Contemporary art is the domain of the Museum of Modern Art, but its temporary seat (Pavilion on the Vistula, from 2016) has space only for temporary exhibitions. Also, the Ujazdowski Castle Centre for Contemporary Art and Zachęta Gallery, although they have collections of contemporary art, do not present them in the form of permanent exhibitions. Bratislava is still waiting for a space in which to present the collection. There is no contemporary art museum in the city; Kunsthalle Bratislava is a space for temporary exhibitions. Therefore, MNW and SNG bear a special responsibility. In this respect, the situation is much better in Prague and Budapest. Trade Fair Palace, a branch of the National Gallery, is the capital museum of modern and contemporary art with a grand permanent exhibition of Czech and international art. In the city, Museum Kampa showcases modern art (although since 2015 in a limited scope). In Budapest, collections of modern and contemporary art are well exposed in the Hungarian National Gallery (Hungarian art) and in the Ludwig Museum (Hungarian and international art).

Notes

1 The interior half of the brick was removed by the museum staff after a week; the exterior piece, after over a year.
2 Two discussions took place in 2010: in March, there was a public debate on filling the post of the Director-General of the Slovak National Gallery, and in April, there was a discussion entitled "Public institutions for contemporary art. Problems and models" in which guests from abroad participated.

8 Contemporary art in the provinces
Case study of the "Znaki Czasu" (Signs of the Time) program in Poland

In 2004, Polish cultural policy was directed specifically towards contemporary art. After decades of neglect with respect to collecting the newest art, as well as inadequacies in museum and gallery infrastructure appropriate for the type, state authorities launched a nationwide program that offered an organizational framework and financial assistance for creating regional collections. It was also motivated to cultivate permanent places for their presentation. The National Culture Program "Znaki Czasu" (Signs of the Time) was one of the stimuli for the art museum boom. This chapter is a case study of that program. I reconstruct the motives for its creation, describe its origins and place in state cultural policy, and point out sources of inspiration both within and outside Poland. It was the only (albeit short-lived) program in the contemporary history of the region in which public authorities planned – in a deliberate manner and on a national scale – to support the building of a contemporary art collection and to encourage the creation of permanent exhibition spaces to house it.

The "Znaki Czasu" program was included in the "Strategy for the Development of Culture in the Regions for the Years 2004–2013"; however, when the document was adopted its plan of action plan was limited to the years 2004–2006. The starting point for the development strategy was to analyze the contemporary cultural sphere and its dissemination. The document indicates that there are no so-called "museums of modernity" in Poland which

> in an innovative way present civilizational achievements, including cultural achievements. Museums of this type require audience participation during viewing. Their important functions are the viewer's comprehensive education, as well as the selection of the range of information they receive. Characteristically they combine elements of leisure and entertainment while making the collections accessible. This is one of the most beloved forms of popular culture and education, which at the same time effectively competes with entertainment.
>
> (Strategia rozwoju kultury w regionach 2003: 8)

Research carried out for the purposes of the strategic document showed that the regions lack the will to create contemporary art centers. Among the provincial cities, only Krakow and Wrocław declared their readiness to create them.[1] Minister of Culture Waldemar Dąbrowski, who initiated the program, stated:

> We do not have a single collection of twentieth-century art in Poland that could be considered complete. I am not saying world art, I am not even saying European; I am saying, Polish. Nor do we even have the cultural infrastructure that would permit presentations of contemporary, living artists. [. . .] We neglect to shape public space, which always results from the quality of people who live in this city.
> (Narodowy Program Kultury "Znaki Czasu" 2004)

The program announced by the Ministry of Culture in 2004 outlined six main objectives for implementation: 1) creating, on the basis of regional collections, a representative national collection of contemporary art; 2) promoting Polish contemporary art; 3) restoring the tradition of artistic patronage; 4) engaging many social groups in cultural and artistic activity; 5) making art an instrument of social dialogue and the development of civil society; and 6) developing the art market in Poland. At its foundation lay the desire to create a regional art collection – one in each province, to be built by civic organizations specially created for this purpose. They were to refer to the tradition of the Society for the Encouragement of Fine Arts (see Chapter 1), but France served as the direct model for creating a central program promoting regional collections of contemporary art.

The beginnings of the French program date back to 1982, but the circumstances related to its introduction already existed in the 1960s. The first minister of culture, André Malraux, who took office in 1959 for ten years, led the creation of so-called cultural centers throughout the country. These represented a form of cultural decentralization aimed at the reduction of disparities between Paris and the provinces. In sum, one hundred were created with funding from the Ministry of Culture as well as department, municipal, and regional authorities. Eventually, due to difficulties with their financing, they were transformed in the 1970s into the Centers for Cultural Action (Kowalski 2005: 90). "Apart from the precursory museums in Grenoble, Saint-Étienne or Marseille, as well as cultural centers in Rennes, Grenoble, Amiens, and Chalon-sur-Saône, a specific model of a museum institution focused on contemporary art was established only at the end of the 1960s" – noted Katia Baudin, director of FRAC Nord-Pas-de-Calais, who summed up the French institutional landscape on the eve of the program's launch (Une histoire au présent 2003: 9). In the 1970s, individual and local public initiatives then began to emerge outside of Paris, such as CAPC in Bordeaux, Coin du Miroir in Dijon, and Nouveau Musée in Villeurbanne. However, initiatives by state authorities and local governments in the field of contemporary art were sporadic until 1981.

Decentralization in the field of contemporary art institutions, simultaneously with the promotion of contemporary art, took the form of Regional Funds for Contemporary Art (Fonds régionaux d'art contemporain, abbreviated as FRAC). In total, twenty-two such funds were created – one in each region. The state obliged the regions to establish associations that would manage funds directed at the purchase of works of modern art, subsidized by the state and region. The structure of FRACs is based on the activities of two bodies: a technical committee that makes proposals for purchases, and an administrative committee that evaluates the proposals and makes purchases. Most of the committees are comprised of local officials, but state-level representatives also serve. Each fund has its director, who together with the committee creates a vision for the collection. Regions should allocate finances at the same level as the state, but in practice, financial parity was rarely respected (Urfalino and Vilkas 1995: 13–16). State and regional subsidies are renewed from year to year, and the amounts are always negotiated with the Ministry of Culture.

The original goals of the FRACs were enumerated in a circular issued by the culture minister, Jack Lang to the regional directors on 23 June 1982. It contains three basic goals (Urfalino and Vilkas 1995: 16):

1   The development and dissemination of all forms of contemporary creation. Regional funds are designed to create a collection of paintings, sculptures, photography, graphics, decorative arts, and crafts, and purchasing committees ensure that photography, graphics, and crafts are properly represented.
2   The policy of original purchases. Each region was obliged to define its purchasing policy, which may appeal to regional artists, artists from other regions or foreign artists, whereby concentrating purchases on artists' works from one region should not be disproportionate.
3   The social awareness of contemporary forms of visual arts in the regions, ensuring the purchased works reach the widest possible audience. This should be done through traveling exhibitions, loans granted to local collectives, and loans to museums, public places or places of culture.

The emphasis in purchase planning was placed on living artists. Over the years, most FRACs have also developed a production policy that has been linked to the nature of purchasing policy. Director of FRAC Bourgogne, Eva González-Sancho, stated that FRAC is "a sure way for us to fuel the creativity of contemporary artists" (Próba zdefinowania przedmiotu 2003: 16). Initially, the emphasis on a more general orientation created a historical platform through the acquisition of 1960s (and even earlier) avant-garde art. In some cases, as Baudin pointed out, the historical platform translated to minimalism, conceptual art or *arte povera*, which at that time was still not very conspicuous in French museums, but still affordable (Próba zdefinowania przedmiotu 2003: 14). As a consequence, ten years of activity in regional collections resulted in a total of eight thousand works; after twenty years, more than fifteen thousand; and at the beginning of 2011, there were over twenty-two thousand.

At the time of their establishment, FRACs were a new proposal. It was assumed that the collections should have a nomadic character without a fixed location, that they would be mobile, enabling them to be shown in various places and to reach a wide audience. In addition to temporary exhibitions, there were also other types of artistic projects. One of the most interesting ideas for the circulation of art comes out of Metz, where due to the shortage of exhibition space, works of art have been loaned out to willing residents. The flats in turn would be open to the public on a particular day, thus creating a kind of gallery scattered across the city (Morawińska 2003: 9). FRACs were appointed to collect modern art and to promote it in society, facilitated by the art's mobility.

It turned out, however, that a collection's mobility does not necessarily preclude the establishment of a permanent foothold for other types of artistic and educational exhibition projects. Their permanent headquarters are: FRAC Midi-Pyrénées in Toulouse (since 1994 located in the former slaughterhouse Les Abattoirs, part of an institution created from a combination of modern and contemporary museums), FRAC Normandie in Sotteville-lès-Rouen (since 1998 in a former 1930s-era warehouse for tram parts, called "Trafic"), FRAC Lorraine (since 2004 in a twelfth-century building in Metz), FRAC Aquitaine (from 2005 in Hangar G2 in the port of Bordeaux), FRAC Poitou-Charentes (operating in two locations; since 2008 it has possessed a permanent place for exhibitions, documentation, and administration in Angoulême, and in 2009 the warehouse with exhibition space opened in Linazay), FRAC Nord-Pas-de-Calais in Dunkirk (since 2013 located in the port building, which is a combination of existing and new architecture), FRAC Bretagne (a new building opened in 2012), FRAC Franche-Comté (since 2013 in the port building), FRAC Provence-Alpes-Côte d'Azur in Marseille (in a new building opened in 2013), FRAC Alsace (since 1995 in the Alsace Culture Agency building), FRAC Champagne-Ardenne (since 1990 in a former Jesuit college in Reims), and FRAC Limousin (since 1991 in the basement of a late-nineteenth-century trade union building in Limoges formerly used as a wine cellar).

There are still exhibitions in France, the largest being *Trésors publics*, whose aim was to attract social attention. It traveled to four cities in 2003: Avignon, Nantes, Strasbourg, and Arles, before traveling to several venues abroad: in Italy and Poland (2003), Scotland (2004), Slovakia and Spain (2005), Czech Republic (2006), Israel (2007), and Lithuania and Belgium (2008). The exhibition, *Rzeczywistości. Kolekcje bez granic II/Réalités: Collections sans frontières II* from the collection of five FRACs (Alsace, Franche-Comté, Lorraine, Burgundy, and Champagne-Ardennes) and organized in

Zachęta, marked the introduction of the French idea to Poland (the proposal for which was made by the French in 2001).[2] Associations or foundations were established (some of them taking the name "Zachęta" [encouragement] as a reference to the historical association) in the individual voivodships. Independent of each other and fully autonomous, they were founded in order to build collections of works of art of the highest quality. Coordination of the program at the national level has been entrusted to the National Center for Culture. The Ministry undertook to provide financial support to the level of half of the amount allocated for purchases of works in a given year, which was obtained in individual voivodships from other sources (city authorities, the region, or sponsors). In addition to building regional collections, the program assumed that in every region there would be so-called Interdisciplinary Centers of Modernity, defined as bodies combining artistic, social, educational, recreational, and entertainment functions. The program also provided for the organization of so-called itinerant exhibitions and accompanying seminars, workshops, and publications, as well as undertaking educational and promotional activities for contemporary art. In 2004 and 2005, in individual provincial cities, the associations launched a purchasing policy (with the exception of the Mazowieckie voivodship, which possesses the largest number of contemporary art institutions, and the Podkarpackie voivodship, where no one was willing to run the association; in the Śląskie voivodship, the association was established in Katowice and Częstochowa). Each minister symbolically donated the first work of art, often seen as indicative of the direction of acquisitions and character of the future collection. Particular associations have defined their purchasing policies individually, but the customary temporal limit or point of reference is 1989 – the date of political, economic, and conscious change.

At the center of the Polish project, as in France, creating a contemporary art collection in each region as well as the promotion art remain central goals. The direct similarities end there, however, because the terms in France and Poland were completely different. In France, each region has been required to set up a repository that receives regular funding from the ministry and regional authorities for business, whereas in Poland, the establishment of associations was arbitrary; they are also civic in nature, reminiscent of the historical Zachęta. It was specified only that founding committees of regional societies are to consist of fifteen people, and members of the association may be people known for their involvement in cultural and artistic affairs: collectors and art lovers, as well as representatives of institutions providing financial backing to the program (the marshal, voivode, mayor), chief editors of regional media, personalities in the culture and science worlds, rectors of art schools, social leaders, curators and art historians, journalists, lawyers, artists, PR specialists, economists, or pedagogues. Financing in kind by the ministry and regional authorities or sponsors was provided only at the program's inception; it did not guarantee financial continuity. Another difference is related to the proposal for the creation of Interdisciplinary

Centers of Modernity: in the French program, there were no stipulations for permanent institutions, although they appeared over time as a result of regional needs. In Poland, their necessity stemmed from great deficiencies in the infrastructure dedicated to contemporary artistic activity, especially in the provinces.

Those in the cultural milieu referred to the "Znaki Czasu" skeptically, for fear that the central program would duplicate the way the Bureaus of Art Exhibitions functioned during the previous regime. However, the program quickly produced the intended results. Five years after its establishment, at the end of 2009, over 1,800 works were acquired across the collections, including twenty-one works by foreign artists; individual associations and foundations organized a total of seventy exhibitions. Statistics show the scale of the entire undertaking, and individual initiatives cannot be reduced to a common denominator; they differ from one another in terms of the nature of the collections, plans, and activities related to their exhibition. In 2017, many of the organizations established under the program were already historical in nature; they either ceased to exist or ceased operations, storing collections in existing museums within a given city. Some of the resulting organizations were extremely local, while others aspired to play an important role on a national scale. Regionalism was understood differently, either as a collection of works by regional artists or a collection of national undertones intended for the local public. Some of the organizations attempted to create their own exhibition spaces, while others supported existing permanent collections; still others presented their collections in other institutions. Some have specialized in specific themes or media. The collections in Białystok, Katowice, Krakow, Wrocław, Olsztyn, Łódź, and Lublin gathered the largest number of works by top-shelf national artists. Six collections also extended their scope beyond Polish art, introducing works of foreign artists mainly from the countries of Central and Eastern Europe into their collections.

In the case of the collection in Szczecin, current art was defined as art created not only in contemporary times, but also anchored in them, participating in debates critical to the present and sensitive to the specific context in which they arise (Szczecin – Stowarzyszenie Zachęta Sztuki Współczesnej). The specificity of individual collections has been focused on various themes, media, or geographical areas. According to Agata Zbylut, president of the Zachęta Contemporary Art Association in Szczecin, "the collection is to be a regional collection, that is, works within it are to follow the changes in art since 1989 as fully as possible and thus serve the region as a kind of textbook of Polish history of art collected in Pomorze Zachodnie" (Jagodzińska 2008: 23). The uniqueness of this collection is the spatial installations and sound objects as well as classical scores that were purchased, among other things, following composers' competitions organized by Zachęta. The axis of the collection of the Dolnośląskie Society for the Encouragement of Fine Arts in Wrocław in the first period of operation were installations, and in the new decade, works related to the performative trend in the visual arts. A special place in the collection of the Silesian Society for the Encouragement of Fine Arts in Katowice has been occupied by works referring to social issues, cultural identity and historical memory specific to Upper Silesia. In building its collection, the Lublin Society for the Encouragement of Fine Arts focused on two themes: "Matter (in) space", which includes reflections on the autonomy of a painting, its status, matter and presence in space, and "Art of ideas – ideas of art". The Lublin collection referred to a locale that was understood in a specific way: "It is not about creating a collection of artists from the Lublin region, but inscribing within the collections the tradition charted by the creators and institutions operating in Lublin in the last half-century" – wrote Piotr Kosiewski (2008). The Łódź Society for the Encouragement of Fine Arts described its collection as "historical" – a collection of its time, i.e. the past 15–20 years. In Białystok, the collection of the Podlasie Society for the Encouragement of Fine Arts was conceived as a continuation of the Collection II of the Arsenal Gallery (see Atlas 3.1). The main purpose of the society was to complement and promote the gallery's collections; hence, both collections must be treated together. Works by Central and Eastern European artists were among those purchased by the society. The Warmia and Mazury Society for the Encouragement of Fine Arts in Olsztyn declared that it wanted to create a representative collection of a national character, as there is no collection of contemporary art in the region. The Lubuskie Society for the Encouragement of Fine Arts in Zielona Góra has set itself the goal of covering the most important tendencies in Polish art of the last twenty years, including significant local phenomena, and at the same time complementing two museums operating in the region: the Lubuskie Museum in Gorzów Wielkopolski and the Museum of the Lubuskie in Zielona Góra. The societies in Opole and Kielce focused on regional artists. The Opole Society for the Encouragement of Fine Arts adopted the goal of promoting the local artistic environment through the purchase of works from the annual presentations of the region's creators and analogous presentations of young artists.

The Minister, when inaugurating the program, stated that he wanted it to "lead to the creation of numerous collections of contemporary art by ambitious artists, not exclusively regional and not exclusively Polish. The sum of these collections will be representative of our times" (Inauguracja 2004). However, not all regional societies interpreted this appeal in the same way. In 2008, Piotr Sarzyński, commenting in the weekly newspaper *Polityka* on the project of establishing regional collections, divided the collectors' strategies into three categories. He described the first, represented by Opole and Kielce, as "nurturing its own garden" by "nurturing the local artistic environment"; the next included the activities of societies that "decided to create their own small museums of contemporary Polish art, reaching for big names from the top ranking lists" (Krakow, Białystok, Olsztyn, Szczecin); and the third is a mixed variant, where about half of the artists are locals (Gdańsk, Częstochowa, Wrocław, Łódź) (Sarzyński 2008: 90).

The only building erected for artistic needs on the initiative of the local association was established in Toruń. In Krakow, the MOCAK Museum of Contemporary Art (see Atlas 3.8) was inspired by the local foundation, the Małopolska Foundation of the Museum of Contemporary Art (the building opened in 2010), and in Wrocław, the Society contributed to the creation of Contemporary Museum (see Atlas 3.19). These institutions and their headquarters should be considered the successors of the Interdisciplinary Centers of Modernity. In Toruń and Krakow, there were formal problems regarding acquisitions – namely, both cities created a new institution independent of the association or foundation for assembling the collection. In Toruń, this process took several months; the institution acquired Association's collection in the form of a loan, and creates its own collection from it, none of which is presented in the form of a permanent exhibition. In Krakow, both the marshal of the province and the mayor of the city tried to create a museum. The Foundation, as part of the "Znaki Czasu" program, was established by the Marshall's Office of the Małopolska Region, while the mayor established the museum. Due to the fact that the collection could be in the museum only in the form of a loan, the institution was not interested adopting it (Wrzos-Lubaś 2010: 5). Finally, the collection found institutional support in the BWA Tarnów (see Atlas 3.15), where it is presented in the form of rotating scenes in a gallery located at the railway station. The regional Society for the Encouragement of Fine Arts in Częstochowa in 2007 managed to acquire for its activity the historic Konduktorownia building, which remained after serving the Viennese-Warsaw line and was renovated by the city. The Dolnośląskie Society had made use of the space of the Museum of Architecture in Wrocław to house its collection, which is to be located in the new building erected next to the Contemporary Museum (originally the possibility of rebuilding the Royal Castle in Wrocław for the exhibition was considered). The Society is located in the temporary headquarters of the MWW, where the collection is presented in the form of temporary exhibitions. The Association in Szczecin loaned the works acquired under the program to the local National Museum. Independently of the collection, the association made efforts to obtain a municipal transformer house for the purposes of exhibition. In 2013, TRAFO Trafostacja Sztuki (see Atlas 3.14) was opened there. The Olsztyn association was seeking a permanent exhibition space from the start of its activity. Its collection was to be located in the area of the historic cavalry barracks; however, the city in 2008 abandoned the plans for their revaluation. The Society is located in the Museum of Warmia and Mazury in the Olsztyn castle, which lends warehouse and exhibition space. The Silesian Zachęta attempted to obtain a permanent place for its collections in a post-industrial building. The initial plans envisaged their location at the old railway station in Katowice, where one exhibition of the collection and a number of cultural events had taken place. But the city authorities showed no interest in purchasing the building for a center of modern art. Another potential location in an unfinished building in the Provincial Park of Culture and Recreation in Chorzów turned out to be insufficient for the growth of the collection. The idea of acquiring one of the historic buildings of the "Katowice" coal mine (on whose territory the new Muzeum Śląskie was created) for exhibition purposes also did not come to pass. The collection continues to seek a place for itself and is not presented publicly. One of the main tasks set by the Lublin society was the creation of the Museum of Modern Art in Lublin. Eventually it acquired a gallery for its activity, named Galeria Lipowa 13 (it operated in 2010–2014 at the Lublin Plaza shopping center). In Gdańsk, the Pomeranian Association for the Promotion of Fine Arts originally planned the construction of the Museum of Contemporary Art on Granary Island, but the idea quickly fell apart, the company suspended its activities, and the works went to storage at the National Museum in Gdańsk and the Państwowa Galeria Sztuki w Sopocie (State Art Gallery in Sopot). Similarly, the plan to create the Opole Center for Contemporary Art was not implemented, and the works were temporarily exhibited at the Opole Philharmonic. This list of real and desirable locations for the collection illustrates the powerful museum building impulse in Poland; combined with other objects erected and planned for contemporary art, they represent a wealth of institutions that on one hand must be maintained, and on the other encourage visitors to take advantage of their offerings.

A separate group constitutes societies that, instead of pursuing the ambition of creating a contemporary art institution with its own exhibition space, have begun to work for already-existing institutions in the region and to create collections that are complementary to their own. There are also those whose work philosophy does not require institutional support. The Society in Łódź signed a cooperation agreement with the Muzeum Sztuki, to where it moved its headquarters and deposited a collection, several pieces of which are presented within a permanent exhibition in ms² (see Atlas 3.10). Similarly, Podlaska Zachęta supported the long tradition of the exhibitors' and collectors' Arsenal Gallery with its purchases. The National Museum in Kielce presented the collection of the Świętokrzyskie Society in 2006. The collection was deposited there in 2009, but its status is not clear; the society suspended its activities in 2007. The association having the most individual character was the one in Poznań. Initially, it worked to enrich the permanent exhibition of the local National Museum, and in 2005, it began a cooperation with the Provincial Public Library and the Regional Center for the Animation of Culture for the creation of a representative collection. The Wielkopolskie Society became involved in the Poznań City of Arts project to free art from the confines of the gallery walls. The axis of the collection is sculptures and installations. The works purchased by Zachęta are located at the Poznań airport, on the streets, squares, and in parks. One with which the association was involved – the monumental *Agora* by Magdalena Abakanowicz consisting of 106 cast iron figures – was installed in Chicago's Grant Park.

The program accomplished its main objective – that is, initiating the construction of regional collections. However, the associations did not prove to be robust enough everywhere, in terms of program and finances, to be able to survive and grow without support from the ministerial program. The minister's position was changed, and he was demoted. In 2007, the national cultural program was transformed into the "Znaki Czasu" operation, to which institutions and organizations could apply for programming funds. But these funds were not reserved only for the fifteen organizations created to collect art in the regions – all art institutions in the country could apply. This procedure clearly weakened associations and foundations, because they had no guarantee of obtaining funds for purchasing works of art; moreover, they had to compete with larger and older institutions. With the passage of time, less and less was spent on the operational program. Finally, at the end of 2008, after another change in the ministerial post, it was liquidated.

The presidents of the regional associations, invited in 2008 for its evaluation (I collected their opinions for the article Jagodzińska 2008: 16–23), mostly agreed that this kind of initiative was very much needed in Poland. "I think that the 'Znaki Czasu' program has changed a lot in Poland; it definitely has revived the art market, made prices for works more realistic, and positively influenced the 'authority' of the latest art" – said Monika Szewczyk, president of the society in Białystok. Justyna Zadworna from Zachęta in Poznań also emphasized the positive influence of "Znaki Czasu" on the art market, adding that "thanks to the program [works collected by Zachęta] could be acquired for museums that did not have sufficient funds to build interesting collections", and that "Many activities of the societies caused a positive ferment". However, the authorities of the associations also pointed to the program's deficiencies and errors. The President of the Silesian Zachęta, listing its advantages, added: "This program lacked vision and consistency. What's next, since so much has already been done?"

Initially, the National Center for Culture played the role of liaison. However, after the Ministry's total resignation from the program's implementation, Zachęta remained connected only nominally (though not in all cases, as the Krakow organization contains neither "Zachęta" nor "association" in its name). The ArtKontakt.pl online service run by the Lublin Zachęta was the only initiative bringing all regions together, though the information on individual collections and associations is incomplete and not always up to date. The ArtKontakt website is similar in character to that of the Platform association founded by FRAC in 2005.

Depriving regional associations of financing meant that the development of collections was severely limited and even prohibitive. The problem was not only the lack of budgetary funds, but also the lack of understanding on the part of local authorities. The associations' confrontation with the free market divided them clearly into those which, despite problems and unfavorable circumstances, are operating dynamically, and those that are falling into disrepair and inertia – not only for reasons of insufficient funding, but also because of a lack of cooperation with local authorities, interpersonal conflict, and bad management. In most cases, the associations decided to close their operations. In 2018, few of them were still in operation. Monika Szewczyk rightly noticed that most likely not all Zachęta associations will survive, for they were not necessary everywhere. Lech W. Leszczyński, vice-president of the Society in Łódź who was also diagnosing the policy of purchasing contemporary art in public collections (or rather the lack thereof), came to a similar conclusion:

> Until the political changes in Poland, museums and public galleries complemented their collections to a more or less satisfactory degree, then collapsed. Since then, that is, the 1990s, we have seen the all but universal abandonment of the purchase of works of modern art for Polish public collections. In such a situation, we consider the creation of regional collections to be very necessary. The question is only whether this "regionalism" was not exaggerated. Would it not be better to limit things to a few strong (artistically and organizationally) centers in which the societies created would be supported by existing strong structures and cultural environments [?].
>
> (Statement for the Jagodzińska 2010 article,
> not quoted in this article)

At the moment when such a large network of associations emerges, each operating under different social, political, and economic conditions, and each to varying degrees belonging to the region's artistic traditions, it would be inappropriate to expect that collections are everywhere created with equal vigor, or that they will each seed autonomous art institutions from within their own exhibition spaces. This is how it is in France: "Each FRAC, depending on the needs of a given region, has another mission before it", FRAC director of Franche-Comté, Anne Dary pointed out (Próba zdefiniowania przedmiotu 2003: 21). In large provincial cities that are simultaneously strong artistic centers, "Znaki Czasu" became the *spiritus movens* for the creation of contemporary art museums – Wrocław and Krakow. In smaller towns, the program revealed strong artistic ambitions that led to, or at least advanced, plans aimed at creating art institutions with their own building – Toruń, Szczecin, and Częstochowa. In cities with extensive artistic traditions, there was no need to create a new institution, and the associations undertook to support the existing institutions and their collections – Łódź, Białystok. In Poznań, the fifth largest Polish city, with its strong artistic traditions, there were no plans to create a contemporary art museum, and the local Zachęta found its own way to fill the niche in terms of presenting the latest art. In many other cities, "Znaki Czasu" caused a positive ferment, which translates to dynamic collection development – and in Katowice, efforts to obtain a permanent headquarters.

The French FRACs are also not immune to criticism. Ami Barak pointed out that, for example, they are accused of building a collection solely on the basis of redundant names and following changing fashions (Une histoire au présent 2003: 15). Dorota Jarecka referred to this situation in Poland to some degree only in retrospect, suggesting a balance between locality and universality in collections, as opposed to over-representing regional artists (Jarecka 2006a: 14).

An important goal of the "Znaki Czasu" program, as signaled in the Minister's inaugural speech, was to generate a public debate on contemporary art in Poland. This debate has come full circle and developed on an unprecedented scale in Polish culture. Its contribution was an enormous discussion about the construction of the Museum of Modern Art in Warsaw, and on a smaller scale about the location of the Museum of Contemporary Art in Krakow, as well as that accompanying the creation of museums and historical exhibitions: the Museum of Polish History in Warsaw, the Museum of the Second World War in Gdańsk, and the historical exhibition in the Muzeum Śląskie in Katowice.

Notes

1 The survey asked the voivodship marshals and presidents of provincial cities to consider how they would allocate an additional PLN 30 million in their budget. Only the respondents from the Małopolska, Wielkopolska, and Zachodniopomorskie provinces expressed a desire to finance a Center for Contemporary Art; among the voivode cities surveyed, only Krakow and Wrocław declared a willingness to spend additional funds to create such a center. (Strategia rozwoju kultury w regionach 2003: 11).
2 The exhibition was also accompanied by a seminar organized at the French Institute in Warsaw dedicated to the FRACs and creation of a similar structure in Poland.

9 Museums of Central Europe
A Central European identity?

The museum boom did not happen overnight. I do not apply the term exclusively to new institutions and new buildings, but more broadly to the development of museums, and by extension the modernization of existing buildings, their expansion, the dynamic development of collections, or new unveilings of permanent exhibitions. The impetus for creating new art institutions came with the advent of the new century. Its driving forces would be the entrance of Central European countries into the European Union, and the availability of new sources of financing for construction projects. Sudden, often turbulent and massive, it is associated with the need to catch up. Museums and centers dealing with the arts of the twentieth and twenty-first centuries are one type of institution appearing in the Central European cultural landscape during this period after the political transformation, but it must be remembered that they are not the only type representing dynamic changes. In Poland, for example, new historical and city museums are emerging with equal dynamism.

Inspiration for spatial and architectural solutions is very often derived from Western countries and mainstream culture; in this respect, museums are no exception. The opening of borders along with political transformation has led to the adoption of Western standards in many areas of life, including various cultural fields. The aim has been to offer vague notions of "European" or "international" standards in Central Europe, as well as to demonstrate that the achievements of this region are an integral part of European and world culture. Extensive museumization is also underway in Western countries, but there the cultural ecosystem is supplemented with new museums, often housing private collections. In contrast, in Central Europe, there is an imperative to create or significantly develop this ecosystem by building or extending major encyclopedic museums, regional and local museums, art centers and Kunsthallen, and private museums.

The overview of museum investments from Central Europe made on the pages of this book shows that these institutions are no different than museums or art centers being built in other parts of the world. Local architects reach for foreign sources; also, international architectural firms build here. The juries of architectural competitions, among which there is no shortage of foreign experts, implement buildings that could be built in any other latitude. Museologists discuss issues that are current in museums around the world. Central European museums of art (though this applies to all types of museums) are global with respect to their spatial and functional layout, management strategies, education strategies and communication with the public. In this respect, the research hypotheses that I set for myself and which I have formulated in the Introduction are true. In Central Europe, Western patterns arrived belatedly. An illustrative example is the discussion about the architectural form of the Museum of Modern Art in Warsaw (a spectacular icon vs. a minimalist building that fits in with the surroundings). This does not mean, however, that Central European museums lack local specificity. Securing collections is the foremost priority, followed by the creation of a program of exhibitions and artistic projects, cooperation with artists, and a research agenda.

In this chapter, I will focus on regional specificity, and will consider to what extent the art of Central Europe is attractive for local institutions. Are their collections and program activities built around the geographical category "Central Europe"? Does Central European art appear problematic in programming, or is the category "Central Europe" (which is unlike any other geographic region) ultimately irrelevant? The point of reference for these considerations will be the concept of "glocalization" that situates Central European museums and art centers between the local and global with respect to the artists represented in their collections and exhibitions, and attendant issues.

The notion of glocalization has been discussed in the literature of various disciplines since the 1990s, and refers to the concepts of the global and the local; depending on the approach, these terms sometimes are treated together (wherein one encompasses the other; Robertson 1992), and at other times, separately (Ritzer 2003). According to Encyclopedia Britannica, the term means:

> the simultaneous occurrence of both universalizing and particularizing tendencies in contemporary social, political, and economic systems. [. . .] Glocalization indicates that the growing importance of continental and global levels is occurring together with the increasing salience of local and regional levels. Tendencies toward homogeneity and centralization appear alongside tendencies toward heterogeneity and decentralization.
>
> (Blatter n.d.)

In the case of relations between art institutions and the region of Central and Eastern Europe, glocalization means settling in the region and accentuating its distinctiveness, while simultaneously looking at and reacting to various current tendencies around the world. Glocalism construed regionally – using Central European, not national, optics – could be the value that defines this region, but to what extent is the adoption of this concept interesting for museums in Central Europe?

A strong voice rang in the need for a holistic view of the region in 2000 in Ljubljana on the occasion of the exhibition, *Arteast 2000+ The Art of Eastern Europe in Dialogue with the West*. The Museum of Modern Art (Moderna Galerija) organized the exhibition in a building which at that time was being prepared for adaptation to a contemporary art museum.[1] It marked the public inauguration of an international collection whose strategy was based on dialogue between East and West. The museum director, Zdenka Badovinac, also one of the most highly regarded critics and curators of art in the region, indicated that "the Arteast 2000+ is not merely a collection of works by Eastern European artists. It aims to transcend the spaces that were until recently isolated, and to establish dialogue as a pre-condition for the ultimate bridging of the division between the East and the West" (Badovinac 2000: 17). Importantly, this collection began to appear next to, not in isolation from, the collection of local art assembled at the museum. It was conceived as a response to Western collections filled with the canonical names of art history, showing those artists from post-socialist countries who were disenfranchised from wider representation (and in many cases were lacking any representation whatever). Therefore, the goal of this collection, continues Badovinac, is "to help the idea of Eastern Europe as a blind spot of history to finally disappear [sic] from the map of Europe. We wish that Ljubljana would become the place where one could obtain relevant information about art that remains largely unknown in the wider international space" (Badovinac 2000: 19). The creation of this collection was simultaneously "a pioneering work in the self-definition of the art of the former socialist countries" (Badovinac 2011: 45). To what extent has Moderna Galerija achieved its goal? Is Eastern Europe still a blind spot of history? The answer may be found in an overview of the region's collection and program strategies in relation to regional optics.

Art collections in the museums of individual Central European countries – museums of modern and contemporary art, as well as collections in encyclopedic museums – focus on local (national) art. This is undoubtedly the result of the availability and affordability. But it cannot be assumed that if the budgets for purchases of works were higher, art from the region would automatically be more widely represented. Scholars of Eastern European art emphasize that during the socialist period there was more interest in Western than in Eastern European art. Piotr Piotrowski indicates that,

> Due to official policy, the Eastern Communist authorities were more favourably disposed towards building walls, particularly among Eastern societies, than building bridges between our countries. Eastern artists and intellectuals were also more interested in Western art than in their own neighbourhood, looking at the West as a sort of redemption, neglecting to look around in the other Eastern European countries.
>
> (Piotrowski 2000: 24)

The regional ignorance embedded in the previous system – ignorance as well as low interest in art in neighboring countries – continues to this day. As Vladimír Beskid indicates,

> In the 1990s, the "wild" years of transformation, we all thrust ourselves towards the West and were not interested in what was happening with our neighbours. It is only a pity that we did not sufficiently use the potential of and benefits offered by the Soros Centres for Contemporary Art (in Slovakia since 1993). We did not build a stronger common platform for promoting the visual culture of Central and Eastern Europe to the international scene. And we still do not have this platform.
>
> (Interview with Vladimír Beskid 2018)

Beskid is referring to Slovakia, but a similar situation characterizes all countries of the region. In Western museums, apart from individual works, there is no collection of Eastern European art. The Jerke Museum in the Ruhr Area (established in late 2016; see Atlas 3.21), which presents only Polish modern and contemporary art, is a singular example. Scheduled to open in 2019, the Susch Museum in the Swiss Engadine region aims to present art from the Eastern European region – but as an integral part of its thematic profile, defined as "the disruption of power structures" and empowerment of "(a)rtists, movements and ideas that to date have been marginalised or left outside of the canon [. . .]. In particular, though not exclusively, female artists will be offered new contexts and positions" (Muzeum Susch 2018: 1). For this reason, "Those who want to study Eastern art should come to the East", Piotrowski wrote (2000: 24). Here, however, there are not many places offering the art of the region. Eighteen years on, there are more than there were, but still surprisingly few. Apart from the museum in Ljubljana, Central European art has only a few important footholds in the region.

The Ludwig Museum in Budapest, whose uniqueness lies in the encapsulation of international, Western art collections with works from the region, is exemplary. Krisztina Szipőcs admits, "we wanted to show and collect the art of this specific political-cultural region from the beginning, to preserve the cultural, visual memories of the post-Soviet times" (Interview with Krisztina Szipőcs 2017). The Central European collection constitutes about 20 percent of the museum's holdings; it provides a context for the international inventory, which came from the Ludwig collection and includes works by Hungarian, Slovak, Polish, Romanian, and other artists from the former Yugoslavia. "We cannot really buy the works of big international stars, due to financial reasons", admits Szipőcs. "The Central-Eastern-European prices are still more affordable. On the other hand, it was not only a practical, but a strategic decision, too". The curator's decision is therefore the result of what was possible; it is the product of budgetary constraints. The statistics of exhibitions focused on the creative work of the region are impressive, especially since the museum systematically has been continuing on this trajectory in its exhibition policy since its inception in 1996.

MODEM (see Atlas 2.4) in Hungary is also interested in Central Europe. Though the Antal-Lusztig collection presented here includes only Hungarian art, the Central European accent comes into view with a program of exhibitions not specifically connected to the region. It is not without significance that the main curator, Ábel Kónya, studied at the Academy of Fine Arts in Krakow and speaks excellent Polish; this has translated into exhibitions of Polish artists. "We want to show the most important phenomena in the region in Central Europe as much as possible – I will mention here Poland, the Czech Republic, Slovakia, Austria, Romania, Serbia, Hungary – because here a very interesting art is being born", Kónya says, pointing to lively contacts between Hungarian and Polish artists in the 1970s and 1980s. "It was natural. Now these contacts are not so frequent. And it does not have to be that way. MODEM will try to initiate as many projects as possible in the future, in which artists from these countries could show together at exhibitions" (Interview with Ábel Kónya 2018). This thinking from a regional perspective is now developing at MODEM (though was present in the first period of the institution's operation before it was harnessed to the structure of the local museum). Together with the subsequent organizational changes formally made in 2018, the team is rebuilding MODEM's position in the region.

In the Czech Republic, the collection of Meda and Jan Mládek bears the most Central European stamp. It contains works not only by Czech artists, but also by Slovak, Polish, Hungarian, and Yugoslav artists. As Jiří Pospíšil, member of the board of directors of the Jan and Meda Mládek Foundation points out, the collection "is based on both aesthetic values and political values" (Interview with Jiří Pospíšil, Helena Musilová and Sandra Průša 2015). It includes the works of artists whom Meda Mládek met personally and whose work appealed to her. It was important, as Sandra Průša says, that "she identified with the artists that were not supported by the communist government", and this pertained not only to Czechoslovakia, but also other communist countries. Due to the limited space and change of the program strategy (connected with Meda Mládek's resignation from her position as chair of the board of directors), the exhibition of the Prague collection has been reduced to a minimum for a more extensive presentation at the castle in Moravský Krumlov. There, however, this collection is generally invisible (information about it is lacking even on the organizers' websites), and the show in the Czech provinces was not promoted. The Central European direction also is hardly visible in the program of temporary exhibitions. The exhibitions presented by the Museum Kampa are not the products of cooperation with museums (either within or outside the region), and past attempts to show collections in other institutions have not been successful. Průša noticed: "We tried to get into the United States or Hungary, but there is not enough interest in our collection. Those museums always want just Kupka". In 2015, the Museum Kampa employed a chief curator for the first time in its history. Assuming this function, Helena Musilová admitted, "It will be my task to build a strong connection between Museum Kampa and, for example, the National Gallery here in Prague, a Hungarian, and any other Central European museum. Our collection is very good, but it seems nobody knows what we have inside, except Kupka" (Interview with Jiří Pospíšil, Helena Musilová and Sandra Průša 2015). Central Europe has also gained an important position in the National Gallery in Prague since being under Jiří Fajt's direction (from 2014). Due to the national character of the institution, Czech art will always form the core of the collection. But the Central and Eastern European direction in art, in its status as art of the former Soviet bloc states, is also important for him. This direction is related to Fajt's scholarly interests in medieval and early modern art from Central and Eastern Europe. "When I came to the National Gallery, I indeed gave my full attention to the Trade Fair Palace", Fajt confessed (Interview with Jiří Fajt 2018).

The Central European Forum Olomouc was to be dedicated to art after the Second World War, conceived as part of the local Museum of Modern Art in Olomouc. It was supposed to create a collection of art that included works by Czech, Slovak, Polish, and Hungarian artists, complemented with works from Austria and Germany; to organize exhibitions as well as cyclical events; and to act as an information center, library, and multimedia archive (Zatloukal 2009: 23). According to its objectives, it was to play an important role in preserving the region's historical memory. It was established in 2008 during a meeting of the Ministers of Culture of the Visegrad Group countries, but it did not advance beyond the program and architectural concept (ultimately it did not receive political backing or funding).

The importance of the region's art captured the interest of Petr Pudil, founder of Kunsthalle Praha, whose opening is planned for 2020. He stated that "it is one of the most important regions that we would like to cover" (Interview with Petr Pudil 2018).

Among the Polish museums, the Museum of Modern Art in Warsaw emphasizes the region the most. Joanna Mytkowska, taking over the position of the director 2008, stated in an interview: "Until now, confirmation of the value of works of art from Eastern Europe took place in large global centers. An attempt at changing this tendency needs to be made. The Museum in Warsaw can become an important place of research on the region with which we share historical experience" (Jarecka 2007e: 14). MSN inaugurated that activity with an exhibition of Yugoslavian art in 2008. In the program, however, MSN supplemented Eastern Europe as one of the key words with another, embracing a slogan of transformation. Eastern Europe, said Mytkowska ten years later, "is a historical duty. Of course it is very interesting, but in the context of transformation in different parts of the world. Transformation is much more important than Eastern Europe" (Interview with Joanna Mytkowska 2017). Geography is therefore important, as long as it is coupled with other categories in defining program.

In 2006, Kamil Kopania suggested that the Arsenal Gallery in Białystok, which had become a hotspot on the map for contemporary art in Poland, should start to collect works by artists from geographically proximate countries. He stated,

> The very location of Białystok is in this respect very convenient. Moreover, the Baltic art market is significantly more accessible from our point of view than the American or Western American markets. It would be just as tempting as needed [sic; necessary] to create in the city a center which would have a collection or art from the Ukraine, Czech Republic, Slovakia, Hungary and – generally speaking – Eastern and Central Europe.
>
> (Kopania 2006: 60)

In accordance with the mission of the so-called Collection II, which has been building its gallery since 1992, "Presenting leading phenomena in Polish art, it reflects on traces of post-system transformation changes to culture. Concurrently, for reasons rooted within the Gallery's programme as such, it depicts fundamental tendencies and changes in Belarussian, Ukrainian, Czech, and Armenian art" (Kolekcja n.d.). In addition, projects involving the Partnership of Central and Eastern European Countries occupy an important place in the gallery's program, illustrating the trends and changes in contemporary art in these regions.

Central Europe occupies a central place in the activities of the International Cultural Centre in Krakow. A strategic document and informational materials emphasize this geographical area stating, "Central Europe is the point of departure and point of reference for all our projects. It is through the prism of our geographical location and by comparison with our neighbours, both immediate and more distant, that we observe the processes unfolding at the intersection of culture, heritage, art, politics, economics and social phenomena" (Jagodzińska 2014: 4). One of the objectives is formulated as: building the image of Poland as a promoter of cultural cooperation in Central Europe (Strategia 2012–2020, 2013: 27). The ICC does not have a collection of art, but the ICC Gallery holds temporary exhibitions of modern and contemporary art that include broadly Central European works.

Central European art does not play a big part in programs in museums or art centers in Slovakia. It was mostly visible in the first period of operation of Kunsthalle Bratislava (before it was transferred to the umbrella of SNG). Richard Gregor, former chief curator, explains: "we were interested in the region of Central Europe trying to contribute to the debate on contemporary art in the region. We had more plans for the future, we wanted to bring other international shows as well and be a little wider than Central Europe" (Interview with Richard Gregor 2018). Following this line, only four big exhibitions were organized, including one coproduction devoted to Central European art taking place in Johannesburg (*Between democracies*

1989–2014: memory and commemoration, 2015), which was meant to be transferred to Bratislava afterwards (2016). However, due to the change in organizational framework of Kunsthalle and its management, this ultimately did not happen. Katarína Rusnáková, researcher, curator, and former museum director, admits with bitterness: "lately most of Slovak art museums have been focused on local art from the reason of the lack of money and enthusiastic curators including the missing infrastructure" (Interview with Katarína Rusnáková 2018). Alexandra Kusá says that interest in the region is rather a result of individual curators' interests (see Interview with Alexandra Kusá, Chapter 2). The region's art is visible in the Danubiana Meulensteen Art Museum exhibition program: in 2007–2010, it organized annual exhibitions of Hungarian, Russian, Slovak, and Hungarian and Czech art, respectively. Vincent Polakovič emphasizes: "due to our location on the Danube River which flows through ten countries, we are primarily a Slovak and European museum" (Interview with Vincent Polakovič 2017). However, he does not specifically refer to this part of Europe. While there are also presentations of the art of individual countries or their national artists, there are no cross-sectional presentations of art from this region.

Regional features are visible in a number of other Central European institutions, but they are of a less systematic or even incidental character. Such institutions include MOCAK and the Muzeum Sztuki in Łódź, which in 2010 organized a large exhibition of Central and Eastern European art entitled *Modernisations 1918–1939. The Future Perfect*, rounded off by a rich accompanying program and an extensive scholarly publication.

In 2017, an international project entitled, *New Dictionary of Old Ideas* began (to be completed in 2020), the central theme of which is Central Europe. The MeetFactory in Prague leads the project; other institutions from the region have been invited; for example, TRAFO in Szczecin, Transit in Vienna, ODD in Bucharest, Visual Culture Research Center in Kiev, and HIT Gallery in Bratislava. This is a residential research project that will culminate in a conference, exhibition, and publication. Participant Stanisław Ruksza, director of TRAFO, says:

> We will discuss the changes that have taken place in recent years, for example, whether we are going West or building our separate position in the context in which we find ourselves. We all agree today that Europe has several speeds and that we have not responded so much to certain issues in our region in the period of catching up with the West.
>
> (Interview with Stanisław Ruksza 2017)

Several Central and Eastern European collections can also be identified outside the Visegrad countries. The Slovenian Museum of Contemporary Art Metelkova possesses and systematically displays the largest collection, but private collections are no less important. In 2004, on the initiative of the Austrian Erste Bank, "Kontakt. The Arts and Civil Society Program of the

Erste Bank Group in Central Europe" was formed, and within whose parameters, a collection of Central and Eastern European art took shape. The collection is co-created by banks in the Czech Republic (Česká spořitelna) and Slovakia (Slovenská sporiteľňa), which are part of this financial group. The starting point is the conceptual tendencies and artistic movements of the 1960s and 1970s, and the core consists of current works with an emphasis on conceptualism and performance. The goal of the collection's creators is to include key works by artists and groups important for the region. It is described as a "work in progress", and reflects the political and historical changes taking place in Central, Eastern, and South-Eastern Europe. Another goal is "bringing works from the region into contact with each other as a way of formulating a broader and hitherto non-existent shared historical context, allowing the works to appear and be interpreted in a new light" (Marte and Seidl 2006: 18), as well as telling "the history of contemporary art of this region as a history of *neighbourhoods* – i.e., of more of less isolated and unstable systems of reference" (Schöllhammer 2006: 25, emphasis as in original). Members of the collection advisory board emphasize that one reason for the collection's creation is the fact that representative art collections of the region have not been created in this part of Europe, whether by local museums or other institutions. The fact that most of the work was bought directly from artists shows the lack of public and private sector interest in these artists. (Schöllhammer 2006: 25).

The continuation of the ideas guiding the creators of the Erste Bank collection is ART FOND – Central European Art Fund created in 2014 in Bratislava. Its initiator was Andrej Zaťko, director of the Slovak branch of J & T Bank, and from 2016 a chairman of the Board of Directors and a Managing Director of Post Bank in Slovakia. The collection includes the work of artists from the 1960s to the present. According to the objectives, "the mapping, promotion and support of the Central European art scene will [. . .] allow its renewed understanding and integration into the international art history" (Central European Contemporary ART FUND n.d.). The construction of the collection began with Slovak and Czech art, but the ambition of its creators is also to include artists from the region.

In his publications on the subject of the museums of Central and Eastern Europe, Gábor Ébli looks at the region more broadly, including the countries of the former Yugoslavia, Lithuania, Latvia, Estonia, Russia, and even Austria, where he identifies museums that canonize Eastern European art. "Now, a quarter-century after the Iron Curtain came down, there is significant interest in identifying shared trends in the art of the past forty-fifty years in Eastern Europe" he writes (Ébli 2016a). In particular, he identifies nine as being art-focused: the Ludwig Museum in Budapest; the Moderna Galerija in Ljubljana; the Museum of Contemporary Art (MSU) in Zagreb; four museums in Poland: MOCAK, the Muzeum Sztuki in Łódź, the Museum of Modern Art in Warsaw, and the Wrocław Contemporary Museum; the collection created by the ERSTE bank in Vienna; and, to a lesser extent, the

Museum Moderner Kunst Stiftung Ludwig Wien (Interview with Gábor Ébli 2018). Even if my selection of institutions is slightly different, the number of museum collections and exhibition spaces that focus on the art of the region – Central or Eastern Europe – is not large, and fluctuates between ten and fifteen places. Perhaps if looking from a distance at these institutions as literal points on the map, one has the impression that Central European art (both overall or cross-sectional, and as individual presentations by artists working in the region) is both important for and widely represented in the region. Upon closer inspection, however, its voice is very weak.

The interest of curators, critics, and art historians in the art of the region has never been extensive, but geography is much less important to people who create the program of these institutions than the problems they would like to refract through the lens of the work of art. Today, I have the impression that despite various local initiatives, the attractiveness of Central and Eastern Europe as a framework for program activities and collections is diminishing. There is no doubt that Piotrowski was one of the biggest (if not the largest) promoters of the notion of the region's appealing distinctiveness when it comes to the art offered in museums. He wanted an exceptional museum for Poland in the region; his vision of a critical museum tailored for the National Museum in Warsaw was to constitute a new standard for museums with historical collections (see Chapter 7). The model was taken from the museum of contemporary art, and its implementation in an encyclopedic, historical, or any other kind of museum had to enable the "updating" of its collections through interpretation from the perspective of contemporary problems and challenges. In his idea for institutional programming, Piotrowski drew from the experience of working on the concept of MSN, on whose council he sat from 2005–2007. He admitted: "The critical mission of a contemporary art museum is not new, although the institutions rarely treat it as their main program. But the introduction of criticality into the historical museum is a novelty" (Instytucja krytyczna 2014: 171). Piotrowski tried to transform the peripheral museum and collections based on local and Polish art into an asset. The MNW offered a good perspective on this part of Europe, and its use in program activities was to constitute an attractive counter-proposal for mainstream cultural museums grounded in masterpieces. He wrote: "we were interested in a different artistic geography – not an orientation to the West, which threatens to make the region a province of the West, but Central and Eastern Europe, as a starting point for building in the future – a global vision of museum culture" (Piotrowski 2011b: 73).

Such a vision of the national museum did not please everybody, but Piotrowski's failure as director (lack of support from the board of trustees and, as a result, his resignation from the post) was not solely related to this programming strategy. Anda Rottenberg, a member of the council who suggested Piotrowski for this position, said that Piotrowski "treated the museum as a battlefield, he said: 'storm Bastille and put up an opera', and probably intuited how it would end. This revolution had been made" (Już trudno 2013: 173). Finally, under different directorship, the MNW went the other way, for as Rottenberg herself admitted, changing such a large, conservative, and incumbent museum is possible only through evolution (Wczesne lata 2014: 127).

The exhibition, *As soon as I open my eyes I see a film. Experiment in the art of Yugoslavia in the 1960s and 70s* organized for the opening of the MSN was a kind of program manifesto of the nascent institution. It was accompanied by the following description (interestingly, the version of the text in English was different from the one in Polish; the Polish translation of the description appears here):

> There is no doubt that the eyes of the world's largest artistic institutions are directed to our part of the continent. World museums more and more often fill blind spots in the universal history of art, but at the same time they impose their own, obviously western, research perspective. The Museum of Modern Art in Warsaw, joining in this process, strives to make the Central European point of view and the Central European historical experience enrich authentically this new history of art.
>
> That is why the Museum of Modern Art in Warsaw begins its exhibition activities just from the presentation of art not yet included in the universal canon of artistic heritage of the second half of the twentieth century.
>
> (Kiedy rano otwieram oczy 2008)

However, the exhibition met with much less interest than its creators assumed. This resulted in a quick reformulation of the museum's program and its turn to local matters in Warsaw (e.g. urban issues).

The owner and director of the Prague DOX art center, Leoš Válka, refrains from expressing geographical preferences. He says:

> Artists from Central Europe are not more important than others. Because they are coming from a similar culture and they have similar political burden – I mean that they have the Communist past and totalitarian regime experience – we feel close to them, but they do not have a preferential status. Each exhibition has to justify its own position.
>
> (Interview with Leoš Válka 2015)

Does this emphasis on the region still need to be essential in post-transformation Europe, where the boundary between West and East has largely faded; in which other geographical categories seem to carry more weight (like the Baltic States and the former Yugoslavia), and in which many other problems and issues require art institutions to take positions (such as on migration or the break-up of the EU)? In my opinion, yes, still. I believe that – following Piotr Piotrowski's thought – emphasizing the art of the region in collections and programming strategies offers an interesting alternative to the institutions of the Western world, in which the recurring names of the (Western) art canon dominate. At this point, the number and scale of exhibitions and collections as well as institutional strategies focused on the region is too small to be able to be deemed characteristic. It seems that individual institutions lack faith in the idea that building an identity based on the geographical category of this part of Europe will gain popularity among both locals and visitors from more or less distant places. Falling into excessive locality (which is often enforced by financial constraints) and situating local art almost exclusively in the local context – and by extension excluding a regional one (geographically closer, historically, culturally as well as financially more accessible) – causes these institutions to remain on Europe's periphery.

Known and recognizable names in the international circulation of art act as a magnet for the Central European and general public alike. On the other hand, the scarcity of places where the art from the region can be known results in ignorance, which in turn converges with some – and not other – preferences of the public. An interesting proposal are two "Polish" private museum initiatives in Germany and Switzerland. Their location in Western countries immediately situates Polish art in an international context comparable to that at the Ludwig Museum in Budapest. As Werner Jerke, owner of the Jerke Museum in Recklinghausen, explained the reasons for his decision (Interview with Werner Jerke 2018):

> I wondered once whether to show my collection permanently in Poland, but it is easier to run it this way. If I had a museum in Gliwice or Pysko-wice, where I come from, I do not know if there would be much interest. There are many museums of Polish art in Poland, but in Germany the museum of Polish art is unique.

The exhibition strategy of the Susch Museum, in which Polish and Eastern European art is not emphasized in any way, seems to refer to a situation in which the blind spots of history have already been obliterated and the art of the region has become an integral part of global art circulation. These museums, on the one hand, are part of the growing interest of the West in the art of the East; on the other, they can create and fuel interest. The idea of a museum of Polish art in the Czech Republic or Hungarian art in Poland is much less realistic and would rather require the involvement of public funds. That structure seems to be quite artificial and probably also difficult to promote (it is worth noting that the Jerke Museum was established in a region where a large part of the population has Polish roots; it is also open only three days a week). However, the idea of a museum of Central European art that does not favor the art of the state in which it was created has much greater potential. Furthermore, an identity based on geography would not preclude the possibility of looking at art and the world in more complicated terms.

"Post-1989 Central Europe is a Europe in search of identity – between national revival and globalisation", writes Jacek Purchla (2008: 333). One of the functions of museums is to strengthen identity. Maybe, then, there is a place for such a museum. Where? Krakow – as Purchla has stated on many occasions – is located in the heart of Central Europe and is its essence (Purchla 2008: 335). The distance from Krakow to Warsaw is comparable with that to Budapest, Bratislava, and Prague. A city of museums, which Krakow certainly is, will surely accommodate another one. But the question is whether the will to invest in regional identity is strong enough in the region itself.

Note

1 The Museum of Contemporary Art Metelkova (+ MSUM) was opened in 2011; together with Moderna Galerija, it forms one institution (MG + MSUM).

Atlas of museums and centers of contemporary art in Central Europe after 1989

Contents

1 The Czech Republic

1.1 Brno: Wannieck Gallery

activity: 2006–2015
name changes: from 2013 Richard Adam Gallery, then shortened to Adam Gallery
adapted building
investment type: private
exhibition space: 3,800 m²
former address: Ve Vaňkovce 2, Brno
www.adamgallery.cz

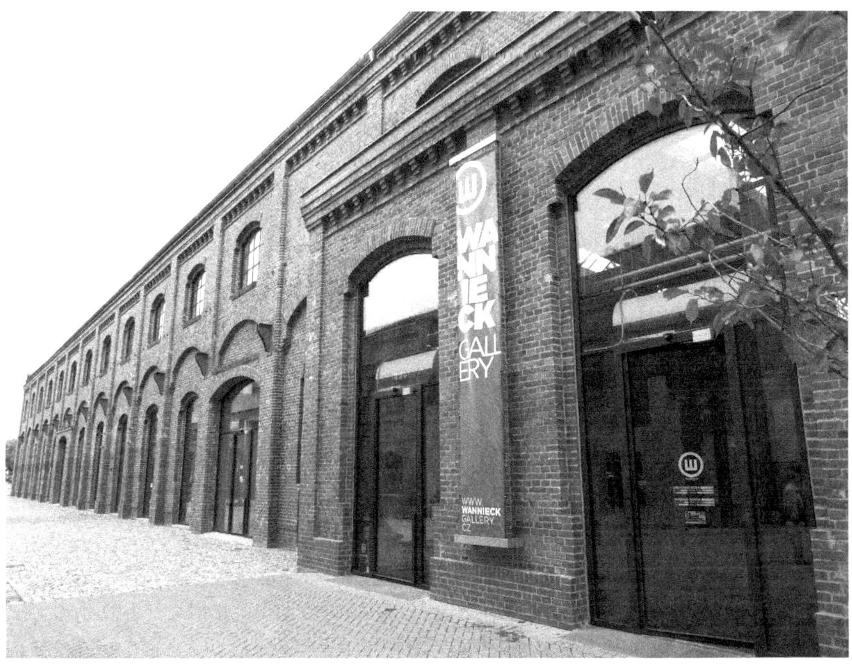

Wannieck Gallery in Brno.
Photo: Katarzyna Jagodzińska

Wannieck Gallery was created for Richard Adam's collection of contemporary Czech art. The gallery was located on the site of the former Wannieck factory in Brno which was divided into two parts at the beginning of the twenty-first century; the larger was demolished for the construction of a shopping center, and the smaller (the former machine plant building) was revitalized and adapted for the gallery of contemporary art. The building is managed by a city-owned company, from which the space is rented. Adam was the first tenant.

During the time of the gallery's existence, it was the largest publicly accessible private collection of contemporary Czech painting in the Czech Republic. It is also not limited to Czech art. As Richard Adam has said, "Initially, the collection focused exclusively on Czech artists, but now [2009] we are also trying to collect images of artists from Slovakia, Germany, Austria, Poland, Hungary, and Russia" (Interview with Richard Adam 2009).

High rent forced the gallery to close. The gallery has moved to the virtual realm, and the collector and gallery running the foundation now want to "be focused on collection, show the collection to foreign institutions and galleries, make contacts with foreign curators, [and] support young artists" (Personal communication with Petra Lekešová 2016).

Fait Gallery is another tenant in this space, and operates on the basis of a similar model: it has a collection of Czech modern art and organizes exhibitions of contemporary art. The gallery was founded by entrepreneur Igor Fait from Brno in 2012; initially it was located in the former malt house of the Královo pole brewery in Brno University of Technology premises. In 2016 it moved to a vacant gallery space at the Wannieck factory.

For more on the revitalization of the Wannieck factory, see Chapter 4.

1.2 Český Krumlov: Egon Schiele Art Center (Egon Schiele Art Centrum)

established in 1992, opened in 1993
adapted building
investment type: private
address: Široká 71, Český Krumlov
www.schieleartcentrum.cz

The Egon Schiele Art Center was founded on the initiative of Hana Jirmusová-Lazarowitz from the Czech Republic and Gerwald Sonnberger, director of the Museum of Modern Art in Passau, Austria. Later, they were joined by the collector Serge Sabarsky from the United States, who became the chairman of the foundation's leading institution. The city donated the Renaissance building of the brewery chosen for the center's seat.

The central figure here is Egon Schiele; the artist was associated with Český Krumlov, as his mother come from this town, and he were there many times. The center presents a permanent exhibition of drawings, graphics, the artist's own furniture, memorabilia, documentation about his stays in Krumlov, and the motifs on his paintings and drawings. Its main activity is temporary exhibitions of modern and contemporary art – primarily exhibitions of Czech and international artists devoted to a particular topic in a given year. The connection with Egon Schiele is demonstrated in exhibitions of other Expressionist artists. "We are also interested in great talents who died prematurely – like Egon Schiele. In this category we could name Keith Haring or Jindřich Prucha", says director Hana Jirmusová-Lazarowitz (Personal communication with Hana Jirmusová-Lazarowitz 2017).

In addition to the exhibition space, the center has studio spaces which are rented to artists on a ten-year basis.

1.3 *Humpolec: 8smička*

opening: 2018
adapted building
investment type: private (non-profit institution)
exhibition space: 350 m² (main space) + 600 m² (additional space)
address: Kamarytova 97, Humpolec
http://8smicka.com

8smička is run by a Foundation established in 2017 by Zdeněk Ryzner and his wife Barbora, and David Staněk. The founders refer to it as an "art zone", which according to Marcela Straková, "its executive director, allows to communicate broader focus [to an art gallery]. We hope people will accept 8smička as a platform for education, meetings, both artistic and local community etc." (Personal communication with Marcela Straková 2018).

The institution is located halfway between Prague and Brno, in Humpolec, a center of cloth production in the nineteenth century. It is situated in adapted building of a textile factory from the end of the nineteenth century.

The inaugural exhibition entitled *A homage to broadcloth: Textiles in the context of fine art* symbolically built a connection between the history of the place and its present function. There are planned high quality exhibitions of modern and contemporary art that are meant to attract visitors to the town from other parts of the Czech Republic, as well as to attract a local audience.

8smička holds a collection of modern and contemporary Czech art, from the mid-twentieth century to the present. It is not presented at the permanent exhibition, but mostly loaned to other institutions.

See more on the building in Chapter 4.

1.4 *Kutná Hora: GASK – the Gallery of the Central Bohemian Region (GASK – Galerie Středočeského kraje)*

opening in Kutná Hora: 2010
adapted building

investment type: public
investor: the Czech state (Ministry of Culture) and the Central Bohemian
   Region
exhibition space: 3,000 m²
address: Barborská 51–53, Kutná Hora
http://gask.cz

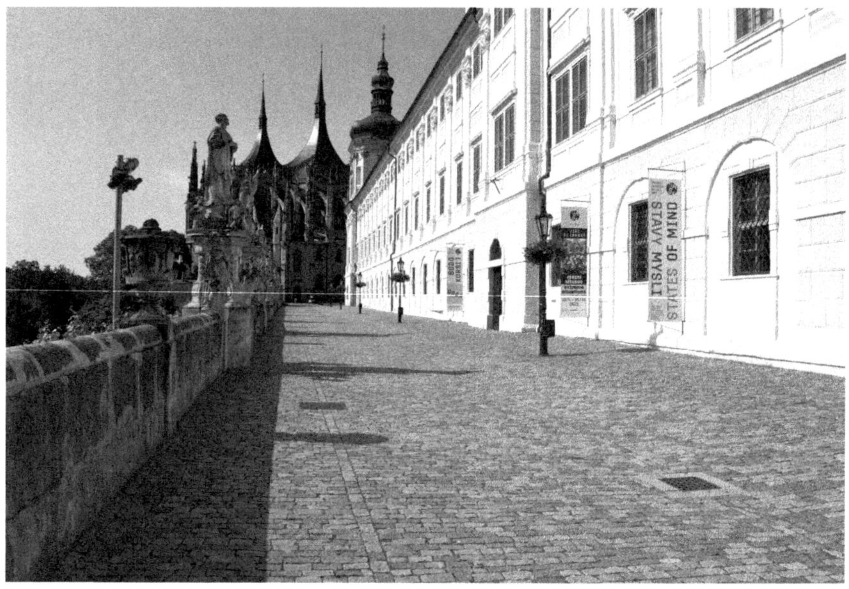

GASK – the Gallery of the Central Bohemian Region in Kutná Hora.

Photo: Katarzyna Jagodzińska

GASK – the Gallery of the Central Bohemian Region is a new chapter in the history of an institution established in 1963 as the Central Bohemian Gallery, originally located in Prague and with a depository and permanent exhibition at the restored Nelahozeves Castle about 35 km from Prague. In 1965, the first permanent exhibition of modern art from the collection of galleries was opened, and temporary exhibitions of modern and contemporary Czech art were organized. The exhibition was shown at the castle until 1971. From the 1960s to the 1980s, the museum organized temporary and long-term exhibitions at various locations around central Bohemia, and between 1991 and 1995, it staged exhibitions in the cloister halls of Carolinum in Prague, the historical seat of Charles University. From 1973, the museum was located in three internally connected historical houses in the center of Prague, on the route connecting Prague Castle with the Old Town Square. In 1993, the museum changed its name to the Czech Museum of Fine Arts, Prague. The change was motivated on the one hand by the desire to occupy a place on the international stage and on the other by the desire to break with the past, specifically with the gallery's previous role as a cultural organ of post-1968 hard-line ideology. Until 2000, the museum was administered by the Ministry of Culture, and then from 2000 the newly established regional government of Central Bohemia took over responsibility. Due to the modest exhibition space, the extensive museum collection was presented only occasionally, in the form of temporary exhibitions. The Jesuit College building in the historical town of Kutná Hora, about 70 km away from Prague, transferred to the museum in 1998 for depository spaces and a permanent presentation of the collection, was the intended solution.

The museum opened in 2010 under new management and staff. The name was changed to GASK, and the gallery headquarters was moved to Kutná Hora as opposed to the original plan to keep it in Prague.

The collection is now presented in the form of long-term displays. The theme of the first exhibition, *Collection 1 2 3. The Tracks of History in Acquisitions* (2010–2014) was to show how political changes in Czechoslovakia/the Czech Republic influenced the museum's acquisition policy. The second exhibition from the collection *States of Mind/Beyond the Image* (from 2014, updated in 2017) is ahistorical and based on contrasting thematic pairs such as: solitude/friendship, courage/fear, irony/respect, confinement/freedom, alienation/meditation, independence/obsession and idealism/cynicism.

> For more on the politics behind opening GASK in Kutná Hora, see Chapter 1.
>
> For more on the adaptation of the Jesuit College, see Chapter 4.

1.5 Prague: Artbanka Museum of Young Art (AMoYA)

activity: 2011–2013
adapted building
investment type: private
exhibition space: 4,000 m²
former address: Karlova 2, Praha 1

The museum opened in 2011 and operated for only a year and a half. It was created by Petr Šec and Olga Dvořák, and was located in the Baroque Colloredo-Mansfeld palace rented from the Municipal Gallery on the Royal Route in Prague. The aristocratic palace had been associated with art in the past. From the beginning of the nineteenth century, it housed the Colloredo-Mansfeld art gallery. In 1818, the gallery was opened to the public, and in 1840, the first annual exhibition of the resurrected Union of Fine Arts was held here. The palace's decoration occupies a two-story, oval ballroom boasting a rococo ceiling painting. In 1953, the archives of the Academy of Sciences were located here, and the building itself, without concern for its historic fabric, was adapted for office use. Walls were either taken down or new ones were installed, wiring was installed, and the parquet was covered with linoleum.

Before the museum was opened, the building underwent only a basic adaptation. Exposed past uses of the building became an integral part of the presentation of contemporary art. A ticket office and store were installed. So-called Part A of the building was assigned to important names in Czech and international art. Parts B and C were flats that give the impression of recently having been abandoned. Wallpaper, carpets, tiles, and washbasins became the background for the art being created today: in Part B, these were works by artists from the Czech and Slovak art academies, while Part C contained curatorial projects of an alternative nature.

See more in Chapter 4.

1.6 *Prague: DOX Centre for Contemporary Art (Centrum současného umění DOX)*

opening: 2008
adaptation project: Ivan Kroupa
investment type: private
exhibition space: 2,510 m² + 614 m² terrace for external installations
address: Poupětova 1, Praha 7
www.dox.cz/cs

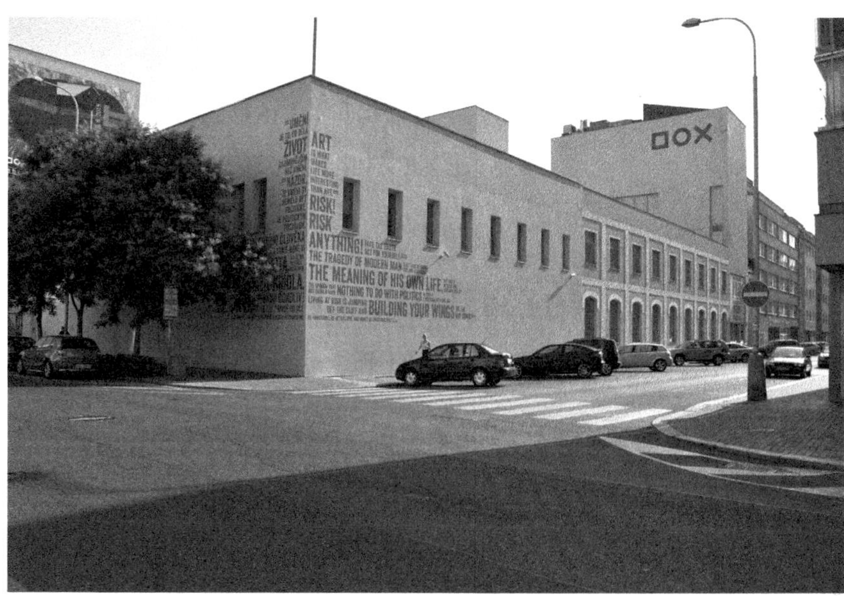

DOX Centre for Contemporary Art in Prague.
Photo: Katarzyna Jagodzińska

The beginnings of the DOX Centre for Contemporary Art date back to 2002. Its initiator was the developer Leoš Válka. Originally, he planned to create a loft complex in the post-industrial building; however, captivated by the potential of post-industrial architecture, he decided to open a center of contemporary art. He took on partners to implement his idea. The opening, anticipated for several years, took place in 2008.

The name DOX derives from the Greek word, *doxa*, meaning opinion, glory, faith, point of view, reputation, and paradox. It refers to the nearby port (docks) and the industrial heritage of the Holešovice district (DOX 2008: 1).

The Center presents international contemporary art, architecture, and design. It does not have a collection; its curators produce the exhibitions, or they are hosted from other venues. The model for DOX is MAK – the Austrian Museum of Applied Arts/Contemporary Art in Vienna. Válka emphasizes that the full spectrum of art is to be shown in DOX. As at MAK, it is to be presented alongside contemporary design and architecture (Skřivánek 2008). The DOX specialty is problem-based exhibitions. Válka explains:

> We focus on projects with a critical stance and a wider social agenda that extends beyond the often too self-contained domain of contemporary art. [. . .] There are other places that do the more conventional exhibitions and they do them well. So we want to do things which are more challenging, more difficult – not for difficulty's sake, but because they pose questions which are difficult to communicate.
>
> (Interview with Leoš Válka 2015)

In 2016, a new space, Airship Gulliver, was opened on the roof of DOX, serving primarily as a site for literary gatherings related to the exhibitions. Gulliver is a 42-meter-long wooden construction resembling a zeppelin. In 2018 a new multi-functional space DOX+ for performing arts was opened.

1.7 Prague: FUTURA Project

opening: 2003
adapted building
investment nature: private
exhibition space of the Center for Contemporary Art: over 1000 m²
address: Center for Contemporary Art – Holečkova 49, Praha 5; Karlín
    Studios – Kasárna Karlín, Prvního pluku 2, Praha 8
www.futuraproject.cz

Center for Contemporary Art FUTURA (Centrum pro současné umění FUTURA) was founded by Italian architect Alberto Di Stefano. The institution was conceived as a link between small commercial galleries and large institutions (Horáková 2003). It is part of the so-called FUTURA Project, next to the Karlín Studios, where there are workshops for artists and gallery activities, and the Třebešice Castle, which holds the artists residency program and an art collection.

The center is located in a post-industrial building; it is not directly accessible from the street, but hidden behind the façade of a tenement house. Access is via a locked gate and staircase, behind which a post-industrial building rises in a spacious yard. Its adaptation for the purposes of the art gallery under the direction of Di Stefano was carried out at a very quick pace (three months). The spare nature of the halls was the consequence of limited financial resources. In the garden there is a permanent installation by David Černý, *Brownnosing*, unveiled at the center's opening in 2003.

Karlín Studios in its original building, former ČKD machine factory, rented out between 2005–2016 sixteen spaces to local and international artists as the first project of its type in the Czech Republic. Alberto Di Stefano adapted the post-industrial building for the artists' ateliers after the studio complex at Wenceslas Square was sold in 2004. One of the artists who lost his studio there was Jiří David, who turned to Di Stefano for help in finding new accommodations. Together, they sought out the building owned by M2 real estate company and agreement was set according to which each of the artist would donate to this company a work of art each year. The Karlín Studios building has also become the seat of two galleries. In 2017, it moved to a new post-industrial location in the same district, the Kasárna Karlín former barracks, original building of Karlin Studios was demolished and complex offices and flats is being built there instead.

1.8 Prague: MeetFactory

> activity: 2001–2002, reopened in 2007
> adapted building
> investment type: private
> exhibition space: 300 m² (gallery)
> address: Ke Sklárně 15, Praha 5
> www.meetfactory.cz

MeetFactory was conceived by the Czech artist David Černy, who gained international fame with his controversial sculptures. It was opened in 2001 in a former slaughterhouse located in the post-industrial district of Holešovice. The institution's name is a play on words responding to the building's previous function: meat, meet, meat factory, meeting factory. The Prague flood of 2002 forced the creators of MeetFactory to close. In 2005, it managed to acquire a new structure (also post-industrial) in the Smíchov district. It is now housed in a former railway building situated on a degraded plot between the train tracks, the city's multi-lane highway and viaduct. Adjacent to the tracks there is a tram line that provides transportation to and from the city center.

MeetFactory interprets contemporary art widely, integrating various fields of artistic activity and media under one roof: visual arts, theater, music, film.

It is not only an exhibition space, but above all a place where art is created: artists' studios occupy two floors; some studios are more or less permanent, and some are rented as part of a residency program.

1.9 Prague: Museum Kampa – The Jan and Meda Mládek Foundation (Nadace Jana a Medy Mládkových)

opening: 2001
adapted building
investment type: private and public
exhibition space: 3,800 m², courtyard 430 m²
address: U Sovových mlýnů 2, Praha 1
www.museumkampa.cz

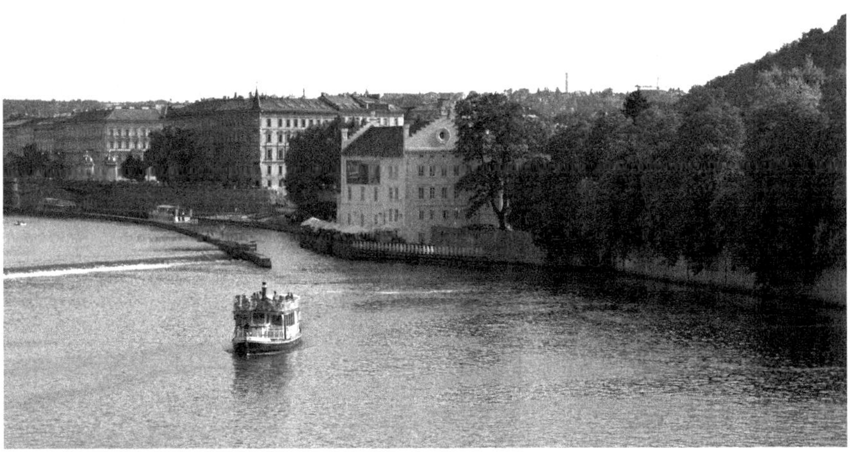

Museum Kampa – The Jan and Meda Mládek Foundation in Prague.

Photo: Katarzyna Jagodzińska

The Kampa Museum was established for the art that Meda and Jan Mládek collected while in exile. Meda Mládek donated her share to the city of Prague after the Velvet Revolution. The collection includes the work of artists from Czechoslovakia and Central Europe, which the Mládeks have been collecting since the 1960s. The purchase of art and its exhibition in the United States were intended to assist artists who were unable to exhibit in Czechoslovakia.

The ruined Sova's mill complex in the Kampa district was chosen for its headquarters. The city financed the restoration of the Renaissance-Baroque building, adding elements of contemporary architecture through Mládek's initiative. The building began services in 2001; however, due to flooding, the official public opening took place in 2003.

The museum's mission statement notes that "[a] collection of Central European art serves not only as a reminder of the so called Eastern Bloc but also contributes to the awareness of modern Czech culture" (The Jan and Meda Mládek Foundation n.d.).

The Kampa Museum is the custodian of three collections:

1   The Jan and Meda Mládek Collection, which includes the works of František Kupka, Otto Gutfreund, Jiří Kolář, and the Collection of Central European Art. The latter includes works by Czech, Slovak, Polish, Hungarian, and Yugoslav artists predominantly from the 1960s and 1970s. The works of 1950s Czech and Slovak artists, which Mládek from 1967 bought directly from artists' studios, constitute the largest portion of this collection (The Art of Jan and Meda Mládek n.d.).

2   Jiří and Běla Kolář collection. It consists of several sections: classic works by Czech artists, key figures of the avant-garde from the first half of the twentieth century, works of the Group 42, to which Kolář belonged, and works of artists representing various "experimental" approaches debuting at the turn of the 1950s and 1960s (The Jiří and Běla Kolář Collection n.d.).

3   The Jindřich Chalupecki collection. This tribute to Jindřich Chalupecki was assembled from 1989 to the beginning of 1990 with a view to sales, the proceeds from which were to be used to purchase a dialysis machine for a gravely ill art historian. The show hung for two weeks in the National Gallery and presented works by artists from several generations. Ultimately, two-thirds of the cost of the machine was covered by the Karta 77 Foundation, and Meda Mládek paid for the rest. After the exhibition was closed, the work was moved to the Prague castle. In 2001–2003 it was transferred to the Mládek foundation (Collection for the Renowned Theoretician Jindřich Chalupecký n.d.).

The history of this collection is described in more detail in Chapter 7.
The issues related to the adaptation of the Sova's mill are presented in Chapter 5.

1.10 *Prague: National Gallery – Trade Fair Palace (Národní galerie – Veletržní palác)*

opening: 1995
adapted building
investment type: public
exhibition space: 20,000 m²
address: Dukelských hrdinů 47, Praha
www.ngprague.cz

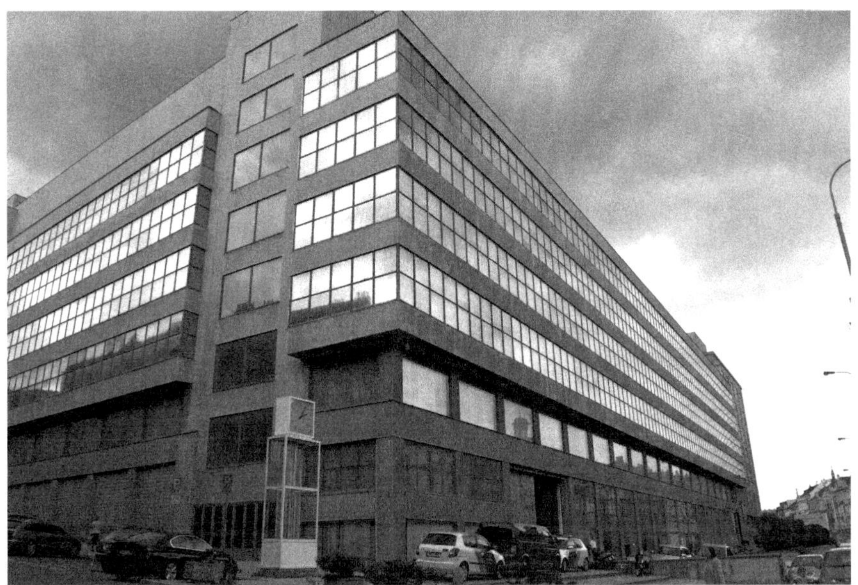

National Gallery – Trade Fair Palace in Prague.
Photo: Katarzyna Jagodzińska

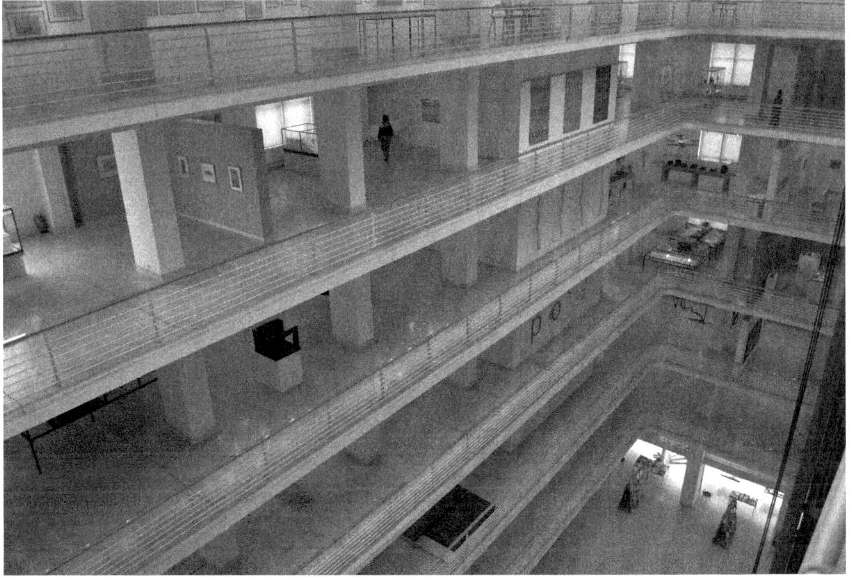

National Gallery – Trade Fair Palace in Prague. Interior.
Photo: Katarzyna Jagodzińska

The National Gallery in Prague was founded in 1796. It has been operating under this name since 1949. The history of its modern art collections dates back to 1902, when Emperor Franz Joseph I founded the Contemporary Gallery of the Kingdom of Bohemia. The Trade Fair Palace was chosen in 1978 after the Prague technical trade building was destroyed by fire in 1974. It holds the departments of art of the end of the nineteenth, twentieth, and beginning of the twenty-first centuries. As Jaroslav Anděl points out, then-director Jiří Kotalík chose to follow the Parisian Centre Pompidou, creating a vision for a contemporary department (Working Session: Second 1997: 48).

Originally, the trading complex in the Holešovice district was to cover a much larger area. In 1924, a closed competition for the architectural design of the trade fair headquarters was announced. Six architects entered; the architects earning the highest appraisals were Alois Dryák, Josef Fuchs, and Oldřich Tyl. The investment was to consist of four buildings: the two main structures (A and B) were to house offices, exhibition spaces, warehouses, and restaurants. Building C was to accommodate flats and office space, and Building D, a hotel. In the second stage of the competition, the management commissioned Tyl and Fuchs to develop the plans for Building A, which was to become a prototype for the other structures (Masák, Švácha and Vybíral 1995: 9–13). Its economically unjustified momentum, high maintenance costs, competition from the fair complex in Brno, and the economic crisis completely hampered the project's implementation (and explains why fewer foreign exhibitors participated in the event after 1929). Finally, only Building A – Veletržní palác (construction 1925–1928) was completed. It was the first large public building (dimensions: 140×75 meters, 37 meters high, central hall 15 meters high) in the Czech Republic designed in the functionalist style (Masák, Švácha and Vybíral 1995: 24–26, 35).

The building fulfilled its trade function until 1951. In 1974, a fire consumed a significant portion of it such that the authorities considered demolition. Eventually, in 1978, the building was handed over to the National Gallery by government decree. Construction plans were prepared in 1985–1989 by the SIAL office. The modernization and reconstruction of the building, which had been planned for four years, began in 2018. It will provide better conditions for presenting contemporary art (including increasing the story height to enable the installation of large-scale works) and will be open to the public to a greater extent (e.g. creating a public space in front of the building).

The collection of modern art of the National Gallery consists of works by Czech and international artists. Among the latter is a renowned collection of French art created in the late 1920s, when with the support of the Czechoslovak president Tomas Guarrigue Masaryk the National Gallery made purchases directly from artists' studios (including twenty-five paintings by Pablo Picasso). Towards the end of the second decade of the twenty-first century, the art of Central Europe began to play an increasingly important role in the gallery's program activities.

On the adaptation of Trade Fair Palace, see Chapter 4.
On the activities of the Trade Fair Palace, see Chapter 7.

2 Hungary

2.1 *Budapest: KOGART*

opening: 2004
adapted building
investment type: private
exhibition space: 1,600 m²
address: 112. Andrássy út, Budapest
www.kogart.hu

The creator of the KOGART Gallery is the economist, businessman, and private collector Gábor Kovács, whose passion for art led him to establish the foundation Kovács Gábor Művészeti Alapítvány (Gábor Kovács Art Foundation) in 2003, followed by an institution under the name, KOGART in 2004. Kovács is one of the wealthiest people in Hungary. He was the vice-president of Citibank in London, and after returning to Hungary, he became the president of Bankár Holding. He began collecting art in the early 1990s.

The institution's mission is to increase the accessibility and understanding of contemporary art among the Hungarian public. The goals of KOGART include the promotion of art, especially fine arts, supporting talented young artists, and the creation of an internationally valued collection of contemporary art composed mainly of works by Hungarian artists. These objectives were implemented by establishing a new model of art patronage in Hungary with the participation of the private sector (on the basis of materials for sponsors provided by KOGART).

The Gábor Kovács collection and the foundation collection exist independently. The latter focuses on contemporary art from the mid-twentieth century to the present, created from purchases of works by Hungarian artists. In 2018, the collection contained 2,500 works.

The headquarters of KOGART is a nineteenth-century villa on the stately Budapest boulevard. In 2013, the KOGART House branch was opened in the holiday resort of Tihany at Lake Balaton. Since 2015, KOGART organizes exhibitions in the Castle Garden's Guard's Palace based on the cooperation agreement with the Hungarian government.

For more on the collection, see Chapter 6.

2.2 Budapest: Ludwig Museum – Museum of Contemporary Art (Ludwig Múzeum – Kortárs Művészeti Múzeum)

opening: 1991 in Building "A" of the Royal Palace (Ludwig Museum, Budapest)
re-opening: 1996 in Building A of the Royal Palace (Ludwig Museum – Museum of Contemporary Art)
re-opening: 2005 at the Palace of Arts
project: Zoboki, Demeter and Associates (Palace of Arts)
investment type: public
exhibition space: 3,300 m²
address: Palace of Arts – Komor Marcell u. 1, Budapest
www.ludwigmuseum.hu

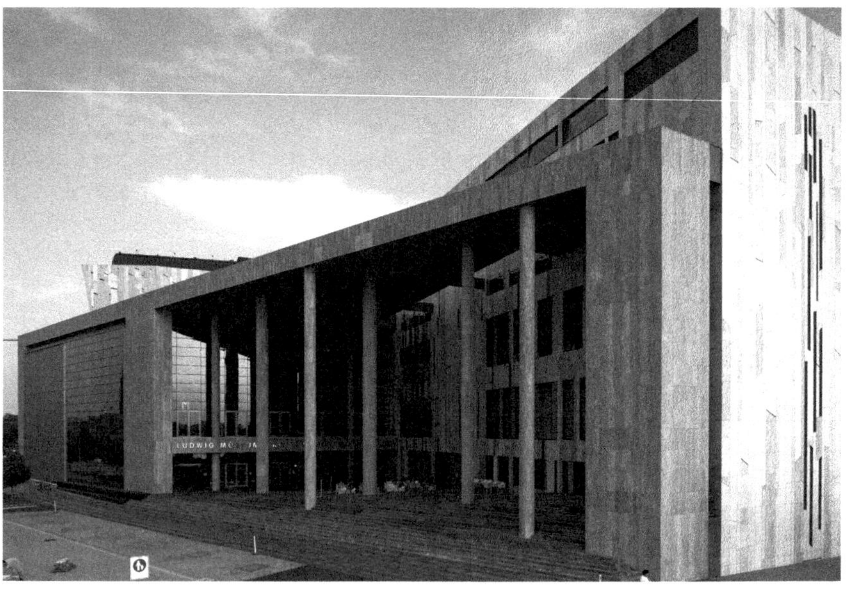

Ludwig Museum – Museum of Contemporary Art in Budapest.

Photo: Balázs GLÓDI © Ludwig Museum – Museum of Contemporary Art, Archives

The Ludwig Museum was formally established in 1989, and gained independence in 1996. Its beginning is marked by the gift of seventy works of contemporary international art for the Hungarian state from German collectors Peter and Irene Ludwig. The work was transferred in 1989. The collection was deposited at the Buda Castle, and the Hungarian National Gallery took over its care until the independent museum was established. The collection exhibition, opened in 1991, was supplemented with further works donated in the form of a long-term loan by the Ludwig Foundation and the works of contemporary Hungarian artists from the National Gallery. The new museum received three floors of the so-called Building A of the Royal Castle, and achieved its institutional and financial independence in 1996, when the government founded Museum of Contemporary Art on the basis of the Ludwig Museum. The new museum started to build an independent Hungarian and Eastern European collection (from the late 1960s onward), related to the international collection.

In 2005, the museum was moved to a new building – the Palace of Arts (Müpa) in the new cultural district of Millennium City Center, where it was located next to the Béla Bartók National Concert Hall and the Festival Theater.

The new building was not originally designed with the Ludwig Museum in mind; hence, the museum was located in a space that was not adapted for its collection. The architectural design of the Palace of Arts is the Budapest architectural office of Zoboki, Demeter and Associates, which in 2000 won a closed competition to design a monumental building for cultural purposes in the Millennium City Center. The museum joined the planning process from 2003.

The collection includes works by international, Central European and Hungarian artists.

See more on the Palace of Arts in Chapter 5.
See more on the beginnings of the museum in Chapter 6.
See more on the Central European sketch of the collection in Chapter 9.

2.3 Budapest: MEO Contemporary Art Collection (MEO Kortárs Művészeti Gyűjtemény)

activity: 2001–2007
adapted building, design of reception building: István Bényei
investment type: private
exhibition space: 2,600 m²
address (institution closed): József Attila u. 4–6, Budapest

The MEO art center was founded by entrepreneurs and collectors Lajos Kováts and Márton Winkler. On the site of Táncsics's nineteenth-century tannery, in which the Quality Control Department functioned, two buildings were erected for the center's headquarters. Its name in Hungarian is Minőség Ellenőrzési Osztály; taking its name from this, MEO opened in 2001. To the former factory buildings in which the exhibition halls were located, a small reception building was added which shimmered with color after dark.

The center was a place where Kováts's collection of contemporary art was presented and a space for temporary shows.

Due to unprofitability and misunderstandings between the owners associated with the operation and artistic program, the MEO closed in 2006 (Rácz 2006). At the end of 2006, its activity was reactivated under the name WAX for a period of one year.

2.4 *Debrecen: MODEM Modern and Contemporary Arts Centre (MODEM Modern és Kortárs Művészeti Központ)*

opening: 2006
project: András Kováts (Keletterv)
investment type: public
exhibition space: 3,000 m²
address: Baltazár Dezső tér 1, Debrecen
www.modemart.hu

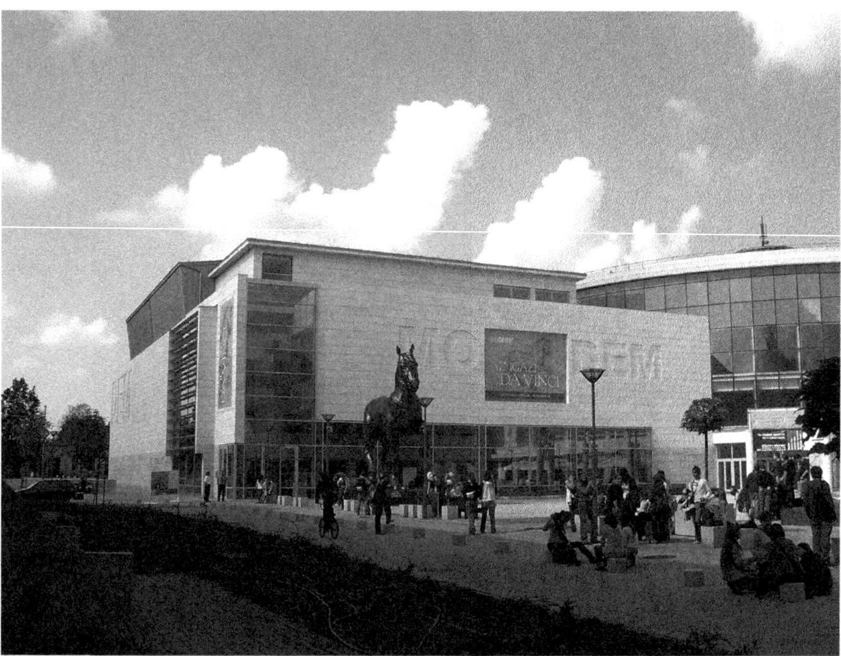

MODEM Modern and Contemporary Arts Centre in Debrecen.

Photo: Katarzyna Jagodzińska

In 2005, Debrecen took part in the competition for the European Capital of Culture; the application described plans to create a modern art gallery in the city. It was to become a place for the permanent display of a private collection of Hungarian modern and contemporary art belonging to the local collector, Péter Antal. Antal deposited the collection with the city authorities, who in turn placed it under the aegis of the newly created MODEM Modern and Contemporary Arts Centre.

MODEM was opened in 2006 on the site of the Kölcsey Központ Conference Center, hotel, and restaurant, a new building complex erected at the time the largest in eastern Hungary. Originally, office space was planned for the portion of the complex MODEM would occupy.

Until 2015, MODEM was run by a public company, then for three years it lost its organizational independence and was harnessed to the structure of the Déri Múzeum. The change was intended to facilitate the acquisition of funds for activities (MODEM could act as a museum, not a center of art) or care for collections; but it led to the departure of a part of the team, the breaking of previously established contacts, and the weakening of the institution both in Hungary and the international arena. In 2018, it returned to the earlier organizational arrangement.

At the beginning of the twentieth century in Debrecen, Sámuel Lusztig started the collection on which MODEM's activity is based. His collector's passion continued with his grandson Péter Antal. After ten years, the collector resigned from the mode of collection deposits and it is available instead as part of temporary exhibitions; the collector is in charge of storage. The collection, comprised of Hungarian art of the twentieth and twenty-first centuries, as well as a host of monochromatic works, contains over four thousand objects. MODEM also accumulated a small collection of art.

One of the themes that is gaining prominence in the temporary exhibition program is the art of artists from Central Europe.

2.5 Dunaújváros: Institute of Contemporary Art (Kortárs Művészeti Intézet), ICA-D

opening: 1997
expansion project: Péter Juhász
investment type: public
exhibition space: 450 m²
address: Vasmű út 12, Dunaújváros
www.ica-d.hu

The Institute of Contemporary Art, Dunaújváros – ICA-D was founded in 1997. The beginnings of the institution reside in the proposal of a former local entrepreneur living in Sweden, Lajos Takács, for the organization of Salvador Dalí's works from his collection in the city. The exhibition, showing works from his collection, as well as works from several Swedish galleries, was held in 1989 in a Uitz Hall managed by the local cultural center. The success of the exhibition meant that the collector offered to donate the collection to the city if a suitable place for it could be found. The Foundation for Modern Art, whose aim was to create a museum and build a collection based on works on loan, was established in 1990. In 1992, Uitz Hall went under the management of the foundation, and Takács loaned his collection. Part of this loan was also the work provided by contemporary Hungarian artists. In the same year, the foundation also began to acquire its own art collection. Works from both collections were presented at temporary exhibitions. The museum was opened in the expanded Uitz Hall according to plans by Péter Juhász.

A Dalí Museum or Hungarian Museum of Modern Art was originally planned, but an institute of art was ultimately established following Western patterns. The opening of an independent institution also meant the end of cooperation with the collector (Interview with Nóra Deák 2017).

At the very beginning, the institute's collection focused on the work of young contemporary Hungarian artists. Together with output from the period of artistic development, later work created by artists added to the collection at the start of their careers was also accessioned.

2.6 Paks: Gallery of Paks (Paksi Képtár)

> opening: 1991 (2007)
> adaptation project: Gyula Kiss and Irén Járomi (Kiss és Járomi Építésziroda)
> investment type: public
> exhibition space: 1,100 m²
> address: Tolnai út 2, Paks
> http://paksikeptar.hu

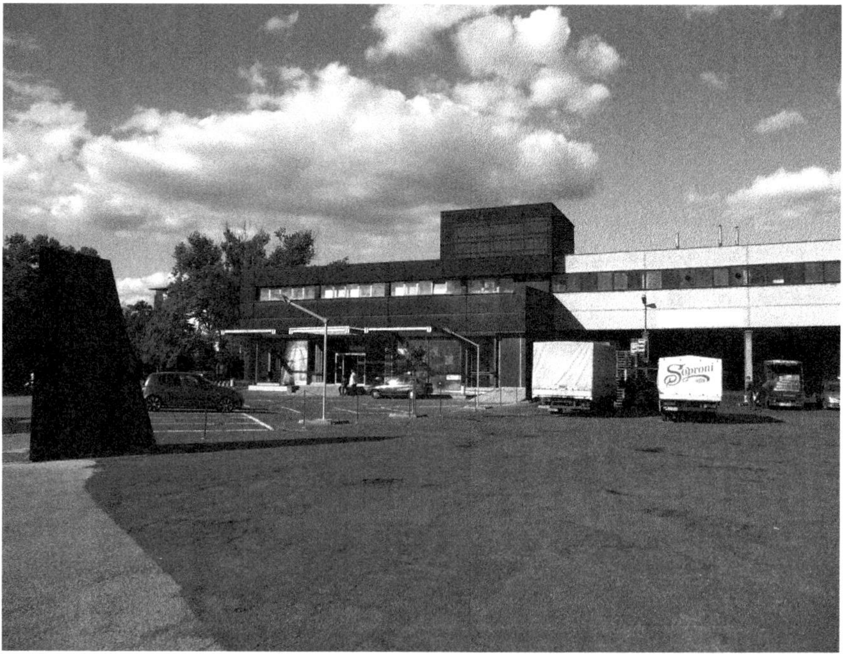

Gallery of Paks.

Photo: Katarzyna Jagodzińska

The Gallery of Paks was created on the initiative of local artist Károly Halász, who persuaded the city council to establish a gallery in Paks, a town of barely fifteen thousand inhabitants. The aim of the institution from the very beginning was not only the presentation of contemporary art, but also the building of a collection. The gallery started its activity in the neoclassical building of the former Erzsébet hotel. Due to the growing size of the collection, the building proved too small, and it became necessary to seek out a new space. In 2007, a new gallery headquarters was opened on the premises of the adapted vegetable preserves factory.

The gallery's priority is artistic education. Cooperation with schools takes place within the city of Paks and surrounding villages.

Initially, only local and regional artists' works were included in the collection, but with the passage of time, the collector's strategy began to encompass the entire territory of Hungary. Temporary exhibitions focus on the art of constructivism and geometric abstraction.

3 Poland

3.1 Białystok: Arsenal Gallery (Galeria Arsenał)

opening: 1965
adapted buildings
investment type: public
exhibition space: 350 m² + 650 m² in power plant
address: ul. A. Mickiewicza 2 and Arsenal Gallery Elektrownia: ul. Elektryczna 13, Białystok
http://galeria-arsenal.pl

Arsenal Gallery was established in 1965 as a gallery in the network of the Bureaus of Art Exhibitions (BWA). Ten years later, it gained a permanent seat in the building of the former eighteenth-century arsenal. In 1994, the gallery subject to the provincial authorities passed to the management of the municipal authorities, and two years later, its name was changed to Arsenal Gallery. Since 1990, Monika Szewczyk has been running the gallery continuously, creating from the local gallery one of the most important institutions of contemporary art in Poland (also active on the international stage).

The gallery contains two separate art collections. The first, *Three Streams. Realism – Metaphor – Geometry* was from the period 1965–1985, while the second named *Collection II* was created from the beginning of the 1990s and covers the most important phenomena in Polish art, and reflects the traces of changes that took place in culture after the period of systemic transformation – as well as the most important tendencies in contemporary art of Belarus, Ukraine, the Czech Republic and Armenia. In 2005–2016, *Collection II* was complemented by the Podlasie Society for the Encouragement of Fine Arts (created as a part of the program "Znaki Czasu") with its purchases.

In 2011, the gallery acquired a second exhibition space – a power plant building from the early twentieth century. The building is awaiting renovation, but exhibitions have been organized there even before the building was officially acquired (since 2008).

3.2 Gdańsk: LAZNIA Centre for Contemporary Art (Centrum Sztuki Współczesnej ŁAŹNIA)

opening: 1998, second headquarters opened in 2012
adapted building
investment type: public
exhibition space: 618 m²
address: LAZNIA 1: ul. Jaskółcza 1, Gdańsk
LAZNIA 2 Art Education Center: ul. Strajku Dokerów 5, Gdańsk
www.laznia.pl

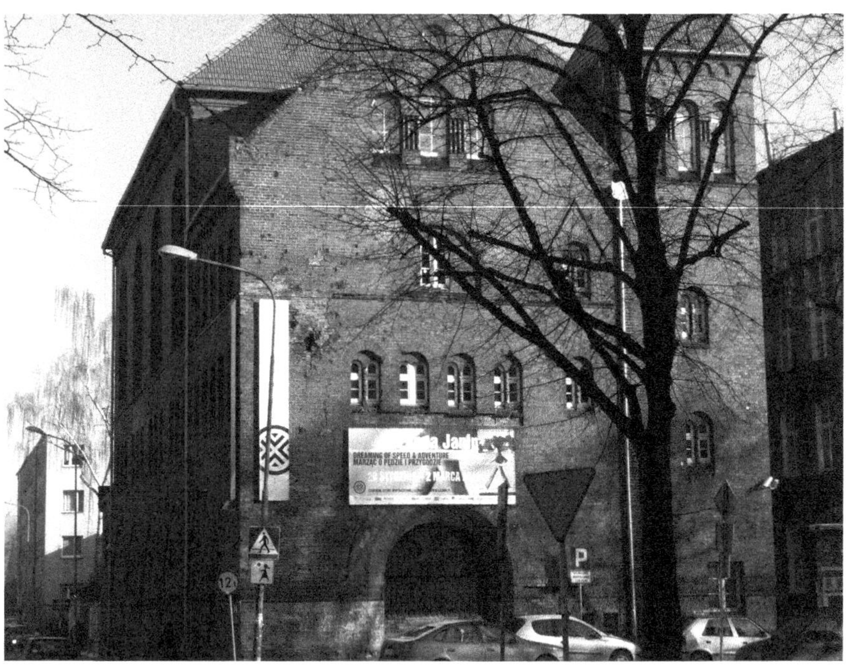

LAZNIA Centre for Contemporary Art in Gdańsk.
Photo: Katarzyna Jagodzińska

The beginnings of the LAZNIA Centre for Contemporary Art are associated with the operation of the Wyspa Gallery established in 1987 by Grzegorz Klaman on Granary Island, in one of the burned-down grain warehouses. In 1992, Klaman together with two artists' associations acquired the building of an abandoned early twentieth-century municipal bathhouse, in which they wanted to organize their studios and run a gallery to present their works. The exhibition, *The Collection of Contemporary Art for the 1000th Anniversary of Gdańsk*, organized in 1997 as part of the official millennium celebrations, paved the way. The title of the exhibition was to provoke discussion on the lack of such a collection in Gdańsk (Szyłak, Klaman and Bartołowicz 1995, Leszkowicz 2008).

LAZNIA, which was created a year later, was charged with the task – as the first director Aneta Szyłak says, of "commenting on political and social reality. Let us remember that Poland was at that time in the period of intense political transformation and strengthening of its democratic institutions. We wanted to participate in this process" (Świerczyńska 2008). The institution was established in the Dolne Miasto district fraught with social problems (unemployment, crime).

The flagship project of LAZNIA is the Outdoor Gallery of the City of Gdańsk (since 2005). It builds a collection of permanent works of art in the urban space (selected through a competitive procedure) that will contribute to the social and architectural transformation of the neglected district.

In 2012, second seat in the Nowy Port district was established under the name LAZNIA 2 Art Education Center. The adaptation of the building, another historical bathhouse, for cultural purposes is again part of the district's revitalization project.

3.3 Gdańsk: Wyspa Institute of Art (Instytut Sztuki Wyspa)

> activity: 2004–2016
> adapted building
> investment type: non-governmental
> investor: Wyspa Progress Foundation
> exhibition space: 600 m²
> address (out of date): ul. Doki 1/145 B, Gdańsk
> www.wyspa.art.pl

The establishment of the Wyspa Institute of Art was preceded by the release of Aneta Szyłak from the position of the director of the LAZNIA Centre for Contemporary Art in 2001, and the closure of Wyspa Gallery, run by Wyspa Progress Foundation. The creators of the foundation, Grzegorz Klaman and Szyłak, started to search for a place that would allow them to continue their current activity. Their choice fell on the former Gdańsk Shipyard area, where they already had the opportunity to work: in 2000, they created the blueprint for the *Road to Freedom* exhibition dedicated to Solidarity. First, in 2002, they acquired the Modelarnia building, in which they created artists' studios; then, in 2004, they acquired the building of the former Naval Shipbuilding School, in which the foundation established IS Wyspa.

The mission of the institute, strongly embedded in the history and identity of the place, was sketched by Szyłak to:

> reveal the complexity of the relationships between people and between the different modi of formatting the Shipyard discourse. [. . .] This was

not only a discourse about the Shipyard as a workplace, an economy, and the possibility of collapse, nor a discourse about the history of Solidarity. We were also interested in the subversive role of individual memory, in alternative economies that might serve as a sort of proposition, and in how we could reflect on the Shipyard's materiality and its underappreciated material heritage. We were curious to see how we could look in a different way at the social relationships and the meaningfulness of the Shipyard people. We were searching for those who had been excluded from the field of visibility and hadn't experienced the process of individuation, liberation from the movement.

(A living experience 2015: 97–99)

The basic objectives of the institute included activities for the Young City (Młode Miasto) district, which includes the shipyard's privatized area – its revitalization, integration with the growing city, and cultural and social activation. This program was implemented through the organization of debates, discussions, seminars, artistic projects, and projects of a social and historical nature.

3.4 Gdańsk: NOMUS New Museum of Art (Nowe Muzeum Sztuki NOMUS) – Muzeum Narodowe w Gdańsku (National Museum in Gdańsk)

creation: 2017
opening at the temporary building: scheduled in 2018
investment type: public
address: ul Jaracza 14, Gdańsk
www.nomus.gda.pl

In 2006, the National Museum in Gdańsk attempted the creation of a branch dealing with contemporary art on a plot adjacent to the museum's main edifice. Due to numerous construction projects the city was undertaking at the time, the construction of the building did not take place. Creation of the new institution begun in 2015, on the site of the former Gdańsk Shipyard, which had begun to grow into a culture district (with The European Solidarity Center and the Museum of the Second World War).

The abbreviation NOMUS – formed from the first syllables and the letters of the Polish words "new art museum" – carries an additional meaning, which was laid out in the Museum's Manifesto, it was:

[p]honetically close to the Greek word NOMUS meaning law, including social law and order of the community, and in the Egyptian tradition, meaning a unit of territorial division. We reach for our law, local law, to write our own art history – from scratch. We do not strive

to make our museum similar to others and to reproduce the canonical image of art.

(Szyłak 2017)

The task of NOMUS will be to document the art of Gdańsk and the region, and to introduce it into the canon of Polish art history (Interview with Aneta Szyłak 2017). The emphasis was placed not on contemporary art, but on the institution. The Manifesto states: "The concept of new art seems a bit of a worn-out idea; rather, it is about a museum that takes a new look at collecting strategies, display methodology, or conducting research. So it is new in the sense of a new programming offer" (Szyłak 2017).

The temporary seat of the museum will be the former seat of the Wyspa Institute of Art, and the target site is to be located in one of the adapted post-shipyard buildings.

3.5 Katowice: Szyb Wilson Gallery (Galeria Szyb Wilson)

opening: 2001
adapted building
investment type: private
exhibition space: 2,500 m²
address: ul. Oswobodzenia 1, Katowice
www.szybwilson.org

In terms of space, this is the largest private art gallery in Poland. It is located on the site belonging to the "Wieczorek" coal mine which dates back to the 1820s. The Wilson shaft, after which the gallery was named, was in use until 1995. Three years later, the entrepreneur Johann Bros bought the building in order to adapt it to the gallery of modern art, which was opened in 2001. The gallery, consisting of three parts, is housed in the buildings of the guild-hall and bathhouse.

The gallery is run by the Eco-Art Foundation. The main purpose of the gallery is to promote the work of young artists, including that of children and youth. The flagship event organized in the gallery is the international Art Naif Festival.

3.6 Katowice: Muzeum Śląskie

opening: 2015
project: Riegler Riewe Architekten
investment type: public
exhibition space: 7,000 m²
address: ul. T. Dobrowolskiego 1, Katowice
https://muzeumslaskie.pl

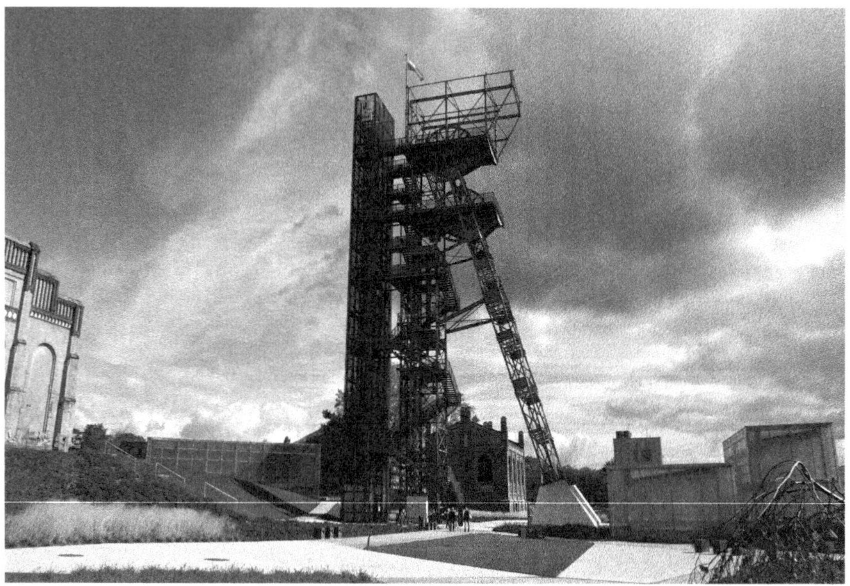

Muzeum Śląskie in Katowice.
Photo: Katarzyna Jagodzińska

The Muzeum Śląskie (Silesian Museum) was established in 1929, but it waited for its proper building until 2015, when the headquarters was opened on the site of the "Katowice" bituminous coal mine. The finished museum building, which the institution had not managed to move into, was demolished during the war by the Nazis. At that time, the museum was liquidated. It resumed operations in 1984 in a converted hotel building located in the city center. Since then, efforts have been made to erect a new building. The project chosen in the architectural competition was not carried out for financial reasons.

In the architectural competition staged in 2007, the design of the Austrian studio Riegler Riewe Architekten was selected. Underground exhibition rooms have been designed, and in the above-ground portion of the building, there are visible structures that capture and bring light into the interior, as well as an office building. These white glass cuboids contrast with the mine's red brick buildings. Historical buildings are successively revitalized and adapted for museum purposes (headquarters of individual museum departments, an educational exhibition for children, a restaurant). The investment symbol, visible from a distance, is the 40-meter-high mine shaft hoisting tower "Warszawa II", which has been transformed into a viewing platform offering a panoramic view of the Katowice city center, the area of the former mine, the seat of the National Polish Radio Symphony Orchestra, and the International Congress Center. Together with the museum and the famous Spodek Sports and Entertainment Arena (1971), these form the Cultural Zone.

The Muzeum Śląskie is multidisciplinary in nature. The Center for Polish Scenography operates under its aegis; it maintains historical, archaeological, and ethnographic collections, and vocational arts. Nevertheless, art occupies a central place in the museum, and the collection of modern and contemporary art is well exposed at the permanent exhibition. The museum also has a space for temporary exhibitions dedicated to contemporary art – a gallery featuring a single work of art which is separated from the main exhibition space. It is intended to resemble the Turbine Hall at Tate Modern. Large-format site-specific works are implemented here. Also, the second, larger exhibition hall often exhibits contemporary art.

The opening of the museum in the new building took place in 2015. It was preceded by controversies surrounding the plans for an historical exhibition that told the complex history of Silesia. Subject to heated debate was the highly political issue of balance between Polish and German traditions in the exhibition. Ultimately, the director of the institution was replaced.

See more on the history of building the museum in Chapter 4.
See more on the architectural design in Chapter 3.

3.7 *Krakow: Cricoteka Center for the Documentation of the Art of Tadeusz Kantor (Ośrodek Dokumentacji Sztuki Tadeusza Kantora Cricoteka)*

opening in the new office: 2014
project: IQ2 Consortium (Piotr Nawara and Agnieszka Szultk from nsMoonStudio and Stanisław Deńko from Vision)
investment type: public
exhibition space: 760 m²
address: ul. Nadwiślańska 2–4, Krakow
www.cricoteka.pl

Cricoteka was founded in 1980 by Tadeusz Kantor. Until Kantor's death in 1990, it functioned as the Cricot 2 Center of Theater. Its headquarters was dispersed in several locations in Krakow, none of which offered the possibility of a wider presentation of Kantor's artistic achievements. In 2005, it was possible to adapt an old power plant of the district of Podgórze located on the Vistula River (erected in the years 1899–1900; after the Second World War, it served as a sanitation facility) for the needs of Cricoteka. In the following year, an international architectural design competition was organized for the adaptation and extension of the building. The historic power plant building was symbolically packed with a new architecture reminiscent of a bridge span, which is a direct reference to the art of Kantor. The new building houses exhibition halls – the Kantor art gallery and the temporary exhibition

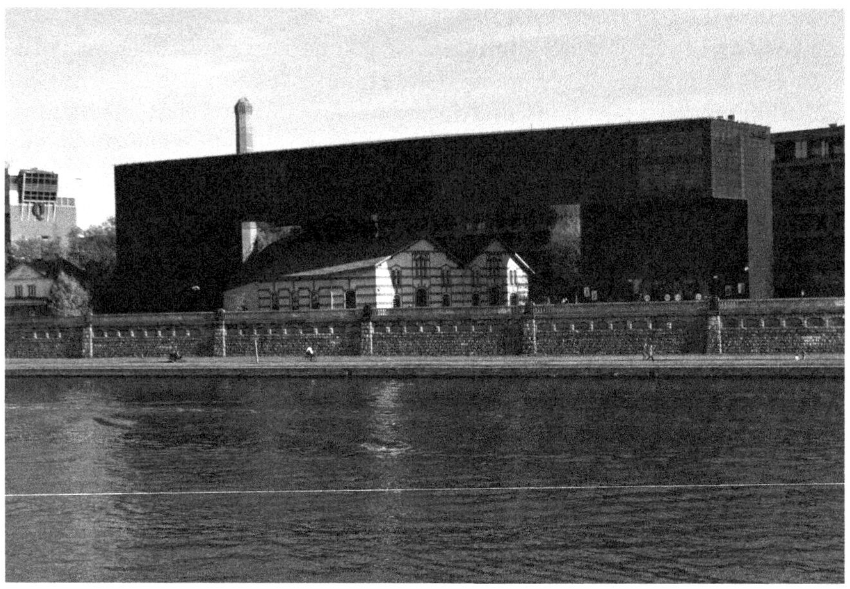

Cricoteka Center for the Documentation of the Art of Tadeusz Kantor in Krakow.
Photo: Katarzyna Jagodzińska

gallery – while the adapted theater building was created in the converted power plant building. Temporary exhibitions offer a context for Kantor's art; contemporary artists, contemporary works, and site specific pieces are shown here.

See more on the architectural design in Chapter 4.

3.8 *Krakow: MOCAK Museum of Contemporary Art in Krakow (Muzeum Sztuki Współczesnej w Krakowie MOCAK)*

opening: 2010
project: Claudio Nardi Architetto
investment type: public
exhibition space: 4,000 m²
address: ul. Lipowa 4, Krakow
www.mocak.pl

The need to establish a museum of contemporary art has been raised repeatedly in Krakow for years. The oldest correspondence with the city authorities on the subject of the establishment of such an institution dates from 1983–1985; in 1993, the city authorities proposed the creation of a Modern Art Department as part of the Historical Museum of the City of Krakow

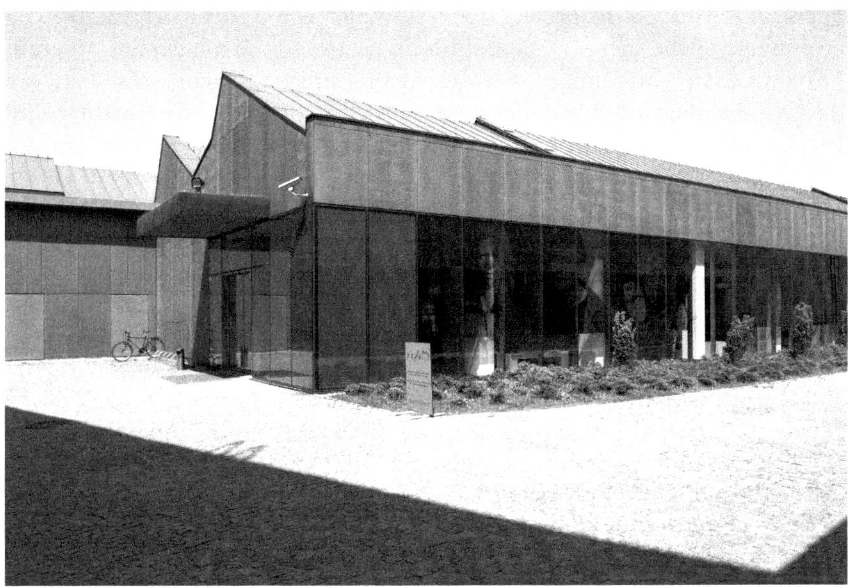

MOCAK Museum of Contemporary Art in Krakow in Krakow.

Photo: Katarzyna Jagodzińska

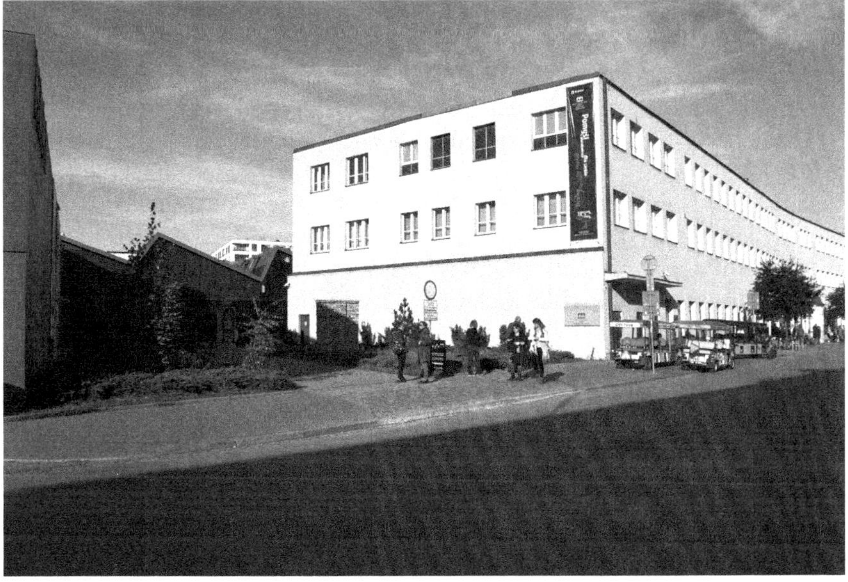

MOCAK Museum of Contemporary Art in Krakow (left) and Schindler's Factory (right).

Photo: Katarzyna Jagodzińska

on the site of the former "Lenin's house". However, due to the lack of financial resources, the project was not implemented (MOCAK 2010). The beginnings of the museum should be connected to the ministerial program "Znaki Czasu", announced in 2004. At that time, a dispute arose between the Krakow magistrate and the voivodship office on who the museum would appoint and where it would be located. Ultimately, the mayor of the city promoted a vision for the museum's creation at the former German Oskar Schindler Enamelware Factory.

Throughout the construction period and in the first years of the operations, the local press conducted a lively discussion about the museum's location. The original intention was to situate operations in the factory front building (performing previous administrative functions), but ultimately the building was handed over to the: Historical Museum of the City of Krakow and the permanent exhibition, *Kraków under Nazi Occupation 1939–1945* is installed there. Maria Anna Potocka, later elected as museum director, commented: "In the architectural competition, it was pointed out that no exhibition halls can be designed in factory buildings. All exhibition halls are new, so they do not interfere with the sacred nature of the place's traditions" (A Speech by Maria Anna Potocka 2010). In 2007, an international architectural competition was announced for the adaptation of Schindler's factory buildings, which the Florentine architect Claudio Nardi won. The public inauguration of the building took place in 2010.

The main museum building with a saw-tooth roof is a reference to the structures of the factory hall. On two levels (ground floor and basement) are galleries for permanent and temporary exhibitions. The adjoining building contains a conservation workshop, Beta Gallery, MOCAK reading room, and the Mieczysław Porębski Library. In 2013, the Re Gallery, an exhibition space designed for students of art schools, was opened.

The collection has been started from scratch. The oldest works date from the 1970s; however, the collection focuses on work created since the 1990s. Potocka also donated her collection of contemporary art in the form of gift, which she amassed over the years with a view to bequeathing it to the museum.

The exhibition of the collection has a changeable nature. Works are presented in a rotational formula, new acquisitions are exhibited, and the exhibition formula also changes to correlate with temporary exhibitions. In 2017, the museum inaugurated a collection of works in the public space around the MOCAK building.

> See more on the history of the factory, location, and issues of revitalization in Chapter 4.

3.9 *Łódź: Atlas Sztuki*

> activity: 2003–2017
> adapted building

investment type: private
exhibition space: 310 m²
address (out of date): ul. Piotrkowska 114/116, Łódź
www.atlassztuki.pl

The originator and creator of the Atlas Sztuki (Atlas of Art) was Andrzej Walczak, an architect by education and co-founder of one of the largest Polish companies in the construction industry, Atlas, which produces mainly adhesives and dry-mix mortars. He is one of Poland's wealthiest individuals. As Jacek Michalak, manager of the institution notes, "Art always interested Andrzej Walczak. He also believed that as a rich man, a man who was successful, he should share that. Being a great fan of Łódź, in trying to make this city change, that it should look better, he decided that this gallery will be on the agenda for the city's promotion and revitalization" (Interview with Jacek Michalak 2017).

The gallery operated in a one-story building of a nineteenth-century market hall located on the city's main pedestrian street, but concealed within a cavernous courtyard.

The program's goal was to show art's variety. Mainly, it showed Polish art by recognized artists, but also held exhibitions of foreign artists and collectors. Once a year, it presented works by artists from Łódź. The gallery was considered one of the most important non-profit galleries in Poland.

3.10 *Łódź: Muzeum Sztuki ms²*

opening: 2008
design: Pracownia Architektoniczna Ferdzynów
investment type: public
exhibition space: 3,600 m²
address: ul. Ogrodowa 19, Łódź
http://msl.org.pl

The Muzeum Sztuki (Museum of Art) was defined by the International Collection of Modern Art that was accumulated for this institution by "a.r.", a group of Polish avant-garde artists and poets. This collection has been open to the public as early as in 1931, making the Muzeum Sztuki one of the first museums of avant-garde art in the world. Since 1946, the museum has been located in the former palace of Łódź's industrialist, Maurycy Poznański, that was supposed to be a provisional seat. A real chance for a new headquarters (following an unsuccessful attempt in 1973) appeared in 2004. At that time, the nineteenth-century Izrael Kalmanowicz Poznański Textile Factory was being adapted to the trading and entertainment center Manufaktura. The museum received one of the buildings from the investor of Manufaktura. After refurbishment completed in 2008, it was transformed into a seat of the twentieth- and twenty-first-century art collections and a space for temporary

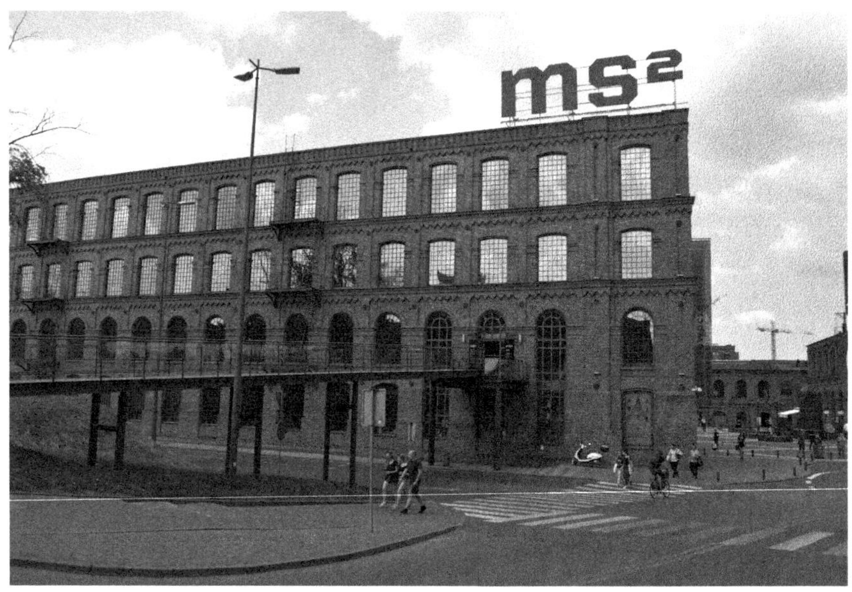

Muzeum Sztuki ms² in Łódź.
Photo: Katarzyna Jagodzińska

exhibitions. Since then, the previous venue has functioned under the name ms¹, while the new one has been named ms².

At the permanent exhibition opened in the new building, the chronological arrangement was abandoned in favor of a thematic approach, manifesting the desire "to establish a correspondence with the most important topics of the present day" (Suchan 2008). The director Jarosław Suchan emphasizes the necessity to constantly work on actualization of the avant-garde legacy and the need to present art of historical avant-garde in dialogue with the contemporary art production: "I believe that thanks to contemporary artists we gain a new insight into the art of predecessors. And vice versa" (Andino Velez and Fudala 2008: 5). The narration of the exhibition has been divided into conceptual triads (in the first exhibition it was "body, injury, prosthesis", "construction, utopia, political", "object, fetish, phantasm", and "eye, image, reality"). Suchan underlines that the new permanent exhibition "illustrates just one possible way of thinking about art and the collection of the Muzeum Sztuki. In no way does it aspire to the role of being the only valid interpretation of it" (Suchan 2008). In the center of the exhibition, there was – for the first time shown in its entirety – a historical collection of the group "a.r."; however, it was not a reconstruction of the historical layout of the collection, which would not have been possible owing to wartime losses. The permanent exhibition has been assumed to be changeable; in 2009, over 80 percent of works were exchanged for others, and similar changes take place on a yearly basis (Mazur 2011). In 2014, the new exhibition of the collection, entitled *Atlas of Modernity* (Atlas Nowoczesności) opened. It was organized around phenomena and ideas that constituted modernity and still remain coordinates defining our reality, such as emancipation, autonomy, industrialization, capital, urbanization, experiment, mechanization, and revolution.

The history of the museum is presented in Chapter 1.
See more about the factory and Manufaktura in Chapter 5.

3.11 Poznań: Art Stations Gallery

activity: 2004–2016
name changes: until 2007 "Stary Browar" Gallery
design: ADS Studio
investment type: private
exhibition space: 475 m²
address (out of date): ul. Półwiejska 42, Poznań
www.artstationsfoundation5050.com

The Art Stations Gallery was run by the Art Stations Foundation (until 2007 as the Kulczyk Foundation). Apart from visual arts, the foundation also dealt with dance, theater, film, and music. Activities in the field of culture were carried out in the "Stary Browar" complex – a shopping center created by Grażyna Kulczyk, who is also the president of the foundation. The activity of "Stary Browar" was based on the 50/50 philosophy, according to which 50 percent of its activity revolves around business and 50 percent around art. The quest to achieve this balance was carried out by introducing works of art into commercial and service activities. They were positioned in the middle of shopping arcades, in the Courtyard of Art and in the designer hotel Blow Up Hall 50 50 (monumental sculptures and installations, including mobile and site specific works).

The objectives of the foundation's exhibition program were to promote and support young local artists as well as outstanding artists from Poland and abroad (Raport roczny Kulczyk Foundation 2007: 9) and present the most interesting achievements of contemporary art with an emphasis on fields that until recently were regarded in Poland as art of lower artistic rank, such as design or photography (Raport roczny Kulczyk Foundation 2004: part 03.01).

The Art Stations Gallery building was located in the middle of the shopping center buildings. It was a new three-story wing that blended with the architecture of the brewery.

In 2007, the selection of over one hundred works from Kulczyk's collection covering mainly contemporary art was presented at the *GK Collection # 1* exhibition.

In 2015, "Stary Browar" was sold, and in the next the gallery was closed. The foundation still operates in the center, but it is limited to the performative program.

See more about the Kulczyk collection and further plans for its presentation in Chapter 6.

3.12 Radom: Elektrownia Mazovian Center for Contemporary Art (Mazowieckie Centrum Sztuki Współczesnej "Elektrownia")

opening: 2005, 2014
project: Andrzej Kikowski, Damian Cyryl Kotwicki, Daniel Cwalina, Marcin Bądaruk, Darek Kwiatkowski, Hubert Trammer, Lech Rowiński, Eng. Arkadiusz Czerniak
investment type: public
exhibition space: 5,000 m²
address: ul. Kopernika 1, Radom
www.elektrownia.art.pl

The initiator of the establishment, the Elektrownia Mazovian Center for Contemporary Art (MCSW) was film director Andrzej Wajda, who spent his youth in Radom. In 2004, together with his wife, he donated a part of their art collection to the Museum of Contemporary Art functioning within the structures of the Jacek Malczewski Museum in Radom, and suggested the creation of an art center that would allow the proper exhibition of works crowded in the small museum and warehouse building. The abandoned building of the former municipal power plant was selected as the future location of the art center.

The formation of MCSW from the beginning met with difficulties in the matter of raising funds from the EU or the Norwegian Financial Mechanism, land ownership, and maintenance of the Museum of Contemporary Art within which the collection operates, as well as personal games at the managerial level.

The building of the red brick power plant was built in 1901 by the Russian Electric Society "Union" from St. Petersburg. The power plant operated in it until 1956, after which it was taken over by the municipal heating plant, which operated there until 1998. The first exhibition in the power plant building was organized in 2006. In the same year, a two-stage competition for an architectural concept for the development of the old power plant building and the adjacent area for the art center was announced, in which Andrzej Kikowski, Damian Cyryl Kotwicki and the team prevailed. In their project, the red brick building was connected with cuboidal modules covered with a black, perforated sheet. It was not until the end of 2010 that construction works began and the building was opened to the public in 2014.

In 2017–2018, MCSW received the collection of works amassed by the Radom Museum of Contemporary Art for a five-year deposit (4,500 works), and assembled its own collection of Polish art after 1989, which was conceived as complementary to the museum holdings. The works at its disposal are described by MCSW as the Radom Collection of Contemporary Art. Their ambition is to "illustrate the continuity of the transformation process of Polish art after 1945" (Bochyński 2014: 25). At the opening of the new building, a cross-sectional exhibition was organized from the merged collection transversal *Specimen: an attempt at a collection*.

3.13 Radom: Museum of Contemporary Art – Jacek Malczewski Museum (Muzeum Sztuki Współczesnej – Muzeum im. Jacka Malczewskiego)

opening: 1990
investment type: public
address: Rynek 11, Radom

The Museum of Contemporary Art was established in 1990 as a branch of the Jacek Malczewski Museum in Radom (founded in 1923). This is the first museum in Poland bearing this name, though it was not autonomous. Its headquarters were two Baroque tenements on the Market Square: Esterka House and Gąska House (in 2018, a major modernization of these building has started). The establishment of the museum had a prestigious quality for the city which had to build its modern image. The museum's creator, Mieczysław Szewczuk writes:

> When I created my museum plan and started creating collections, Radom had been for some time a provincial city and the authorities expected that there would be supra-regional institutions here. The establishment of the first contemporary art museum in Radom was a part of the city's promotion program.
>
> (Szewczuk 2013: 123)

The construction of contemporary art collections began ten years earlier. Purchases were made during the 1980s; however, since the 1990s, the museum's collection – at that time a specialized department – has been growing mainly thanks to donations from artists, their families and collectors. In this way, in the years 1992–2011, the museum obtained 2,500 works (Szewczuk 2013: 119), while in 2013, the entire collection of modern and contemporary art included 4,500 works. Among the donors are Andrzej Wajda and Krystyna Zachwatowicz, who from 1997 donated works from their private collection (Szewczuk 2005: 196, 203). Szewczuk (2016: 18–19) emphasizes the social nature of collection building: "A decisive factor was the time – the 1980s – the time of 'independent culture'. It was then that our close contacts with artists developed. The attitude of selfless service for the benefit of culture was common among them". The collections mainly include Polish art of the second half of the twentieth century.

From the outset, the museum struggled with financial and accommodation problems. The collection was presented once a year in a temporary exhibition, as well as at exhibitions throughout Poland. The problem with the exhibition space was to be solved by the Elektrownia Mazovian Center for Contemporary Art (MCSW) established in the city. In 2008, the dispute flared up – the Museum of Contemporary Art was slated for liquidation, and there were attempts to formally hand over its collections to MCSW, although its construction had not yet begun. As a result of the protestors from within the artistic milieu, including Wajda, it was not liquidated. MCSW was opened in 2014. It began to create its own collection and program unrelated to the Museum of Contemporary Art. In 2016, the collection was shown at the major exhibition *Living for Art*.

3.14 Szczecin: TRAFO Trafostacja Sztuki

opening: 2013
adaptation project: Studio A4 – Jacek Lenart
investment type: public
exhibition space: 600 m²
address: ul. Świętego Ducha 4, Szczecin
http://trafo.art

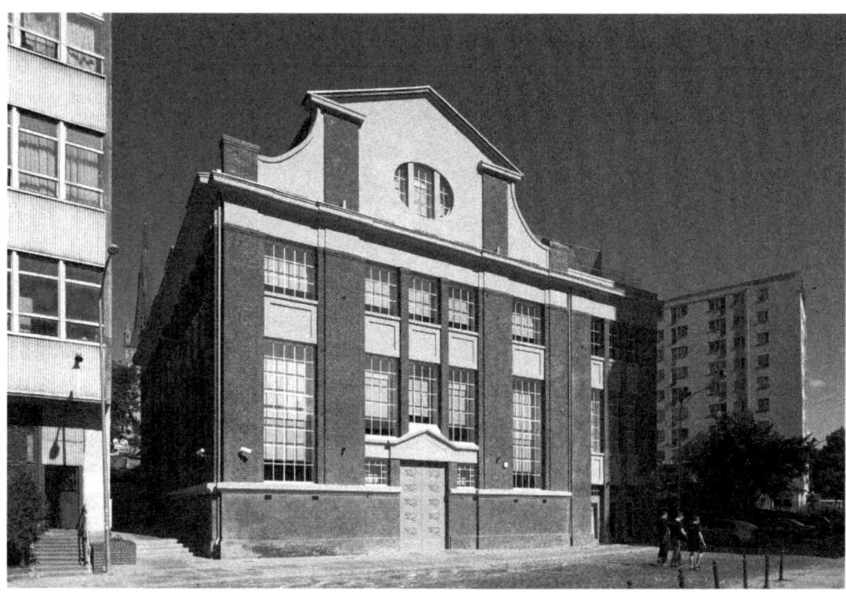

TRAFO Trafostacja Sztuki in Szczecin.
Photo: Piotr Krajewski. Courtesy of the TRAFO Trafostacja Sztuki in Szczecin

In 2004, as part of the "Znaki Czasu" program, the Society for the Encouragement of Fine Arts was established in Szczecin, which quickly began efforts to acquire a permanent seat for its activity. The choice fell on the building of a disused transformer house dating from the beginning of the twentieth century, which was planned as a place for artistic activity in the 1970s. The original plans were to organize a collection exhibition within it, but in the end, an institution independent of the association was established.

In 2012, the City Council of Szczecin established the cultural institution Trafostacja Sztuki, which became the owner of the building. The manager of the institution was selected in a tender procedure, which caused a great deal of controversy. Two entities joined the tender – the Association for the Encouragement and the Baltic Contemporary company. The association's offer was rejected due to a formal error and the company that performed the program activity in 2012–2016 was selected as the manager. The program was criticized by the community of art historians. In 2017, TRAFO became a municipal institution.

According to the philosophy introduced under the new management at that time:

> TRAFO serves as a multifunctional meeting platform for artists and visitors. It introduces the audience to the tools of art by putting them in various contexts and transdisciplinary relationships. Visual works interact with literature, music, theatre, social sciences and new technologies.
>
> (TRAFO Center for Contemporary Art n.d.)

See more on the history of building and architecture in Chapter 4.

3.15 Tarnów: BWA Tarnów

opening: 1975, 2013
adapted building
investment type: public
exhibition space: 200 m²
address: ul. Słowackiego 1, Tarnów
www.bwa.tarnow.pl

The BWA Tarnów (Bureau of Art Exhibitions – Biuro Wystaw Artystycznych) was created as one of the artistic exhibition offices in the then-voivodship of Tarnów. Since 1996, it has maintained its status as a municipal cultural institution. The historical name of the gallery has been retained under the new political conditions; however, from the standpoint of programming, it is a new institution. Since its inception in 1975, it has been in the city center, in different locations. From 1989–2010, it operated in historic tenement houses on the Tarnów market square, and since 2013, in the restored historical building of the Marksmen's Brotherhood in the park. For three years, while the renovation was taking place in the new headquarters, the gallery operated in the building of the Tarnów railway station waiting room. After the move, the space at the station was maintained, and exhibitions from the collection of the Małopolska Foundation of the Museum of Contemporary Art are still being carried out.

Thanks to the new director of Ewa Łączyńska-Widz (since 2012; previously a curator), BWA Tarnów is one of the most interesting and important places for the presentation of contemporary art in Poland. The gallery's program is focused on the classics of Polish contemporary art, searching and presenting the most interesting phenomena of Polish art in recent years, and the artists' local environment.

The gallery has produced ten works in Tarnów's public spaces.

3.16 *Toruń: Znaki Czasu Centre of Contemporary Art (Centrum Sztuki Współczesnej Znaki Czasu)*

opening: 2008
project: Edward Lach
investment type: public
exhibition space: 4,150 m²
address: ul. Wały Generała Władysława Sikorskiego 13, Toruń
http://csw.torun.pl

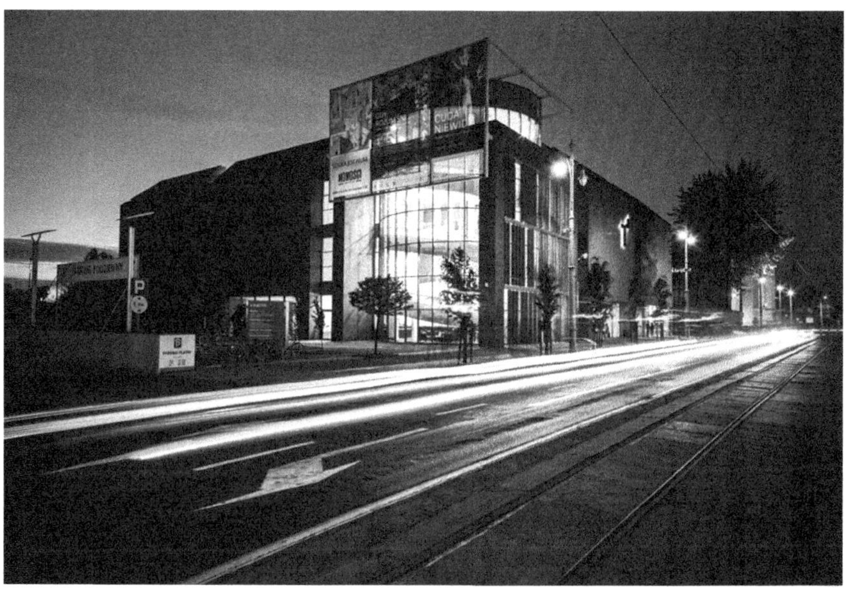

Znaki Czasu Center of Contemporary Art in Toruń.
Photo: Wojciech Olech. Courtesy of the Znaki Czasu Centre of Contemporary Art in Toruń

The creation of the Znaki Czasu Centre of Contemporary Art (CSW) in Toruń is directly connected with the inauguration in 2004 (precisely in Toruń) of the ministerial program "Znaki Czasu" during the seminar *To Each Time, Its Own Art*. In the same year, the regional Association for the Friends of Fine Arts Znaki Czasu was created as part of the program; it began to assemble a regional art collection, but also made efforts to acquire a building for its premises. The city authorities earmarked a plot for this purpose, and in 2004, a competition for an architectural concept was announced. Two years later, the Ministry of Culture established a new institution. The architectural competition selected the concept of Edward Lach, who proposed a building corresponding to the brick architecture of the Toruń Old Town. In 2008, the building was opened to the public. In 2010, the ministry resigned from collaborating on an institution that became municipal.

The program concept of the CSW changes with each change of management, hence the history can be divided into three periods: 2008–2010, 2011–2014, and 2015–present. The program prepared for the opening was based on three pillars: glocality, collection and collecting, and education. In the CSW program, visual arts combine with music, dance, theater, film, architecture, and design.

The collection consists of a body of work donated by the Association and a collection built by CSW. The key word for the expanded collection is performativity.

See more on architecture in Chapter 3.

3.17 *Warszawa: Ujazdowski Castle Center for Contemporary Art (Centrum Sztuki Współczesnej Zamek Ujazdowski)*

opening: 1985*
historical reconstruction
investment type: public
exhibition space: 2,080 m²
address: ul. Jazdów 2, Warsaw
http://u-jazdowski.pl

The Ujazdowski Castle Center for Contemporary Art operates in the building of the Baroque Ujazdowski Castle, dating back to the seventeenth century and rebuilt in the 1970s. The building, which functioned successively as a residence, barracks, school, and hospital, survived the war, but on account of its poor state of preservation, it was dismantled in 1954.

The dynamic development of the Ujazdowski Castle and the building of its position on the international arena occurred thanks to the first director after the systemic transformation, Wojciech Krukowski (1990–2009). Since the beginning of the 1990s, the Ujazdowski Castle has been amassing an art collection. The premise was that a current art collection be created whose nature "should be directly determined by the exhibition curriculum and identified with the Ujazdowski Castle's current mission of *presenting art in the process of transformation*" (Krukowski 2005: 16). From the beginning, the collection has had an international character. It was presented in the form of changing exhibitions – selections from the collection seven times. Works located in the surroundings of the castle comprise part of the collection.

During Fabio Cavalucci's directorate (2010–2014) – he was the first foreign director of the Polish art institution – the Ujazdowski Castle found itself in a state of collapse (due to conflicts with employees, and financial problems that resulted in the cancellation of exhibitions).

According to the vision of the subsequent director (from 2014), Małgorzata Ludwisiak, the Ujazdowski Castle is "a place where we try to think about the world through art. The world understood as your own backyard, as well as vast spaces beyond its borders" (U-jazdowski – Program n.d.).

In the years 1989–2016, part of the Ujazdowski Castle was the famous Laboratory of Creative Education (Laboratorium Edukacji Twórczej).

> *Note*: This is the only institution presented in the list that was founded before 1989, and its headquarters was not changed after the political transformation, or significantly modified, or expanded. Director Wojciech Krukowski explained that in practice CSW has been operating since 1990: "Since this time the presentation program has been continuous and systematic in all fields of an interdisciplinary artistic institution."
>
> (Krukowski 2005: 14)

3.18 *Warszawa: Museum of Modern Art (Muzeum Sztuki Nowoczesnej)*

> opening: 2008 in the temporary office, opening in the new office planned for 2021
> project: Thomas Phifer and Partners
> investment type: public
> exhibition space: ultimately 4,500 m^2
> address: ultimately Plac Defilad, Warsaw
> https://artmuseum.pl/pl

In 2005, the Minister of Culture and the Mayor of Warsaw signed an agreement on the creation of the Museum of Modern Art (MSN) in the capital. A plot of land in the center of Warsaw was selected for its headquarters – on Defilad Square, in the immediate vicinity of the Palace of Culture and Science. At the end of 2005, an international architectural competition for a museum building was opened (repeated twice for formal reasons). In the conditions of the architectural competition, it was written that the winning project should be on the one hand a counterpoint to the Palace of Culture, and on the other, a new symbol of Warsaw. The first prize was awarded to the Swiss architect Christian Kerez (ratio of votes 7:6). The project had the shape of a sublime, minimalist (although the architect declined to use this term) box on an L-shaped plan. The choice of this project aroused great controversy in the environment of museum workers, architects, people of culture, and the inhabitants of Warsaw.

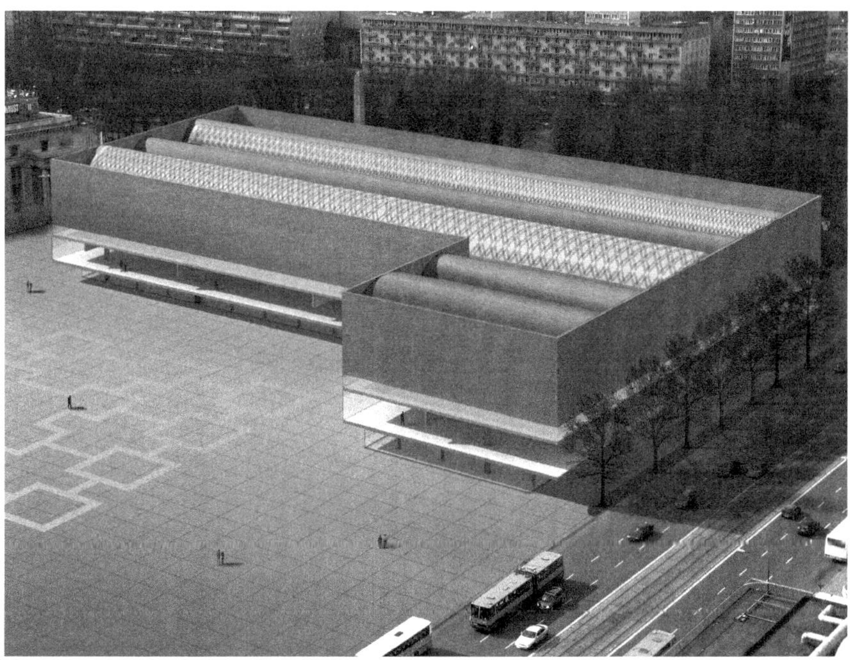

Visualization of the project of the Museum of Modern Art in Warsaw, Christian Kerez, 2006.

Courtesy of the Museum of Modern Art in Warsaw

The Mayor of Warsaw did not give in to the demands to withdraw from the implementation of the Kerez project. In 2008, a contract was signed between the city and the architect. At the request of the clients, the spatial arrangement of the building was significantly changed three times. In 2009, the investor commissioned the architect to fit the building infrastructure for yet another institution – the Rozmaitości Theater. In 2010, Kerez proposed a completely new museum and theater project, only maintained in a competition style. The problem was the unexplained ownership of land for the construction. After an impasse lasting one and a half years, which resulted in the reciprocal recrimination online of the architect and city hall, in 2012, the city terminated the contract with the architect and the case was taken to court.

In the following year, a new architectural competition was announced. The problem of land ownership had also been resolved. In 2014, the American

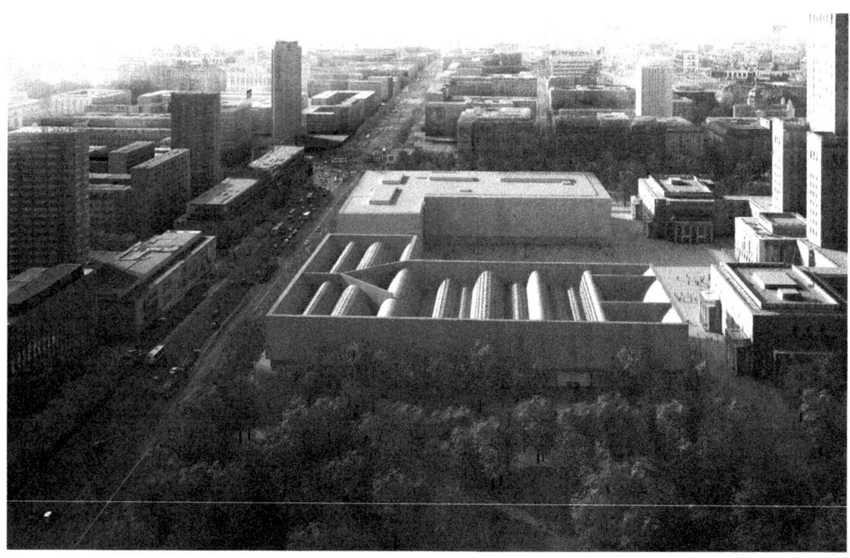

Visualization of the project of the Museum of Modern Art in Warsaw, Christian Kerez – changed design, 2010.

Courtesy of the Museum of Modern Art in Warsaw

studio Thomas Phifer and Partners was chosen. The basis for this architectural concept is the openness of the building to the city space. It is provided by a glazed portion of the ground floor, allowing access to the exhibition halls from the street perspective, as well as museum entrance located on all four sides. Between the buildings of the museum and the theater, which will function independently of each other, there is a courtyard-forum enabling the implementation of artistic and social activities outside the space of both institutions.

In 2008, the museum began its activity at the temporary office located in the immediate vicinity of the Palace of Culture and the plot intended for the new building – at the back of the furniture pavilion "Emilia". In 2012, the museum acquired for its operation another, larger temporary seat in the same furniture pavilion, with an area of 4,300 square meters. In 2016, "Emilia" was demolished for the construction of an office building, while the museum moved to a temporary pavilion located on the Vistula River.

The prolonged wait for the museum building has been used to get to know its neighborhood and public. Director Joanna Mytkowska admits that at the time,

> we have learned what a museum can be. We were not working, of course, from the perspective of a well-organized institution, but at the beginning

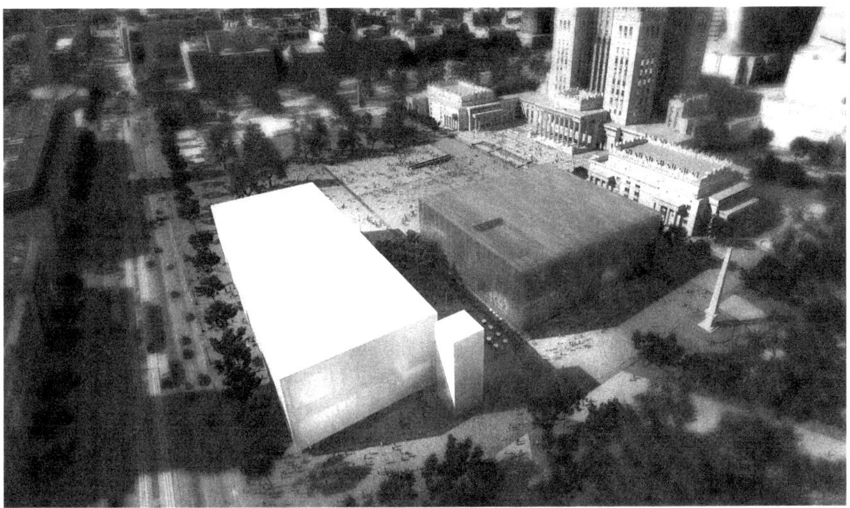

Visualization of the project of the Museum of Modern Art in Warsaw and TR Warszawa theater, Thomas Phifer and Partners studio, 2015. Bird's-eye view.
Courtesy of the Museum of Modern Art in Warsaw

> it was rather a collective that had to cope with all the problems that affect the average citizen. It brought the museum so close to its audience. [. . .] Throughout these years, we learned from the mistakes that really were committed on a small scale. This is definitely priceless. It also forces us to be extremely creative – this comes from the simple fact that in the absence of many things or solutions, so you had to find them yourself.
>
> (Interview with Joanna Mytkowska 2017)

Since 2009, every year, the museum has been implementing the design festival *Warsaw Under Construction* (since 2013 in cooperation with the Warsaw Museum). At the same time, as a result of the joint initiative of the artist Paweł Althamer, Targówek, and MSN district authorities, the Sculpture Park in Bródno was created.

Since 2008, the museum has been building a collection of art. Mytkowska admits that for objective reasons, the museum "will not collect with the aspiration of full representation. The Museum's task is to modernize this canon, to see it from a new angle, which in art is marked by 1989" (Mytkowska z zespołem 2007: 2). An important part of the collection are the archives of artists.

> See more on the circumstances of the creation of the museum and architectural competitions in Chapter 3.

3.19 *Wrocław: Wrocław Contemporary Museum (Muzeum Współczesne Wrocław)*

opening: 2012 at the temporary office
project: Nizio Design International and DCK – Design Studio Damian
   Cyryl Kotwicki
investment type: public
exhibition area: 4,500 m² (3,500 m² in temporary office)
address: pl. Strzegomski 2a, Wrocław
http://muzeumwspolczesne.pl

The impetus for the creation of the Wrocław Contemporary Museum was the creation of the Dolnośląskie Society for the Encouragement of Fine Arts in 2004 as part of the ministerial program "Znaki Czasu". The statutory aim of the Society, apart from building the collection of contemporary art, was to establish a cultural institution in Wrocław called the "Center for Contemporary Art". In 2007, the program concept of the museum was developed; the following year, an international architectural competition for the building was announced. Winners of the first prize in the architectural competition, decided in 2008, explained that in the museum's design they referred to the artistic traditions of Wrocław (concepts and expressions: "shadow art", "material architecture", "relation of light and space" (Konkurs na opracowanie koncepcji n.d.)) and to the shape of the plot intended for construction. The body is shaped like a cube twisted around its own axis.

In 2009, the idea appeared to create a temporary museum seat in an air-raid shelter from the time of the Second World War, which, after opening the headquarters, would serve as a studio warehouse. The museum was opened in the temporary building in 2011. In turn, the construction of the building was postponed to an indefinite time in the near future.

An important element determining the identity of the institution is its name, "Contemporary Museum". According to the program assumptions, it underlines the contemporary nature of expectations and the challenges posed to the museum, while at the same time distancing itself from the disputes over the concepts of "contemporary art" and "modern art" (Krajewski and Monkiewicz 2007: 5).

The collection of the museum consists of its own works, as well as others from the holdings of the Society. The collection program is focused "around the most important achievements of the Wrocław art scene from the mid-1960s, among which visual and conceptual art, feminism and gender issues were of great importance, and from the 1980s the active involvement of creators in public debate" (Kolekcja Muzeum Współczesnego Wrocław n.d.). An important place is occupied by art from the area of then – Czechoslovakia, Hungary, and the former Yugoslavia.

See more on the architecture of the new edifice in Chapter 3.
See more on the temporary residence in Chapter 4.

3.20 Wrocław: Four Domes Pavilion, Museum of Contemporary Art – National Museum in Wrocław (Pawilon Czterech Kopuł, Muzeum Sztuki Współczesnej – Muzeum Narodowe we Wrocławiu)

opening: 2016
adapted building
investment type: public
exhibition space: 5,500 m²
address: ul. Wystawowa 1, Wrocław
http://pawilonczterechkopul.pl

The Museum of Contemporary Art, a branch of the National Museum in Wrocław, was created for a presentation of more than twenty thousand exhibits of the collection of Polish art of the second half of the twentieth century. The historic Four Domes Pavilion erected in 1912 for the Centennial Exhibition was adapted to the museum's seat. Designed by Hans Poelzig, the building was conceived from the very beginning as a place for organizing exhibitions. In the second half of the twentieth century, it housed the Feature Film Studios and after its collapse, in a very poor condition, it was taken over by the National Museum.

The opening of the museum in the restored building took place in 2016. The aim of the first collection exhibition was to present the most interesting and valuable works from the collection, which would show the diversity and interwoven-ness of Polish modern art. Part of the exhibition was the presentation of the art of artists from the Wrocław community (Banaś 2016).

3.21 Recklinghausen (Germany): Museum Jerke

opening: 2016
project: Werner Jerke
investment type: private
exhibition space: 400 m²
address: Johannes-Janssen-Straße 7, Recklinghausen, Germany
www.museumjerke.com

The Jerke Museum is the only one in the Atlas that is not located in Central Europe. It is an investment of major importance – the only private museum devoted to art from the Central European region (specifically Polish) located in Western Europe. Its creator is Dr. Werner Jerke, art collector, doctor, owner of an ophthalmology clinic in the heart of the Ruhr area, Recklinghausen. Jerke comes from a German family, but he was born and raised in Górny Śląsk and studied, among other places, in Krakow.

The Ruhr area is one of the most saturated with museums and collections of modern and contemporary art in Germany. Recklinghausen itself also possesses traditions in the field of art and theater. The museum is a small

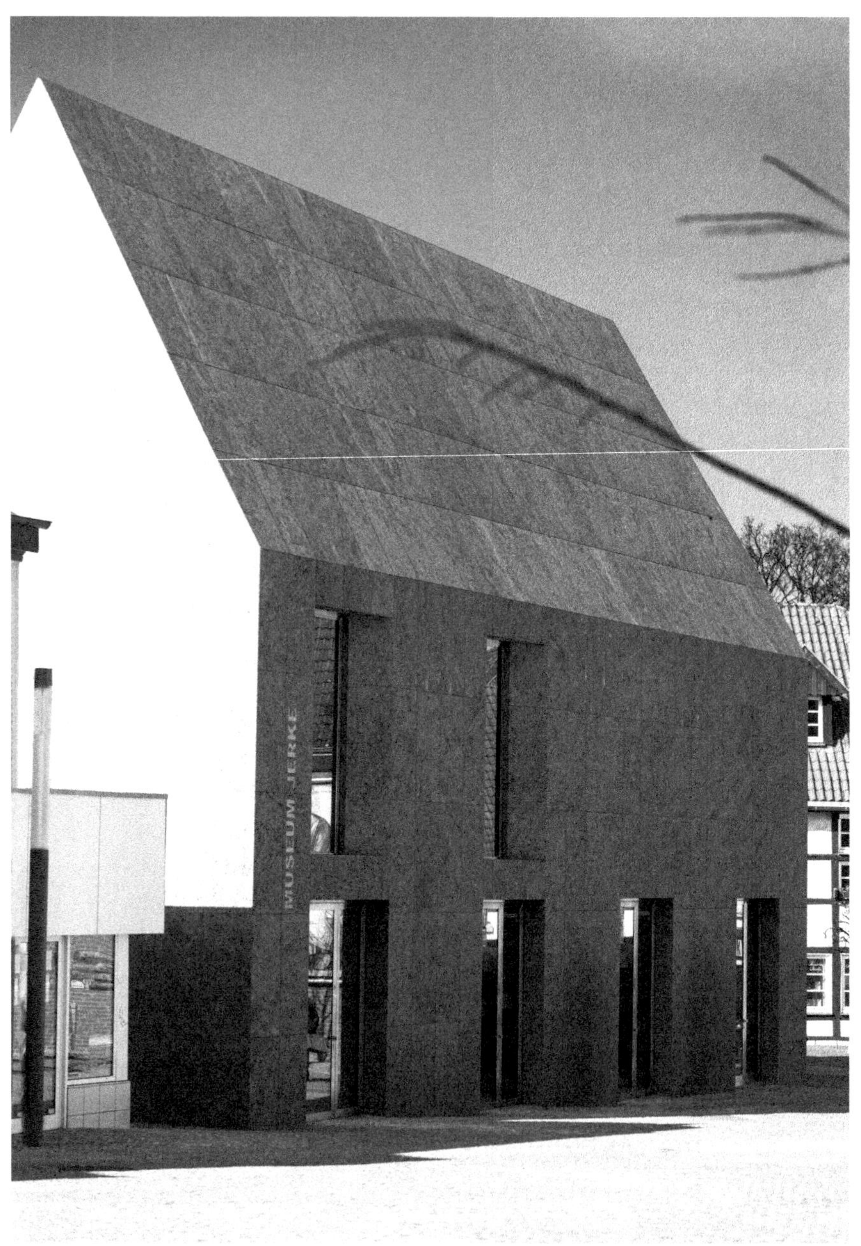

Museum Jerke in Recklinghausen (Germany).
Photo: Museum Jerke archive

building located in the city center, by the market square. It was designed by Jerke himself, selecting a slab of gray-blue granite for the façade cladding. The façade is decorated with a stained glass designed by Wojciech Fangor.

The museum was created to accommodate the Jerke collection. Its core is Polish avant-garde art. As the collector himself says: "I buy works that were provocative at the time they were created and were something new" (Interview with Werner Jerke 2018). Twice a year, the museum organizes an exhibition of a Polish artist, while for the rest of the time the collection occupies the exhibition rooms.

4 Slovakia

4.1 *Banská Štiavnica: Banská St a nica Contemporary*

> opening: 2009
> investment type: non-governmental
> exhibition space: 200 m²
> address: Trate mládeže 6, Banská Štiavnica
> www.banskastanica.sk/c/home

Banská St a nica Contemporary (BSC) is a project implemented by Zuzana Bodnárová (curator and culture manager) and Svätopluk Mikyta (visual artist) who after six years in Prague moved to Banská Štiavnica, where in 2008 they established the NGO Stokovec Space for Culture. In the following year, they began artistic activity in the still-functioning railway station. The building was half empty, serving only as a waiting room and a place to sell railway tickets. In 2011–2017, the tickets were sold by members of the association. "This work, selling the tickets, was an interesting social experiment for us. No big money, but interesting interactions" – explains Zuzana Bodnárová (Personal communication with Zuzana Bodnárová). In 2017, the railway abandoned the sale of tickets at the station and closed the waiting room, with the consequence that St a nica is open only twice a week. Once a year, a monumental work of art is created in the space of the waiting room. This space is also a space for work, as well as a place where concerts take place.

BSC Contemporary organizes residences, exhibitions and concerts, produces new artworks and editions, and publishes art books. Studios for artistic residencies are located in the building of the station. Every year, the artists create a work for the waiting room spaces.

4.2 *Bratislava: Kunsthalle Bratislava*

> opening: 2014
> adapted building
> investment type: public
> investor: Ministry of Culture

exhibition space: 2,000 m²
address: Námestie SNP 12, Bratislava
www.kunsthallebratislava.sk

Kunsthalle Bratislava was founded in 2014 and is located in the House of Arts. Its creation was the result of many years of artists' efforts. It was established by the Ministry of Culture and initially functioned in the structures of the National Educational Center. Due to management problems in 2016, Kunsthalle became part of the Slovak National Gallery.

The Kunsthalle mission is "to map visual art and make it approachable to domestic and foreign audiences" (Kunsthalle Bratislava n.d.). The institution attaches great importance to education in the field of contemporary art.

For more on the history of this institution, see Chapter 7 and in an interview with Alexandra Kusá in Chapter 2.

4.3 Bratislava: Milan Dobeš Museum (Múzeum Milana Dobeša)

activity: 2001–2016
adaptation project: Gabriel Svitok and Ondrej Chrobák
investment type: private
exhibition space: 450 m²
address (out of date): ul. Zámočnícka 13, Bratislava

The Milan Dobeš Museum was founded in 2001 on the initiative of collector and art dealer Peter Sokol. It presented the owner's collection and works loaned by the artist. The temporary exhibitions showed the works of other artists representing the current in geometric abstraction that provided the context for the collection's exhibition.

A tenement house within the historical city of Bratislava was chosen for the museum's seat. Adaptation for exhibition purposes was carried out according to the design of Gabriel Svitok and Ondrej Chrobák, who introduced elements of the new architecture into the interior: a skylight at the attic register that brings light to the other levels through their glazed floors.

In 2016, the museum was closed and the collection was sold to a Czech investor.

See more about the museum in Chapter 6.

4.4 Bratislava: Nedbalka Gallery

opening: 2012
adapted building: 1995 extension designed by Viktória Cvengrošová and Virgil Droppa
investment type: private
exhibition space: 1,500 m²

address: Nedbalova ulica 17, Bratislava
www.nedbalka.sk

The gallery was created with the aim of presenting a private collection of Slovak art from the late nineteenth century to the present acquired by philanthropists Peter and Miloslava Paško and their friend Artúr Bartoška. It is located in a converted tenement house in the city center. Previously, it housed a bank, Slovenská sporiteľna; in 2011, it was bought by Peter Paško to open an art gallery there.

The purpose of the gallery, as explained by director Lucia Gunišová Pavuková, "is to allow the broad public to discover the masterpieces by great Slovak artists who significantly contributed to Slovak national heritage" (Personal communication with Lucia Gunišová Pavuková 2018). The collection includes about a thousand works, mainly paintings, as well as sculptures and graphics. It is presented in the form of a permanent exhibition distributed across four floors of the building, and concurrently with temporary exhibitions.

4.5 *Čunovo: Danubiana Meulensteen Art Museum*

opening: 2000, 2014
project: Peter Žalman, extension Jan Kukula
investment type: private
exhibition space: 2,500 m²
address: Čunovo vodné diela
www.danubiana.sk

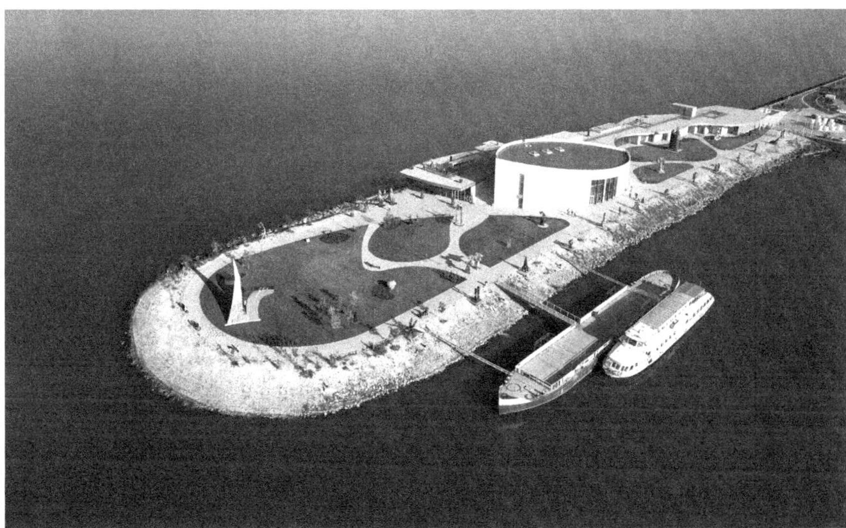

Danubiana Meulensteen Art Museum in Čunovo.

Photo: Danubiana archive

The Danubiana museum of modern art was established in 2000 on the picturesque peninsula on the Danube near Bratislava. Its creation was possible thanks to the determination of the art dealer Vincent Polakovič and the involvement of the Dutch investor Gerard Meulensteen, whose own name became an integral part of the institution's name. The building was designed by the Slovak architect Peter Žalman, who relied on the vision of the Roman galley with oars presented to him by Polakovič and painter Peter Pollág. The idea of a museum in the shape of a ship refers to its location – the Danube connects countries; the ship connects the banks, allowing circulation; and the museum also links nations and cultures through art. The museum on the peninsula was planned as a place of recreation and family leisure. Its integral part is the sculpture park arranged in the garden around the building. There is also a marina on the peninsula, thanks to which one may reach the museum by boat or ship. In 2013, construction was undertaken to expand the building for new exhibition and reception areas. The new wing made it possible to open the collection as planned from the beginning.

In 2014, the status of the museum changed; Meulensteen decided to transfer it to the Slovak state. The museum is run by a foundation, almost half the resources of which is provided by the Ministry of Culture. Selected works from the Meulensteen collection will be presented in the museum for twenty years. This time will, in turn, allow the museum to expand its own collection.

See more on the museum architecture in Chapter 3.
See more on the nature of the private investment in Chapter 6.

4.6 *Košice: Kunsthalle Košice/Hala umenia*

opening: 2013
adapted building
investment type: public
exhibition space: 1,950 m²
address: ul. Rumanova 1, Košice
www.k13.sk

Kunsthalle was one of the investments carried out in Košice in connection with the title of the European Capital of Culture which the city carried in 2013. For this purpose, the building of the disused indoor swimming pool built in 1957–1962 according to the design of the Košice architect, Ladislav Greč, was adapted. This object was considered one of the most beautiful swimming pool buildings in the former Czechoslovakia. The interiors were designed by Herta Ondrušová-Viktorínová. The indoor pool was closed in 1992, and currently only an outdoor summer swimming pool operates through a separate entrance on the side of the park.

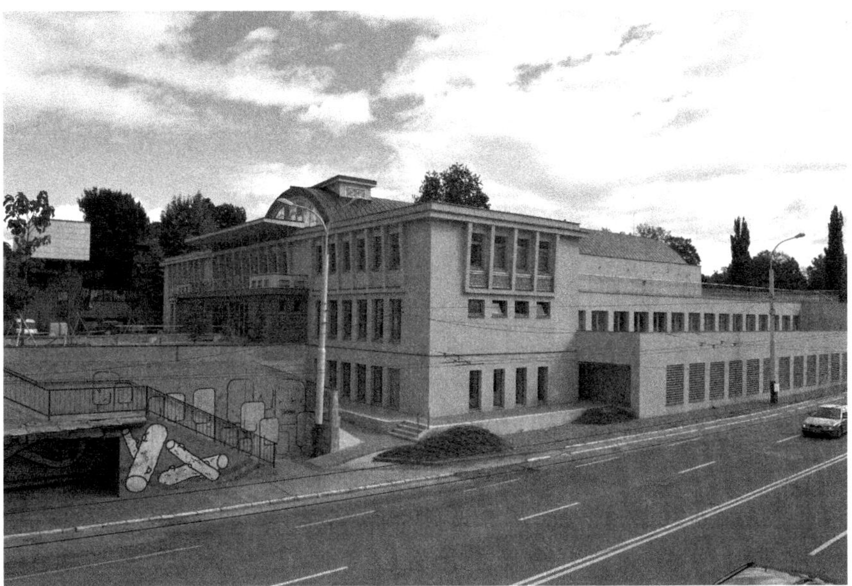

Kunsthalle Košice.
Photo: Katarzyna Jagodzińska

Construction work began in 2012, and in 2013 the building was opened to the public.

Kunsthalle is not a separate institution, it operates within the urban organization k13 – Košické kultúrne centrum. This organizational model worked well during the festival, when the city was filled with cultural events, but the lack of autonomy and artistic leadership in later years meant that the institution has not had its own program line. It presents not only contemporary art exhibitions, but also concerts and theatrical and dance performances.

4.7 Modra: ZOYA Gallery and ZOYA Museum

opening: 2005 (gallery) and 2009 (museum)
project: Cakov + Partners
investment type: private
exhibition space: 700 m² (gallery) and 1,000 m² (museum)
address: Erdődyho palác, Ventúrska 1, Bratislava and ELESKO Wine
   Park, Partizánska 2275, Modra
www.zoyamuseum.sk

The ZOYA Gallery and then the ZOYA Museum were created as places for the presentation of exhibitions of the private collection of Slovak art from

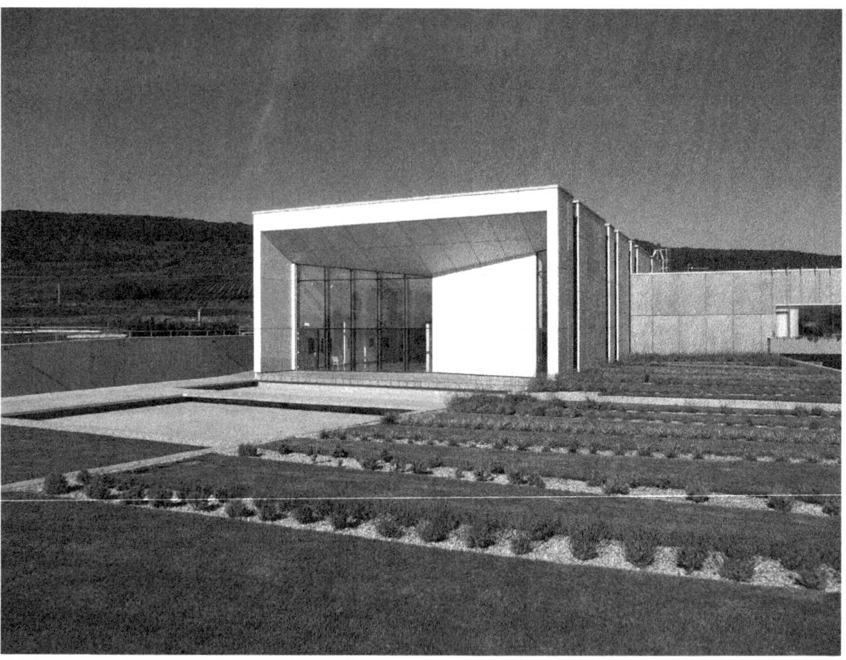

ZOYA Museum in Modra.
Photo: Katarzyna Jagodzińska

the twentieth and twenty-first centuries gathered by the Slovak collector Iveta Ladecka and her husband. The gallery is located in the center of Bratislava, on the first floor of the Baroque House of Erdődy. Four years later, in 2009, a museum was opened in the ELESKO winery in the village of Modra. It occupies a separate wing in a large complex, where, in addition to wine production and facilities for wine tasting, there is a popular restaurant. The museum presents a selection of Andy Warhol's work in the form of a permanent exhibition; the owners emphasize his Slovak roots.

4.8 Medzilaborce: Andy Warhol Museum of Modern Art (Múzeum moderného umenia Andyho Warhola)

opening: 1991
investment type: public
exhibition space: 1,000 m²
address: Andyho Warhola 748/36, Medzilaborce
www.muzeumaw.sk

The museum owes its creation to the determination of a local patriot, Michal Bycko. During the communist period, he sought to establish an Andy Warhol museum in Medzilaborce (Warhol's parents came from the nearby village of Miková). At that time, the beginnings of museum collections (documents and family photos) were established and contact was made with the artist's brother, John Warhol, who lived in the United States. In 1989, the first exhibition devoted to Warhol took place, and in the same year, the new museum's statute was approved. The museum was established in 1991 by the Ministry of Culture. Originally, the old post office was to be converted into its headquarters, but finally the museum was located in a newly built cultural center. The activity of the museum under the name Warhol Family Museum of Modern Art (Múzeum moderného umenia rodiny Warholovcov) inaugurated the exhibition *Andy Warhol in his Parents' Country* (his paintings for the museum's collection were also transferred to the museum by Andy Warhol's oldest brother, Paul, and his son, James). In 1997, the name was changed to Andy Warhol Museum of Modern Art. Since 2002, the museum has been run by the authorities of the Prešov region (História Múzea moderného umenia).

The collection holds about two hundred works by Warhol and one hundred by other artists. Some of the presented works have been borrowed from the Andy Warhol Foundation for Visual Art in New York, and memorabilia and artifacts related to the artist and his family are also displayed.

4.9 *Žilina: Nová synagóga Žilina – Center of Contemporary Art and Culture (Centrum pre súčasné umenie a kultúru)*

opening: 2012–2017
adapted building
investment type: non-governmental
exhibition space: 700 m²
address: J.M. Hurbana 11, Žilina
www.novasynagoga.sk

In 2011, the Jewish kehilla in Žilina sought a new tenant for the building of a decommissioned synagogue. The proposal for the adaptation of the building for exhibition purposes came to the organizers of the cultural hub Stanica Žilina-Záriečie, which serves as a cultural and performing arts center and a waiting room for a constantly functioning railway station. The creators of the project are Marek Adamov, co-founder of the non-governmental organization Truc sphérique; Fedor Blaščák, critic and curator; and Martin Jančok, architect. Adamov recalls, "We started because of the responsibility to the Jewish community and the architecture of famous Peter Behrens. Really, without a need for another space" (Interview with Marek Adamov 2015).

The project involves a group of activists – designers, researchers, architectural historians – who worked for seven years on a voluntary basis. "We had our eye on the building of the synagogue a few years ago, when the cinema was still there. We were impressed by its beauty and at the same time annoyed

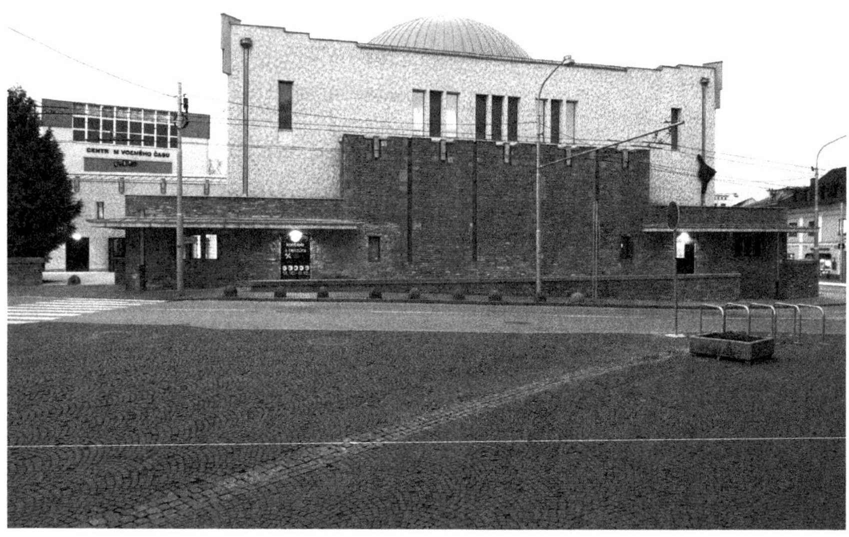

Nová synagóga Žilina – Center of Contemporary Art and Culture.
Photo: Daniela Dostálková. Courtesy of the Nová synagóga Žilina

by its status as an almost forgotten monument", remember the creators of Nová synagóga (Unpublished interview).

Nová synagóga, like Stanica associated with it, is primarily an independent initiative. Adamov emphasizes, "It is a lively project, not an institution. We did not start with a director and curators. It is a different way of doing things. Activistic" (Interview with Marek Adamov 2015).

The synagogue was erected in 1928–1931 according to the design of the German architect Peter Behrens. In 1963, it was entered in the register of monuments in Slovakia. The adaptation works consisted in removing accretions dating from the second half of the twentieth century. The original dome was unveiled and the height of the building was restored, reaching 17 meters. The official opening of the almost fully restored edifice took place in May 2017, although the "pre-openings" and first events and exhibition ran since 2012. The construction work naturally limited artistic activity for a time.

Originally a Kunsthalle was planned, as this type of institution was missing in Slovakia. Eventually, following creation of Kunsthallen in Košice and Bratislava, this term was dropped from the institution's name.

Bibliography

Adamov, M., 2012. Žilina-Záriečie Railway Station. In Miejsca kulturalnego wrzenia. *Herito* 9, pp. 187–188.

Anděl, J., 2008. Introduction. In J. Anděl and L. Válka (eds.), *DOX Centrum současného umění/Centre for Contemporary Art. Start.* Prague: DOX Centre for Contemporary Art, pp. 16–18.

Andino Velez, M., 2007. Architektura sama w sobie, rozmowa z Christianem Kerezem. *Muzeum*, 2, pp. 1–4.

Andino Velez, M., 2008. Supermarket of the Avant-Garde. In M. Küng (ed.), *Conflicts, Politics, Construction, Privacy, Obsession: Material on the Work of Christian Kerez.* Ostfildern: Hatje Cantz, pp. 83–91.

Andino Velez, M. and Fudala, T., 2008. Trzy przestrzenie Muzeum Sztuki, rozmowa z Jarosławem Suchanem. *Muzeum*, 3(1), pp. 5–7.

Apel Obywatelskiego Forum Sztuki Współczesnej w sprawie Trafostacji Sztuki [online]. Available at: <www.change.org/petitions/ofsw-apel-obywatelskiego-forum-sztuki-wsp%C3%B3%C5%82czesnej-w-sprawie-trafostacji-sztuki> [Accessed 5 October 2018].

Aronsson, P. and Elgenius, G. eds., 2015. *National Museums and Nation-building in Europe 1750–2010: Mobilization and Legitimacy, Continuity and Change.* London and New York: Routledge.

The Art of Jan and Meda Mládek, n.d. Available at: <www.museumkampa.com/en/The-Jan-and-Meda-Mladek-Collection-120.htm> [Accessed 5 October 2018].

Ash, T.G., 1999. Kanonierki i kanony. Translated from English by S. Kowalski. *Gazeta Wyborcza*, 21–22 August, pp. 8–11.

The Athens Charter for the Restoration of Historic Monuments. Athens 1931, ICOMOS, Available at: <www.icomos.org/en/charters-and-texts/179-articles-en-francais/ressources/charters-and-standards/167-the-athens-charter-for-the-restoration-of-historic-monuments> [Accessed 5 October 2018].

Azua, J., 2005. Guggenheim Bilbao. "Competitive" Strategies for the New Culture: Economy Spaces. In A.M. Guasch and J. Zulaika (eds.), *Learning From the Bilbao Guggenheim.* Reno: Center for Basque Studies, pp. 73–95.

B.a., 2008. Powstanie Muzeum Współczesne. *Wrocław 24.net*, 20 June [online]. Available at: <http://wroclaw24.net/wyniki.php?action=add> [Accessed 6 August 2010].

Badovinac, Z., 2000. Introduction. In M. Briški (ed.), *Arteast 2000+ The Art of Eastern Europe in Dialogue with the West: From the 1960s to the Present. Exhibition of Works for an Emerging Collection.* Catalogue. Ljubljana: Moderna Galerija Ljubljana, pp. 16–19.

Badovinac, Z., 2011. The Museum of Contemporary Art. In T. Hansen (ed.), *(Re) staging the Art Museum.* Berlin: Henie Onstad Art Centre and Revolver Publishing, pp. 37–55.

Bajcurová, K., 2008. Introduction. In D. Buran and K. Müllerová (eds.), *111 diel zo zbierok/111 Works of Art from the Collections.* Bratislava: Slovak National Gallery, pp. 8–31.

Banaś, B. ed., 2016. *The Collection of the Polish Art of 20th Century and Early 21st Century: The Four Domes Pavilion: A Guide.* Translated from Polish by K. Dorocińska. Wrocław: Muzeum Narodowe we Wrocławiu.

Bartoszewicz, D., 2009. Muzeum Historii Polski: Supermarket czy ikona? *Gazeta.pl,* 6 December [online]. Available at: <http://warszawa.gazeta.pl/warszawa/1,34889, 7335594,Muzeum_Historii_Polski__supermarket_czy_ikona_.html> [Accessed 5 October 2018].

Bartoszewicz, D., 2016. GraŻyna Kulczyk chciała budować muzeum w Warszawie. Buduje w Szwajcarii. *Wyborcza.pl Warszawa – Magazyn Stołeczny,* 4 November [online]. Available at: <http://warszawa.wyborcza.pl/warszawa/1,150427,2092 9966,grazyna-kulczyk-chciala-budowac-muzeum-w-warszawie-buduje-w.html> [Accessed 5 October 2018].

Bâtiments anciens . . . Usages nouveaux (Images du possible), 1978. Paris: Centre Georges Pompidou.

Baudrillard, J., 1994. *Simulacra and Simulation.* Translated from French by S. Faria Glaser. Ann Arbor: University of Michigan Press.

Bencsik, B., 2007. Ninety-Nine Years. 20th-Century and Contemporary Hungarian Art. The Antal-Lusztig Collection in Modem. In *Kilencvenkilenc év. Az Antal-Lusztig gyűjtemény a Modemben/Ninety-Nine Years. The Antal-Lusztig Collection in the Modem.* Debrecen: Modem Modern Debreceni Művészeti Közhasznú Társaság, pp. 10–14.

Beskid, V., 2011. Exhibition Concept. In *Artbanka Museum of Young Art. AMoYA.* Prague: Art. Deposit, pp. 10–11.

BHP. Zakładając nową instytucję sztuki na terenach dawnej Stoczni Gdańskiej/Heath & Safety. Implementing a new art institution on the former Gdansk Shipyard premises. Fundacja Wyspa Progress, 4 September–3 October 2004 (exhibition booklet).

Blatter, J., Glocalization, n.d. In *Encyclopaedia Britannica Online* [online]. London: Encyclopædia Britannica (UK). Available at: <www.britannica.com/topic/glocal ization> [Accessed 5 October 2018].

Bochyński, R.K., 2014. Kolekcja Mazowieckiego Centrum Sztuki Współczesnej "Elektrownia" w Radomiu. In Z. Belowski, W. Pujanek, M. Jończy, and R.K. Bochyński (eds.), *Specimen – próba kolekcji.* Radom: Mazowieckie Centrum Sztuki Współczesnej ELEKTROWNIA, pp. 25–35.

Bogner, D. ed., 2004. *A Friendly Alien. Ein Kunsthaus für Graz.* Ostfildern-Ruit: Hatje Cantz.

Bohlen, C., 1991. Budapest Gets Cold Feet in Big Fair with Vienna. *The New York Times,* 22 January [online]. Available at: <www.nytimes.com/1991/01/22/world/ budapest-gets-cold-feet-on-big-fair-with-vienna.html> [Accessed 5 October 2018].

Bomanowska, M., 2008. Sztuka kołem zamachowym, rozmowa z prof. Marią Poprzęcką. *Gazeta Wyborcza Łódź – Co Jest Grane,* 19 November [online].

Available at: <http://lodz.wyborcza.pl/lodz/1,35135,5962483,Sztuka_kolem_zamachowym.html> [Accessed 5 October 2018].

Bordovský, J. ed., [2008]. *Industriální stavby – Pivovary: 1. rekonstrukce a konverze pivovarů*. Bordovský. [Ostrava].

Bourdieu, P. and Darbel, A., 1969. *L'Amour de l'art. Les musées d'art européens et leur public*. Les Éditions de Minuit. English edition: Bourdieu, P. and Darbel, A., 1991. *The Love of Art: European Art Museums and their Public*. Translated from French by C. Beattie and N. Merriman. Cambridge: Polity Press.

Brix, E., 2001. The Future of Central Europe. In J. Purchla (ed.), 2003. *Central Europe: A New Dimension of Heritage*. Cracow: International Cultural Centre.

Bude v Bratislave Kunsthalle? Rozhovor s Richardom Gregorom. *Flash Art CZ/SK*, December 2007–May 2008, Vol. 2, pp. 18–20.

Budowa Muzeum Tadeusza Kantora i nowej siedziby CROCOTEKI, Projekt. Available at: <http://cricotekawbudowie.pl/pl,i-nagroda> [Accessed 27 December 2017].

Budúcnosť premostenia, 2001. Budúcnosť premostenia – budúcnosť SNG? *Projekt*, 2.

Bulkacz, V., 2004. A Lifetime of Preserving Central Europe's Art Heritage. *Prague Club Magazine*, 3.

Cantacuzino, S., 1989. *Re-Architecture. Old Buildings/New Uses*. London: Thames & Hudson Ltd.

Cantacuzino, S., 1975. *New Uses for Old Buildings*. London: Whitney Library of Design.

CBOS, 2007. *Opinie warszawiaków o projektach budynku Muzeum Sztuki Nowoczesnej*. CBOS, Public Opinion Poll, 26–28 February 2007.

Central European Contemporary ART FUND, n.d. Available at: <www.artfond.sk/en/home/more-about-art-fond/> [Accessed 5 October 2018].

Chrabąszcz, R., Hausner, J., and Mazur S., 2003. *Administracja publiczna w wybranych krajach Europy Środkowo-Wschodniej*. Kraków: Uniwersytet Ekonomiczny w Krakowie.

Christian Kerez New Projects of the Museum of Modern Art in Warsaw. 15 July–14 September 2008. Available at: <https://artmuseum.pl/en/wystawy/christian-kerez/> [Accessed 5 October 2018].

Chuchma, J., 2010. Česká kultura platí za věčnou pubertu Milana Knížáka vysokou cenu *iDNES.cz*, 11 June. Available at: <http://zpravy.idnes.cz/ceska-kultura-plati-za-vecnou-pubertu-milana-knizaka-vysokou-cenu-10n-/kavarna.asp?c=A100610_133518_kavarna_chu> [Accessed 5 October 2018].

Collection for the Renowned Theoretician Jindřich Chalupecký, n.d. Available at: <www.museumkampa.com/en/The-Collection-for-Jindrich-Chalupecky-122.htm> [Accessed 5 October 2018].

Collection II, Galeria Arsenał. Available at: <http://galeria-arsenal.pl/o-kolekcji-ii> [Accessed 5 October 2018].

Concept for More Efficient Support of the Arts in 2007–2013, 2006. Prague: Ministry of Culture of the Czech Republic.

Craig-Martin, M., 2008. Towards Tate Modern. In F. Morris (ed.), *Tate Modern: The Handbook*. London: Tate Publishing, pp. 44–51.

Cultural Policy, 2001. *Cultural Policy*. Praha: Ministry of Culture (February).

Cymer, A., 2015. Oddam dworzec w dobre ręce. *Wysokie Obcasy*, 41, 17 October, pp. 22–26.

Czernichowska, K., 2009. Muzeum w bunkrze przy pl. Strzegomskim. *MM Moje Miasto – Wrocław*, 25 May. Available at: <http://wroclaw.naszemiasto.pl/artykul/

muzeum-w-bunkrze-przy-pl-strzegomskim,2895784,art,t,id,tm.html> [Accessed 5 October 2018].

Davis, D., 1990. *The Museum Transformed: Design and Culture in the Post-Pompidou Age*. New York: Abbeville Press.

Declaration of Prime Ministers of the Czech Republic, the Republic of Hungary, the Republic of Poland and the Slovak Republic on Cooperation of the Visegrad Group Countries After their Accession to the European Union. 12 May 2004. Available at: <www.visegradgroup.eu/documents/visegrad-declarations/visegrad-declaration-110412-1> [Accessed 5 October 2018].

Delanty, G., 1995. *Inventing Europe: Idea, Identity, Reality*. Basingstoke: Palgrave Macmillan.

Dobrzynski, J.H., 1999. Travel Advisory. Massachusetts Home for Contemporary Art. *The New York Times*, 30 May. Available at: <www.nytimes.com/1999/05/30/travel/travel-advisory-massachusetts-home-for-contemporary-art.html> [Accessed 5 October 2018].

DOX, 2008. *Opening DOX*. Press Release, DOX Centre for Contemporary Art, 23 October 2008, p. 1. Available at: <www.doxprague.org/doc.php?id=080930094554_LPT0_Press%20release%20260908%20Opening%20DOX.pdf> [Accessed 2 March 2009].

Dvadsať Rokov od Nežnej Neprebehlo: Kunsthalle. Available at: <http://sites.google.com/site/dvadsatrokovodneznej/rozne/fakty/kauzy/kunsthalle> [Accessed 5 October 2018].

Ébli, G., 2016a. Collecting Contemporary Art in Eastern Europe, I. Museums in Regional Rivalry? *Revista ARTA*, 10 February. Available at: <http://revistaarta.ro/en/collecting-contemporary-art-in-eastern-europe-i-museums-in-regional-rivalry/> [Accessed 5 October 2018].

Ébli, G., 2016b. Collecting Contemporary Art in Eastern Europe, II: Do Institutionalised Private Collections Measure Up with Museums? *Revista ARTA*, 22 February 2016. Available at: <http://revistaarta.ro/en/collecting-2/> [Accessed 5 October 2018].

Ébli, G., 2016c. *Múzeumánia. Egy kulturális élménygyár európai modelljei*. Budapest: L'Harmattan.

Elvert, J., 2003. Manowce "Mitteleuropy". Niemieckie koncepcje nowego kształtu Europy w okresie międzywojennym. In J. Kłoczowski and S. Łukasiewicz (eds.), *O nowy kształt Europy. XX-wieczne koncepcje federalistyczne w Europie Środkowo-Wschodniej i ich implikacje dla dyskusji o przyszłości Europy*. Lublin: Instytut Europy Środkowo-Wschodniej.

Eunamus Research, n.d. Available at: <www.ep.liu.se/eunamus/research/research-research.html> [Accessed 5 October 2018].

Fabiański, M., 2000. How Can an Artistic Region Be Defined? The Case of Early-Modern Cenral Europe. In K. Murawska-Muthesius (ed.), *Borders in Art: Revisiting "Kunstgeographie" (Proceedings of the Fourth Joint Conference of Polish and English Art Historians, University of East Anglia, Norwich, 1998)*. Warsaw: Institute of Art.

Falvey, Ch., 2010. Highest State Awards Given to Twenty-Two Outstanding Men and Women. *Český rozhlas 7 – Radio Praha*, 29 October. Available at: <www.radio.cz/en/section/curraffrs/highest-state-awards-given-to-twenty-two-outstanding-men-and-women> [Accessed 5 October 2018].

Fertőszögi, P., 2008. Salute. In P. Fertőszögi (ed.), *KOGART Kortárs Művészeti Gyűjtemény/KOGART Contemporary Art Collection*. Budapest: KOGART.

Fialová, I. and Tichá, J., 2008. *PRG / 20 / 21: Contemporary Architecture*. Praha: Zlatý řez.

Folga-Januszewska, D., 2005. Zbiory sztuki XX wieku i sztuki współczesnej w muzeach polskich. In D. Folga-Januszewska (ed.), *Nowe muzeum sztuki współczesnej czy nowoczesnej?* Warszawa: Krajowy OŚrodek Badań i Dokumentacji Zabytków, pp. 139–145.

Frank, J., 2000. Fourty Years of the Műcsarnok. In K. Keserü (ed.), *Műcsarnok/ Kunsthalle*. Budapest: Műcsarnok.

Fundacja im. Stefana Batorego 15 lat. s.l., n.d.

Gábor, E., 2000. The Building of the Műcsarnok. In K. Keserü (ed.), *Műcsarnok/ Kunsthalle*. Budapest: Műcsarnok.

gas, cig, 2007. Elektrownia ma budynek na własnoŚć. *Gazeta.pl*, 22 March. Available at: <www.gazeta.pl/radom/2029020,44313,4007170.html> [Accessed 16 July 2009].

gg, 2006. Symboliczne rozpoczęcie budowy CSW. *Gazeta.pl Toruń*, 27 October. Available at: <http://torun.gazeta.pl/torun/1,35576,3707442.html> [Accessed 29 January 2012].

Giebelhausen, M., 2011. Museum Architecture. A Brief History. In S. Macdonald (ed.), *A Companion to Museum Studies*. Malden, Oxford: Wiley-Blackwell.

Głaz, J., 2005. Stary Browar najlepszy na Świecie. *Gazeta Wyborcza*, 11 December. Available at: <http://gospodarka.gazeta.pl/gospodarka/1,52981,3060886.html> [Accessed 5 October 2018].

Greub, T., 2008. Museums at the Beginning of the 21st Century: Speculations. In *Museums in the 21st Century: Concepts, Projects, Buildings*. Munich et al.: Prestel.

Gruszczak, A., 2004. Czecho-Słowacja: aksamitny rozwód. In M. Bankowicz et al. (eds.), *Historia polityczna świata XX wieku 1945–2000*. Kraków: Wydawnictwo Uniwersytetu Jagiellońskiego.

Gruza, M. and Pinkas, O., 2010. Muzeum: pudło czy ikona? *rp.pl*, 19 January. Available at: <www.rp.pl/artykul/55362,421844_Muzeum__pudlo_czy_ikona_.html> [Accessed 5 October 2018].

György, P., 2004. A múzeumi örökség. *Népszabadság*, 6 September.

Hajok, D., 2005. Niepewne losy Muzeum Sztuki Współczesnej? *Gazeta.pl Kraków*, 3 March. Available at: <www.archiwum.wyborcza.pl/Archiwum/1,0,4891405, 20070609KR-DLO,Niepewne_losy_Muzeum_Sztuki_Wspolczesnej,.html> [Accessed 5 October 2018].

Hajok, D., 2010. Sztuczne płuco Zabłocia. *Gazeta Wyborcza Kraków*, 19 November, p. 6.

Herman, Z., 2008. Przestrzeń publiczna i dekonstrukcja. Christian Kerez w Warszawie. *Muzeum*, 3(1), pp. 14–16.

História Múzea moderného umenia Andyho Warhola v Medzilaborciach. Available at: <www.muzeumaw.sk/clanok/historia-muzea> [Accessed 5 October 2018].

Hlaváček, L., 2000. Art in an Open Society. In *Sorosovo Centrum současného umění – Praha, 1993–1998 / Soros Center for Contemporary Arts – Prague, 1993–1998*. Praha: Nadace pro současné umění.

Hołda, K., 2007. IleŻ ikon moŻe mieć jedno miasto na jednym placu? Afirmacja projektu Ch. Kereza dla MSN. *Obieg.pl*, 27 February. Available at: <http://archi wum-obieg.u-jazdowski.pl/teksty/1006> [Accessed 5 October 2018].

Horáková, P., 2003. A Tour around Futura – A New Centre for Contemporary Art in Prague. *Český rozhlas 7 – Radio Praha*, 8 August. Available at: <www.radio.cz/en/section/arts/a-tour-around-futura-a-new-centre-for-contemporary-art-in-prague> [Accessed 5 October 2018].

House, J., 1987. Orsay Observed. *The Burlington Magazine*, 129, February.

The I Prize, 2008. In P. Wilkosz, W. Stefanik, and K. Woźniak (concept), *Tender for an Architectural Concept of Museum of Contemporary Art in Wrocław*. Wrocław.

Ilczuk, D. and Pro Cultura Foundation Collaborators, 2015. *COMPENDIUM of Cultural Policies and Trends in Europe: Poland. Country Profile*. Council of Europe/ERICarts, Issue 17.

Inauguracja Narodowego Programu Kultury "Znaki Czasu" – wystąpienie ministra Waldemara Dąbrowskiego, 2004. Toruń, 13 March.

Inkei, P. and Szabó, J.Z., 2011. *COMPENDIUM Cultural Policies and Trends in Europe: Hungary. Country Profile*. Council of Europe/ERICarts, Issue 12.

Inkei, P. and Vaspál, V., 2014. *COMPENDIUM Cultural Policies and Trends in Europe: Hungary. Country Profile*. Council of Europe/ERICarts, Issue 16.

Instytucja krytyczna. Z Piotrem Piotrowskim rozmawiają Zofia Waślicka i Artur Żmijewski. In P. Althamer et al. (eds.), 2014. *Instytucja krytyczna*. Warszawa: Wydawnictwo Krytyki Politycznej, pp. 156–172.

Insurance Policy. Z Piotrem Piotrowskim rozmawia Adam Mazur. *Obieg*, 30 September 2010. Available at: <http://archiwum-obieg.u-jazdowski.pl/wydarzenie/19756> [Accessed 5 October 2018].

International Charter for the Conservation and Restoration of Monuments and Sites (The Venice Charter 1964). IInd International Congress of Architects and Technicians of Historic. Monuments, Venice, 1964. Adopted by ICOMOS in 1965. Available at: <www.icomos.org/charters/venice_e.pdf> [Accessed 5 October 2018].

Internetowy Serwis Architektoniczny Ronet.pl, Results of the Competition, 23 February 2007. Available at: <www.a-ronet.pl/index.php?mod=konkurs&k_id=28> [Accessed 5 October 2018].

Interview with László Baán, the Government Commissioner in Charge of Developing of "MuseumPark", n.d. Museum of Fine Arts. Available at: <www.szepmuveszeti.hu/background_materials_articles/interiew-with-laszlo-baan-the-government-commissioner-in-charge-of-developing-of-museumpark-897> [Accessed 5 October 2018].

Introduction, 2000. In *Sorosovo Centrum současného umění – Praha, 1993–1998 / Soros Center for Contemporary Arts – Prague, 1993–1998*. Praha.

Jagodzińska, K., 2008. BWA w cieniu wolnego rynku. *Art & Business*, 1–2, pp. 20–25.

Jagodzińska, K., 2010. Zachęceni do kolekcjonowania. *Art & Business*, 3, pp. 16–23.

Jagodzińska, K., 2012. Budapest – A Political Museum District. *Herito*, 6, pp. 146–151.

Jagodzińska, K., 2014. *International Cultural Centre* [Guidebook]. Krakow: International Cultural Centre.

Jagodzińska, K., 2014. *Czas muzeów w Europie Środkowej. Muzea i centra sztuki współczesnej (1989–2014)*. Krakow: International Cultural Centre.

The Jan and Meda Mládek Foundation, n.d. Available at: <www.museumkampa.com/en/Museum-104.htm> [Accessed 28 January 2018].

Jarecka, D., 2006a. Sztuka lokalna idzie do Zachęt. *Gazeta Wyborcza*, 3 February, p. 14.

Jarecka, D., 2006b. Jak nowe muzeum odmieniło Graz. *Gazeta Wyborcza*, 21 April, p. 16.

Jarecka, D., 2007a. DoŚĆ rzeźby w Warszawie. *Gazeta Wyborcza*, 21 February, p. 14.

Jarecka, D., 2007b. JeŚli nie Kerez, to kto? *Gazeta Wyborcza*, 26 February, p. 14.

Jarecka, D., 2007c. To muzeum będzie niesamowite. Rozmowa z Adamem Szymczykiem. *Gazeta Wyborcza*, 2 March, p. 17.

Jarecka, D., 2007d. Architektura jako źródło cierpień. *Gazeta Wyborcza*, 12 March, p. 16.

Jarecka, D., 2007e. Być nowym centrum Europy Wschodniej. Rozmowa z Joanną Mytkowską. *Gazeta Wyborcza*, 8 June, p. 14.

Jasiński, A., 2008. Uwagi na marginesie konkursu na koncepcję głównego gmachu Muzeum Śląskiego w Katowicach. *Architektura & Biznes*, 1, p. 76.

Jencks, Ch., 2006/2007. The Iconic Building Is Here to Stay. In P. Dean (ed.), *Hunch 11: Rethinking Representation (The Berlage Institute Report)* (Winter). Rotterdam: Episode Publishers.

Jencks, Ch., 2008. *The Iconic Building*. New York: Rizzoli.

The Jiří and Běla Kolář Collection, n.d. Available at: <www.museumkampa.com/en/The-Jiri-and-Bela-Kolar-Collection-121.htm> [Accessed 5 October 2018].

Joanna Mytkowska o nowym budynku muzeum w rozmowie z Łukaszem Stępnikiem, 7 September 2015. Available at: <http://artmuseum.pl/pl/news/joanna-mytkowska-o-nowym-budynku-muzeum> [Accessed 5 October 2018].

Jurkiewicz-Eckert, D., 2006. "Międzynarodowa Kolekcja Sztuki Nowoczesnej" Muzeum Sztuki w Łodzi i jej znaczenie dla dziedzictwa kulturowego Europy. *Studia Europejskie*, 4. pp. 121–143.

Jurkovičova tepláreň, 2017. Jurkovičova tepláreň bude dominantou mestského parku v komplexe Sky Park. *Bratislava24*, 17 February. Available at: <http://bratislava.dnes24.sk/jurkovicova-teplaren-bude-dominantou-mestskeho-parku-v-komplexe-sky-park-263206> [Accessed 5 October 2018].

Już trudno. Z Andą Rottenberg rozmawia Dorota Jarecka, 2013. Warszawa: Wydawnictwo Krytyki Politycznej.

Kaufmann, T.D., 2004. *Toward a Geography of Art*. Chicago and London: The University of Chicago Press.

Keresztély, K., 2005. Cultural Investments in a City in Transition: The Budapest Case. In G. Barta et al. (eds.), *Hungarian Spaces and Places: Patterns of Transition*. Pécs: Centre for Regional Studies.

Kerez, Ch., n.d. *Opis autorski*. Available at: <www.museumcompetition.pl/download/Konzept_Polnisch_Beschreibung.pdf> [Accessed 8 March 2007].

Kiedy rano otwieram oczy, widzę film. Eksperyment w sztuce Jugosławii w latach 60. i 70., 25 April–22 June 2008. Available at: <https://artmuseum.pl/pl/wystawy/kiedy-rano-otwieram-oczy-widze-film-2> [Accessed 5 October 2018].

Kifner, J., 2000. Museum Brings Town Back to Life. *The New York Times*, 30 May. Available at: <www.nytimes.com/2000/05/30/us/museum-brings-town-back-to-life.html> [Accessed 5 October 2018].

Kizáková, Z., 2010. Metropola bez Kunsthalle nie je metropola. *kultura.pravda.sk*, 21 April. Available at: <https://kultura.pravda.sk/galeria/clanok/34014-metropola-bez-kunsthalle-nie-je-metropola/> [Accessed 5 October 2018].

Knell, S., 2016. *National Galleries: The Art of Making Nations*. New York: Routledge.

Kolekcja Muzeum Współczesnego Wrocław, Muzeum wirtualne, n.d. Available at: <www.muzeumwirtualne.pl> [Accessed 5 October 2018].

Kolozsváry, M., 2005. From a Budapest Villa to an Esterházy Palace. In M. Kolozsváry (ed.), *Hungarian Art 1900–1950. Radnai Collection, Győr*. Budapest: Kieselbach, pp. 48–53.

Konkurs na opracowanie koncepcji architektonicznej Muzeum Sztuki Współczesnej we Wrocławiu. I nagroda, n.d. *Serwis Architektoniczny Ronet.pl* <http://www.a-ronet.pl/index.php?mod=nagroda&n_id=906> [Accessed 5 October 2018].

Konopelska, W. *Galeria Sztuki Współczesnej ELEKTROWNIA*, n.d. Available at: <www.galeria-elektrownia.pl/onas.htm> [Accessed 6 September 2009].

Kopania, K., 2006. *Arsenał sztuki. Galeria Arsenał w Białymstoku i jej Kolekcja II*. Białystok: Podlaskie Towarzystwo Zachęty Sztuk Pięknych.

Kosiewski, P., 2008. Lokalność i uniwersalizm. O lubelskiej i innych Zachętach. *ArtKontakt.pl*. Available at: <www.artkontakt.pl/Lokalnosc_i_uniwersalizm_O_lubelskiej_i_innych_Zachetach-a-12-3.html> [Accessed 11 September 2014].

Kowalewicz, K., 2008. ms² czyli sztuka spotęgowana, rozmowa z Jarosławem Suchanem. *Gazeta Wyborcza – Muzeum Sztuki* – suplement to *Gazeta Wyborcza – Łódź*, 14 November.

Kowalski, K., 2005. Francja. In B. Gierat-Bieroń and K. Kowalski (eds.), *Europejskie modele polityki kulturalnej*. Kraków: Małopolska Szkoła Administracji Publicznej Akademii Ekonomicznej.

Krajewski, P. and Monkiewicz, D., 2007. *MWW Muzeum Współczesne Wrocław. Koncepcja Programowa*. Wrocław: Urząd Miejski.

Kráková, D. and Gurová, D., 2009. Z teplárne bude možno galéria. *SME*, 23 February. Available at: <https://bratislava.sme.sk/c/4275021/z-teplarne-bude-mozno-galeria.html> [Accessed 5 October 2018].

Krukowski, W., 2005. CSW Ujazdowski Castle International Collection. In A. Mazur (ed.), *Collection 04 2001–2005*. Warszawa: Centre for Contemporary Art Ujazdowski Castle, pp. 14–21.

Krzysztofek, K., 1999. Ewolucja założeń i programów polityki kulturalnej w Polsce w latach dziewięćdziesiątych. In T. Kostyrko and M. Czerwiński (eds.), *Kultura polska w dekadzie przemian*. Warszawa: Instytut Kultury.

Kukurová, L. and Makara, T. eds., 2013. *Kasárne/Kulturpark 2008/2011*. Košice.

Kundera, M., 1984. The Tragedy of Central Europe. *The New York Review of Books* (pre-1986), 26 April, pp. 33–38.

Kunsthalle Bratislava, n.d. Available at: <www.kunsthallebratislava.sk/en/khb/kunsthalle-bratislava> [Accessed 5 October 2018].

Kunsthalle Praha. Available at: <www.pudilfamilyfoundation.org/en/kunsthalle-praha> [Accessed 5 October 2018].

Kupfer Schneider, A., 1998. *Creating the Musée d'Orsay: The Politics of Culture in France*. University Park: Pennsylvania State University Press.

Kusiński, J., Bonisławski, R., and Janik, M., 2009. *Księga fabryk Łodzi*. Łódź: Wydawnictwo Jacek Kusiński.

Lampugnani, V.M., 2011. Insight versus Entertainment. Untimely Meditations on the Architecture of Twentieth-Century Art Museums. In S. Macdonald (ed.), *A Companion to Museum Studies*. Chichester: Wiley-Blackwell.

Larry's List Ltd. and AMMA eds., 2016. *Private Art Museum Report*. Modern Arts Publishing.

Lehmannová, M. and Březinová, A., 2011. Moravian Industrial Museum/Moravian Museum of Applied Arts in Brno. In P. Tomášek (ed.), *National Gallery of Moravia*. Brno: Moravská galerie v Brně, pp. 280–281.

Lenartowicz, J.K., 2006. Smok szalony w Bilbao. In M. Popczyk (ed.), *Muzeum sztuki. Od Luwru do Bilbao*. Katowice: Muzeum Śląskie.

Leszkowicz, P. ed., 2008. *Łaźnia. Architektura, sztuka i historia/Laznia – The Bathhouse: Architecture, Art and History*. Gdańsk: Centrum Sztuki Współczesnej Łaźnia.

Liget Budapest Competition Programme, 24 February 2014.

Liget Budapest Néprajzi Múzeum – Tervpályázat Zárójelentése, Városliget Zrt. [2016].

A living experience that was a transformative one: Aneta Szyłak Talks to Edwin Bendyk. In A. Szyłak and K. Sikorska eds., 2015. *Garden of Everyday Errors: Alternativa Book of Practices*. Gdańsk: Fundacja Wyspa Progress, Fundacja Alternativa, pp. 87–121.

Lorente, J.P., 1998. *Cathedrals of Urban Modernity: The First Museums of Contemporary Art, 1800–1930*. Farnham: Ashgate.

Lorente, J.P., 2011. *The Museums of Contemporary Art: Notion and Development*. Farnham: Ashgate.

Lorentz, S., 1999. Filozofia muzeów. In A. Rottermund, D. Folga-Januszewska, and E. Micke-Broniarek (eds.), *Przeszłość przyszłości . . . Księga pamiątkowa ku czci Profesora Stanisława Lorentza w setną rocznicę urodzin*. Warszawa: Muzeum Narodowe, Zamek Królewski.

Ludwiński, J., 2008. Muzeum Sztuki Aktualnej we Wrocławiu (koncepcja ogólna), [1966]. *Muzeum*, 3, p. 1.

Machalická, J., 2008. Skupina Knížák se představuje. *Lidové noviny*, 23 January. Available at: <www.lidovky.cz/kultura/skupina-knizak-se-predstavuje.A080123_104634_ln_kultura_nev> [Accessed 5 October 2018].

Małgorzata Ludwisiak – rozmowa z Małgorzatą Piwowar, 2014. *Rzeczpospolita*, 21 August. Available at: <www.rp.pl/artykul/1134901-Malgorzata-Ludwisiak-rozmowa.html> [Accessed 5 October 2018].

Malkowski, T., 2006. Śląsk szczęśliwie poprzemysłowy. *Gazeta Wyborcza*, 22–23 July, p. 10.

Mansfeld, J., 2003. Centralne Biuro Wystaw Artystycznych. In G. Świtek (ed.), *Zachęta 1860–2000*. Warszawa: Zachęta Narodowa Galeria Sztuki.

Marr, A., 2008. The Magic Box. In F. Morris (ed.), *Tate Modern: The Handbook*. London: Tate Publishing, pp. 12–19.

Marte, B. and Seidl, W., 2006. Towards a New Understanding. Kontakt. The Art Collection of Erste Bank Group. In N. Krick and W. Seidl (eds.), *Kontakt . . . aus der Sammlung der Erste Bank-Gruppe/Kontakt . . . Works From the Collection of Erste Bank Group*. Wien: König, Walther.

Masák, M., Švácha, R., and Vybíral, J., 1995. *The Trade Fair Palace in Prague*. Prague: National Gallery.

Mazur, A., 2011. Okulary do patrzenia w niebo. Rozmowa z Jarosławem Suchanem. *Dwutygodnik*, 69. Available at: <www.dwutygodnik.com/artykul/2802-okulary-do-patrzenia-w-niebo.html> [Accessed 5 October 2018].

McClellan, A., 2008. *The Art Museum from Boullée to Bilbao*. Berkeley, Los Angeles, and London: University of California Press.

MacLeod, S., 2013. *Museum Architecture: A New Biography*. London and New York: Routledge.

Meschnik, M., 2001. *Biuro Wystaw Artystycznych w Katowicach 1949–1999*. Katowice: Galeria Sztuki Współczesnej BWA.

Metz, K., 2005. Átadták a Művészetek Palotáját. *Magyar Hírlap*, 16 March.

Miała być nowa ikona Warszawy, będzie minimalizm, 2007. *Gazeta Wyborcza*, 19 February, p. 14.

Michałowicz, T., 2004. Muzeum Sztuki z przyszłoŚcią. *Gazeta Wyborcza Łódź*, 19 January.

Millenniumi Városközpont – Részletes programterv, 2002. Duna Sétány kft./Tri-Gránit rt., March.

Minca, M., 2009. Tepláreň ako galéria dizajnu, architektúry a vizuálneho umenia? *Stavebné forum.sk*, 15 May.

MOCAK, 2010. *Oddanie budynku Muzeum Sztuki Współczesnej w Krakowie*. Press Release, 16 November 2010.

Montaner, J.M. and Oliveras, J., 1986. *The Museums of the Last Generation*. London and New York: St Martins Press.

Montaner, J.M., 1990. *New Museums*. New York: Princeton Architectural Press.

Morawińska, A., 2003. Wstęp. In M. Guzowska (ed.), *Rzeczywistości. Kolekcje bez granic II*. Warszawa: Zachęta – Narodowa Galeria Sztuki.

Morrison, G., 2004. Look at Me! *The Guardian*, 12 July. Available at: <www.guardian.co.uk/artanddesign/2004/jul/12/architecture.regeneration> [Accessed 5 October 2018].

ms², 2007. *Nowe miejsce dla sztuki*. Press Release, 4 September 2007.

Murawska-Muthesius, K. and Piotrowski, P. eds., 2015. *From Museum Critique to the Critical Museum*. Farnham: Ashgate.

Murzyn-Kupisz, M., 2013. Potencjał "dzielnic kultury" we wzmacnianiu roli kultury w rozwoju oŚrodka metropolitalnego. DoŚwiadczenia Krakowa. In A. Klasik (ed.), *Rozwój gospodarki kreatywnej na obszarach metropolitalnych*. Katowice: Wydawnictwo Uniwersytetu Ekonomicznego.

Museum competition. Available at: <www.museumcompetition.pl/forum.php?did=1&id=1020> [Accessed 5 October 2018].

Museum Policy in Hungary, National Report 2003, 2003. NEMO Annual Meeting (Network of European Museum Organizations), 25 November. Manuscript.

Muzeum bez kuratorów. Z Marią Anną Potocką rozmawia Adam Mazur, 2010. *Obieg*, 30 November. Available at: <http://archiwum-obieg.u-jazdowski.pl/wydar zenie/19609> [Accessed 5 October 2018].

Muzeum krytyczne to nie dyskursywny ornament. Rozmowa z Piotrem Piotrowskim (Magdalena Ziółkowska), 2011. *Dwutygodnik*, 58:6. Available at: <www.dwutygodnik.com/artykul/2290-muzeum-krytyczne-to-nie-dyskursywny-orna ment.html> [Accessed 5 October 2018].

Muzeum Susch [2018]. *Muzeum Susch to Open in January 2019*. Press Release.

[Muzeum Sztuki Nowoczesnej w Warszawie] Pierwsza nagroda, 2007. *Architektura-Murator*, p. 5.

Mytkowska, J. z zespołem, 2007. Muzeum w procesie. *Muzeum*, 1, pp. 1–2.

Narodowa Strategia Rozwoju Kultury na lata 2004–2013, n.d. Ministerstwo Kultury.

Narodowy Program Kultury "Znaki Czasu" – Conversation between Minister of Culture Waldemar Dąbrowski, Aneta Szyłak, Dorota Monkiewicz, Dorota Jarecka, Waldemar Braniewski, Piotr Krajewski, held by Jerzy Kisielewski, 2004. *Polskie Radio Program 2*, 30 March.

Naumann, F., 1915. *Mitteleuropa*. Berlin: Verlag von Georg Reimer.

Néray, K., 1998. *The Social Role of Contemporary Art and the Ludwig-Phenomenon*. In AICA Symposium, Culture and Politics, Bratislava, November 1998. [manuscript].

Néray, K., 2003. English Insert. In *Selected Works From the Collection*. Budapest: Ludwig Museum Budapest – Museum of Contemporary Art, 2000.

Néray, K., 2006. *Destination, New Museum, Building*. Paper presented in Zagreb in 22–24 June. [manuscript].

Neumann, I., 2001. The Jesuit College. Its Reconstruction and New Role. In *Kutná Hora Arts Centre: Past, Present and Future*. The Czech Museum of Fine Arts, Prague. s.l.

Newhouse, V., 2006. *Towards a New Museum*. Expanded Edition. New York: The Monacelli Press.

Nie uŻywam flesza – rozmowa z Christianem Kerezem, zwycięzcą konkursu, 2007. *Architektura-Murator*, 5, pp. 72–73.

Niedziela, Z., 1995. *Słowacja znana i nieznana: szkice z dziejów literatury słowackiej*. Kraków: Międzynarodowe Centrum Kultury.

O Kolekcji, Centrum Sztuki Współczesnej w Toruniu. Available at: <http://csw.torun.pl/o-kolekcji-sztuki-csw/> [Accessed 5 October 2018].

OFF-Biennale Budapest, Available at: <https://offbiennale.hu/en/off/off-biennale-budapest> [Accessed 5 October 2018].

Ojrzyński, J., 1991. Międzynarodowa Kolekcja Sztuki Nowoczesnej. Kalendarium 1931–1991. In U. Czartoryska (ed.), *Kolekcja sztuki XX wieku w Muzeum Sztuki w Łodzi*. Warszawa: Wydawnictwo Galerii Zachęta.

Ojrzyński, J., 2004. Wprowadzenie. In J. Ojrzyński et al. (ed.), *111 dzieł z kolekcji Muzeum Sztuki w Łodzi*. Łódź: Muzeum Sztuki w Łodzi.

Ondrušeková, A., 2008. Tatra Gallery Poprad. In *Art Museums in Slovakia*. Bratislava.

A Person Working in Independent Culture in Slovakia Must Be Fighter. Interview with Peter Radkoff, [w:] Kasárne/Kulturpark 2008/2011, red. Lenka Kukurová, Tomáš Makara, Košice, 2013.

Petrová, P., 2011. *COMPENDIUM Cultural Policies and Trends in Europe: Czech Republic. Country Profile*. Council of Europe/ERICarts, Issue 12.

Piątek, G., 2007. Krajobraz po konkursie – Opinie o zwycięskim projekcie. *Architektura-Murator*, 5, pp. 66–71.

Piotrowski, P., 2000. Constructing a History/Constructing a Contemporaneity. In M. Briški (ed.), *Arteast 2000+ The Art of Eastern Europe in Dialogue with the West: From the 1960s to the Present*. Exhibition of Works for an Emerging Collection. Ljubljana: Moderna Galerija.

Piotrowski, P., 2011a. *In the Shadow of Yalta: Art and the Avant-garde in Eastern Europe, 1945–1989*. Translated from Polish by A. Brzyski. London: Reaktion Books.

Piotrowski, P., 2011b. *Muzeum krytyczne*. Poznań: Dom Wydawniczy Rebis.

Piotrowski, P., 2012. *Art and Democracy in Post-Communist Europe*. Translated from Polish by A. Brzyski. London: Reaktion Books.

Piotrowski, P., 2015. Making the National Museum Critical. In K. Murawska-Muthesius and P. Piotrowski (eds.), *From Museum Critique to the Critical Museum*. Farnham, Burlington: Ashgate, pp. 137–146.

Plevoets, B. and Van Cleempoel, K., 2011. Adaptive Reuse as a Strategy Towards Conservation of Cultural Heritage: A Literature Review. *WIT Transactions on The Built Environment*, 118, pp. 155–164.

Pode Bal 1998–2008, 2008. Praha: DIVUS.

Polityka w muzeum. Z Piotrem Piotrowskim rozmawia Jacek Maj, 2012. *Znak*, April, 683, pp. 96–99.

Pollág, P., 2001. How It All Began. In P. Žalman (ed.), *Muzeum moderno umienia Danubiana*. s.l.

Pomian, K., 2005. Kolekcja wszystkich gustów. *Gazeta Wyborcza*, 19–20 March 2005, p. 26.

Pracownia Thomas Phifer and Partners zaprojektuje zespół budynków Muzeum Sztuki Nowoczesnej i TR Warszawa, 31 July 2014. Available at: <http://artmu seum.pl/pl/news/pracownie-thomas-phifer-and-partners-zaprojektuje-zespol> [Accessed 5 October 2018].

Prezentacja projektów budynków Muzeum Sztuki Nowoczesnej i TR Warszawa, 18 September 2015. Available at: <http://artmuseum.pl/pl/news/prezentacja-projek tow-budynkow-muzeum-sztuki-nowoczesnej-i-tr> [Accessed 5 October 2018].

Próba zdefiniowania przedmiotu nieidentyfikowalnego i nieustannie zmieniającego swój kształt, 2003. In M. Guzowska (ed.), *Rzeczywistości. Kolekcje bez granic II*. Warszawa: Zachęta Państwowa Galeria Sztuki.

Pučerová, K. ed., 2008. *New Face of Prague: Contemporary Architecture in Prague After 1989*. Praha: Galerie Jaroslava Fragnera.

Purchla, J., 2008. *Cracow in the European Core*. Translated from English by T. Bałuk-Ulewiczowa. Olszanica-Kraków: Bosz.

Purchla, J., 2009a. Biblioteka Europy Środka. In C.G. Kiss (ed.), *Lekcja Europy Środkowej. Eseje i szkice*. Kraków: Międzynarodowe Centrum Kultury.

Purchla, J., 2009b. Medyceusze naszej transformacji. In B. Gierat-Bieroń (ed.), *Ministrowie kultury doby transformacji, 1989–2005 (wywiady)*. Kraków: Towarzystwo Autorów i Wydawców Prac Naukowych Universitas.

Rácz, J., 2006. Az újitó gyűjtő. *Manager*, 1. Available at: <www.managermagazin.hu/magazin.php?page=article&id=933> [Accessed 9 December 2010].

Raport roczny Kulczyk Foundation 2004. Poznań: Kulczyk Foundation.

Raport roczny Kulczyk Foundation 2007. Poznań: Kulczyk Foundation.

Regős, A., 2000. First Decades of the Műcsarnok. In K. Keserü (ed.), *Műcsarnok/Kunsthalle*. Budapest: Műcsarnok.

Regulamin konkursu na opracowanie koncepcji architektonicznej budynku Muzeum Sztuki Nowoczesnej w Warszawie, 2005. Warszawa: Urząd Miasta Stołecznego Warszawy, Biuro Naczelnego Architekta Miasta.

Regulamin Konkursu na Opracowanie Koncepcji Architektonicznej Specjalnej Strefy Sztuki w Ramach Specjalnej Strefy Kultury, [2008]. Łódź: Biuro do spraw Realizacji i Nadzoru Inwestycji.

Ritzer, G., 2003. *The Globalization of Nothing*. London: SAGE Publications.

Robertson, R., 1992. *Globalization: Social Theory and Global Culture*. London: Sage.

Róka, E., 2002. Lajos Ernst and the Ernst Museum. In K. Keserü (ed.), *The Ernst Museum*. Budapest: Ernst Museum.

Sachs, A., 2008. Nelson-Atkins Museum of Art Expansion. In *Museums in the 21st Century: Concepts, Project, Buildings*. Munich et al.: Prestel.

Salwiński, J., 2011. *Wokół ulicy Lipowej*. Kraków: Muzeum Historyczne Miasta Krakowa.

Saraczyńska, A., 2008. Architekci, zaprojektujcie nam muzeum. *Gazeta Wyborcza Wrocław*, 5 June.

Sarzyński, P., 2008. Zniechęcanie Zachęt. *Polityka*, 6 September, pp. 90–91.

Schöllhammer, G., 2006. Kontakt, 1960 ff. In N. Krick and W. Seidl (eds.), *Kontakt . . . Works From the Collection of Erste Bank Group*. Wien: Museum Moderner Kunst Stiftung Ludwig Wien.

Schubert, K., 2002. *The Curator's Egg: The Evolution of the Museum Concept From the French Revolution to the Present Day*. London: One-Off Press.

Šenk, F., 2011. New National Gallery Director. Vladimír Rösel Discusses His Critics, Future Plans. *The Prague Post*, 1 June. Available at: <www.praguepost. com/tempo/8861-new-national-gallery-director.html> [Accessed 11 September 2014].

Sepioł, J., 2005. Miejsce, które prowokuje. *Gazeta Wyborcza Kraków*, 14 January, p. 7.

Silver, N., 1994. *The Making of Beaubourg: A Building Biography of the Centre Pompidou, Paris*. Cambridge, MA and London: The MIT Press.

Skřivánek, J., 2008. Jak se staví galerie. *Art+Antiques*, June, pp. 38–41.

Skřivánek, J., 2009. Deset let s Knížákem v Národní galerii. *Art+Antiques*, pp. 7–8.

[Slovenská národná galéria], 2005. *Projekt 3*.

Smatlák, M., 2011. *COMPENDIUM Cultural Policies and Trends in Europe: Slovakia. Country Profile*. Council of Europe/ERICarts, Issue 12.

Smolar, A., n.d. Z perspektywy 15 lat. In *Fundacja im. Stefana Batorego 15 lat*. s.l.

Soćko, R., 2009. Pomysł na Transformatorownię. *W Szczecinie.pl*, 16 July. Available at: <https://wszczecinie.pl/index.php/aktualnosci,pomysl_na_transformatorownie, id-16096.html> [Accessed 5 October 2018].

A Speech by Maria Anna Potocka in a Panel Discussion Organized by MOCAK. *Co to jest program muzeum?*, 28 April 2010. Center for the Humanities Studies of the Jagiellonian University.

Springer, F., 2017. Biały prostopadłoŚcian nad Wisłą. Prowokacja, instalacja, performance czy po prostu zbieg okolicznoŚci? *Gazeta.pl Weekend*, 27 February. Available at: <http://weekend.gazeta.pl/weekend/1,152121,21592829,bialy-prostopadloscian-nad-wisla-prowokacja-instalacja-performance.html> [Accessed 5 October 2018].

Starmach, A., 2005. Tylko centrum, tylko plac Na Groblach. *Gazeta Wyborcza Kraków*, 4 March, pp. 10–11.

Stepnowska, T.A., 2003. Współczesna kolekcja Zachęty. In G. Świtek (ed.), *Zachęta 1860–2000*. Warszawa: Zachęta Narodowa Galeria Sztuki.

Strategia 2012–2020: Twórcza kontynuacja. Międzynarodowe Centrum Kultury, 6 May 2013.

Strategia działalności i rozwoju 2010–2020, Muzeum Narodowe w Warszawie, September 2010 – Final Conclusions (short version of the document available on the *Obieg* website wnioski końcowe (wersja skrócona dokumentu udostępniona na stronie czasopisma "Obieg"). Available at: <archiwum-obieg.u-jazdowski.pl/files/ Fragmenty%20STRATEGII%20MNW.doc> [Accessed 5 October 2018].

Strategia rozwoju kultury w regionach. Narodowy program kultury "Znaki Czasu" na lata 2004–2013, 2003.

Stratton, M., 2000. Reviving Industrial Buildings: An Overview of Conservation and Commercial Interests. In M. Stratton (ed.), *Industrial Buildings: Conservation and Regeneration*. London: Taylor & Francis.

Suchan, J., Information issued by the Muzeum Sztuki in Łódź at the Occasion of the Opening of the ms^2 Building, 20–22 November 2008.

Sudjic, D., 2003. Landmarks of Hope and Glory. *The Observer*, 26 October, Arts, p. 6.

Sudjic, D., 2005. Can We Still Believe in Iconic Buildings? *Prospect*, 19 June. Available at: <www.prospectmagazine.co.uk/2005/06/canwestillbelieveiniconicbuildings> [Accessed 5 October 2018].

Summary of the Debate Forum on the Modern Hungarian Museum, 2002. *exindex*, 11 June. Available at: <http://exindex.hu/index.php?l=en&page=3&id=413> [Accessed 5 October 2018].

Suzuki, H., 2005. Journey to the Origin. In *Chichu Art Museum. Tadao Ando Builds for Walter de Maria, James Turrell, and Claude Monet*. Ostfildern: Hatje Cantz.

Świerczyńska, J., 2008. Z Anetą Szyłak rozmowa o sztuce. *Trójmiasto.pl*, 6 June. Available at: <http://kultura.trojmiasto.pl/Z-Aneta-Szylak-rozmowa-o-sztuce-n28387. html> [Accessed 5 October 2018].

Szále, L., 2005. Egy nagyon hasznos luxusberuházás. *Ahogy tetszik*, 30 July.

Szanto, A., 2001. Art/Architecture; Museum Building in the Budapest Style. *The New York Times*, 26 August. Available at: <www.nytimes.com/2001/08/26/arts/ art-architecture-museum-building-in-the-budapest-style.html> [Accessed 5 October 2018].

Szczecin – Stowarzyszenie Zachęta Sztuki Współczesnej. Available at: <www.artkontakt. pl/infobiz_server.php?mod=products_category&pcid=20> [Accessed 29 January 2012].

Székély, M., 2014. Contemporary Art Museums in Central Europe. Between International Discourse and Nation (Re)building Strategies. *Études du CEFRES*, 17.

Szeląg, M., 2005. Muzeum sztuki współczesnej – topos powojennego Życia artystycznego. In D. Folga-Januszewska (ed.), *Nowe muzeum sztuki współczesnej czy nowoczesnej?* Warszawa: Krajowy OŚrodek Badań i Dokumentacji Zabytków, pp. 27–37.

Szentpéteri, M., 2005. Művelődés a Soroksári úton. Az ördög a részletekben. *Magyar Narancs*, 13 January, reprinted in *Építészfórum*, 17 January 2005. Available at: <www.epiteszforum.hu/node/2134> [Accessed 5 October 2018].

Szewczuk, M., 2005. Program i wizja Muzeum Sztuki Współczesnej w Radomiu. In D. Folga-Januszewska (ed.), *Nowe muzeum sztuki współczesnej czy nowoczesnej?* Warszawa: Krajowy OŚrodek Badań i Dokumentacji Zabytków, pp. 195–210.

Szewczuk, M., 2013. Muzeum Sztuki Współczesnej w Radomiu po dwudziestu dwóch latach. *Muzealnictwo*, 54, pp. 117–124.

Szewczuk, M., 2016. Polish Art After 1945: Between the Idea of Modern Art and Reality and Memory. In M. Szewczuk (ed.), *Living for Art: Contemporary Art Collection at the Jacek Malczewski Museum in Radom. Painting/Drawing/Sculpture/ Graphics/Photography/Objects*. Radom: Wojciech Janik and Jacek Malczewski Museum in Radom, pp. 17–29.

Szlendak, T., 2008. *Otwieranie wielkiej szafy. Odbiór sztuki współczesnej i zapotrzebowania na kulturę wysoką w Toruniu i w regionie. Raport z badań dla Centrum Sztuki Współczesnej "Znaki Czasu"*. April–May. [unpublished]

Szmygin, B., 2003. Teoria zabytku Aloisa Riegla. *Ochrona zabytków*, 3–4, pp. 148–153.

Szoboszlai, J., n.d. *Irokez Collection Come on the Scene*. Available at: <www.irokez-collection.hu/index.php?> [Accessed 5 December 2010].

Szybowicz, A., Ślusarczyk, W., and Woźniak, M., 2009. Muzeum na wyspie. Nowa jakość bydgoskiego muzeum. *Muzealnictwo*, 50, pp. 104–115.

Szyłak, A., 1995. *Wyspa. The Site of Ideas: The Idea of Site*. In [w:] A. Szyłak, G. Klaman, and J. Bartołowicz (eds.), *Wyspa. The Site of Ideas: The Idea of Site*. Gdańsk: Galeria Wyspa, Fundacja Wyspa Progress.

Szyłak, A., 2017. *NOMUS Manifest*. Available at: <www.nomus.gda.pl/pl/blog/ nomus-manifest/> [Accessed 5 October 2018].

Szyłak, A., Klaman, G. and Bartołowicz, J. eds., 1995. *Wyspa. The Site of Ideas: The Idea of Site*. Gdańsk: Galeria Wyspa, Fundacja Wyspa Progress.

Takáts, J., 2005. *Borderless City: European Capital of Culture – Pécs2010*. Pécs: Pécs2010 Application Centre.

Tali, M., 2018. *Absence and Difficult Knowledge in Contemporary Art Museums*. London and New York: Routledge.

Tali, M. and Pierantoni, L., 2011. New Art Museums in Central and Eastern Europe and the Ideologies of Urban Space Production. *Cultural Trends*, 20(2), pp. 167–182.

Tomášek, P., 2011. National Gallery of Moravia. In P. Tomášek (ed.), *National Gallery of Moravia*. Brno: Moravská galerie v Brně.

Torbicka, I., 2009. GraŻyna Kulczyk nie zbuduje muzeum! *Gazeta.pl Poznań*, 9 October. Available at: <http://poznan.gazeta.pl/poznan/1,36037,7126194,Grazyna_Kulczyk_nie_zbuduje_muzeum_.html> [Accessed 5 October 2018].

TRAFO Center for Contemporary Art, n.d. Available at: <http://trafo.art/en/about/institution/> [Accessed 28 January 2018].

Travers, T., 2005. Renewing London. In M. Gayford et al. (eds.), *Tate Modern: The First Five Years*. London: Tate Publishing.

Turowski, A., 1998. *Muzeum – instytucja awangardy*. In A. Turowski (ed.), *Awangardowe marginesy*. Warszawa: Instytut Kultury.

U-jazdowski – Program, n.d. Available at: <http://u-jazdowski.pl/program [Accessed 28 January 2018].

Une histoire au présent. Conversation entre Ami Barak, Katia Baudin et Bernard Blistène, 2003. In S. Philippon (ed.), *Trésors publics. 20 ans de création dans les Fonds régionaux d'art contemporain*. Paris: Flammarion.

Unwin, R., 2011. Budapest "Mega-Project" to Defy the Downturn. *The Art Newspaper*, November, p. 229.

Urfalino, Ph. and Vilkas, C., 1995. *Les Fonds régionaux d'art contemporain. La délégation du jugement esthétique*. Paris: L'Harmattan.

Urok zamkniętego zaułka, Katarzyna Bik talks to Jacek Majchrowski, 2005. *Gazeta Wyborcza Kraków*, 14 January, p. 7.

Várkonyi, G., 2005. To the Portrait of Béla Radnai: Foreward – Afterwards. In M. Kolozsváry (ed.), *Hungarian Art, 1900–1950. Radnai Collection, Győr*. Budapest: Kieselbach, pp. 54–67.

Városliget Zrt., *Liget Budapest Competition. Architectural Design Competition for the Building of New National Gallery and Ludwig Museum*. Closing Report, 12 April 2015.

Vlastník, J., 2001. Meda Mládková. *Travel in the Czech Republic*.

[Vlnas, V.], [1995]. *200 let Národní Galerie v Praze 1796–1996*. [Praha].

Volf, P., 2003. Obsession. *The Heart of Europe Magazine*, p. 3.

Wczesne lata. Z Andą Rottenberg rozmawia Artur Żmijewski, 2014. In P. Althamer et al. (eds.), *Instytucja krytyczna*. Warszawa: Wydawnictwo Krytyki Politycznej, pp. 110–133.

Willoughby, I., 2008. Ambitious New Privately Owned Gallery Opens in Prague. *Český rozhlas 7 – Radio Praha*, 24 October. Available at: <www.radio.cz/cn/section/arts/ambitious-new-privately-owned-gallery-opens-in-prague> [Accessed 5 October 2018].

Winner Announced for 320fok Cultural Centre, Siófok, Hungary, 2010. *Bustler*, 5 August. Available at: <www.bustler.net/index.php/article/winner_announced_for_320fok_cultural_centre_siofok_hungary> [Accessed 5 October 2018].

Working Session: Second, 1997. In *The Curator, the Museum, the Collection*. CIMAM Annual Meeting Barcelona, 22–24 September. Barcelona.

Wrzos-Lubaś, M., 2010. Bezdomna kolekcja cennych dzieł. *Polska Gazeta Krakowska*, 11–12 December, p. 5.

Wstępna koncepcja warszawskiego Muzeum Sztuki Nowoczesnej, 2005. Warszawa: Muzeum Sztuki Nowoczesnej w Warszawie, 28 sierpnia.

Wyspa, n.d. Available at: <www.wyspa.art.pl/title,Wyspa,pid,43.html> [Accessed 28 January 2018].

Wytyczne programowe dla wspólnej siedziby Muzeum Sztuki Nowoczesnej w Warszawie i TR Warszawa, 2014. Warszawa, 1 April.

Zabel, I., 2004. Intimacy and Society: Post-Communist or Eastern Art? Contribution at the Conference Conditions, 10–12 June 2004, Berlin. In I. Zabel (ed.), *Contemporary Art Theory*. Zurich: JRP|Ringier 2012.

Zaczyński, M., 2007. Architektura rozsądku. *Newsweek*, 9 December, pp. 112–114.

Žalman, P., 1999. Muzeum na objednávku – Danubiana. Architektúra ako symbol. *Projekt*, 2.

Zapletal, T., 2011. The Origin of the Moravian Gallery in Brno or the MG as the Unintended Product of the Totalitarian State's Gallery Policy. In P. Tomášek (ed.), *National Gallery of Moravia*. Brno: Moravská galerie v Brně, p. 282.

Zatloukal, P., 2009. *Olomouc Central European Forum – Architectural Design*. Olomouc 2009.

Zielniewicz, T., Borkowski, G., and Mazur, A., 2006. Muzeum Sztuki Nowoczesnej, Współczesnej, Transformacji a nawet Negocjacji. *Obieg.pl*, 6 July. Available at: <http://archiwum-obieg.u-jazdowski.pl/rozmowy/5702> [Accessed 5 October 2018].

Żygulski, Z. jun., 1982. *Muzea na świecie*. Warszawa: Państwowe Wydawnictwo Naukowe.

Żygulski, Z. jun., 2004. Przemiany architektury muzeów. *Muzealnictwo*, 45, pp. 106–124.

Interviews conducted by Katarzyna Jagodzińska

(name of the interlocutor, function, institution, date)

Interviews with * were published in Jagodzińska, K., 2019. *Nowe miejsca nowej sztuki w Europie Środkowej*. Kraków: Towarzystwo Autorów i Wydawców Prac Naukowych Universitas.

Adam, Richard. Artistic Director, Wannieck Gallery, Brno, 18 February 2009.

Adamov, Marek. Co-founder, Stanica Žilina-Záriečie and Nová synagóga Žilina, 25 July 2015.*

Baán, László. Director, Museum of Fine Arts, Budapest, Government and Ministerial Commissioner for the Liget Project Budapest, 15 November 2017.* [full version]

Beskid, Vladimír. Art Director of the European Capitol of Culture Košice 2013, 17 January 2018.*

Charzyńska, Jadwiga. Director, LAZNIA Centre for Contemporary Art, Gdańsk, 23 October 2017.*

Deák, Nóra. General Director, Institute of Contemporary Art, Dunaújváros, 5 December 2017.

Drury, Richard. Chief Curator, GASK – Gallery of the Central Bohemian Region, Kutná Hora, 17 July 2015.*

Ébli, Gábor. Museologist, Institute of Theoretical Studies at Moholy-Nagy University of Art and Design, Budapest, 6 February 2018.*

Fajt, Jiří. General Director, National Gallery, Prague, 5 January 2018.* [full version]

Folga-Januszewska, Dorota. Long-standing President ICOM Poland, 12 October 2017.

Gregor, Richard. Former Chief Curator, Kunsthalle Bratislava, 1 May 2018.*

Jelinek, Balázs. Project Director, Városliget Ltd., Budapest, 30 August 2017.

Jerke, Werner. Owner, Museum Jerke, Recklinghausen, 15 April 2018.*

Klaman, Grzegorz. President of Wyspa Progress Foundation, Gdańsk, 30 January 2011.

Knížák, Milan. Director-General, National Gallery, Prague, 29 September 2008.

Kónya, Ábel. Senior Curator, MODEM Modern and Contemporary Arts Centre, Debrecen, 7 February 2018.*

Kusá, Alexandra. Manager of thc Gallery of Modern and Contemporary Art, Slovak National Gallery, Bratislava, 12 March 2009.

Kusá, Alexandra. Director, Slovak National Gallery, Bratislava, 22 November 2017.* [full version]

Lahoda, Vojtěch. Director of the Institute of Art History, Czech Academy of Sciences, and lecturer, Institute of Art History, Charles University in Prague, 29 September 2008.

Márta, István. Managing Director, Zsolnay Cultural Quarter, Pécs, 6 August 2014.

Mélyi, József. Art Historian, Art Critic, Curator. Department of Art Theory of the Hungarian University of Fine Arts, Budapest, 15 February 2018.*

Michalak, Jacek, Manager, Atlas Sztuki, Łódź, 9 October 2017.*

Mytkowska, Joanna. Director, Museum of Modern Art, Warsaw, 30 December 2017.*

Polakovič, Vincent. Director, Danubiana Meulensteen Art Museum, Čunovo, 10 October 2017.*

Pospíšil, Jiří (Member of the Board of Directors of The Jan and Meda Mládek Foundation), Musilová, Helena (Chief Curator) and Průša, Sandra (Head of Exhibitions and Collections). Kampa Museum, Prague, 16 July 2015.

Potocka, Maria Anna. Director, MOCAK Museum of Contemporary Art in Krakow, 31 December 2017.*

Pudil, Petr, Co-founder, Kunsthalle Praha, Prague, 23 April 2018.*

Ruksza, Stanisław. Director, TRAFO Trafostacji Sztuki, Szczecin, 25 October 2017.*

Rusnáková, Katarína. Art Historian, Curator. Department of Theory and History of Fine Arts at the Academy of Arts, Banská Bystrica, 9 February 2018.*

Suchan, Jarosław. Director, Muzeum Sztuki in Łódź, 11 May 2018.*

Székely, Miklós. Art Historian, Research Fellow. Institute for Art History, Research Centre for the Humanities, Hungarian Academy of Sciences, 13 February 2018.*

Szipőcs, Krisztina. Deputy Director, Ludwig Museum – Museum of Contemporary Art, Budapest, 23 November 2007.

Szipőcs, Krisztina. Deputy Director and Chief Curator of the Collection, Ludwig Museum – Museum of Contemporary Art, Budapest, 17 September 2008.

Szipőcs, Krisztina. Deputy Director of Collections and Exhibitions, Ludwig Museum – Museum of Contemporary Art, Budapest, 18 December 2017.*

Szyłak, Aneta. Proxy, NOMUS New Museum of Art, Gdańsk, 27 October 2017.*

Válka, Leoš. Director, DOX Centre for Contemporary Art, Prague, 17 July 2015.*

Personal communication by e-mail

Bodnárová, Zuzana. Curator and Culture Manager, BANSKA ST A NICA Contemporary, Banská Štiavnica, 4 March 2018.

Gunišová Pavuková, Lucia. Director, Nedbalka Gallery, Bratislava, 5 February 2018.

Inkei, Péter. Director, The Budapest Observatory, 20 June 2018.

Jirmusová-Lazarowitz, Hana. Director, Egon Schiele Art Centrum, Český Krumlov, 25 October 2017.

Lekešová, Petra. Nadační fond současného umění, Adam Gallery, Brno, 14 March 2016.

Němcová, Magda. Specialist in the Department for the Protection of Cultural Goods, Ministry of Culture in the Czech Republic, Prague, 28 June 2018.

Straková, Marcela. Executive Director. 8smička, Humpolec, 17 August 2018.

Names index